CHRISTIANIZING
THE SOCIAL ORDER

CHRISTIANIZING
THE SOCIAL ORDER

BY

WALTER RAUSCHENBUSCH

PROFESSOR OF CHURCH HISTORY
IN ROCHESTER THEOLOGICAL SEMINARY

AUTHOR OF "CHRISTIANITY AND THE SOCIAL CRISIS" AND
"PRAYERS OF THE SOCIAL AWAKENING"

WIPF & STOCK · Eugene, Oregon

Wipf and Stock Publishers
199 W 8th Ave, Suite 3
Eugene, OR 97401

Christianizing the Social Order
By Rauschenbusch, Walter
ISBN 13: 978-1-60608-572-1
Publication date 3/9/2011
Previously published by Macmillan, 1914

To

HILMAR, PAUL, AND KARL

MY BOYS

WITH A FATHER'S LOVE AND HOPES

FOREWORD

WHEN "Christianity and the Social Crisis" was published in 1907, I thought I had said all that God had given me to say on our social problems, and might henceforth with a clear conscience leave that line of work to those who carry less handicap than I do. So I went to Europe for a year and devoted myself to the historical studies which are my professional duty and my intellectual satisfaction.

But meanwhile the social awakening of our nation had set in like an equinoctial gale in March, and when I came home, I found myself caught in the tail of the storm. "Christianity and the Social Crisis" had won popular approval far beyond my boldest hopes, and the friends of the book drew me, in spite of myself, into the public discussion of social questions. Naturally my mind worked on problems which had been raised in my book, but had not really been taken in hand there. I had urged a moral reorganization of social institutions, a christianizing of public morality. Men asked: "What must we do? And what must we undo? What social ideal should guide us? What methods can we safely use in realizing it?" The most varied audiences followed the discussion of these problems with an intensity of interest that was quite new to me. Without the spiritual coöperation and stimulus of others this book would never have been written.

In 1910 and 1911 I had the honor of delivering the Earl Lectures at the Pacific Theological Seminary at Berkeley, Cal., and the Merrick Lectures at Ohio Wesleyan University. The latter lectureship carried the obligation of publishing the lectures in book form. I take this opportunity to express my obligation to the Faculties and Officers of both institutions for courtesies which I shall never forget, and for providing the incentive to work out my thought in written form. These two lecture courses created the nucleus of this book; the form, however, and much of the contents are new.

The subject of the book needs no such apology as is implied in the foregoing statements. If there is any bigger or more pressing subject for the mind of a Christian man to handle, I do not know of it. The problem of christianizing the social order welds all the tasks of practical Christianity with the highest objects of statesmanship. That the actual results of our present social order are in acute contradiction to the Christian conceptions of justice and brotherhood is realized by every man who thinks at all. But where do the sources of our wrongs lie hidden? What has wrought such deadly results from a civilization that has such wonderful promises of good? How can we cease to produce evil in despite of our right intentions? How can the fundamental structure of society be conformed to the moral demands of the Christian spirit?

The First Part of the book describes the present social awakening in the organizations of religion. Outsiders misjudge the part which the churches are taking in the impending social transformation because they are ignorant of the quiet revolution that is going on in the spirit and aims of the American churches. Few, probably, even of those who are taking an active part in their social awakening, realize fully the far-reaching importance of this great historic movement.

Part Two seeks to show that the christianizing of the social order was the very aim with which Christianity set out. That aim has long been submerged and almost forgotten, but it has reëmerged simultaneously with the rise of modern life, and now demands a reckoning with every religious intellect, offering us all a richer synthesis of truth and a more distinctively Christian type of religious experience.

Part Three subjects our present social order to a moral analysis in order to determine what is Christian in the structure of society, and what is not. This traverses some of the ground covered in my previous book, but from new angles. In spite of its critical character the net results of the analysis, to me at least, are immensely cheering.

Part Four follows up this muster by showing that the unregenerate elements of our social organization are not quietly waiting till we get ready to reform them, but are actively invading God's country and devastating the moral achievements built up by centuries of Christian teaching and sacrifice.

In Part Five I have tried to trace in advance those fundamental lines of moral evolution along which society must move in order to leave its inhumanities behind and to emerge in a social order that will institutionalize the Christian convictions of the worth of manhood and the solidarity of mankind.

Part Six, finally, suggests the methods of advance, the personal and social action by which our present conditions can be molded into a juster and happier community life in which the Christian spirit shall be more free to work its will.

If this book was to be written at all, it had to deal searchingly with the great collective sins of our age. Evangelism always seeks to create a fresh conviction of guilt as a basis for a higher righteousness, and this book is nothing if it is not a message of sin and salvation. But its purpose is not denunciation. It is wholly constructive. Of "Christianity and the Social Crisis" it has been said that it is a book without any hate in it. So far as I know my own soul that is true of this book, too.   I have written it as a follower of Jesus Christ.   My sole desire has been to summon the Christian passion for justice and the Christian powers of love and mercy to do their share in redeeming our social order from its inherent wrongs.

WALTER RAUSCHENBUSCH.

ROCHESTER THEOLOGICAL SEMINARY,
     October 4, 1912.

CONTENTS

PART I

THE SOCIAL AWAKENING OF THE CHURCHES

PART II

THE REVOLUTIONARY DESTINY OF CHRISTIANITY

PART III

OUR SEMI-CHRISTIAN SOCIAL ORDER

xi

PART IV

THE INVASION OF GOD'S COUNTRY

PART V

THE DIRECTION OF PROGRESS

PART VI

THE METHODS OF ADVANCE

CHRISTIANIZING
THE SOCIAL ORDER

CHRISTIANIZING THE SOCIAL ORDER

PART I

THE SOCIAL AWAKENING OF THE CHURCHES

CHAPTER I

THE AWAKENING OF THE NATION

FOR the last ten years our nation has been under conviction of sin. We had long been living a double life, but without realizing it. Our business methods and the principles of our religion and of our democracy have always been at strife, but not until our sin had matured and brought forth wholesale death did we understand our own obliquity.

Most of us were eager to get the better of our fellows by seizing some advantage which the rest could not get. Our vast continent offered unrivaled chances for this great American game. But of late we have begun to realize that some have played the game according to the accepted rules, but with unexpected effectiveness. The natural resources of the country are passing into the control of a minority. An ever increasing number of people are henceforth to live in a land owned by an ever decreasing number. The means of traffic are the arteries of the social body; every freight car is a blood corpuscle charged with life.

We have allowed private persons to put their thumb where they can constrict the life blood of the nation at will. The common people have financed the industry of the country with their savings, but the control of industry has passed out of their hands almost completely. The profits of our common work are absorbed by a limited group; the mass of the people are permanently reduced to wage-earning positions. The cost of living has been raised by unseen hands until several millions of our nation are unable to earn even the bare minimum which social science declares necessary for health and decency, and all families living on a fixed income have felt a mysterious and suffocating pressure.

All this was the necessary outcome of our economic system, but it was a sore surprise to most of us when the process began to culminate and we saw the end of our own doings.

When the people in anger turned to the means of self-defense provided by our political democracy, they found the weapons on which they relied in the hands of their opponents and leveled against themselves. The will of the people expressed through the ballot was often directly frustrated by election frauds and bribery. Even when the votes were properly registered and counted, they were as ineffectual as a blow on the surface of a pond. They merely served to give legal sanction to the manipulations of a political oligarchy whose will was the real force in shaping our affairs. When the popular will did succeed in framing a party platform, the men elected to carry it out balked like Balaam's ass, because some mysterious presence (not angelic) blocked the way, and the people had no means of compelling their servants to obey them, or even of punishing the guilty with any precision. The most august and powerful body in the nation, the Senate of the United States, had become a fortification of predatory interests, and great States were shamed for long years by the contemptible men who were supposed to be their ambassadors at Washington. The federal courts, holding the final veto power over all laws passed in the land, were filled with men satisfactory to politicians and big business.[1] All courts had become so tangled in their own antiquated methods of procedure, and were still so permeated with conceptions inherited from the age of despotism, that the institutions of justice are to-day the chief props of social maladjustment.

The history of American politics in recent years has been a history of the reconquest of political liberty. Our nation has been in the position of a city that wakes up to find an insurrectionary minority in military control, with barricades erected at all strategic points. For a decade the people have been storming these barricades and seeking to overthrow the unconstitutional powers which had become our *de facto* government. The States are now barring out sinister financial influences by compelling the publication of election expenses and limiting their amount. They are trying to weaken the political oligarchies by direct nomination. They hope to cleanse and rejuvenate the Senate by direct election. They are sweeping and ventilating the worst corners of our common home, the cities, by uniform accounting and commission government. They are turning our so-called representative government into self-government by the initiative, referendum, and recall.

All this is nothing less than a political revolution. It is a second war of independence. It goes on all over the country with a curious unanimity of impulse which proves that it is not the artificial product of party agitation, but an awakening of the better self of the nation.

When the people began to regain political power, they

[1] See William Allen White, "The Old Order Changeth," Chapter VIII, and Appendix, pp. 255–262.

used it to get at the facts. A series of legislative investigations furnished X-ray photographs of our national in-
wardness and threw them on a screen big enough for all
to see. The magazines lectured us on the scientific material
furnished. We saw the bribed voters of respectable coun-
ties in the Middle West startled by sudden publicity, as
a lot of cockroaches in a dirty kitchen scamper away when
the light is turned on. We saw the legislators of great
States crowding around the jack-pot as hungry as pasture
cattle for the pail of salt. We saw a great corporation
compelled to pay back huge sums stolen from the government. We followed private wires running from land frauds
in the West way up into the dome of our government
edifice at Washington. We saw the most imposing institutions of banking and insurance caught in crookedness
that had grown almost venerable and beautiful with age,
like the patina that gathers on ancient bronze.

The insurance investigation in which Charles E. Hughes
gained national fame in 1905 was the beginning of enlightenment for great numbers. Subsequent inquiries were
less epoch-making because they merely corroborated and
expanded popular information. The sense of national sin
and dishonor has become a settled conviction. Only the
report of the Chicago Vice Commission has been able to
wring a new groan of shame and desperation from the whole
nation.

It has been a terrible process of national education. If
in 1890 a prophet, personally conducted and introduced
by an archangel, had predicted accurately one half of the
facts which are now common knowledge, public opinion
would have dismissed him with incredulity.

It is proof of the moral soundness of our people that when
they did understand, there was a revulsion of feeling.
The standards of collective morality rose almost with a
snap. Some men died broken-hearted when they found

themselves fixed by the stern gaze of this new moral feeling. Others are to-day looking in this new light at the fortunes they gathered by the old methods, and are wishing that their hands were emptier.

Sin is the greatest preacher of repentance. Give it time, and it will cool our lust in shame. When God wants to halt a proud man who is going wrong, he lets him go the full length and find out the latter end for himself. That is what he has done with our nation in its headlong ride on the road of covetousness. Mammonism stands convicted by its own works. It was time for us to turn.

We are turning.

The other day I was walking along the seashore. A broad stretch of sand and slimy stones was between me and the water. Dead things lay about, stranded, limp, and gray. It was ebb tide.

When I returned after a few hours, a magic change had taken place. Over the stagnant flats the waves were rolling briskly and eagerly, as if they were young. The gulls were dipping and screaming. Gray ripples far out showed where fish were schooling. All the world smelled and felt differently. The tide was coming in.

The same sense of a great change comes over any one who watches the life of this nation with an eye for the stirring of God in the souls of men. There is a new shame and anger for oppression and meanness; a new love and pity for the young and frail whose slender shoulders bear our common weight; a new faith in human brotherhood; a new hope of a better day that is even now in sight. We are inventing new phrases to name this new thing. We talk of the "social feeling" or "the new social consciousness." We are passing through a moral adolescence. When the spirit of manhood comes over a boy, his tastes change. The old doings of his gang lose interest. A new sense of duty, a new openness to ideal calls, a new capacity of self-sacrifice surprise those who used to know him. So in out conventions and clubs, our chambers of commerce and our legislatures, there is a new note, a stiffening of will, an impatience for cowardice, an enthusiastic turning toward real democracy. The old leaders are stumbling off the stage bewildered. There is a new type of leaders, and they and the people seem to understand one another as if by magic.

Were you ever converted to God? Do you remember the change in your attitude to all the world? Is not this new life which is running through our people the same great change on a national scale? This is religious energy, rising from the depth of that infinite spiritual life in which we all live and move and have our being. This is God.

CHAPTER II

THE American churches are part of the American nation. They are not a foreign clerical organization grafted on our national life, but an essential part of it from the beginning, a great plastic force which has molded our public opinions and our institutions from the foundation up. They are organizations of the people, by the people, and for the people. When a great spiritual movement like the social awakening shakes our nation to the depths, we may be sure that the churches will respond to it and have an active part in it. And so we find it.

Outside of the churches the social awakening is remarkable for the religious spirit which it creates in men who thought they were done with religion. They are getting a faith once more. They show all the evidences of religion, — love, tenderness, longings mysterious to themselves, a glad willingness to sacrifice time and money for the salvation of their fellows. What is this but religion?

On the other hand, with the people in the churches, who have long been consciously religious, the new thing is the social application of their religious life. The old current of their religion is pouring into a broader channel of social purpose, and running with a swift flow toward the achievement of public justice and love. Feelings and enthusiasms, doctrinal ideas and moral purposes, which to a former generation would have seemed to have but a slender connection with religion, are now felt to be an essential part of the spiritual life and, in fact, the great business of religion.

7

All this is big with meaning and hope. It has come over the churches so swiftly that even their leaders hardly realize the extent of this social awakening and the significance of the movement of which they are part. Many outsiders still talk as if they had heard nothing about it. If we are to discuss the christianizing of the social order, we must know the spiritual forces which are rallying and volunteering for the task.

Every great movement begins in the hearts of a few. "The soul is still oracular." Amid the din [of the market some listen to the voice within. They are usually the young men whom the world has not yet dulled and debased; the able men whose large minds look beyond immediate need and profit; the natural idealists predestined by heredity for noble ends; and the religious hearts in whom the inner light has created an intuitive comprehension of present wrong and future righteousness. The best are those in whom these qualities combine.

These prophetic minds condense the unconscious longings of the mass of men in concrete experience and thought. They become centers of new light and energy. They awaken and lead the rest because they utter clearly what others feel dimly.

Social Christianity has had a brilliant succession of prophets in the older nations of Europe. Our own country has lagged a generation behind. The modern social problem is the problem of capitalistic industrialism and becomes acute only when a country becomes industrialized. We have been an agricultural nation until recently, and where industry did develop, the people still had the vastness of our land to ease the pressure of population and keep up the standard of living. Yet some foresaw what was coming. Abraham Lincoln and Wendell Phillips, fighting for the emancipation of an enslaved race, foresaw a wider industrial conflict still to come.

I want to pay the tribute of honor to three men who were pioneers of Christian social thought in America twenty-five years ago: Washington Gladden, Josiah Strong, and Richard T. Ely. These men had matured their thought when the rest of us were young men, and they had a spirit in them which kindled and compelled us.

But all whose recollection runs back of 1900 will remember that as a time of lonesomeness. We were few, and we shouted in the wilderness. It was always a happy surprise when we found a new man who had seen the light. We used to form a kind of flying wedge to support a man who was preparing to attack a ministers' conference with the social Gospel. Our older friends remonstrated with us for wrecking our career. We ourselves saw the lions' den plainly before us, and only wondered how the beasts would act this time. In 1892 Terence V. Powderly, Grand Master Workman of the Knights of Labor, then the most powerful organization of labor in the country, said, "You can count on the ends of your fingers all of the clergymen who take any interest in the labor problem." Mr. W. D. P. Bliss, editor of the brave Christian Socialist paper, the *Dawn*, replied by enumerating sixty-two ministers of his own acquaintance who were not only interested, but deeply interested, in the cause of labor. (I count it one of my chief titles to mercy in the day of judgment that I was on that roll of the elect.) This was a triumphant reply to Mr. Powderly's assertion, but even Mr. Bliss, who probably had a wider personal contact with the Christian social movement at that time than any other man, knew only sixty-two names in the whole country, and padded the list by adding sixty other ministers who were members of the American Economic Association and therefore "presumably interested" in social problems.

It is the contrast with those early days which makes the present situation in the churches so amazing. The able ministers who were not already physically or mentally old by 1900, and who were not rendered impervious by doctrinal rubber-coating of some kind, have been permeated by the social interest almost in a body. With the young men the social interest has become a serious rival of the old ministerial calling. Some turn to the settlements or to Y.M.C.A. work because it seems to offer more opportunities for social usefulness than the pastorate of a church. When students in the seminaries are free to choose their own topics for Commencement addresses, a very large proportion of them give evidence that the social enthusiasm has affected them. The addresses often come closer to being real confessions of their faith than the creeds to which they may subscribe at their ordination. The imprudences of some social preachers are at least proof that the heroic spirit is being evoked in the ministry. Their unnecessary vehemence is often the psychological form which fear takes in a sensitive soul that nerves itself for a shock of assault. Very many ministers in recent years have entered into living sympathy with the old prophets who felt "the word of Jehovah" burning within them.

Perhaps the most convincing proof of the spread of the social interest in the ministry is the fact that the old men and the timid men are falling in line.

It is always a splendid victory of the spirit over the body when an old man compels his brain to overcome the physiological inertia of age and receive new ideas and convictions. In doing so, he comes out of the shelter of a system of thought which he has built in a long life and which hitherto seemed complete and sufficient, and takes his staff in hand once more to go in quest of the Holy Grail of truth. When a man of ripe years, whose religious horizon was formerly bounded by routine church work, soul-saving, and the premillennial hope, now opens his heart to the social hope of the new age, we may well feel the deepest reverence for such spiritual energy. But we may also be sure that these old men would not see visions unless a new pentecostal spirit had been poured out on all the disciples.

And when the time-serving brother, who had so long been discreetly silent on social questions, wrapped in the fur-lined consciousness of being that highest type of the Christian apostle, a "safe man," grew thunderous on child labor and meat prices, we felt that our labors had not been in vain in the Lord, and were willing in love to suppress the surprised query of John the Baptist under similar circumstances: "And who taught *you* to flee from the wrath to come?"

The social interest in the Church has now run beyond the stage of the solitary pioneer. It has been admitted within the organizations of the Church. Formerly some determined spirit would force his ideas on a ministers' conference and be treated with good-humored condescension as a rider of hobbies. To-day the concerted study of social problems has become a common thing in ministerial clubs and conferences. Adult Bible classes and study groups turn by preference to books on the social teachings of Jesus. A valuable literature is being created to supply the need for cheap teaching material.[1] Men's clubs, social unions, Chautauquas, and church conventions have created an active demand for competent speakers on topics of social Christianity. But the most astonishing change is in the temper of church audiences. Formerly speakers compelled the people to take their medicine whether they liked it

[1] "The Gospel of the Kingdom," edited by Josiah Strong, published by the American Institute of Social Service (Bible House, New York City), was begun in 1909, has a circulation of 6000 copies, and is used by about 500 classes and 12,000 students. The material has also been printed in the *Homiletic Review*. "Studies in American Social Conditions," a series of compact pamphlets, with an excellent classified bibliography in each, are published for the same purpose by Rev. R. H. Edwards. (Can be ordered at University bookstore, Madison, Wis.)

or not, and became adepts in sugar-coating their pills. To-
day speakers have to be on their guard lest they be swept
along by their hearers. Utterances that would have
seemed shockingly radical ten years ago are now applauded.

Under the pressure of the social awakening the churches
are officially seeking to get in touch with organized labor.
In 1904 Rev. Charles Stelzle first attempted an exchange
of delegates between the Ministerial Association and the
Central Labor Council of Minneapolis. The idea was
indorsed by the Presbyterian General Assembly and the
American Federation of Labor. Probably about one
hundred and fifty ministers of various denominations are
now attending the meetings of union labor with more or
less regularity. They have the right to the floor, are often
called on, and in some cases have won marked popularity
and influence.[1] In this way they come into sympathetic
contact with the great industrial working class, whose aims
and moral qualities have hitherto been like an unexplored
continent on the map of the churches. Under the advice
of the Federal Council of the Churches of America thousands of churches have set aside the Sunday before Labor
Day as Labor Sunday; in 1910 the American Federation
of Labor cordially indorsed this idea and advised its
members to attend such services in a body. Some day we
may see the ministers march in the Labor Day parade with
the other workers, to assert their solidarity with the great
fellowship of productive labor.

In the last five years nearly all the great denominations
have discussed the social situation and the duty of the
Church at their national conventions. This in itself is a
notable proof of the spread of the social awakening. Some
of the national bodies meet only once in three or four years,

---

[1] Information about the exchange of "fraternal delegates" can be obtained
from the Presbyterian Department of Church and Labor, 156 Fifth Avenue,
New York City.

and every hour of the time is jealously claimed by the
established denominational interests. If the social questions are given the right of way, there must be a strong
public opinion demanding it. The meetings devoted to
these discussions have repeatedly stood out above all the
rest by their size and enthusiasm, and the barometric
pressure felt by all. The General Assembly of the Presbyterian Church has had a noble history of more than a hundred years, but it never saw a greater meeting than that at
Kansas City in 1908, when 12,000 people met to consider
the relation of the Church and Labor.

Since 1908 the denominations have begun to adopt
formal declarations defining their attitude to the social
problems. Of course resolutions are often cheap bluster
at an absent foe. But resolutions condemning the actions
of its own wealthy and powerful supporters are not likely
to come to a vote in any convention unless the moral conviction behind them is mature and irresistible. The
masters of church assemblies are usually more than willing
to let sleeping dogs lie without prodding them. The resolutions of recent years may settle nothing, but they indicate
a great deal.

The honor of making the first ringing declaration in a
national convention belongs to the Methodist Church
North. Every General Convention of the Church since
1892 had been memorialized by some minor body pleading
for action. In 1908 no less than thirteen annual conferences besides various preachers' meetings presented me-
morials. The bishops in a cautious way devoted a large
part of their episcopal address to the subject.[1] The Committee on the State of the Church presented a brave and
outspoken report, culminating in a kind of Bill of Rights
for labor, and ending in a splendid summons to all the mili-

[1] *General Conference Journal of the Methodist Episcopal Church*, 1908,
pp. 130–137.

tant forces of this great Church to do their part in the pressing duty of the hour.[1]

Immediately after the Methodist General Conference, in December, 1908, the Federal Council of the Churches of Christ in America was organized at Philadelphia, representing and uniting thirty-three Protestant denominations. This organization marked an epoch in the history of American Protestantism. But no other session created so profound an interest as that devoted to "Social Service." The report of the Commission was heard with tense feeling, which broke into prolonged and enthusiastic applause at the close. The Bill of Rights adopted by the Methodist Convention was presented with some changes and adopted without the slightest disposition to halt it at any point. The following declaration, therefore, has stood since 1908 as the common sense of the Protestant churches of America : —

"We deem it the duty of all Christian people to concern themselves directly with certain practical industrial problems. To us it seems that the churches must stand —

For equal rights and complete justice for all men in all stations of life.

[1] *General Conference Journal of the Methodist Episcopal Church*, 1908, pp. 545–549. "And now we summon our great Church to continue and increase its work of social service. We summon all our ministry, bishops, presiding elders, and pastors, to patient study of these problems and to the fearless but judicious preaching of the teachings of Jesus in their significance for the moral interests of modern society. We look to the press of our Church for enlightenment and inspiration. We look to our Sunday Schools and Epworth Leagues to awaken and direct the spirit of social responsibility. We demand of every agency and organization of the Church that it shall touch the people in their human relationships with healing and helpfulness, and, finally, be it remembered that we cannot commit to any special agencies the charge that all the Church must keep. Upon every member rests a solemn duty to devote himself with his possessions, his citizenship, and his influence to the glory of God in the service of the present age. And thus by their works, as by their prayers, let all 'the people called Methodists' seek that kingdom in which God's will shall be done on earth as it is in heaven."

For the right of all men to the opportunity for self-maintenance, a right ever to be wisely and strongly safeguarded against encroachments of every kind.

For the right of workers to some protection against the hardships often resulting from the swift crises of industrial change.

For the principle of conciliation and arbitration in industrial dissensions.

For the protection of the worker from dangerous machinery, occupational disease, injuries, and mortality.

For the abolition of child labor.

For such regulations of the conditions of toil for women as shall safeguard the physical and moral health of the community.

For the suppression of the 'sweating system.'

For the gradual and reasonable reduction of the hours of labor to the lowest practicable point, and for that degree of leisure for all which is a condition of the highest human life.

For a release from employment one day in seven.

For a living wage as a minimum in every industry, and for the highest wage that each industry can afford.

For the most equitable division of the products of industry that can ultimately be devised.

For suitable provision for the old age of the workers and for those incapacitated by injury.

For the abatement of poverty.

To the toilers of America and to those who by organized effort are seeking to lift the crushing burdens of the poor, and to reduce the hardships and uphold the dignity of labor, this Council sends the greeting of human brotherhood and the pledge of sympathy and of help in a cause which belongs to all who follow Christ."[1]

Nearly every great denominational convention since that time has felt the obligation to make a serious pronouncement on the social questions. In several cases the social creed of the Federal Council was adopted; for instance, by the

[1] "The Social Creed of the Churches," edited by Harry F. Ward, is an exposition of the planks in this platform.

Congregational Council in 1910. When any change was made, it was in the direction of still more radical emphasis. Thus the Northern Baptist Convention in 1911 added: "The control of the natural resources of the earth in the interests of all the people; the gaining of wealth by Christian methods and principles, and the holding of wealth as a social trust; the discouragement of the immoderate desire for wealth, and the exaltation of man as the end and standard of industrial activity." The Unitarians later in the same year adopted these Baptist additions and declared further "for proper housing; for the proper care of dependants and criminals; for pure food and drugs; for wholesome recreation; and for international peace; for such safeguarding and extension of the institutions of democratic government as will permit and insure the maintenance of the rights of all against the encroachment from the special interests of the few." Instead of the abatement, they demanded "the abolition of poverty."

It was my intention to sum up the action taken by the various denominations in order to furnish evidence here of the spread and strength of the social awakening in the churches. But when I began to collect the documentary material, I found it so abundant that I could not do justice to it in the space available here. Some one ought to compile it all and give the historical setting in each case. These resolutions have registered the rise of a new moral intelligence and purpose, at least among the leaders, and have committed the churches to the solemn obligation of assisting in the public enforcement of these standards of conduct. They are vital material for American church history henceforth.

The leaders of the social awakening are now creating permanent organizations to educate the rank and file of the churches and to give practical effect to the new convictions. As early as 1901 the Protestant Episcopal Church appointed a Standing Commission on Church and Labor, and since 1907 Diocesan Commissions have been at work in a dozen dioceses.[1] The League for Social Service is officially recognized as the Methodist organization for propaganda and is carrying on a very effective work of stimulation.[2] The Methodist Church North requires its ministerial candidates to study designated books on social questions. The Northern Baptist Convention has appointed a Social Service Commission, which has issued a series of pamphlets and compiled an excellent course of reading.[3] The Congregationalists have a Social Service Department.[4] The most effective work has been done by the Presbyterian Department of Church and Labor, organized in 1903.[5]

The rise of social Christianity is felt in all the institutional agencies of the American churches. Those movements which are distinctively modern and devised to meet present-day needs are completely dominated by it. In union efforts it is also very marked because here the combined intelligence of all denominations is massed. The Religious Education Association, for instance, has from the first dealt with its large problems from the social point of view, and the social emphasis seems to grow stronger every year. The Young Men's Christian Association used to stand for religious individualism. The mere mention of "sociology" once excited ridicule. To-day the association has devel-

[1] See *Journal of the General Convention* of 1910, Appendix X; publications of the Christian Social Union, especially No. 106.

[2] See the publications of the Methodist Federation for Social Service, published by Eaton and Mains, New York.

[3] See Social Service Series, and "A Course of Social Reading for Ministers and Workers," both published by the American Baptist Publication Society, Philadelphia.

[4] See the Report of the National Council of Congregational Churches, 1910.

[5] See publications of the Presbyterian Department of Church and Labor, obtainable of the Board of Home Missions, 156 Fifth Avenue, New York.

oped a splendid machinery for constructive social service, and its leaders are grappling with the problems of entire communities and of great social groups in a brave and far-sighted way. Its financial strength and its interdenominational leadership are largely due to the fact that it had faith and sagacity enough to take hold of the social needs with reasonable promptness. The Young Women's Christian Association is naturally a more conservative body, but in 1911 it definitely committed itself to the business of securing a living wage and a maximum working day for the women workers for whose welfare it exists.

In the older religious movements there has been a shifting of motive and appeal in response to the rise of the social conceptions of Christianity. We can remember the time when the demand for men and money for foreign missions was based almost wholly on the ground that millions of heathen souls were dying without the saving knowledge of Christ. To-day the leaders of the missionary movement are teaching a statesmanlike conception of the destiny of Christianity as the spiritual leaven of the East and the common basis of a world-wide Christian civilization. On the foreign field the Christian Church is not yet a conservative force, but a power of moral conquest. There it really embodies the finest spiritual purposes of the Christian nations in the effort to uplift the entire life of the backward peoples. There is no doubt that the influence of the English and American Protestant missions was one of the chief forces at work in the Turkish and the Chinese revolutions. In Japan the government seems to scent some sort of connection between the native Christians and the spread of socialist ideas. The ablest missionaries, when they return to their home country, resent the tameness with which the Church has submitted to our own unchristian conditions and demand the application of the missionary attitude and faith to our mammonistic heathenism. Wherever the leaders of the cause have confronted the young, the educated, and the masculine sections of the community, as in the Student Volunteer Movement and the Laymen's Missionary Movement, they have been compelled to lay stress on the social conception of missions. In turn the stress laid on that aspect of mission work has contributed to the new grip which this cause has laid on the educated laity. Men of affairs have a natural affinity for social points of view, provided no selfish interests of their own cloud their minds. Thus the whole tone and spirit of missionary thought to-day, as compared with that of a former generation, is proof that the social awakening has arrived.

The Men and Religion Forward Movement of 1911–1912 is another evidence of the ascendency of social Christianity. It was the most comprehensive evangelistic movement ever undertaken in this country and was planned with consummate care and ability. Its leaders were determined to win the men back to religion by meeting the distinctively masculine interests; therefore they had to be bold. On the other hand, they needed the financial support of men of wealth and the moral support of all kinds of churches; therefore they had to be cautious. When the leaders got together, before ever a gun was fired, it became clear that there was only one message with which all expected to go before the men of the country. All the varied departments of the movement found their spiritual center and unity in the idea of the Kingdom of God on earth, which is the doctrine of social Christianity. When the movement began to be tried out, it grew increasingly plain that it was the trumpet call of the social gospel which rallied the audiences and brought men under moral and religious conviction. The men selected as "social service experts" stopped short of socialism and to that extent disappointed and even antagonized some portion of their audiences, but they set forth the social ideals of organized labor with tremendous freedom and force. Nor was the social message confined to the "social service" sections. "Boys' Work" and "Community Extension" were closely allied in subject matter. It is safe to say that the promoters of the movement had no intention at the outset to give such prominence to the social message. But that makes the actual course of developments all the more instructive. The movement has probably done more than any other single agency to lodge the social gospel in the common mind of the Church. It has made social Christianity orthodox. But in turn it has shown what spiritual power lies stored in the Kingdom ideal, and has proved that the present generation, in the nation and in the Church, will not be satisfied with any kind of Christianity that does not undertake to christianize the social order.

The movements to which reference has been made in their nature embody the progressive forces of the Church. On the other hand, the denominational publishing houses and the theological seminaries are usually citadels of conservatism. They make a specialty of what is "safe." To-day the publishing boards of several denominations are putting forth literature which really sets forth the forward thought of the Church on social questions. Twenty-five years ago only one or two seminaries offered an articulated course on the relation of Christianity to the organic life of society.[1] To-day there are few seminaries of first-class

[1] So far as I know, Andover Seminary deserves the wreath of the pioneer. In 1879 Professor W. J. Tucker, now president of Dartmouth College, annexed a perfunctory lectureship in pastoral theology and turned it into a sociological course. An outline of the course was published in the *Andover Review*, 1889–1892, and stimulated other professors to attempt a similar work. The Andover House, at Boston, 1891, was an outcome of these impulses; it is now the South End Settlement, still under Robert A. Woods, as its wise and beloved head. Union Theological Seminary established Union Settlement in 1895 and made the headworker lecturer in Practical Christianity. Graham Taylor's stimulating work at Chicago Theological Seminary began in 1892. Dr. Francis G. Peabody's first course was given at Harvard as early as 1880.

rating that do not have a chair devoted to "Social Ethics" or "Christian Sociology." Not that seminary education is now fully adjusted to the social conception of Christianity. When that conception gets through with its reconstructive influence on the theological curriculum, every department of our seminaries will have a changed alignment and a new vocabulary. But young men are no longer sent out to that highest form of social service, the Christian ministry, without some knowledge of the social nature and life of men.

As a crowning demonstration of the social awakening I offer the fact that the new social convictions have come near to getting lodgment in a creed. In every formative age the Church has felt the need of defining and anchoring its orthodoxy in formal statements of belief. If in all these stately documents there is any trace of social consciousness, or any sense that the Christian Church has the divine mission to change this sad old earth into the Kingdom of God, I should be glad to have it pointed out.[1] But in 1906, when the Congregationalists, the United Brethren, and the Methodist Protestant bodies, together comprising over a million members, were on the point of entering into organic union, a creed was adopted in which one of the five articles was wholly devoted to the social duty of the Church : —

"We believe that according to Christ's law men of the Christian faith exist for the service of man, not only in holding forth the word of life, but in the support of works and institutions of pity and charity, in the maintenance of human freedom, in the deliverance of all those that are oppressed, in the enforcement of civic justice, and in the rebuke of all unrighteousness."

By 1905 it had reached the dignity of a Department with five instructors and eleven courses.

[1] The material for such a study can be found readily in Schaff, "Creeds of Christendom" (three volumes).

We are tempted to add the damnatory clause so often occur-
ring in older creeds: "Si quis autem contrarium senserit,
anathema sit."

Our religious denominations are like a group of composite
personalities. Each has its own inheritance of principles
and historic traditions, its own form of organization, its
own understanding of the Gospel. Like the character of
an individual, this constitutes its sacred endowment and
equipment. When some historian a hundred years hence
undertakes to describe the present social transition, it will
be an interesting task for him to make a comparative estimate of the influence which the various denominations have
exerted on the awakening of the nation and the founding
of a new social order.

The Protestant Episcopal Church, for instance, failed
to take any leading part in the older social conflicts with
alcoholism and with slavery, but in the present struggle
against industrial extortion it has furnished far more than
its share of workers and leaders. The Church Association for the Advancement of the Interests of Labor
(C.A.I.L.), organized by a few ministers in 1887, was probably the first organization of social Christianity in this
country. The close contact of the Episcopal Church with
the Anglican Church brought it abreast of the advanced
social movements in England. Its conceptions of the
Church made it easier to outgrow Protestant individualism.

By the establishment of its Department of Church and
Labor the Presbyterian Church has won a preëminence
which all may envy, but which none will grudge, for its
work has been nobly free from denominational selfishness
and has benefited all. That a Church so conservative
by reason of wealth, social standing, and doctrinal traditions has been able to set the pace for all in establishing
friendly relations with organized labor, shows what
capable leadership can do. Thousands of ministers have

come from the ranks of labor. Why have not hundreds of them remained in working contact with it, as Charles Stelzle has done ?

The Congregationalists, Baptists, Disciples, Unitarians, and Universalists, with their sib and kin, represent the principles of pure democracy in church life. That is their spiritual charisma and their qualification for leadership in the democratization of the social order. Their loose-jointed organization makes united action more difficult for them than for other churches, but they have been prolific of men whose freedom of thought and resolute love of justice showed that they had been suckled with the milk of inde-pendency. These denominations are apt to get less credit for their public service than those of strong church con-sciousness, like the Catholics and Episcopalians, because they insist less on having the activities of their members put forth under church auspices. For instance, the Broth-erhood of the Kingdom, formed in 1893, was one of the earliest organizations of social Christianity in the country. Its early members were all Baptists, and it might have become the organization of Baptist radicals, but it chose the broadest interdenominational basis on principle, and the denomination thus gets no credit for an enterprise born of its best spirit.

The Methodists are likely to play a very important part in the social awakening of the American churches. They combine the democratic spirit of the Congregation-alist group with a much stiffer and more centralized organ-ization. Their field has always been among the plain people. They comprise about 28 per cent of the Protestant membership and a much larger per cent of the conscious religious experience and conviction of the country. They have rarely backed away from a fight when the issue was clearly drawn between Jehovah and Diabolus. How hard they can hit, the liquor trade will ruefully testify.

Both North and South their leaders are fully determined to form their *bataillons* on this new line of battle, and when they march, the ground will shake.

The awakening of the churches is far from complete. The American churches, all told, had about thirty-three million enrolled members in 1906. To arouse and educate so vast a body is an enormous task. A large percentage of that number is either too young or too old to be interested in the new social ideas. It will require at least one generation under the most favorable conditions to make this enlargement of the religious conceptions the common property of all.

Some denominations have not yet awakened. For instance, the Lutherans have beautiful institutional charities, but it is hard to discern any trace that as a body they are sharing in the new social enthusiasm. Large portions of them are isolated by their use of the German and Scandinavian languages. They have kept aloof from some of the older moral enthusiasms of American Christendom. They rank third in point of numbers among the Protestant bodies and claim more than two million members, but they have never exercised the influence in public life to which their numbers, the splendid qualities of their Teutonic stock, and the ability of their leaders would have entitled them. Their ministry is faithful to the older doctrinal issues of the Reformation and declines on principle to let the Church concern itself with social questions. They hold that the Church should preach the Gospel, administer the sacraments, and leave it to the individual to do his duty in society and the State. The largest and most conservative of the Lutheran bodies, the Missouri Synod, even declines as a Church to organize institutions of charity, leaving it to associations of individuals outside of the Church. "The real business of the Church is to preach the Gospel. It is not the mission of the Church to abolish physical misery or to help men to earthly happiness. Jesus says, If any man will follow me, let him deny himself and take up his cross daily." [1] In theory this position leaves individuals free for christianizing activity in society; in practice it leaves them unstimulated, uninstructed, and even sterilized against social enthusiasms. American Lutheranism might have rendered a great service to social Christianity in America by transmitting to us the mature results of social experience and thought of the German Church, just as the Episcopalians have transmitted the impulses of the Anglican Church. But thus far Lutheranism has buried its ten talents in a tablecloth of dogmatic theory and kept its people from that share in the social awakening which is their duty and their right.

This is an illustration of the obstacles which the social awakening encounters in its spread.

One of the most important practical questions is the attitude of the Roman Catholic Church to the social movements. It is bound to be a powerful factor in the future of American society. In 1906 its members constituted 36.7 per cent of the total church membership. In addition very many of that great majority of the population which is out of connection with the churches have come from the Catholic Church and still feel its spiritual influence. It is especially strong among the industrial working class. Probably a majority of the trades-unionists and of the labor leaders belong to it. It exerts a far stronger control over the social affiliations and the ideas of its members than the Protestant churches, and does not hesitate to use its terrible disciplinary powers where the authority of the Church is at stake.

Is the Roman Catholic Church affected by the social awakening, and will it do its full share in the moral work imposed on the Church? It is hard for an outsider to

[1] President F. Pfotenhauer in *Der Lutheraner*, 1911, p. 150.

judge. This Church is peculiarly many-sided, a complexity of the most ancient and modern elements, a mixture of reactionary and progressive forces.

As an international body, governed from the Vatican, the Roman Church is the greatest conservative force in the Western world. Its dogma, its theology, its philosophy, its ritual, its hierarchy, and its spirit of authority would certainly never come into existence if Christianity originated to-day in the modern world. They are remnants of a social life that is dead or dying except where the Church keeps it alive. By virtue of this inheritance from an older social order Catholicism is monarchical and hierarchical in its organization, and not even a century of development among the democracy of America has been able to wrest any serious concession from it. The official exponents of its thought are selected abroad for their conservatism, and they instinctively lean toward conservative opinions on public questions. When Cardinal Gibbons in his Jubilee sermon condemned the Initiative, the Referendum, the Judicial Recall, and the direct election of United States Senators, the climax of his appeal was, "What has been good enough for our fathers ought to be good enough for us."[1] There spoke the conservative spirit of Roman Catholicism.

On the other hand, this Church excels Protestantism in its institutional charities, and there is always but a short step from remedial charity to preventive justice. Many of its priests live with and for the poor, and are splendid incarnations of personal democracy. If the entire Catholic Church in America could follow its own Christian and American spirit, unhampered by foreign tendencies and influences, there would certainly be a sudden and splendid spurt toward democracy.

[1] Oct. 1, 1911, on the occasion of the fiftieth anniversary of his priesthood and the twenty-fifth of his cardinalate. See *Literary Digest*, Oct. 14, 1911.

The Church seems to be committed to a fight against the Socialist Party, at least as it now is. The American Federation of Catholic Societies makes a systematic anti-socialist propaganda one of its prime objects. "Let our societies everywhere keep up the fight against socialism, which was born in the brain of atheistic agitators and which, if permitted to gain a foothold, will bring in a state of revolution and bloodshed." [1] Catholicism and Socialism are the two most powerful voluntary organizations in modern life, and the impending duel between the two is of deep concern to us all. It will tangle the natural course of our political development.

But its opposition against Marxist Socialism does not stamp the Catholic Church as a purely reactionary force. Indeed, it will be compelled to uphold trades-unionism and radical social reform in order to give moral justification to its anti-socialist attitude and to neutralize the socialist influence among its working-class constituency. There has been a decided increase in social interest among the priesthood in recent years. Several bishops have issued pastoral letters on social issues. The church papers discuss social questions freely. The Central-Verein of the German Catholics has a bureau for the study of social problems and the spread of literature. Professor John A. Ryan of St. Paul has put forth a far-reaching program of reform, which has been approved by many Catholic professors of ethics and would probably have the indorsement of the majority of the priests. He demands a legal minimum wage, an eight-hour law, relief for the unemployed, provision against accident, illness, and old age, the housing of working people, public ownership of public utilities, adequate control of monopolies, taxation of the future increase of land values, and prohibition of speculation on the exchange.

[1] Annual Report of the Secretary for 1910.

The social awakening is an epoch in the history of the American churches, and it will move with the slow tread of great historic events.

When the call of foreign missions came to our fathers a century ago, it was obeyed slowly and dubiously. It imposed heavy burdens on young churches that already had the enormous task of keeping pace with the nation in its westward march. It collided with cherished doctrinal convictions in some denominations. So a few admitted it to their hearts joyfully; important factions repudiated it altogether; the larger part acknowledged its claims in theory, but left it to a minority to sustain this new interest. The substantial laymen have surrendered to it only within a few years. Yet it was a movement born of the Christian spirit, and destined to christianize our home churches by the sacrificial heroism generated by it.

In the same way the social mission of the Church to-day is accepted haltingly. It seems to load our weakening churches with a burden which no secular government on earth has yet handled adequately. This call too collides with firmly cemented doctrinal convictions about the supposed functions of the Church. Once more it takes great faith to believe that the Church will gain life by losing life. But as surely as the law of the cross is the supreme law of the Church, she will sicken and die of old age if she shrinks from her burden and quenches the spirit which is plainly speaking in her soul; and she will renew her youth and mount to a Christlike spirituality never reached before, if she will freely and without compulsion take up the cause of the people and follow her Lord on the *Via Dolorosa*.

No fair-minded man should demand that a great composite body like the Christian Church shall be wide-awake and intelligent at the dawn of a new era, while political parties, the Law, the Press, the colleges, and the working class itself are just beginning to rub the sleep from their eyes. For years to come this new social interest in the churches will be vague, groping, sentimental, timid, and inefficient. We shall follow false cries and watchwords, like the mob at Jerusalem that shouted for Barabbas, when really they meant the freedom and glory of their country. We shall be like an army moving against a hill-side before the enemy's batteries are unmasked.

But the Church is moving, and the Master of the Church is behind it. "He has sounded forth the trumpet that shall never blow retreat." Even in these first uncertain days the Church has builded better than it knew. It has created the situation that is to educate it. Those who come after us will judge how well or ill we played our part, but when-ever men hereafter write the story of how Christendom became Christian, they will have to begin a new chapter at the years in which we are now living.

I confess that my faith falters in the very act of professing it. The possibilities are so vast, so splendid, so far-reaching, so contradictory of all historical precedents, that my hope may be doomed to failure. The American churches may write one more chapter in the long biography of the disappointed Christ, which our sons will read with shame and our enemies with scorn. But for the present the East is aflame with the day of Jehovah, and a thousand voices are calling. If failure comes, may it find our sword broken at the hilt.

CHAPTER III

WE are apt to think that progress is the natural thing. Progress is more than natural. It is divine.

Men are impatient with the moral forces which are changing the social order, because they have never comprehended the terrible tenacity and vigor of the social forces that resist progress.

We are to smite a pathway for the Almighty in human affairs. What powers of resistance will we encounter? With what obstacles must we reckon? When a railway engineer plans a cut through a mountain-side, he first finds out what material must be removed. Is it loose dirt and gravel? A steam shovel will serve. Is it granite? He must order up drills and dynamite.

The most important and persistent obstacle of progress is the conservative stupidity and stolidity of human nature. In history, as in physics, the *vis inertiæ* rules. Possession is nine points of sociology as well as of law. There are nations and races that have not changed appreciably for ages. To a student of history the astonishing thing is not that the people occasionally rioted and raged, but that they stood all this awful oppression and injustice with such patience and passiveness. Even a highly sensitive and mobile nation like our own rarely budges when the house next door is burning. It waits till its own roof is on fire. For proof I refer to the history of our tariff and labor legislation.

The passive indifference of the mass of men is backed by the active conservatism of the most influential social

classes. In every social order the ablest individuals rise
to controlling positions and intrench themselves in the
places they have attained. Their effort is to preserve for
themselves and their children the power and wealth which
they have acquired. Knowing the power of the State,
they seek to control politics. Knowing the power of public opinion, they influence the press and the schools. Their
house is built on things as they are; therefore they are
against any change, — except change that will further
fortify their position.

The financial and political forces which the upper classes
have been able to manipulate in all past eras have been
enormous, and the skill with which they handled them was
always the best that could be hired. It is hard to see that
all the sufferings of the revolutionary movement in Russia
have seriously shaken the power of the classes in control.
In our own country the demand for tariff reform ran for years,
indorsed by both parties, yet it was always put off. When
things finally came to the point of action in 1909, the beneficiaries of the tariff were found to be in control of the
Congress that was to reform it, and the tariff was lowered
upward, while the nation looked on, open-mouthed and
stuttering with astonishment. It was a brilliant object
lesson on the power of the conservative interests.

We might expect considerations of justice and mercy
to thaw through the icy indifference of class selfishness.
But moral suasion is strangely feeble where the sources
of a man's income are concerned. Few are impervious to
public opinion, but the only public opinion that strikes
men with full force is that of their own social class. When
their own class supports them in a given moral attitude,
they can afford to disregard the judgment of all other
classes. Students, for instance, act on a code of honor laid
down by the student community, and jest at the judgment
of outsiders. The feudal nobility were very sensitive to

any slight put upon their honor, but utterly regardless of the hatred and condemnation of the classes whom they exploited and oppressed. The justest and most moderate demands of the hungry multitudes have been treated by the privileged classes as wicked attempts to destroy the foundations of society and religion.

In our country the absence of class demarcations and the intensity of public opinion make such an isolation and indifference far more difficult, but the same law holds. The working class leaders are preaching the duty of class consciousness. The leaders of the business class do not need to preach it. An eminent sociologist recently said that the capitalist class is a hundred times more class conscious than the working class. Let us be moderate in our statements and say ten times.

Another element in the general conservatism of society is the physiological conservatism of age. As we age, we are less and less responsive to new needs and ideas. We linger spiritually in the world that surrounded us when we were young and plastic. Only 13 per cent of the population is over fifty years of age, but this aging section of the community is the most influential section. Wealth, learning, reputation, and social standing come to us slowly as we pass through life. We come to hold positions of trust, and can put others in places of power according to our judgment. No one need fear that society will ever lack conservative forces. The physiological laws of age will always steady us against innovation. Indeed, unless death released us when we age, society itself would age and die. The Angel of Death and the Angel of Birth are the guardian angels of progress. Without them any rejuvenation of society would be hopeless.

Add to these personal forces of inertia the power of institutionalized tradition. We are most familiar with that power in the case of the Church. When theology or ritual are institutionalized, and formulated as creeds, rubrics, and ordinals, they outlast the eternal hills. Untold spiritual and physical sufferings have been necessary to break through such codified conservatism and secure any change in religion. But Law has the same conservative bent as theology. Its customs and precedents and traditions are as faithful and clinging as an hereditary disease.[1] But if precedents are not tough enough, we institutionalize them in law, and if law proves revocable, we put it in the Constitution. After that we can rest from our labors, and our works will follow us. Law needs reformation quite as much as theology, and in our country it has received far less of it. Our nation has come to the point where the Constitution of the United States urgently needs revision, but before we get it, we shall discover what it signifies when tradition is institutionalized.

If to all this interlaced network of forces that bind down the mobility of society we have to add the power of a reactionary Church, the case becomes desperate.

Time was when the clergy could match their power with that of kings and emperors. Their influence has declined, but even to-day no government defies them willingly. No city administration in our country would care to have the pulpits of the city reverberate against it. A preacher enjoys a unique immunity from contradiction. To some extent he can invest his personal ideas with the authority of religion itself. However it may be in our own

---

[1] Goethe in "Faust" : —

> "Es erben sich Gesetz' und Rechte
> Wie eine ew'ge Krankheit fort ;
> Sie schleppen von Geschlecht sich zum Geschlechte
> Und rücken sacht von Ort zu Ort.
> Vernunft wird Unsinn, Wohltat Plage ;
> Weh dir, dass du ein Enkel bist !
> Vom Rechte, das mit uns geboren ist,
> Von dem ist, leider ! nie die Frage."

D

country, none will deny that in other countries and in past times the clergy have often fanaticized the people against their own liberation.   They have inspired the ruling classes with a firmer conviction that the maintenance of their rights was the will of God.   Most of us can understand to some degree the accumulated resentment with which the common people in the old countries regard their clergy.

The power of religion is almost illimitable, but it is not necessarily beneficent.   Religion intensifies whatever it touches, be it good or evil, just as electricity turns a magnet into an electromagnet.   There is no love so tender, no compassion so self-sacrificing, no courage so enduring, as the love and compassion and courage inspired by religion. But neither is any hatred so implacable or any cruelty so determined as religious hatred and cruelty.   Mormon polygamy still persists in the face of law, public sentiment, and social evolution, because it is supported and sanctioned by Mormon religion and theology.   When we pray for more religion, let us pray for a religion that is dedicated to the better future and not to an evil past.

We realize so strongly that the Christian spirit is the most progressive of all moral forces that we are apt to forget that the Church in the past has been the most conservative of all institutions.   It is venerable with age and it venerates its own venerability.   It carries a great body of traditional thought for which it claims divine wisdom and authority.   It has claimed divine rights even for its official form of organization.   Consequently it has kept up fossil customs for a thousand years.   The Russian Church and the Roman Church each perform their ritual in a language that was living when each Church was young, but which has now been unintelligible to the people for many centuries.   This is a symbol of far larger facts.   The Church identifies itself with the social conditions of an age and then clings to them when they are passing away.   So it helps to conserve them.   This is a power both for good and for evil, but always for conservatism.   The Church has a mission and duty of leadership, and it never willingly surrenders its people to any movement not controlled by itself.   Thus, wherever the Church is ancient and identified with the past, it is apt to be a conservative force.

All the great national churches of Europe have opposed the conquering march of political democracy.   They all execrated the French Revolution and fought its spiritual influences.   Nothing in the history of the nineteenth century is more thrilling than the passionate longing of Italian patriots for the freedom and unity of Italy.   Yet the ancient Church of Italy, whose secular dominion had been the chief obstacle to Italian unity, not only resisted the final achievement of that desire, but forty years later still stood aside while Italy was celebrating the jubilee of its union.   The irreligion so prevalent in France is in part due to the fact that the Church is identified in the common mind with opposition to democracy and fraternity.   Long after the establishment of the present republic, the French bishops had to be warned by the pope to transfer their loyalty from the dead monarchy to the existing government. The recent condemnation of the Sillon was a condemnation of the principles of democracy.[1]   The Protestant State Churches of Germany have insisted on loyalty to the

[1] The Sillon, *i.e.* the Furrow, organized by an earnest and brilliant young Catholic, Marc Sangnier, sought to plow the atheistic soil of France for the sowing of religious faith by combining Catholic belief with the aspirations of democracy.   The Church at first favored the Sillon, but soon feared it, and the Pope condemned it by a sensational pronouncement in 1910.   He said the Sillon sought to apply the principles of the philosophers of the eighteenth century "by exalting the dignity of human nature, by working in favor of the abolition of social inequality and of the destruction of class differences, and by suppressing all authority," and had sought to upset "the historical and natural foundations of society in order to substitute for them individual autonomy, general equality, and universal brotherhood."   Sangnier submitted.

monarchy and to the reigning dynasties as an essential part of a Christian life, and set themselves both against the political democracy of the first half of the nineteenth century, and the social democracy of the second half. The Church of England, too, has long been Tory in its sympathies and political influence.

It is, therefore, a vital question for the social progress of our country what fundamental attitude the churches of America are likely to take to the forces that are striving to renovate our social order.

If the American churches cover the existing order with the shield of their protection and call on their people in the name of God and religion to keep things as they are, they will make of the short march from Egypt to the Promised Land a weary forty years' pilgrimage in the desert of Sinai. It will take incomparably longer to get results, and the results will be less complete and less stable after they are obtained. The social engineering forces will not be digging through loose gravel beds, but through gravel into which liquid cement has been poured.

On the other hand, if our churches take the side of the people and back the demands for social justice and fraternity in the name of Christ and the Gospel, the whole situation is changed. The influence of religion would weaken the confidence of the possessing classes in their own moral position. Under the pressure of social compunction and sympathy Christian men who hold power and wealth would be disposed to make concessions in practical cases where they cast the decisive vote. Some members of the upper classes would go over to the people's cause with banners flying, and add a powerful intellectual, financial, and moral reënforcement. When Moses leaves the palace of Pharaoh, the chances of Israel to get out of Egypt are considerably improved.

The sympathy of the churches would also hearten the

forward forces. The working classes would feel greater confidence in the justice of their cause, more hope in its triumph, and consequently greater patience in their struggle. Consideration for the friendship and support of the churches would check any inclination to headlong action and desperate methods. Their cause would be less threatened by the malign influence of violent tactics. It rests largely with the churches whether the emancipation of the working classes will come by a gradual and peaceful evolution of society, or whether we are to have the folly and woe of our Civil War over again.

We have a demonstration close at hand what it means whether the Church marches with a great popular movement or stands against it.

When our country cut loose from England and established republican institutions, the really powerful religious organizations, including the Roman Catholic, were heart and soul on the side of the Revolution. The memory of ecclesiastical oppression suffered in Great Britain, and the fear of Anglican domination in America, aligned the religious interests with the common patriotic feeling. In the weary struggle of the Revolutionary War the churches were the moral aids of the government in nerving the people to bring the necessary sacrifices. Their influence helped to secure stability for the raw institutions of the Union when the war was over. The American churches have always accepted heartily the principle of democracy on which our government is based and have invested it with religious sanction. They have themselves been small democracies, built on the same pattern as our civic institutions, and thereby have helped to train our people in the practice of self-government.

The movement for democracy which blazed up in the French Revolution affected Latin America too, and between 1810 and 1825 most of the Spanish colonies gained their independence and established republican governments. But here the Church was not on the side of democracy. The Catholic Church had suffered deeply through the Revolution in Europe. It saw in the revolutionary leaders a spirit of unbelief and revolt against authority. It found its extensive property, its inherited privileges and exemptions threatened by the political changes. Its own constitution and spirit are monarchical and in sympathy with firm authority and reverence for inherited order. For these and other reasons the Church set itself against the modernizing influences of democracy. The conservative forces which exist everywhere in human society were here reënforced by the personal resources and institutional interests of the Roman Catholic Church, and the Church became the stronghold of the reactionary elements. Consequently the history of these nations is not like the track of a marching army, but like the sands of an arena where powerful antagonists have circled in a long-drawn grapple. We are often told that the Latin peoples have less genius and hereditary training for self-government than we. Perhaps the difference in our history is at least partly due to the fact that our republic had the churches with it; their republics had the Church against them.

Cassandra, the daughter of Priam, had the fatal gift of prophecy, and long before the downfall of Troy her spirit was plunged in gloom as she saw from afar the flare of the burning city of her fathers. There are thousands of patriot hearts to-day heavy with similar foreboding as they see the opposing interests, massive and relentless, drawn up for the inevitable conflict. As we realize the solidity and efficiency of the social forces controlled by privilege, we understand the immense importance of the spiritual awakening that is now going on in the heart of the Christian Church. She cannot fight the battle alone, but where the forces are evenly matched she can decide the issue.

Four centuries before Christ a host of Gauls plundered Rome and for seven months besieged the Capitol. At last the Romans purchased their departure. When the gold was being weighed in the balances, the Gallic chieftain Brennus threw his huge sword into the scale containing the weight agreed, and bade the conquered balance the iron with added gold.

Once more the fate of a nation is rocking in the balance. Let the Church of Christ fling in, not the sword, but the cross, not against the weak, but for them!

PART II

THE REVOLUTIONARY DESTINY OF CHRISTIANITY

CHAPTER I

WANTED : A FAITH FOR A TASK

A GREAT task demands a great faith. To live a great life a man needs a great cause to which he can surrender, something divinely large and engrossing for which he can live and, if need be, die. A great religious faith will lift him out of his narrow grooves and make him the inspired instrument of the universal will of God. It is the point at which the mind of man coincides with the mind of the Eternal. A vital faith will gradually saturate a man's whole life and master not only his conscious energies, but his subconscious drifts. The religious revolution in Paul's life was due to a new faith which seized him and made him over, and ever after he knew that a man is justified by a faith more than by any doings. He had made proof of the fact.

Our entire generation needs a faith, for it is confronting the mightiest task ever undertaken consciously by any generation of men. Our civilization is passing through a great historic transition. We are at the parting of the ways. The final outcome may be the decay and extinction of Western civilization, or it may be a new epoch in the evolution of the race, compared with which our present era will seem like a modified barbarism. We now have such scientific knowledge of social laws and forces, of economics, of history that we can intelligently mold and guide the evolution in which we take part. Our fathers cowered before the lightning; we have subdued it to our will. Former generations were swept along more or less blindly toward a hidden destiny; we have reached the point where we can make history make us. Have we the will to match our knowledge? Can we marshal the moral forces capable of breaking what must be broken, and then building what must be built? What spiritual hosts can God line up to rout the Devil in the battle of Armageddon?

Our moral efficiency depends on our religious faith. The force of will, of courage, of self-sacrifice liberated by a living religious faith is so incalculable, so invincible, that nothing is impossible when that power enters the field. The author of the greatest revolution in history made the proposition that even the slightest amount of faith is competent to do the unbelievable; faith as tiny as a mustard seed can blast away mountains.

"Every great revolution demands a great idea to be its center of action; to furnish it with both lever and fulcrum for the work it has to do."[1] What great idea has the Christian Church which will serve as the religious lever and fulcrum for the engineering task of the present generation? What great faith has it which will inspire the religious minds of our modern world in the regeneration of society?

The chief purpose of the Christian Church in the past has been the salvation of individuals. But the most pressing task of the present is not individualistic. Our business is to make over an antiquated and immoral economic system; to get rid of laws, customs, maxims, and philosophies inherited from an evil and despotic past; to create just and brotherly relations between great groups and

[1] Mazzini, "Faith and the Future," in his Essays, Camelot Edition.

classes of society; and thus to lay a social foundation on which modern men individually can live and work in a fashion that will not outrage all the better elements in them. Our inherited Christian faith dealt with individuals; our present task deals with society.

The Christian Church in the past has taught us to do our work with our eyes fixed on another world and a life to come. But the business before us is concerned with refashioning this present world, making this earth clean and sweet and habitable.

Here is the problem for all religious minds: we need a great faith to serve as a spiritual basis for the tremendous social task before us, and the working creed of our religion, in the form in which it has come down to us, has none. Its theology is silent or stammers where we most need a ringing and dogmatic message. It has no adequate answer to the fundamental moral questions of our day. It has manifestly furnished no sufficient religious motives to bring the unregenerate portions of our social order under the control of the Christian law. Its hymns, its ritual, its prayers, its books of devotion, are so devoid of social thought that the most thrilling passions of our generation lie in us half stifled for lack of religious utterance. The whole scheme of religion which tradition has handed down to us was not devised for such ends as we now have in hand and is inadequate for them. We need a new foundation for Christian thought.

The straits of the churches in their present social awakening are both interesting and pathetic. They are in the position of a middle-aged American in Paris suddenly plunged into trouble with the police, and feeling around in his mind for the French vocabulary he forgot when he was a sophomore.

Twenty-five years ago the social wealth of the Bible was almost undiscovered to most of us. We used to plow it six inches deep for crops and never dreamed that mines of anthracite were hidden down below. Even Jesus talked like an individualist in those days and seemed to repudiate the social interest when we interrogated him. He said his kingdom was not of this world; the things of God had nothing to do with the things of Cæsar; the poor we would always have with us; and his ministers must not be judges and dividers when Labor argued with Capital about the division of the inheritance. To-day he has resumed the spiritual leadership of social Christianity, of which he was the founder. It is a new tribute to his mastership that the social message of Jesus was the first great possession which social Christianity rediscovered. A course of lectures on the social teachings of Jesus is usually the earliest symptom that the social awakening has arrived. Is it another compliment to the undischarged force of his thoughts that we handle them so gingerly, as if they were boxed explosives? We have also worked out the social ideas of the Old Testament prophets. But that is about as far as the popular comprehension of the Bible has gone. We have let Paul severely alone. The Apocalypse is not yet printed in red, as it might be. Few commentaries show any streaks of social insight. We have no literature that introduces the ordinary reader to the whole Bible from the social point of view.

In its systematic doctrinal teaching the Church is similarly handicapped. It is trying old tools to see if they will fit the new job. It has done splendidly in broadening certain principles developed under religious individualism and giving them a social application. But more is needed.

With true Christian instinct men have turned to the Christian law of love as the key to the situation. If we all loved our neighbor, we should "treat him right," pay him a living wage, give sixteen ounces to the pound, and not charge so much for beef. But this appeal assumes that we are still living in the simple personal relations of the good old times, and that every man can do the right thing when he wants to do it.   But suppose a business man would be glad indeed to pay his young women the $12 a week which they need for a decent living, but all his competitors are paying from $7 down to $5.   Shall he love himself into bankruptcy?   In a time of industrial depression shall he employ men whom he does not need?   And if he does, will his five loaves feed the five thousand unemployed that break his heart with their hungry eyes?   If a man owns a hundred shares of stock in a great corporation, how can his love influence its wage scale with that puny stick?   The old advice of love breaks down before the hugeness of modern relations.   We might as well try to start a stranded ocean liner with the oar which poled our old dory from the mud banks many a time.   It is indeed love that we want, but it is socialized love.   Blessed be the love that holds the cup of water to thirsty lips.   We can never do without the plain affection of man to man.   But what we most need to-day is not the love that will break its back drawing water for a growing factory town from a well that was meant to supply a village, but a love so large and intelligent that it will persuade an ignorant people to build a system of waterworks up in the hills, and that will get after the thoughtless farmers who contaminate the brooks with typhoid bacilli, and after the lumber concern that is denuding the watershed of its forests.   We want a new avatar of love.

The Church has also put a new stress on the doctrine of stewardship, hoping to cure the hard selfishness of our commercial life by quickening the sense of responsibility in men of wealth.   This also is wholly in the right direction, but here, too, the Church is still occupying the mental position of the old régime.   The word "stewardship" itself comes down to us from an age of great landed proprietors.

It has an antique dignity that guarantees it as harmless. The modern equivalent would be trusteeship. But a trustee does not own; he merely manages. If he mismanages or diverts trust funds to his own use, he is legally liable. If that is what we mean when we preach stewardship, we should be denying the private property rights on which capitalism rests, and morally expropriating the owners. In that case we ought to see to it that this moral conception of property was embodied in the laws, and that the people would get orderly legal redress against stewards who have misused their trusteeship. That would mean a sort of Recall for business men. But in fact the Church puts no such cutting edge on the doctrine. It uses it to appeal to the conscience of powerful individuals to make them realize that they are accountable to God for the way they spend their money. The doctrine is not yet based on modern democratic feeling and on economic knowledge about the sources of modern wealth. It calls for no fundamental change in economic distribution, but simply encourages faithful disbursement of funds. That is not enough for our modern needs.

The Golden Rule is often held up as a sufficient solution of the social problem. "If only all men would act on the Golden Rule!" But curiously enough men find it hard to act on it, even when they indorse and praise it. There seem to be temptations of gain or of fear in our modern life before which our good intentions collapse. But even as a standard to guide our moral intelligence the Golden Rule is not really adequate for our needs. It is a wonderfully practical guide in all simple, personal relations. It appeals to our imagination to put ourselves in the other man's place and thus discover how we ought to treat him. It turns the flank of our selfishness, and compels that highly developed instinct in us to put itself into the service of love. Like the span measure of our right hand we can carry this rule about with us wherever we go, but it is hardly long enough to survey and lay out the building site of the New Jerusalem. Jesus probably did not intend it for more than an elementary method of figuring our duty.

The Church has also revived the thought of following Jesus in daily conduct, living over again the life of Christ, and doing in all things as he would do in our place. That has been an exceedingly influential thought in Christian history. In the life of Saint Francis and his brotherhood, in the radical sects, and in single radiant lives it has produced social forces of immense power. In our own time the books of Mr. Charles M. Sheldon have set it forth with winning spirit, and we have seen thousands of young people trying for a week to live as Jesus would. But it is so high a law that only consecrated individuals can follow it permanently and intelligently, and even they may submit to it only in the high tide of their spiritual life. To most men the demand to live as Jesus would, is mainly useful to bring home the fact that it is hard to live a Christlike life in a mammonistic society. It convicts our social order of sin, but it does not reconstruct it.

These are all truly religious ideas, drawn from the teaching of Jesus himself, and very effective in sweetening and ennobling our personal relations. But they set up no ideal of human society, demand no transformation of social institutions, create no collective enthusiasms, and furnish no doctrinal basis for a public morality. They have not grown antiquated, and never will. But every step in the evolution of modern society makes them less adequate for its religious needs. The fact that the Church is leaning so hard on them at present shows how earnestly it is trying to meet the present need, and also how scanty is the equipment with which it confronts the new social task.

So we return to the question: What is the religious basis for the task of Christianizing and regenerating the social order? Suppose that a Christian man feels a throbbing compassion and fellow-feeling for the people, and a holy anger against the institutionalized wrong that is stunting and brutalizing their lives, converting the children of God into slaves of Mammon. Suppose that he feels this so strongly that he hardly cares what becomes of his own soul if only he can help his nation and race. Suppose that a whole generation is coming vaguely to feel that way. What great word of faith does historic Christianity offer to express and hallow and quicken this spiritual passion which is so evidently begotten of the spirit of Christ? Must he go to materialistic Socialism to find a dogmatic faith large enough to house him, and intellectual food nutritious enough to feed his hunger? Thousands have left the Church and have gone to Socialism, not to shake off a faith, but to get a faith.

I raise this challenge because I believe Christianity can meet it. My purpose is not critical, but wholly constructive. If I did not believe in the vitality and adaptability of the Christian faith, I should sit down with Job on the ashes and keep silence.

But let no one take the challenge lightly. It points to no superficial flaw in the working machinery of the Church, but to the failure of our religious ideas to connect with our religious needs, and that is fundamental. Religion, to have power over an age, must satisfy the highest moral and religious desires of that age. If it lags behind, and presents outgrown conceptions of life and duty, it is no longer in the full sense the Gospel.

CHAPTER II

THE Christian religion, in the form in which our fore-fathers transmitted it to this modern world, was strong in creating a conviction of personal sin, an assurance of personal forgiveness and adoption, and a firm hope of personal immortality, but it was weak in social hopes and aims. In the relations of man to man, and in the relation of man to his own soul, Christianity was the salt of the earth, the great antiseptic against vice and passion, the spur to justice, the motive of neighborly kindness, and the comfort of the poor and helpless. But it furnished no really effective religious conception of redemption for the organic life of human society. It presented no working program by which the social institutions might be transformed in accordance with the will of God and the mind of Christ. The creation of a distinctively Christian social order was not what Christianity was commonly supposed to stand for. Those who did stand for it were men apart. Orthodox theology hardly considered the Christianizing of the social order as part of the scheme of redemption. The pulpit rarely proclaimed it. The hymns of the Church did not give voice to the desire for it. Its liturgies did not direct the power of united prayer toward its achievement.

When Christianity was in its infancy, there were diverse expectations about its future, but it is safe to say that few would have expected this charge to be raised against it. It was born of revolutionary lineage. Its cradle was rocked by the storm wind of popular hopes. What was it that brought the multitudes to the Jordan to hear John and that thrilled the throngs that followed Jesus about in Galilee? Was it the desire to go to heaven one by one when they died? What inspired the early disciples and lent wings to the Gospel? It was the hope of a great common salvation for all the people, the belief that the Kingdom of God on earth was at last in sight.

Christianity was pure and unperverted when it lived as a divine reality in the heart of Jesus Christ. But in his mind its purpose was summed up in one great word: the Reign of God. To this he dedicated himself in baptism. This set him the problems which he faced in the wilderness temptations. This was the center of his parables and prophecies. This explains the ethical standards which he set up in the sermon on the mount. It was the Reign of God on earth for which he consumed his strength, for which he died, and for which he promised to return.

The Kingdom of God is the first and the most essential dogma of the Christian faith. It is also the lost social ideal of Christendom. No man is a Christian in the full sense of the original discipleship until he has made the Kingdom of God the controlling purpose of his life, and no man is intellectually prepared to understand Jesus Christ until he has understood the meaning of the Kingdom of God. The Reformation of the sixteenth century was a revival of Pauline theology. The present-day Reformation is a revival of the spirit and aims of Jesus himself.

When we undertake to restate the conception of the Kingdom of God precisely as it lived in the mind of Jesus, we are beset by a hundred difficulties of criticism and interpretation which only the specialist can estimate. Fortunately most of them are academic, interesting to the scholar, but of slight importance for the practical and modern questions with which we are here concerned. By far the greatest hindrance to a right understanding of the

E

essential purpose of Christ is the ecclesiastical and theological conception of him which eighteen centuries have
superimposed on the historical records of his life and
teachings. That acts as a refracting and distorting medium
of vision, and until a man has to some degree cleared that
away and learned to read the gospels as they stand, he is
not likely to comprehend the social significance of Jesus
and of the gospel of the Kingdom of God.

The safest and surest way of understanding the faith of
Jesus is to understand the faith of his people.[1] He did
not invent his idea of the Kingdom, but received it as a
heritage from the past of his nation. If it had been a
new invention, it could not have exerted such prompt and
widespread power when he proclaimed it. New moral
and religious conceptions usually get little intelligent response at first. They have to ferment in the common
mind for at least one generation before they can move the
masses. Jesus felt no need of defining or explaining the
idea of the Kingdom; he simply announced that it was at
last on the point of realization, and the people understood.
The idea was a common spiritual possession of the Jewish
people, just as belief in democracy is an axiom in the common thought of America.

The hope of the Kingdom of God had been wrought into
the tissue of Jewish thought by the Hebrew prophets.
They had quickened the whole nation to an attitude of
expectancy and hopeful erectness. In other nations religion consisted mainly in faithful adherence to ancient
customs. It turned its face backward. In Israel the
prophets had been a driving force which put religion and
morality on the march to the future. This was a wonderful spiritual achievement. We still feel the impact of their
power. In reading them I feel awed by the presence of

---

[1] In "Christianity and the Social Crisis," Chapter I, I have discussed the
Hebrew prophets more fully.

the living God, as when Moses saw the thorn bush ablaze. These men were so alive to God and felt his righteousness so overpoweringly that they beat their naked hands against jagged injustice and inhumanity. They were centers of religious unrest, creators of a divine dissatisfaction, and the unsparing critics of all who oppressed and corrupted the people.

The prophets were religious reformers demanding social action. They were not discussing holiness in the abstract, but dealt with concrete, present-day situations in the life of the people which were sometimes due to the faults of the people themselves, but usually to the sins of the ruling classes. They demanded neighborly good will and humane care of the helpless. But their most persistent and categorical demand was that the men in power should quit their extortion and judicial graft. They were trying to beat back the hand of tyranny from the throat of the people. Since the evil against which they protested was political, their method of redress was political too. Their religion did not displace politics, but reënforced it. If any modern preacher had told them to disentangle their religion and their politics and keep them in separate compartments, they would not have known what he meant.

They all had a radiant hope of a future when their social and religious ideals would be realized. Emancipation from foreign tyranny, peace and order throughout the land, just and humane rulers, fertility of the soil, prosperity for all, a glorious capital city with a splendid temple in it — it was the social utopia of an agrarian nation. Hardly an ingredient of human life is missing in their ideals, except the hope of immortality. In the prophets before the Exile there is harldy a side-long glance at life after death. With men so religious their hope was religious to the core, as a matter of course. God himself was to be the great mover of events. The more their moral demands were

baffled by brutal power, the more they threw their hope
back on God for fulfillment.   He himself would make bare
his holy arm and put down his enemies, cleanse the nation
in a day of judgment, pour out his spirit to create new
moral forces, and write his law — not on stone, but in
the living hearts of men as a new national constitution.

This reign of God for which they hoped was therefore a
social hope on fire with religion.   Their concern was for
the largest and noblest social group with which they were
in contact, — their nation.   In all their discussions they
take the social solidarity and collective personality of their
nation for granted.   They sought to knit their countrymen together in the bonds of a social order based on divine
rights and sanctions.   They were men and dealt with men,
but they focused not souls, but society.   They called their
coming age the Reign of Jehovah; but his reign, when set
over against the power of the oppressors, meant the emancipation of the people.   To speak frankly, the prophets
were revolutionists.   If they appeared in Russia to-day,
they would get short shrift.   Some of them set their hope
on the invasion of a foreign power like Assyria, which was
to serve as an instrument in God's hands to break the
existing social order to pieces and clear the way for a new
order to be organized by "the remnant" of the plain and
righteous people.   How the writings of these radicals ever
came to be treasured as the sacred literature of their nation
is one of the mysteries of history.   Other nations would
have killed the men and destroyed every vestige of their
writings.   But now that the social wrongs against which
they protested are long dead, we can listen to them im-
partially, and we rightly feel that these men were inspired
by the living God, and were everlastingly right in smiting
wrong as they did.

It is a mistake to assume that the Kingdom of God
meant the same thing to all the prophets.   They were

generations apart. Each stood within his own historical situation, and each saw the future from his own angle of vision. They differed in spiritual purity and elevation just as modern religious leaders differ, and each saw the Kingdom of God as he had it in him to see it. The ideal has a different smile of beauty for every worshiper, but to each it means the fairest and sweetest that he knows.

Moreover, since the ideal of the Kingdom of God was a social possession of the nation, it rose and declined with the outward condition and the inner spirit of the whole people. When the nation lost its independence, its home, its neighborhood life and social coherence in the great Exile, its national hope gained in passion, but lost in sanity. It had to grow in the dark and it changed, as if a flower of the noon were transformed into a night-blooming cereus of mystic fragrance. The prophets before the Exile stood with both feet on the realities of national life. They expected the reign of Jehovah to come by an act of God, but to connect with present conditions and grow out of them. The patriots of the Exile felt that only a miraculous intervention could bridge the chasm between the present misery and the future splendor, and they leaned back with a kind of passive ardor to wait for God's vengeance on their oppressors. All their optimism was projected far into the future. The present era of the world seemed so embedded in evil, that only the hand of God could break it up and create the new era. Sitting in enforced helplessness, history seemed to them like a predetermined scheme. The great change was all fixed in advance by the divine counsels, like the opening of a bank vault by a time clock, and they bent their devout ingenuity to puzzle out the combination of the divine mechanism in advance.

A still more decisive change came about at the same time as a consequence of the contact of the Jews with the great Babylonian and Persian monarchies and the Persian religion. Their horizon was widened by it. The national judgment enlarged into a world judgment; the national salvation into a cosmic renewal; the Messiah of the Davidic line into a heavenly deliverer. We are familiar with the fact that in the first century of our era the Jewish faith mingled with Greek religious philosophy in Alexandria and other centers and created a syncretistic religion of which Philo is the conspicuous example. A similar mixture apparently took place when the Jewish communities mingled with the life of the Eastern empire. Persian dualism deeply affected later Judaism. In the Old Testament there is hardly a glimpse of a Satan and of evil angels. After the Exile, a great hierarchy of darkness was the counterpart of God and the angelic hosts in popular Jewish thought. These new ideas connected with politics. It was clear now why heathen powers were able to hold Israel down. Demonic forces lurked behind them and would have to be overthrown if the Kingdom of God was to be set up. It was no longer a plain human fight against bloody wrong, but a supernal contest against spiritual principalities and powers. Against that black and Titanic background the old hope of the reign of God stood out with high lights and lurid colors.

Under these influences the prophetic hope was worked over into the scheme of what is called apocalypticism, and embodied in a prolific literature. The apocalyptic scheme was not a product of pure Hebrew thought, but an exotic growth. In fact, its dualism and transcendentalism were a radical departure from Hebrew religion. Apocalyptic ideas are to-day one of the special marks of the most conservative biblical school; at that time they were a "new theology" of questionable paternity.

Even in this debased condition the hope of the Kingdom was still a great religious conception, a brave faith holding on tenaciously in an age of gloom. But its influence was full of danger. Those who drank the cup of apocalypticism henceforth moved in a world of unrealities, always expecting what never happened, and "followed wandering fires, lost in a quagmire." The flame of fanaticism which flared up in the Jewish War and in the later revolts against Rome was fed by the fuel of these ideas.

Apocalypticism is of more than academic interest, for it is still a living force. It passed from contemporary Judaism into primitive Christianity. Jewish apocalyptic books were turned into Christian writings by slight changes or additions, and constituted a considerable portion of the early floating Christian literature. Two apocalyptic books of great beauty and power, which we should never want to lose, were embodied in the Old and New Testament canon: the Book of Daniel and the Apocalypse of John. Since it was an axiom of biblical interpretation that all the sacred writings were equal in value and without any contradiction in their contents, it was assumed that all the prophetic writings in the Bible meant what these two books mean. Apocalypticism had the great advantage over prophetism that it was more coherent and systematic. It presented a theology and a philosophy of history. So the apocalyptic thought-world spread from these two books to all the prophetic sections of the Bible and obscured the thought of the prophets beneath their brilliant colors.

So apocalypticism came to dominate the Christian view of future history. Whenever men looked down the future to gain a religious outlook, they saw it in the artificial lay out of apocalyptic dualism and determinism. The apocalyptic hope has always contained ingredients of religious force and value, but its trail through history is strange and troubled reading. It has been of absorbing fascination to some Christian minds, but it has led them into labyrinths from which some never emerged. It has been the inspiration of earnest Christian men in some lines of

Christian activity, but it has effectively blocked their minds with strange prejudices against other important lines of work. It has turned the enthusiasm of great historical movements into injurious fanaticism. It has spawned hopeless little sects. It has been one chief cause why the Kingdom hope has not gained the wide practical effectiveness which it might have, for in this debased and irrational form it is hopelessly foreign to modern life and thought. I know that this charge will pain some devout Christian minds whom I would not willingly hurt, but in the interest of the very hope for which they stand I have to say that the idea of the Kingdom of God must slough off apocalypticism if it is to become the religious property of the modern world. Those who hold it must cease to put their hope in salvation by catastrophe and learn to recognize and apply the law of development in human life. They must outgrow the diabolism and demonism with which Judaism was infected in Persia and face the stern facts of racial sin. They must break with the artificial schemes and the determinism of an unhistorical age and use modern resources to understand the way God works out retribution and salvation in human affairs.[1]

We have our warrant for modernizing and purifying the inherited conceptions of the Kingdom from Jesus himself.[2] He did not deal with men whose minds were a blank on the Messianic future, but with people who held a mass of variegated hopes and expectations and demanded of him that he should fulfill them. The true way of understand-

---

[1] The Rev. I. M. Haldeman has reviewed my book, "Christianity and the Social Crisis," in a booklet published by C. C. Cook, New York, which I should like to commend to the attention of all who are interested in the subject. It is an emphatic condemnation of my positions and an uncompromising statement of the apocalyptic scheme and spirit in all its dogmatic assurance and artificiality. If any one will read the book and the pamphlet side by side, he will face two kinds of Christianity and can make his choice.

[2] For a fuller discussion of the teachings of Jesus, see "Christianity and the Social Crisis," Chapter II.

ing him is to watch him as he makes his way through this popular thought, accepting, rejecting, correcting, elevating, enlarging, and hallowing. Every true leader of humanity has exerted his power in that method. He must take the right impulses and convictions already existing among the people and weld them into a mightier unity. At the same time he must resist and cut under the misleading and draining ideas and tendencies with which the truth is mixed up. So Jesus accepted the faith in the Kingdom of God which his prophetic forerunners held out to him from the past with unseen hands, and made it the holy content and purpose of his own life. Therewith he gave his full indorsement to the social hope which is an essential part of the Kingdom idea. On the other hand, he accepted it, not as a slave, but as a son, and refashioned it with sovereign freedom. Some of its ingredients that were dearest to the popular heart offended his ethical and religious spirit, and he set himself with forethought to oppose them. These corrections, therefore, embody his most distinctive contributions to the Kingdom ideal. On these points we are sure that we have pure Christian thought and not inherited Judaism. On the other hand, when he lays a corrective emphasis, for instance, on individuality and spirituality, we must not forget that this is balanced by his tacit acceptance of the main idea which he held in common with the people as a matter of course.

The points at which Jesus consciously opposed the current conceptions set up the landmarks of a distinctively Christian ideal of the Kingdom, and I shall attempt to enumerate them. In reading the Gospels from this point of view, we ought to remember, however, that he must have worked out a clear comprehension of these differences gradually. All original minds begin with the stock of ideas common to their social environment and work away from that toward their own formulation of truth as they find themselves. However great the divine ingredient in Christ's nature was, it did not exempt him from the law of growth. As a boy he "advanced in wisdom and stature," that is, in physical and intellectual maturity. Did that process stop when he was thirty years old? Or was it accelerated and intensified when he entered on his public activity? A ready-made Christ who had no need of expanding and trying out his ideas by experience and action would have had no genuine human nature, and it is plain heresy to believe in such. In fact, in the desert temptations we see him in absorbed and concentrated thought in view of the problems he was to meet. We therefore put the problem faultily when we ask: What did Jesus think? We ought to ask: In what direction were his thoughts, working? We want the line of his movement if we are to follow him. His life was cut short in early manhood. John says that at the end Jesus spoke of thoughts which had to remain unuttered, and expressed the hope that the Spirit of God would work on his sayings which lay like germs in their minds, and make them grow.[1] If we want to be faithful to his spirit, therefore, we shall not only have to trace the line along which he moved, but even prolong it beyond the point marked in his recorded teaching.

1. The universal expectation of his people was that the Messiah would hoist the flag of revolt and slay the oppressors either by the breath of his mouth or by the sword of the faithful. Force was apparently the only means by which the tyranny of the present could be overthrown and the Messianic kingdom set up. Yet Jesus repudiated the force revolution from the first. To set up the reign of peace by bloodshed was to accept the kingdoms of the world from the hands of the devil. When his popularity in Galilee was at its height, thousands of pilgrims on their way to the festival at Jerusalem gathered around him on

[1] John xvi. 12–14.

the desert shore of the Lake and tried to make him king by force. It was the psychological moment, but he escaped under cover of the darkness. When they followed him next day, he drenched their fires.[1] During the last days at Jerusalem his power over the people was still such that the Sanhedrin felt that the peace and security of the State were at his mercy.[2] They assumed as a matter of course that the revolution was his aim, but he never lifted the hand that would have summoned it. He even refused the aid of celestial force.[3] When we consider how abjectly kings and statesmen have relied on force to maintain their hold, and how persistently the suggestion of a propaganda of violence has thrust itself on the leaders of popular movements, we can realize what moral firmness and purity of motive is implied in this steadfast refusal to fight evil with evil. He committed himself to death and his cause to apparent failure rather than let the red devil of bloodshed loose.[4] This was not timidity nor squeamishness, but a sagacity centuries ahead of his time. Violence calls out violence. "They that take the sword shall perish by the sword."[5] Evil is not permanently lessened by counter-evil. This must be one of the differentiating marks of those who seek social salvation under the leadership of Jesus: to refuse violent means, however tempting, and to throw all fighting ardor into moral protest.

2. To the Jews the Kingdom of God meant the triumph of Judaism. The kings of the world would become tributary to the Jewish empire. The capital of the world would be shifted from Rome to Jerusalem. To have full share in the Messianic salvation a Gentile must become a Jew. When Gentiles claimed equal rights in the Christian churches, it came with a shock to the Christian Jews, and some could never bring themselves to assent to it. Prob-

---

[1] John vi.   [2] John, xi. 47–48.   [3] Matt. xxvi. 47–56.
[4] John xviii. 36.   [5] Matt. xxvi. 52.

ably Jesus began with the same horizon as his countrymen, but every time he met a Gentile or Samaritan we can
see his horizon in the act of expanding. His heart was so
utterly human that when he felt the touch of a Gentile
hand, he seized the hand of a man and a brother. In the
joy of that discovery he denied the Jewish claim to special
privilege, and reversed the order of merit. He said he had
never found such faith among Jews as in that Roman captain,
and predicted that heathen would come from the ends of
the earth to sit with the Hebrew patriarchs, while their sons
were left in the dark outside. He went out of his way to set
a Samaritan up as a model of humane kindness above the
priest and the Levite. That was sand in the mouth of his
countrymen, just as if an American orator should tell an
Illinois crowd of the superior virtues of the "Dago" and
the "Hunk," or an Alabama crowd of the brotherhood of
a negro. In Jesus we encounter the spirit that beats down
the trammels of a narrow group to seek a wider allegiance;
that reaches out beyond jingo patriotism toward the
brotherhood of nations; that smites race pride and prejudice in the face in the name of humanity; and that refuses
to accept even from religion any obligation to hold ourselves apart from our fellows. That determined breadth
of brotherhood is another permanent landmark of the
Kingdom ideal as Jesus expressed it.

3. The idea of the Kingdom of God was filled with democratic spirit, but it had come down from despotic times
and was cast in monarchical forms. The Messiah was expected as a king, and his followers hoped to rule as his
courtiers. Jesus flatly contradicted such expectations and
laid down the law of service as the fundamental law of his
kingdom.[1] He himself had not come to be served, but to
serve to the death, and all greatness in the Kingdom would
have to rest on the same basis. Modern democracy is

[1] Matt. xx. 20–28.

destined to establish the same principle and to abolish all lordships that cannot show their title on that basis. The Jewish conception of God himself was cast in the mold furnished by human despotisms. When Jesus spoke of God as our Father, he democratized God himself. That substituted happy obedience for the old slavish fear, and free coöperation between man and God for the Jewish mercantile contract ideas. By raising the value of the human soul and its life on the one side, and by bringing God down close to us as our Father, he laid the religious foundation for modern democracy and anticipated the craving of the modern spirit. We to-day conceive of the Reign of God as the Commonwealth of God and Man.

4. To all devout Jews the Mosaic and Rabbinic Law was at the core of religion, much as "the Church" is to pious Catholics. Consequently the Kingdom of God did not mean the abolition of the Law, but its enthronement. The Kingdom would come when the people obeyed the Law; and when the Kingdom came, the Law would be obeyed completely. It was the hope of the Kingdom that made the Pharisee so punctilious and rigid. Jesus, on the other hand, was so indifferent to the ceremonial laws that he struck the earnest religionists of his day as a man of loose life and of destructive influence.[1] All his enthusiasm went out toward justice, mercy, and good will among men. In that respect he revived and surpassed the spirit of the great Hebrew prophets. In the synagogue at Nazareth he set forth the program of the Kingdom from Isaiah; it meant glad news to the poor, release to the captives, sight to the blind, and liberty to the bruised and crushed lives.[2] When John doubted his Messiahship he pointed as proof of it to the fact that human life was being relieved and restored, and that the poor had good news proclaimed to them.[3] . . . All these are phrases of emancipation. In his

---

[1] Matt. xi. 16–19; v. 17.   [2] Luke iv. 16–21.   [3] Matt. xi. 2–6.

wonderful picture of the Messianic judgment there is not a word about sacrifices, prayers, fasting, food laws, or purifications.[1] The Messiah's mete wand is social sympathy. Some have felt the hunger and sickness and loneliness of their fellows; some have not. That alone decides on their fitness for the kingdom of brotherhood. The mercy which Jesus demands here is not the dole of charity, but the sense of solidarity which makes all human life part of our life. He asserts that solidarity for himself by holding that whatever is done to the weakest member of humanity is done to himself. All ethical obligation gets new force and clearness when that oneness is accepted. In this indifference to ceremonial religion and this insistence on human solidarity and its ethical corollaries, he parted company with the ecclesiasticism of his day and of all days and transferred the Kingdom ideal to the plane of ethics inspired by the spirit of God. This is another line of orientation for all who seek the Kingdom of God as real disciples of Jesus.

5. To the great mass of men then and now material plenty and comfort were the real substance of any good time coming. Religious obedience was the price they must pay to get on the inside. Economic wealth was the end; morality and religion the means. Jesus never despised the physical needs of men. Surely he who spent his strength in healing the sick; who remembered the hunger of the multitude; whose first thought for the daughter of Jairus was that the little girl ought to have something to eat; who took pride in the fact that his disciples had never lacked for anything while they were with him; and who put a prayer for the daily bread in the central place amid the brevity of the Lord's Prayer, — was too human and too wise to belittle the physical foundations of human life. But to him eating and drinking were not the end of life. All our

[1] Matt. xxv. 31–46.

hurry and worry that runs after still more property, still more dress, still another automobile, still more sumptuous meals, would seem to Jesus pitiable heathenism and starvation of the God in us. "Seek ye first the Kingdom of God and the righteousness of God, and these things will follow." [1] For overfed men to preach simplicity of living to the underfed is abominable cant. But for the overfed to preach it to themselves is salvation. We are wholly right in demanding a juster and more equal distribution of economic possessions as the A B C of a better social order, but the real good that we are after is not the dollars and cents, but the satisfaction of our craving for justice, the sweep of human fellowship made possible by greater financial equality, the gladness of unhindered brotherhood and humanity. Our mothers were just as happy and quite as noble on ingrain carpet as our daughters on Axminster. The great philosophy and music of Germany were dreamed out on very humble fare. Thousands of Americans every summer plunge back into the wilderness with a sigh of relief to sleep on the ground and scrape frying pans for themselves, and uncounted thousands would like to if only they could. When they revert to simplicity and live like brothers with their guides and friends, they feel that they have a soul and a God. The socialists are right in emphasizing the economic basis of human society; but Jesus is also right in emphasizing its spiritual ends. To exploit no man and to love all men, to be at peace with your brothers and with yourself and with your God, to sing with joy at sight of a sunset or an autumn creeper or a happy child, to prize truth and knowledge, to turn effortless from thought to adoration, and to enjoy prayer as the highest exercise of life, — this is the real thing; the rest is scaffolding. The followers of Jesus should lead all others in protesting against the Dives-and-Lazarus plan of the social order, but not chiefly because

[1] Matt. vi. 19-34.

Lazarus fell short of the normal number of ounces of crumbs, but because they were crumbs and were thrown to him as a dole. A cheese sandwich and an apple make a fair meal if Fletcherized properly, but of equality and freedom we want unlimited rations. Men fear that the amount of goods produced will diminish if socialism should displace the present driving methods of industry. As Christian men we should consider that a slight evil, provided it would purchase social equality and allow us to be brothers to our present superiors or inferiors. This is another mark of the distinctively Christian conception of the Kingdom of God, that the spiritual values of human life are set above all economic aids to life as the real end to be sought.

6. The popular expectation reveled in luscious descriptions of the Messianic age. In the teachings of Jesus there is a marked absence of utopian details, and a marked insistence on present duty. Jesus is the eternal model for the combination of enthusiasm and sanity. The people expected the Messianic revolution to happen with magic suddenness. Jesus in the wilderness temptation declined to set off the fireworks by a miraculous leap from the temple pinnacle. He simply began among his friends and let the thing work its way. Probably at the outset he too expected a mass movement and a swift culmination, but as he tried it out, he realized that this was a matter of slow and patient preparation. The little dogmatist proclaims the invulnerability of his theory long after Humpty Dumpty has fallen from the hard wall of fact. The great minds always bow to the superior sanctity of reality. Jesus proved his sonship by his teachableness. The parables in which he describes the Kingdom of God as an organic growth slowly making its way against hindrances and coming to maturity in its own time were the ripe result of his own observation. These parables clearly express a conscious departure from the current ideas and a cautious

contradiction of them. This is one of the points on which
it is even more valuable for us to know the direction of his
thought than his actual positions. It has taken the intellectual world eighteen hundred years to make some comprehension of the law of growth a part of the working outfit
of the human mind. If Jesus in childhood had entered
into the modern outlook instead of the Jewish, it would
certainly have been easier for him to work out that law
with all its implications. At any rate he differed from his
contemporaries in taking so long a look ahead, and the
combination between far-sighted patience and indomitable
persistence must be counted a peculiar mark of the Christian hope. Apocalypticism presents the utopian form of
the Kingdom hope. Those who hold it are marking time
on a set of ideas derived from pre-Christian Judaism and
incompletely christianized.

7. But while he took the long outlook, he felt the near-
ness of the Kingdom more than they all. To him it was not
merely near, but here, germinating in their hearts, pulsating in their common thoughts, reversing their valuation of
things, sweetening their relations, lifting the least of them
above the highest representative of the old order,[1] and
quietly creating a new world. Apocalypticism had set
up the theory of the two eras, "this age" and "the coming
age," and separated them by a chasm. At least in some of
his sayings we can see Jesus working away from that view
to the thought that the old era was even then passing into
the new. He said, you cannot draw a line, and say, Lo
here, or, Lo there; it is coming without clamor; it is now
among you.[2] When will your boy become a man? Look
into his eyes and see the man now.

[1] Matt. xi. 11.
[2] Luke xvii. 20-21. The Greek phrase may mean either "within you" or
"among you." In either case it is an assertion of the presence of the Kingdom and a contradiction of the catastrophic expectations.

F

These are the points, then, on which Jesus differed from the current expectations, and at which he put his own peculiar stamp on the Kingdom hope. The people expected the Kingdom to be set up by force, either human or celestial; Jesus repudiated the use of force. They regarded the Kingdom as the prerogative of a select group: he insisted on sharing its rights with all, and turned it from a Jewish into a broadly human ideal. They connected it with the hope of self-aggrandizement, which they had learned from human despotisms; he democratized the idea of the Kingdom and put all who sought it under the law of service. They connected it with ceremonial and ecclesiastical religion; he set it within the domain of secular and ethical relations. To many of them the material benefits were the main thing and ethical conformity was the price to be paid; to Jesus fullness of ethical and religious life for all was the real end and substance of the hope. They expected it by catastrophe; he worked toward the law of gradual growth. To them it was future; to him it was both future and present.

But all these corrections of the popular expectation did not involve the least surrender of the inherited hope of a reign of God on earth. Even when he saw death moving down on him to crush both him and his faith, he held fast to it. His promise to return is the form which his invincible faith took in the sight of death.

He never transferred the Kingdom hope from earth to heaven.[1] The Kingdom was so much of this earth that Jesus expected to return to earth from heaven in order to set it up.

Neither did he ever spiritualize the vitality out of the

---

[1] The phrase "the kingdom of the heavens" is constantly used by Matthew and has been the source of a great deal of misunderstanding. Mark and Luke use "the Kingdom of God" in the parallel passages, and the two phrases evidently mean the same thing. "The heavens" was probably used to avoid misuse of the divine name.

Kingdom idea, as the Church has so constantly done. It was never a disembodied ghost to him, but a warm and lovable human reality. "Jesus never held, and never could hold, a purely abstract, internal, spiritualized conception of the Kingdom, which claims only the inner world of the soul and its ethical outflow for God, and leaves the outward organization of the world with its thousand fold wrong and misery intact. To his mind that would have meant a bisection of the world into a spiritual kingdom of God and a material kingdom of the devil, and no sound religious faith can tolerate such a thing." [1]

The purpose of all that Jesus said and did and hoped to do was always the social redemption of the entire life of the human race on earth. If we regard him in any sense as our leader and master, we cannot treat as secondary what to him was the essence of his mission. If we regard him as the Son of God, the revelation of the very mind and will and nature of the Eternal, the obligation to complete what he began comes upon us with an absolute claim to obedience.

The later theology of the Church construed all his life from the point of view of the cross. All his efforts to win his nation for the Kingdom of God moved then toward predetermined failure. Indeed, according to some views, the real redemption would have been frustrated if the people had accepted his leadership. In art, too, his image has been stripped of virility and turned into that of the meek and passive sufferer. But the Jesus with whom his enemies dealt, and from whom they backed away, was never very passive. He was high-power energy from first to last. His death itself was action. It was the most terrific blow that organized evil ever got. He always moved with a purpose and his purpose always was the Kingdom of God. At the beginning he really hoped to win his nation. When he saw

[1] Beyschlag, "Leben Jesu," I, p. 232.

isolation and death impending, he accepted the law of vicarious suffering as part of the method of redemption, and took Death by the hand as God's minister to bring in the Kingdom. His death was his greatest act of social service. His cross was the climax of the world evil and the turning point of history toward a definite and permanent emancipation and redemption of the race. All the great permanent forces of evil in humanity were strangely combined in the drama of his death: bigotry, priestcraft, despotism, political corruption, militarism, and the mob spirit. They converged on him and did him to death.

But he is alive, and now it is their turn.

CHAPTER III

CHRISTIANITY set out with a great social ideal. The live substance of the Christian religion was the hope of seeing a divine social order established on earth. But hardly had the social ideal of Christianity risen above the horizon when it went into a long eclipse. Not that its light was ever wholly obscured. Few eclipses of the sun are total, and even during a total eclipse the brilliant flames of the solar corona encircle the obscuring disk of the moon with a coronet of radiance that tells of the hidden fount of light. For the reverent student of history nothing is more wonderful than to see the Christian ideal misunderstood and perverted, the Christian spirit betrayed, suppressed, and caged, and to watch them bursting forth again with the indomitable energy of divine life.

How was it that the social hope was so early obscured? Why did it move from the center of Christianity to the circumference, and change from a hot and living issue into a decorous relic of the past? That question is of more than merely historical interest, for to-day the process is being reversed. The social ideal is moving back to the center and is getting hot with life. Those of us who want to coöperate intelligently with God in this reversal, ought to understand the causes which obscured the ideal in the early Church, and the causes which are bringing it to new power in modern life.

The explanation which I shall attempt will have to be fragmentary. The matter is so subtly connected with all

69

the main drifts of Christian history that a volume would be required to do justice to the question, and I have only a fragmentary understanding of the process myself. Democracy has but recently begun to prod the scientific mind, and our older historians have only a bungling answer for the questions raised by the new social interest. The next generation will know more than we do about this problem, for the social spirit is beginning to carry the candle of investigation through the cluttered attic of Church History, hunting for the mislaid records of Christian democracy.[1]

The cause which must be ranked first in order of time was the gradual emancipation of Christianity from its earliest Jewish environment. The intense democracy of early Christianity was largely a Jewish inheritance. In Judaism the hope of the reign of God on earth, thanks to such religious teaching as no other nation had, had become a dogma of the popular faith, a common axiomatic conviction. On the other hand, in Greek and Roman life there were only a few academic and poetic glimmerings of such a hope, and Christianity had to create it by its own resources. Consequently the social hope began to fade in intensity as Christianity was assimilated by its new Græco-Roman environment.[2]

The social hope continued to be nourished by Jewish influences even after Christianity had cut loose from living

[1] For an interesting reëxamination of church history, see Conrad Noël, "Socialism in Church History." The various writings of Richard Heath exemplify the spirit in which the material ought to be approached. My book, "Christianity and the Social Crisis," Chapter IV, traverses some of the road traveled in this chapter. Professor H. C. Vedder, "Socialism and the Ethics of Jesus," Chapter XI, has dealt with the same subject.

[2] Albrecht Ritschl: " While the Græco-Roman world was entering the Church, nothing exerted so little influence on its efforts for the moral regeneration of men as the aim of realizing the Kingdom of God in the sense in which Christ had conceived it." Herzog's "Real-Encyclopædie," Vol. XII, 2d edition, the article "Das Reich Gottes."

Judaism. The Old Testament with its social ideals, the Jewish apocalyptic literature with its revolutionary tone, and the inspirational prophetic life in the primitive Church continued the social influence of Judaism. But gradually the concrete social promises of the Old Testament were etherealized by allegorical interpretation. The uncanonical apocalyptic books were shelved as the New Testament canon narrowed down the range of reading in the Church. The "prophesyings" of the early days were discouraged as the Church grew clerical and set on orthodoxy.[1]

The terrible struggles of Jewish patriotism against Roman domination in the Jewish War of A.D. 70 and in the later massacres and revolts created a bitter anti-Jewish feeling in large portions of the civilized world, and this popular sentiment affected the Christians. The Kingdom hope suffered by this, for all the traditional imagery concerning the Kingdom was Jewish in its drapery and coloring. How could a patriotic Greek or Roman make Jerusalem, a ruined city in a despised little country, the center of all his social hopes, and long for the descent of a New Jerusalem? It became a convincing argument against the millennial hope to call it "Judaizing."

Thus the transition from the Jewish to the Greek environment, which constituted the first great crisis and epoch in the history of the Church, was one cause which obscured the social ideal. The form in which the social hope was presented was another cause.

The Kingdom ideal had not remained at the altitude to which Jesus had lifted it, but had relapsed into the crudeness of pre-Christian apocalypticism. Jewish apocalyptic books were edited for Christian consumption by slight additions and changes. The atmosphere of studied mystery, of unreality and stage calcium lights, which char-

[1] See the admirable article by Harnack on the "Millennium," in the "Encyclopædia Britannica."

acterizes all apocalypticism, was doubtless wonderfully attractive to some, but surely also distasteful to others, especially to the educated men. In the conservative and less intellectual Church of the West the millennium remained an undisputed asset of theology even in the third and fourth centuries. It was plainly taught in Scripture; the Gnostic heretics rejected it, and that fact certified its orthodoxy. But it was carried on the books as an incumbrance of theology, much as demonology is in modern theology. It had lost its religious fervor for the educated leaders.

In the Greek Church it was crowded even out of theology. An earthly millennium with rich harvests, fat cattle, and marriage festivities seemed a contradiction of the fundamental Christian aspirations to the theologians of the Alexandrian school. Did not salvation consist in overcoming the carnal lust of the body and the fatal charm of earthly possessions in order to attain the spiritual and eternal life? How, then, could they teach people to desire a thousand years more of earthliness? So Greek theology expurgated the Scriptures of all millennialism. The Apocalypse of John was thrown bodily out of the canon of the Greek Church for centuries. The vine and fig tree of the Old Testament were allegorized and spiritualized till only a disembodied soul could sit under them with comfort. The concrete, human, historic Jesus, whose aim was to establish a righteous life for his people, was supplanted by the heavenly Logos-Christ who gave immortality and made men partakers of the divine nature. In the Eastern half of Christendom theology permanently undermined the social hope.

Throughout the Church the hope for the Reign of God was bound up with the expectation of the visible return of Christ, who was to inaugurate it, and when the first, and the second, and the third generation passed away, and the

Lord had not returned, the millennial hope lost its first freshness and intensity and changed from a religious passion into a theological reminiscence.

Another most important cause for the fading of the social hope was the ascendency of the other-worldly hope. The religious ardor which had glowed in the expectation of the Lord's return to establish his millennial reign now burned with ever increasing intensity in the hope of heaven and immortality. Above the starry firmament was a heavenly world where God was enthroned in glory amid the host of the angels. Thence the Saviour had descended to reveal the laws and impart the powers of that upper world to men, that we too might ascend at death and live forever with the ransomed in his presence. In this world of sin and pain and death there is no abiding city. The true home of the soul is yonder, and we must make our pilgrimage through this vale of tears with ceaseless longing. To love this world and care for its possessions is equivalent to spiritual failure. The soul must be trained by ascetic discipline to detach itself, not only from the sins of the flesh, but even from the desire for food and comfort, from the love of wife and child and home, in order to concentrate all its desires and forces on the attainment of salvation in heaven.

This other-worldly longing was not Hebrew, but Greek in its origin. Belief in life after death played no appreciable part in Jewish religious life till after the Babylonian Exile. In the teachings of Jesus it was firmly lodged, but not at all central in importance. On the other hand, in contemporary Greek life it was intensely strong. All the religions that had real vitality in the first three centuries tried to satisfy the desire for assurance of immortality, and the Greek mind seized on that aspect of the Christian religion above all others. So the Church developed it until it became almost the exclusive content of Christianity. All through

the Middle Ages life was dominated by the belief in a supernatural world. The medieval Church was able to wield
such power because it had the keys of heaven; its doctrine
showed how to get to heaven; its sacraments imparted the
heavenly life. Baptism exorcised the powers of darkness,
sterilized the leaven of original sin, and implanted eternal
life; confirmation conveyed the Holy Ghost; the eucharist
fed the famishing soul with heavenly life; penance and
absolution cleansed away the guilt that would otherwise
condemn to hell; extreme unction prepared the dying soul;
burial in consecrated ground or, if possible, inside of a
church and in holy garments protected against the greedy
fiends that might snatch the soul when the trump of the
archangel summoned all on the *Dies Iræ*. Masses and
indulgences followed the soul even across the chasm of
death to shorten the stay in purgatory and hasten the
entrance to heaven. All the ascetic practices and all the
enormous growth of monastic life were ethical corollaries
of other-worldly religion. The tremendous political power
of the Church and its vast landed wealth during the Middle
Ages were the outcome of the universal desire for heaven
and testify to its absorbing strength. The immortal poem
of Dante proves how completely even the greatest minds of
that age lived in that conviction and desire.

Around this belief the superstitious excrescences of religion sprouted, but the belief itself was not an excrescence,
but the essence of the working creed of Christendom till
our own time. The reformatory sects of the Middle Ages
shared it with the Roman Catholic Church. The Reformation preached more spiritual and intellectual processes
of obtaining salvation, but the other-worldly aim of salvation remained the same. In devout Protestantism a deep
longing for heaven and distrust for the body as an enemy
of the soul were regarded as marks of a Christian frame of
mind. A diluted form of asceticism continued wherever

religion was taken seriously. The Puritan contempt for worldly pleasures, the simplicity of dress among Mennonites and Quakers, the Methodist suspicion of amusements were Protestant forms of the same instinct which had filled the medieval monasteries. "Pilgrim's Progress" tells the story of salvation; but it describes it as a breaking away from this earthly life and as a concentration of all powers on the attainment of heaven. Milton and Bunyan inhabited the same spiritual world as Dante.

This other-worldly concentration of religious desire and energy still dominated the Christian life of the generation just preceding ours. It practically constitutes the gospel now preached in a majority of American churches. The really effective religious ideas are more faithfully mirrored by the hymns of a given time than by its theology and sermons, and a study of our hymnals, especially of the innumerable collections of Gospel hymns which are a really native expression of American Christian life, gives an overwhelming impression of the predominance of other-worldly desires. "In the Christian's home in glory;" "Shall we meet beyond the river?" "I will sing you a song of that beautiful land, the far-away home of the soul;" "That will be glory for me" — what endless variations of the same great theme!

I have no desire to disparage this type of religion. My own youth was nurtured in it, and even its defects have something of dearness to me, like the narrow staircases and sloping ceilings of an old home. It has been the comfort and stay of the bruised and lonely when the wings of the death angel had brushed their doorpost. It makes the eternal choice between right and wrong concrete and tremendous by showing the goal to which each path leads. It strengthens the dawning consciousness of God and the higher life in the young. It has bred strong souls by the self-restraint and discipline it imposed. It has added immeasurably to the valuation put on human life that even the humblest man is an immortal soul, and that in the end the serf and the noble will stand on equal terms before the judgment seat. Strong faith in a life to come has been one of the most powerful forces of social control in the past, a chief influence in making the present life clean, tender, and worth living.

But after all, the desire for rest in heaven is not the social hope of the Reign of God on earth with which Christianity set out. The atmosphere of detachment from this world and of longing for death is not the atmosphere in which Jesus lived in Galilee. He did not estimate the values of life from that point of view, nor lay the emphasis in religion that way. The current of religious energy which made the hope of immortality incandescent was diverted from the hope of a divine social life on earth and left that like a dark lamp. Other-worldly religion developed only those ideas and those ethical motives in religion which served the salvation of the individual in the life to come, and left many of the other talents. of Christianity buried in a napkin. It overdeveloped some sides and underdeveloped others. Thus it contributed to the eclipse of the hope of the Kingdom. If, nevertheless, it has exercised a profound influence on private and public morality and has practically helped to prepare for the Kingdom of God on earth, that proves that the Christian religion is charged with such an amazing social dynamic that even its leakages and by-products have had a revolutionary effect on society. What, then, will it do when it takes the moral renewal of society in hand consciously?

Another chief cause for the eclipse of the social hope was the ascendency of the organized institutional life of Christianity, — the Church. The Kingdom of God is an ideal demanding both the highest spiritual fervor and the most practical sagacity for its realization. The fervor was absorbed by mysticism and the longing for heaven; the sagacity by the tasks of church life and organization. Heaven and the Church together drained the Kingdom ideal of the spiritual force needed for its vitality.

The practical creation of a Christian social order would employ all the constructive social ability of Christian men. It would be the greatest of all political tasks — taking the word "political" in its highest sense. But the organizing ability of Christian leaders from the outset was employed in building up one great social structure within the social order, — the Church. They have always toiled with enormous spiritual energy to organize it, expand it, enrich it, supply it with the material basis of noble buildings, and stimulate and educate its human resources. This task has required all the greater ability because the Church had to rely in the main on voluntary support and effort, while the State can use the easier method of compulsion. How completely the energy of the ministry is absorbed in the task of keeping the Church going, any minister can tell if he stops to consider. Even if a minister wants to employ some of his time in social effort, he often finds himself pulled back by the demands of the organization which has the first claim on his time.

While Christianity was opposed and suppressed by the Roman Empire any effort to reconstruct the social order from a Christian point of view would have met with small thanks. The churches were grateful when they were let alone. They were like socialist locals in the era of repression in Germany, or like Protestant churches in Spain. All they could do was to form small communities, keep their people away from heathenism, knit them together by spiritual cohesion, and educate them in Christian living. Their social achievements along these lines are worthy of all admiration. They created little groups of fraternal democracy, called one another "brother" and acted on the name, purified the relation between husband and wife, gentled the relation of parents and children and of masters and slaves, and made mercy toward the poor so essential a part of their practice that begging in time became actually a virtue.[1] They built up a chain of such organizations so firm that when all the weight of the Empire was thrown on it twice for ten years at a time, it stood the strain.[2] The Church thus built up a State within the State, and its constructive ability was expended on that task. But in thus confining its political activity it limited its political outlook. When the Church emerged from the era of oppression, it had a powerful organization to be maintained and the conviction that to maintain that organization was practically the whole social duty of Christianity. Since that was the formative age of the Church, the precedents and theories then created settled the fundamental policy for subsequent times.

When the era of suppression ended at the beginning of the fourth century, the opportunity to christianize the social life in wider ways had arrived. But by this time much of the revolutionary spirit of Christianity had died away. Some humanizing influence was exerted, but the chief concern of the church leaders was for the Church itself and for the clergy. All human organizations develop a kind of corporate egotism, a collective hunger and self-assertion that endangers the higher ends for which they were created. When our political parties get into power, their first concern is apt to be for "the organization" and not for the country. The Church is only an agency to create the Kingdom of God, but practically it came to regard itself as the Kingdom. Does not Christ reign where his Church reigns? Is not his Kingdom advanced when his Church is strengthened? That practical substitution received theo-

---

[1] On the social efficiency of the early Christian churches see "Christianity and the Social Crisis," Chapter III.   [2] A.D. 250–260 and 303–313.

retical support through the philosophy of history developed in Augustine's "City of God." Far beyond the intention of Augustine men inferred that the *civitas* of carnal men was the State, and the *civitas Dei* which he traced through history was the organized Church. Such an identification involved a terrible condemnation of the State and the existing social order. The present social order was due to sin, governed by Satan, held together by violence, and characterized by private wealth and injustice. No condemnation of capitalism by socialist thinkers has ever been quite so severe as the theory of the State developed by the Catholic Church.[1] On the other hand, the organized Church appeared with the halo of the social ideal. Services rendered to civil society were robbed of most of their moral value and religious motive. The Church stood out as the all-embracing object of Christian devotion and service. That involved an eclipse of the Kingdom ideal, for the Kingdom is the reign of God in the common life. The territory within which it must develop is the social order. The conception that the State is Satanic, discouraged faith in the possibility of a Christian civil order.

The Church did embody a fractional part of the Kingdom ideal. Alongside of a cruel and tyrannical social order it built a duplicate social order which really rested on a nobler foundation. The law of Christ was still its ultimate charter, and appeal always lay to that highest tribunal. De-

---

[1] When the great Pope Gregory VII was engaged in his struggle against the Emperor Henry IV, he wrote, A.D. 1081, to Bishop Hermann of Metz about the nature of civil and ecclesiastical government and the relation of the two, and this is his theory of civil rulers : "Who does not know that kings and princes are descended from those who in ignorance of God, plainly under the impulse of the prince of the world, the devil, by pride, robbery, perfidy, murders, and in short by nearly all kinds of crime sought in blind greed and intolerable presumption to tyrannize over their equals and fellow-men ?" The letter may be found in Mirbt, " Quellen zur Geschichte des Papsttums," 2d edition, pp. 105–112.

generate and tyrannical as many of the clergy were, the best among them were almost the only socialized intellects to be found at that time, the only social workers to whom the common people could turn amid the oppression of civil society. The fact that so many of the best men entered the service of the Church, and that the sins of the Church were felt more keenly than those of the civil governments, prove that it must have been the highest social expression of Christianity which men then knew. It was able to command that devotion which is given only to social ideals connected with religion. Very much of the real good accomplished by the Church it accomplished not as the exponent of revealed religion, nor as the institution of supernatural salvation, nor as the ecclesiastical hierarchy, but as the highest social good that men could discover in their life.

To get a really just estimate of the social value of the Church in the past, we must not measure it by the abstract standards of modern ethics, but compare it with the other social forces and organizations existing in the contemporary social order. We tacitly assume that if the Church had not used its power tyrannically, justice and freedom would have prevailed. On the contrary, some other social organization would probably have used that same power even more tyrannically. In the Eastern half of Christendom the Church never had enough independence and vigor to wrestle with princes and emperors as it did in the West. Consequently, the State used it as a mere tool without the courage or power of protest. Is it accidental, then, that in the domain of the Eastern Church despotism is still unbroken to-day, while in the domain of the Western Church it has been permanently shattered? As compared with the despotic State the Church was still a fulcrum for the lever of God. It kept alive the ideal of a social organization ruled by Christ, and within that organization the forces that were to revolutionize the world first gathered headway.

Yet even within its own organization the Church fell far short of living up to the principles of the Kingdom of God. It became a close replica of the Roman Empire within which its organization had been molded. The popes did their best to copy the Cæsars whose throne they inherited. The early democracy of the Church passed first into an oligarchy, and then into a monarchy, and its official heads took no interest in breeding the spirit of liberty in the people. It is significant that as the laity were suppressed by the clergy, the millennial hope was silenced. "The millennial hope receded step by step in the measure in which philosophical theology advanced and in which the laity passed under the domination of the clergy. The people were deprived of the religion which they could understand and furnished with a belief which they could not understand; or else the old faith and the old hopes faded of themselves and were superseded by the authority of a mysterious creed. In that respect the extermination or the fading of millennialism is perhaps the most momentous fact in the history of Eastern Christianity." [1]

To sum up, the long eclipse of the social ideal was due to a combination of various causes. The decline of the Jewish influence deprived it of the energy which centuries of preparation had given it in Judaism. Its apocalyptic form made it unreal and unpractical. Speculative theology crowded out the social ideas by a wholly different and apparently more "spiritual" set of conceptions. The hope of heaven absorbed the religious fervor which might have reached out for a better life on earth. The organized Church absorbed the constructive ability of Christian men, concentrated their social interest on the work done through the Church, and depreciated the religious value of the social

---

[1] Harnack, "History of Dogma," Vol. II, pp. 294–300.

G

order outside of the Church. The decline of democracy within the Church weakened the religious force of democratic and social aspirations.

The great purpose of Jesus, the reign of God among men on earth, has shared the experience of Jesus himself. Its history has been a long *Via Dolorosa*.

CHAPTER IV

THE REBIRTH OF THE SOCIAL HOPE

To-day the social ideal of Christianity has almost emerged from its eclipse and is becoming once more the great working dogma of our faith.

Its emergence began with the dawn of modern democracy. As soon as the common people came to a collective self-consciousness and understood their own instincts and needs, they struck out for a social realization of the Christian faith.

Beginning with the twelfth century, a series of remarkable religious movements ran through the countries of Western Europe, differing widely in their local aims and doctrinal coloring, but with a strange unanimity of spirit and purpose. Some, like the Franciscan movement, were protected and perverted by the Church; others, like that of the Waldenses, the Lollards, the Taborites, and the Anabaptists, were condemned and persecuted by it. We are accustomed to speak of the latter group as evangelical sects, and to interpret them as forerunners of the Protestant Reformation. It is much closer to historical truth to say that they were the first stirrings of Christian democracy, expressions of lay religion and working-class ethics. They heralded the religious awakening of the common people and their cry for the Reign of God on earth.

These movements combined an ardent hope of a better age with a searching condemnation of the existing social order. They were all inspired by millennial hopes. Apocalypticism revived and got a new meaning from contemporary events. There was to be a new era, a great judgment on the Church, a golden age for all the world. The enthusiasm for poverty which characterized these radical movements before the Reformation and which seems strange to us, gets its real significance as a religious protest against social iniquity. The great institutions of the Church had accumulated enormous landed wealth, and were fat with rents and profits. The higher clergy had secured special privileges, exemptions, and governmental powers, till they were brazen with despotic spirit. The vow of poverty which every monk took had in many cases become a mere sham, for it admitted him to membership in a wealthy monastic corporation and enabled him to live in idleness on the labor of others. When Saint Francis of Assisi wedded the Lady Poverty and refused property for his order as well as for the individual monk, he tried to make parasitic wealth and power impossible for himself and his friends. This most famous and beloved saint of the Middle Ages was the great friend and ideal of the common people, a very incarnation of Christian democracy. In its infancy, before the Church twisted it and wrested it to its own taste and use, the Franciscan movement was charged with an almost revolutionary social sympathy.[1] The Waldensian movement, originating a few years before, was animated by a similar spirit. These men washed their hands of rent and profit, and went to share the life of the people. They headed a social and religious quest for simplicity, sincerity, honesty, and fraternity. In some of these movements none was allowed to hold a government office, because he would thereby become a tool of cruelty and judicial murder and torture. They all held the communistic ideals about property. Wherever voluntary poverty was not the outcome of an ascetic desire for heaven, but an expression of

[1] Sabatier's "Life of St. Francis" is still the classical interpretation of that wonderful soul.

democratic spirit, it stood for the strongest possible condemnation of a selfish and exploiting social order and for an heroic effort to live a truly human and fraternal life. Some bold reformatory spirits, like Arnold of Brescia and John Wiclif, could see no salvation for the entire Church till it ceased to be an exploiter, surrendered its wealth, and adopted the Christian law of simplicity and service.

The fact that these movements were chiefly concerned for the reform of the Church must not blind us to their social significance. The Church is always part of the social order, and in that age it was relatively a far larger part of it than now. It was inextricably tangled up with all the rest of the governing powers. With true instinct the re-awakened democracy turned its forces first on the redemption of the Church. The fact that the Church, the body of Christ, had been seized by the forces that oppressed and exploited the people was the crying shame of the times, more keenly felt than any other horror. All felt that the first step in the creation of a righteous social order was the emancipation of the organized conscience of Christendom. If Christ had a voice once more, all the rest would follow. The course of history in the last four hundred years has proved the correctness of that instinct. The Church was really the strategic key to the emancipation of the people.

The great battle of the Protestant Reformation did not turn on the establishment of the Kingdom of God on earth, but on the question how a man could be justified before God and save his soul now and hereafter. The theology of the Reformation was not modeled on the teachings of Jesus, in which the Kingdom is central, but on the doctrinal system of Paul. It was a discussion of old Catholic problems from new points of view. Some of the minor radical parties did indeed make the ethical and religious teachings of Jesus fundamental and revived the

hope of an earthly reign of Christ, but so far as the great
Reformers are concerned, the social hope was still under
eclipse. The exegetical conscience of Protestantism was
still too numb to make them acknowledge that the Old
Testament prophets and primitive Christianity taught a
reign of righteousness on earth, and the sympathy of the
Reformers with the common people was not sufficiently
active to make the idea lovable to them. Neither Luther
nor Calvin was by nature or conviction a democrat. Melanchthon taught that the Kingdom of Christ is "spiritual
and internal," and all it means is "that Christ is seated
on the right hand of the Father, interceding for us, and
giving his Church forgiveness of sins and the Holy Ghost."
It is significant that both Melanchthon and Calvin, the great
theologians of the Lutheran and Calvinistic churches, shied
away from the Apocalypse of John and let it severely alone.

Nevertheless the Reformation marked a long stride
toward the renaissance of social Christianity. We saw in
the last chapter that among the chief influences obscuring
the social ideal were the dominant place taken by the
Church in the religious consciousness of medieval Christianity, the absorbing intensity of other-worldly desires
and beliefs, and the suppression of the common people and
their instinctive social faith. At these three points the
Reformation inaugurated a profound change. As to doctrine it was a reform; as to the Church it was a revolution. The Reformation broke the hypnotic control over
the intellect and outlook of men which the medieval
Church had exercised, so that they could begin to estimate
the plain secular facts and blessings of life on their own
merits. The Church had been the great institution representing the other world on earth; its priesthood had opened
the gate to heaven; its sacraments had stood for the
miraculous inflow of other-worldly powers. The Reformation shattered the Church, denied the powers of the priest-

hood, and abolished most of the sacraments. It denied the ascetic principle which was the ethical corollary of other-worldly views of life, emptied the monasteries, and did away with clerical celibacy. All this reduced the abnormal other-worldliness of religion and turned a larger portion of the force of religion toward this world and its social interests. By dethroning the hierarchy, giving the laymen equal spiritual standing with the priest, and drawing the laity into the spiritual management of the churches, the Reformation began the process of democratizing religion. But democratic Christianity inevitably means social Christianity. In its final outworkings the Reformation changed the Church in the direction toward which the democratic movements before the Reformation had striven, and in christianizing the Church, it set free the organized conscience of Christendom and made modern science, modern democracy, and modern social renovation possible.

Every Reformation leader of course had some social aims in full view, but the actual social effects of their movement have been vaster and more sweeping than any of them dreamed. The theology for which they fought with all their conscious energy is now slowly fading from the consciousness of the churches they founded. On the other hand, the democracy and equality which they feared or which they abetted unconsciously, are gathering headway with the power of manifest destiny, and are now felt to be more essential in Christianity than the questions about the eucharist or predestination on which churches and nations were rent asunder. These great leaders of men were themselves but tools in the hands of a higher will that was working out a larger end than they knew.

It took a long time for the idea of the Kingdom of God to win a recognized place in Protestant theology, and still longer for it to become a religious force. It was usually regarded as another word for the "invisible Church," the totality of all the regenerate souls scattered through humanity and known to God alone. The coming of the Kingdom meant increasing purity of belief, growing warmth of religious life, and the missionary spread of Christianity. The whole conception was still circumscribed by the walls of the Church. Whenever a bolder note of hope for a reign of peace and justice on earth was sounded, it was usually blown on the old Jewish trumpet of apocalypticism and was a resuscitation of biblical ideas, rather than a spontaneous utterance of present-day faith.

The eighteenth century marked the adolescence of the modern spirit. Science learned to stand erect and to cut that narrow pathway of knowledge which has since broadened into a highway for the nations. A strange enthusiasm for democracy and the rights of man was in the air. The historical method and spirit were taking possession of the world of intellect. The religious principles for which the Reformation fought, but which had so often been obscured under the dust and blood of the battle field, were becoming the assured possession of all. Philosophic minds, like Leibniz, Herder, and Kant, looked backward and forward over the history and the destiny of humanity with a broad sweep of comprehension. They no longer confined the saving work of God to Israel or the Church, but saw the Christ educating all mankind by all the varied agencies of human institutions.

To such men the idea of the Kingdom of God offered itself as the only religious conception capacious enough for thoughts so large, for the Kingdom is an idea as broad as mankind, as inclusive as life itself, and as Christian as the Gospel.[1] The lofty mind of Immanuel Kant was inspired

[1] Johannes Weiss, "Die Idee des Reiches Gottes in der Theologie," Section IV, is especially rich in quotations and references to eighteenth-century thought.

with a religious enthusiasm by contemplating the possibility of an ethical commonwealth, a kingdom of virtue, in which right action would not, as in the State, be due to coercion, but to the free devotion of all. He held that in the past the upward aspirations of the individual have been corrupted or checked by the influence of society, which was a social force dominated by evil; therefore a new organization of society is needed, consciously dedicated to righteousness, which will support and train the weak will of the individual. Such a Kingdom of God would be at once the highest good and the highest duty. Its realization is not like other duties, from man to man, but is a duty that the race owes to the race, the duty of realizing its divine destiny. It is a duty so vast that it transcends the powers of man; God alone can bring it to reality. But because we feel the duty, we may conclude that the Ruler of the moral universe is behind it and is coöperating with us, and each of us must work for it as if all depended on himself.[1]

So the conception of the Kingdom of God has forged to the front as the modern spirit has come to religious self-consciousness, and has been enlarged and modernized to make it the adequate receptacle for the vaster range of present-day knowledge. In recent years it has become the common possession of thoughtful religious men. Every constructive force in modern religion has contributed to its ascendency.

The new historical study of the Bible has put it to the front. We have learned to see each biblical thought in its own historical environment and to let every biblical writer speak out his own ideas. No one has profited more by this willingness than Jesus himself. The eclipse of the Kingdom idea was an eclipse of Jesus. We had listened

[1] Kant, "Die Religion innerhalb der Grenzen der blossen Vernunft," especially Section III.

too much to voices talking about him, and not enough to his own voice. Now his own thoughts in their lifelike simplicity and open-air fragrance have become a fresh religious possession, and when we listen to Jesus, we cannot help thinking about the Kingdom of God. The new study of primitive Christianity has similarly forced on our attention the large place which "the Coming of the Lord" and the millennial hope held in the religious life of the first generations. For four centuries theology has been simultaneously modernizing itself and working backward toward Christ. The Reformation got back to the early Fathers and to Paul. We are getting back to Christ and to his faith in the possibility and certainty of the reign of God on earth.

The spread of evolutionary ideas is another mark of modern religious thought. It has opened a vast historical outlook, backward and forward, and trained us in bold conceptions of the upward climb of the race. There is no denying that this has unsettled the ecclesiastical system of thought, much as the growth of tree roots will burst solid masonry. But it has prepared us for understanding the idea of a Reign of God toward which all creation is moving. Translate the evolutionary theories into religious faith, and you have the doctrine of the Kingdom of God. This combination with scientific evolutionary thought has freed the Kingdom ideal of its catastrophic setting and its background of demonism, and so adapted it to the climate of the modern world.

The practical influence of foreign and home missions has been another constructive influence in modern Christianity which has aided the advance of the social conception of the Kingdom. The leaders of the missionary movement have been compelled to adopt imperial policies and to think in terms of nations and races. Missionaries have been forced by the facts of human life to look beyond the saving of single souls and the establishment of churches to the christianizing of social customs and institutions. The strategy of missions has taught us to reckon with generations in the slow implanting of new powers of spiritual life in great races. The ablest leaders of the missionary propaganda have been among the pioneers of the Kingdom idea, because no other idea was adequate for their needs. The most effective expositions of this revolutionary new theology have come from the platform of missionary conventions, and not from the chairs of theological seminaries.

Another great factor in modern life which has helped to give real vitality to the Kingdom ideal is the enthusiasm for democracy. The gospel of the Kingdom proclaims the kingship of God, but somehow that always means the emancipation and democracy of the people. If God is king, the little kings take their exit. Kings and churchmen have never been taken with the tune of the Kingdom of God when it was accompanied by the reverberating drumbeat of democratic passion. It is a significant fact that in Germany, where Christian socialists have felt bound to remain loyal supporters of the monarchy, the Kingdom of God is made the subject of learned exegetical studies, but is disconnected from the popular social aspirations and seems to awaken no enthusiasm. On the other hand, in the democratic countries, Switzerland, France, England, and America, it has become the great word of Christian socialism.

But the cause which above all others has lent religious power to the Kingdom ideal is its connection with the new social enthusiasm. Wherever men absorb the bolder social purposes and yet keep in loyal connection with historical Christianity, they realize that the idea of the Reign of God on earth combines these two fundamental forces of their life, — and nothing else does. I remember how Father McGlynn, speaking at Cooper Union in the first Single

Tax campaign in New York, in 1886, recited the words, "Thy kingdom come! Thy will be done on earth," and as the great audience realized for the first time the social significance of the holy words, it lifted them off their seats with a shout of joy. In the first century "the Kingdom of God" meant a combination of the religious and the social hopes of the common people. To-day the same elements are fusing once more under new conditions, and the same spirit has taken possession of the ancient word. One of the earliest services of social Christianity has been that it has revitalized that great idea and reintroduced the Church to her own earliest gospel.

That ascendency of the Kingdom idea in modern religious life which I have attempted to trace has been one of the determining facts in my own spiritual experience, and perhaps this personal note may add something to the discussion.

Twenty-five years ago, in the early dawn of the social awakening, we young men were groping in the dark. All our Christian intuitions assured us that this new call for social justice was of God, and that the very spirit of our Master was urging us on. But the older brethren told us that the true function of the ministry was not to "serve tables," but to save the immortal souls of men. One told me that these were "mere questions of mine and thine," and had nothing to do with the Gospel. A young missionary going to Africa to an early death implored me almost with tears to dismiss these social questions and give myself to "Christian work." Such appeals were painfully upsetting. All our inherited ideas, all theological literature, all the practices of church life, seemed to be against us. There was no room in Bethlehem for this new-born interest of ours, and we young men were not yet ready to assert that this was the prince of the house of David coming to claim his ancestral home, and with vastly more rights in the place than most of the furniture with which our wise friends had helped to fill it. So we visited him as he lay in the manger and took comfort in certain humble folk who had strange tales of songs by night and foretellings of great joy to come.

When the forgotten social ideas of the Christian evangel did become clear to us, we felt like young Columbuses taking possession of a new continent. In 1891 I spent a year of study in Germany, partly on the teachings of Jesus, and partly on sociology. That is a good combination and likely to produce results. In the Alps I have seen the summit of some great mountain come out of the clouds in the early morn and stand revealed in blazing purity. Its foot was still swathed in drifting mist, but I knew the mountain was there and my soul rejoiced in it. So Christ's conception of the Kingdom of God came to me as a new revelation. Here was the idea and purpose that had dominated the mind of the Master himself. All his teachings center about it. His life was given to it. His death was suffered for it. When a man has once seen that in the Gospels, he can never unsee it again.

When the Kingdom of God dominated our landscape, the perspective of life shifted into a new alignment. I felt a new security in my social impulses. The spiritual authority of Jesus Christ would have been sufficient to offset the weight of all the doctors, and I now knew that I had history on my side. But in addition I found that this new conception of the purpose of Christianity was strangely satisfying. It responded to all the old and all the new elements of my religious life. The saving of the lost, the teaching of the young, the pastoral care of the poor and frail, the quickening of starved intellects, the study of the Bible, church union, political reform, the reorganization of the industrial system, international peace, — it was all covered by the one aim of the Reign of God on earth.

That idea is necessarily as big as humanity, for it means the divine transformation of all human life. It alone can say without limitation, "Nil humani a me alienum."[1]

In 1892 a number of us, who were all passing through the same molting process, organized the Brotherhood of the Kingdom and dedicated ourselves to the task of "restoring that idea in the thought of the Church and of realizing it in the world."[2] The organization has been too unselfish to become large, but it was a powerful support and stimulus in those early days of isolation. The course of events since then has justified it. Of all the ideas which we were then trying to work out, there is not one but has become a recognized and commanding issue. Of the men who then trusted the inner voice and the outer call an unusual number have risen to positions of acknowledged leadership in the face of a sentiment that was long hostile to their convictions. I attribute this to the fact that the all-inclusive conception of Christianity which they adopted set them large tasks, unified their otherwise scattered interests, inspired them with religious joy, compelled them to fight for God, and so made strong men of them. The experience of this group is typical of that of uncounted others. The triumphant return of the Kingdom idea has marked its line of march by thrice-born men.

Now that the conception of the Kingdom of God has reëntered Christian thought, all religious thinking will have to be done in a new synthesis. In the past the theology of the Church could be stated with scarcely a mention of that purpose which had been the central thought of Christ. Christian hymn books could be compiled without giving expression to this mighty religious hope and motive. Now

---

[1] "Nothing that is human is alien to me."

[2] Information about the Brotherhood of the Kingdom may be secured from the secretary, Rev. Leighton Williams, D.D., Amity House, 312 West 54th Street, New York City.

the Church will have to recast its systematic and practical theology, its ritual, its prayers, its hymns, and its evangelism to make room, not simply for the terminology, but for the aims, the motives, the passions, the philosophy, which are summed up in the phrase "the Kingdom of God." [1] But in thus readjusting itself, it will be working out its own salvation, and will become the organ of a more searching and constructive redemption for modern humanity.

[1] To illustrate my meaning, I may be allowed to refer to a pioneering venture in one of these directions, made in my book, "For God and the People, Prayers of the Social Awakening," published in 1910 by the Pilgrim Press. The response to these prayers, when a few of them were published in the *American Magazine,* and the fruitful use made of them afterward, confirmed me in my conviction that there is a great untapped reservoir of religion in the interests which lie outside of the Church but inside of the Kingdom.

CHAPTER V

WE set out with the proposition that we need a religious faith to inspire and guide us in that task of redeeming the social life of humanity which is clearly laid upon our generation. We have found that faith. Not in traditional theology, Catholic or Protestant, but in the Christianity of Jesus Christ himself. Traditional religion had many scattered social motives and impulses, but it lacked a fundamental dogma of social redemption. The religion that lived in the heart of Jesus and spoke in his words, not only had a social faith; it *was* a social faith. The Church has authority over us only so far as she embodies the mind of Christ; when she has allowed his central purpose to be set to one side or forgotten, we follow the Master.

Our trust in his leadership is once more confirmed by finding that his religious aim, the Reign of God on earth, has quietly risen to new clearness and power simultaneously with the development of modern life. The most ancient dogma of Christianity by an inherent necessity is becoming the instinctive and spontaneous faith of our own age. That fact creates a presumption of God-willed spiritual destiny.

I wish now to show that the faith of the Kingdom of God is fundamentally adapted to inspire and guide us in christianizing the social order.

First of all, it is a religion for this earth and for the present life. The old religious aims overemphasized the other world and undervalued the present world. They taught men to regard the earth as a vale of tears, a place

96

of pilgrimage through which we must hasten, a vestibule of heaven or hell. The body with its instincts was an enemy of the soul. Ascetic suppression of its desires was a logical corollary of this intense concentration on the life to come. The eye of faith was turned upward and saw all its visions beyond the stars.

On the other hand, the faith of the Kingdom puts a new religious value on this earth of ours and on the present life. This earth is even now the habitation of God, and it is ours to make it wholly so. It is not a place to be spurned, but a home to be loved and made clean and holy. The vision of the Reign of God creates a far keener and more impatient sense of the present reign of sin, but the belief in the redemptibility of this earth permits no dumb resignation, but puts the sword into our hands and sends us to the front. This joyful religious acceptance of the present life involves no surrender of the life to come. When our work for God is done and we are tired, when our growth in God has exhausted the opportunities offered by the present life, we can lie down secure in the hope that our life will unfold in greater fullness in a new environment adapted to the garnered results of the present life. But for the present we are here. Here we must see our visions, and here we must realize them. The hope of the Kingdom of God makes this earth the theater of action, and turns the full force of religious will and daring toward the present tasks.

Further, the faith of the Kingdom of God wastes no strength on religious paraphernalia, but concentrates it all on the real task of redemption. Religion in the past has always spent a large proportion of its force on doings that were apart from the real business of life, on sacrificing, on endless prayers, on traveling to Mecca, Jerusalem, or Rome, on kissing sacred stones, bathing in sacred rivers, climbing sacred stairs, and a thousand things that had at

H

best an indirect bearing on the practical social relations between men and their fellows. It is the glory of Christianity that at least in its purer forms it has wasted so little of its driving force on such "religious" actions, and has established so close a connection between religion and ethics. But the old religion of other-worldly salvation necessarily diverted immense currents of energy toward actions that were apart from daily life.

On the other hand, the Kingdom of God calls for no ceremonial, for no specific doings. It insists solely that the natural relations among men which God has created shall be ruled by God's will. It demands an organized fellowship of mankind, based on justice and resulting in love, binding all men together in strong bonds of trust, helpfulness, purity, and good will. Like Jesus, it makes love to God and love to man the sole outlet for the energy of religion, and thereby harnesses that energy to the ethical purification of the natural social relations of men.

We are a wasteful nation. We have long wasted our forests and the fertility of our fields. We pour the precious sewage of our cities into our rivers and harbors to defile and poison the water. We waste child life, the dearest and costliest product of the nation, by needless mortality. We waste the sufferings and pangs of motherhood that brought the children into being. We waste the splendid strength of manhood by industrial accidents and tuberculosis. But the most terrible waste of all has been the waste of the power of religion on dress performances. If that incalculable power from the beginning of time had been directed intelligently toward the creation of a righteous human society, we should now be talking on a level with angels.

Again, the idea of the Kingdom of God on earth will improve our social relations because it gives religious value to the plain man's job. A religion which prepared souls for heaven put a high valuation on professions that dealt with the soul, on the calling of the minister, the teacher, the artist, the mother, and persons in these professions could feel the pride and joy of nobler aims running through their daily work if they were people of religious mind. When they did their daily work, they were aiding the souls of men and serving God. But the "butcher and baker and candlestick maker," who were dealing with coarse and material things, had no such hallowing consciousness of their calling. A man might prove his Christianity by baking an honest pound loaf of bread, but the bread itself did not seem to be a contribution to religious ends.

On the other hand, the Kingdom of God deals not only with the immortal souls of men, but with their bodies, their nourishment, their homes, their cleanliness, and it makes those who serve these fundamental needs of life veritable ministers of God. Are they not serving the common good? Are they not working sacramental miracles by coöperating with that mysterious power which satisfies the want of every living thing by making the grain and the tree to grow? If they do their job well, that job itself is their chief ministry to men and part of their worship of God. Whenever they strive to increase their serviceableness to humanity, they make another advance toward the Kingdom of God. On the other hand, if a man does his job badly, or turns the goods he makes into means of extortion, he is sinning not only against individuals, but against God by breaking down and setting back the Kingdom of God on earth. If the conception of the Kingdom of God came to be the working faith of our modern world, every business man would confront the question whether his business as a total, in the goods it turns out and in the men it employs, is advancing or retarding the Reign of God on earth. Our entire business system would be under the condemnation of religion until it was an institutionalized expression of the Christian law of mutual service. If our business men engaged in reorganizing business for that higher end, they could for the first time in history have the same ennobling sense of serving God which a minister, a teacher, or a mother may now have. They are now a disinherited class in religion. They have a religious sense of worth mainly when they are doing something for their church or their philanthropies outside of their business. The Kingdom faith, once lodged in a man's mind, compels every man to become a redeemer, and his chief redemptive ministry is through his job.

The conception of the Kingdom of God will also demand the development of a Christian ethic for public life. We have none now. Our religion in the past was a religion of private salvation; consequently it developed an effective private morality. It had no ideal of salvation for the organic life of society; consequently it developed no adequate public morality. The conclusive proof of this assertion is the fact that the Christian Church during the nineteenth century allowed a huge system of mammonistic exploitation to grow up which was destructive of human decency, integrity, and brotherhood, and the Church did not realize its essential immorality until its havoc had become a world-wide scandal which even the most blunted conscience could comprehend. Other-worldly religion was sensitive about anything that endangered the salvation of the soul, for that was its one great object. The virulence of sins was measured by their influence on the soul of the sinner rather than by their effect on society. A church member might be disciplined for using the name of God profanely, and be left in peace if he paid his employees sinfully low wages and brutalized the image of God in them. When Christian men are taught to judge all their actions by the effect which they have on the advance of the Reign of God among men, we shall restandardize all our sins according to their social destructiveness, and assign a far greater damnatory value to some of the most respectable sort.

As that religious conception gets a lodgment in any mind, there will be one more recruit available for the common attack against the powers of social destruction.

Every reform would get a higher meaning, and also a more judicious balance, if it were connected with the central purpose of the reign of God.

That great religious hope would put an eternal significance and beauty into the slightest act of unselfish and chivalrous help, just as the cup of cold water becomes a sacrament when it is hallowed by the thought of Christ.

The temptation to use tricky or foul means to attain a reform would be checked if that reform were seen as part of the Kingdom of God. We should realize that the sum total of good cannot be increased by increasing the total of evil.

If the Kingdom of God on earth once more became the central object of religion, Christianity would necessarily resume the attitude of attack with which it set out. When it faced a hostile world and waited for the coming of the Lord and the establishment of his Kingdom, it had the temper of the pioneer. It has had the same spirit wherever it has had to lay the foundations for a Christian social order in heathen nations. But where it has taken the existing social order for granted and has devoted itself to saving souls, it has become a conservative force, bent on maintaining the great institution of the Church and preserving the treasure of doctrine and supernatural grace committed to it. When we accept the faith of the Kingdom of God, we take the same attitude toward our own social order which missionaries take toward the social life of heathenism. Instead of feeling under obligations to defend things as they are, Christian men would be under religious constraint to be the most searching moral judges of the present conditions. They would have a social ideal so large and daring that the program of all other reformers would be only fragments of the Christian program. The Church would have to "about face." The center of gravity in the whole Christian structure of history would be shifted from the past to the future.

As that marching attitude would become common, it would create an instinctive sympathy with all who are championing humane causes. The adventurous and chivalrous spirit would be set free in religion, and that would win the virile spirit of youth. The young always shrink from the ladylike and innocuous saint, and prefer a courageous sinner to a bloodless Christian. But there is a wonderfully swift response whenever any one dares to summon them for some forlorn hope in the service of Christ. The Kingdom of God would evoke the spirit of battle and the finest temper of sport. Indeed the Kingdom of God is the greatest fight for which men ever enlisted, and the biggest game that was ever played. The odds are always against you. It is just as if a lone little eleven on the gridiron should see the whole crowd from the bleachers pouring down into the field and lining up against them. Yet you know in your soul that you are bound to win, for God is playing on your side, and God has unusual staying powers. All who have ever fought for the Kingdom of God know that there is a strange joy in it. The memory of one good fight for freedom or justice gives a thrilling sense of worth for a life-time. There is even a stern sense of humor as you watch the crowd rolling down on you and you wait to be trampled on.

What would it be worth for social redemption to have that spirit become common among religious men?

CHAPTER VI

WE who know personal religion by experience know that there is nothing on earth to compare with the moral force exerted by it. It has demonstrated its social efficiency in our own lives. It was personal religion which first set us our tasks of service in youth, and which now holds us to them when our body droops and our spirit flags. Religion can turn diffident, humble men like Shaftesbury into invincible champions of the poor. All social movements would gain immensely in enthusiasm, persuasiveness, and wisdom, if the hearts of their advocates were cleansed and warmed by religious faith. Even those who know religious power only by observation on others will concede that.

But will the reënforcement work the other way, also? Religion strengthens the social spirit; will the social spirit strengthen personal religion? When a minister gets hot about child labor and wage slavery, is he not apt to get cold about prayer meetings and evangelistic efforts? When young women become interested in social work, do they not often lose their taste for the culture of the spiritual life and the peace of religious meditation? A hot breakfast is an event devoutly to be desired, but is it wise to chop up your precious old set of colonial furniture to cook the breakfast? Would the reënforcement of the social spirit be worth while if we lost our personal religion in the process?

If this is indeed the alternative, we are in a tragic situation, compelled to choose between social righteousness and communion with God.

Personal religion has a supreme value for its own sake, not merely as a feeder of social morality, but as the highest unfolding of life itself, as the blossoming of our spiritual nature. Spiritual regeneration is the most important fact in any life history. A living experience of God is the crowning knowledge attainable to a human mind. Each one of us needs the redemptive power of religion for his own sake, for on the tiny stage of the human soul all the vast world tragedy of good and evil is reënacted. In the best social order that is conceivable men will still smolder with lust and ambition, and be lashed by hate and jealousy as with the whip of a slave driver. No material comfort and plenty can satisfy the restless soul in us and give us peace with ourselves. All who have made test of it agree that religion alone holds the key to the ultimate meaning of life, and each of us must find his way into the inner mysteries alone. The day will come when all life on this planet will be extinct, and what meaning will our social evolution have had if that is all? Religion is eternal life in the midst of time and transcending time. The explanations of religion have often been the worst possible, God knows, but the fact of religion is the biggest thing there is.

If, therefore, our personal religious life is likely to be sapped by our devotion to social work, it would be a calamity second to none. But is it really likely that this will happen? The great aim underlying the whole social movement is the creation of a free, just, and brotherly social order. This is the greatest moral task conceivable. Its accomplishment is the manifest will of God for this generation. Every Christian motive is calling us to it. If it is left undone, millions of lives will be condemned to a deepening moral degradation and to spiritual starvation. Does it look probable that we shall lose our contact with God if we plunge too deeply into this work? Does it stand to reason that we shall go astray from Jesus Christ if we engage in the unequal conflict with organized wrong? What kind of "spirituality" is it which is likely to get hurt by being put to work for justice and our fellow-men? Some of the anxiety about personal religion is due to a subtle lack of faith in religion. Men think it is a fragile thing that will break up and vanish when the customs and formulas which have hitherto incased and protected it are broken and cast aside. Most of us have known religion under one form, and we suppose it can have no other. But religion is the life of God in the soul of man, and is God really so fragile? Will the tongue of fire sputter and go out unless we shelter it under a bushel? Let the winds of God roar through it, and watch it! Religion unites a great variability of form with an amazing constancy of power. The Protestant Reformation changed the entire outward complexion of religion in the nations of northern Europe. All the most characteristic forms in which Christianity had expressed itself and by which its strength had hitherto been gauged were swept away. No pope, no priest, no monk, no mass, no confessional, no rosary, no saints, no images, no processions, no pilgrimages, no indulgences! It was a clean sweep. What was left of religion? Religion itself! At least your Puritans and Huguenots seemed to think they had personal religion; more, in fact, than ever before. Catholics thought it was the destruction of personal religion; really it was the rise of a new type of religion. In the same way the social Christianity of to-day is not a dilution of personal religion, but a new form of experimental Christianity, and its religious testimony will have to be heard henceforth when "the varieties of religious experience" are described.[1]

Nevertheless, conservative Christian men are not

[1] My friend Elie Gounelle has a fine discussion on this in his book, "Pourquoi sommes-nous chrétiens sociaux?" p. 29 (Librairie Fischbacher, Paris). A remarkable little book.

frightened by their own imaginings when they fear that
the progress of the social interest will mean a receding of
personal religion. They usually have definite cases in
mind in which that seemed to be the effect, and it is well
worth while to examine these more closely.

In the first place, personal religion collapses with some
individuals, because in their case it had long been growing
hollow and thin. Not all who begin the study of music
or poetry in youth remain lovers of art and literature to
the end, and not all who begin a religious life in the ardor
of youth keep up its emotional intimacy as life goes on.
Take any group of one hundred religious people, laymen
or ministers, and it is a safe guess that in a considerable
fraction of them the fire of vital religion is merely flickering
in the ashes. As long as their life goes on in the accustomed
way, they maintain their religious connections and expressions, and do so sincerely, but if they move to another part
of the country, or if a new interest turns their minds
forcibly in some other direction, the frayed bond parts
and they turn from their Church and religion. If it is the
social interest which attracts them, it may seem to them
and others that this has extinguished their devotional life.
In reality there was little personal religion to lose, and that
little would probably have been lost in some other way.
This would cover the inner history of some ministers as well
as of church members.

In other cases we must recognize that men become
apathetic about church activities in which they have been
interested, because they have found something better.
The Hebrew prophets turned in anger from the sacrificial
doings of their people; Jesus turned away from the long
prayers of the Pharisees, who were the most pious people of his day; the Reformers repudiated many of the
most devout activities of medieval Catholicism. Wherever
there is a new awakening of spiritual life, there is a dis-

carding of old religious forms, and it is to the interest of
personal religion that there should be. Is there nothing
petty, useless, and insipid in the Catholic or Protestant
church life of our day from which a soul awakened to larger
purposes ought really to turn away? Is it reprehensible
if some drop out of a dress parade when they hear the sound
of actual fighting just across the hills?

It is also true that in this tremendous awakening and
unsettlement some turn away in haste from things which
have lasting value. Few men and few movements have
such poise that they never overshoot the mark. When the
Reformation turned its back on medieval superstition, it
also smashed the painted windows of the cathedrals and
almost banished art and music from its services. When
mystics feel the compelling power of the inner word of
God, they are apt to slight the written word. So when
religious souls who have been shut away from social ideals
and interests and pent up within a fine but contracted religious habitation get the new outlook of the social awakening, it sweeps them away with new enthusiasms. Their
life rushes in to fill the empty spaces. Their mind is busy
with a religious comprehension of a hundred new facts and
problems, and the old questions of personal religion drop
out of sight. In such cases we can safely trust to experience to restore the equilibrium. In a number of my younger
friends the balancing is now going on. As they work their
way in life and realize the real needs of men and the real
values of life, they get a new comprehension of the power
and preciousness of personal and intimate religion, and they
turn back to the old truths of Christianity with a fresh
relish and a firmer accent of conviction. We shall see that
rediscovery in thousands within a few years. No doubt
they are to blame for their temporary one-sidedness, but
their blame will have to be shared by generations of religious individualists whose own persistent one-sidedness

had distorted the rounded perfection of Christianity and caused the present excessive reaction.

The question takes a wider meaning when we turn to the alienation of entire classes from religion. There is no doubt that in all the industrialized nations of Europe, and in our own country, the working classes are dropping out of connection with their churches and synagogues, and to a large extent are transferring their devotion to social movements, so that it looks as if the social interest displaced religion. But here, too, we must remember that solid masses of the population of continental Europe have never had much vital religion to lose. Their religion was taught by rote and performed by rote. It was gregarious and not personal. Detailed investigations have been made of the religious thought world of the peasantry or industrial population of limited districts, and the result always is that the centuries of indoctrination by the Church have left only a very thin crust of fertile religious conviction and experience behind. This is not strange, for whenever any spontaneous and democratic religion has arisen among the people, the established churches have done their best to wet-blanket and suppress it, and they have succeeded finely. When these people cut loose from their churches, they may not be getting much farther away from God. Usually these unchurched people still have a strong native instinct for religion, and when the vital issues and convictions of their own life are lifted into the purer light of Jesus Christ and set on fire by religious faith, they respond.

A new factor enters the situation when we encounter the influence of "scientific socialism." It is true, the party platform declares that "religion is a private affair." The saving of souls is the only industry that socialism distinctly relegates to private enterprise. If that meant simply separation of Church and State, Americans could heartily assent. If it meant that the Socialist Party proposes to be the political organization of the working class for the attainment of economic ends and to be neutral in all other questions, it would be prudent tactics. But in practice it means more. The socialism of continental Europe, taking it by and large, is actively hostile, not only to bad forms of organized religion, but to religion itself. Churchmen feel that a man is lost to religion when he joins the Socialist Party, and socialist leaders feel that a socialist who is still an active Christian is only half baked. When French and German socialists learn that men trained in the democracy and vitality of the free churches of England and America combine genuine piety and ardent devotion to the Socialist Party, it comes to them as a shock of surprise. In May, 1910, about 260 delegates of the English "Brotherhoods" visited Lille in France and were received by the French trades-unionists and socialists with parades and public meetings. The crowds on the streets did not know what to make of it when they saw the Englishmen marching under the red flag of socialism and yet bearing banners with the inscriptions: "We represent 500,000 English workmen;" "We proclaim the Fatherhood of God and the Brotherhood of Man;" "Jesus Christ leads and inspires us." What were these men, Christians or socialists? They could not be both. The Frenchmen lost all their bearings when they heard Keir Hardie, the veteran English labor leader and socialist, repudiating clericalism, but glorifying the Gospel and the spirit of Christ, and declaring that it was Christianity which had made a socialist of him.

The antireligious attitude of continental socialism is comprehensible enough if we study its historical causes dispassionately. Its most active ingredient is anticlericalism. I surmise that if some of us Americans had been in the shoes of these foreign workingmen and had seen the priest from their angle of vision, we should be anticlerical too. But in the old churches religion, the Church, and

the priest mean the same thing; you must accept all or
reject all. Men do not discriminate when they are hot
with ancient wrongs.

Another ingredient in socialist unbelief is modern science
and skepticism. Socialists share their irreligion with other
radicals. They are unbelievers, not simply because they
are socialists, but because they are children of their time.
Great masses of upper-class and middle-class people in Europe
are just as skeptical and materialistic, though they show no
touch of red. Socialists have no monopoly of unbelief.

But in addition to this, materialistic philosophy does
come to socialists embodied in their own literature as part
of socialist "science." The socialist faith was formulated
by its intellectual leaders at a time when naturalism and
materialism was the popular philosophy of the intellectuals,
and these elements were woven into the dogma of the new
movement. Great movements always perpetuate the ideas
current at the time when they are in their fluid and formative stage. For instance, some of the dogmas of the
Christian Church are still formulated in the terminology
of a philosophy that was current in the third and fourth
centuries. Calvin worked out a system of thought that is
stamped with his powerful personality and with the pecul-
iarities of his age. But after it had once become the dogmatic fighting faith of great organized bodies, it was all
handed on as God's own truth. Socialism is the most
solid and militant organization since Calvinism, and it is
just as dogmatic. Thus we have the tragic fact that the
most idealistic mass movement of modern times was committed at the outset to a materialistic philosophy with which
it had no essential connection, and every individual who comes
under its influence and control is liable to be assimilated to
its type of thought in religion as well as in economics.[1]

[1] While I was writing these pages I received a letter from a socialist who
had read "Christianity and the Social Crisis." "Speaking for the proleta-

Those who fear the influence of the social interest on personal religion are not, therefore, wholly wrong. In any powerful spiritual movement, even the best, there are yeasty, unsettling forces which may do good in the long run, but harm in the short run. Atheistic socialism may influence the religious life of great classes as deforestation affects a mountain side.

On the other hand, where the new social spirit combines harmoniously with the inherited Christian life, a new type of personal religion is produced which has at least as good a right to existence as any other type. Jesus was not a theological Christian, nor a churchman, nor an emotionalist, nor an ascetic, nor a contemplative mystic. A mature social Christian comes closer to the likeness of Jesus Christ than any other type.

In religious individualism, even in its sweetest forms, there was a subtle twist of self-seeking which vitiated its Christlikeness. Thomas a Kempis' "Imitation of Christ" and Bunyan's "Pilgrim's Progress" are classical expressions of personal religion, the one Roman Catholic and monastic, the other Protestant and Puritan. In both piety is self-centered. In both we are taught to seek the

rian class, I shall say that we all, who have gone far enough in the study of socialism to become revolutionary, regard the so-called Christian churches as our bitterest enemies. It is an axiom among us that any man who comes into our party must drop his religion (by that, of course, I mean churchianity) before he can become a valuable member of the socialist party. And he always does. I did. It is a fact that most of us are atheists, not because we want to be, but because the churches are always on the side of our enemies. They preach against us. As a consequence, the hardest person to wake up is the workingman who has been chloroformed by the church in the interest of the master class. . . . Personally I do not want to see the churches take your advice. Keep them out of our movement. We have built it so far with blood and tears without their help. I believe in God. I do not know whether I believe in immortality. I would like to, and so would all my comrades. I am by nature religious. Worship is a necessity of the human heart and I am lost without something to cling to." This letter in its mixture of anger and longing doubtless expresses the attitude of a great number.

highest good of the soul by turning away from the world
of men.   Doubtless the religion of the monastery and of
the Puritan community was far more social and human than
the theory might indicate.   Bunyan seems to have felt
by instinct that it was not quite right to have Christian
leave his wife and children and neighbors behind to get rid
of his burden and reach the heavenly city.   So he wrote
a sequel to his immortal story in which the rest of the
family with several friends set out on the same pilgrimage.
This second part is less thrilling, but more wholesomely
Christian.   There is family life, love-making, and marriage on the way.   A social group coöperate in salvation.
Bunyan was feeling his way toward social Christianity.

Evangelicalism prides itself on its emphasis on sin and
the need of conversion, yet some of the men trained in its
teachings do not seem to know the devil when they meet
him on the street.   The most devastating sins of our age
do not look like sins to them.   They may have been converted from the world, but they contentedly make their
money in the common ways of the world.   Social Christianity involves a more trenchant kind of conversion and
more effective means of grace.   It may teach a more
lenient theory of sin, but it gives a far keener eye for the
lurking places of concrete and profitable sins.   A man
who gets the spiritual ideals of social Christianity is really
set at odds with "the world" and enlisted in a lifelong fight
with organized evil.   But no man who casts out devils is
against Christ.   To fight evil involves a constant affir-
mation of holiness and hardens the muscles of Christian
character better than any religious gymnasium work.
To very many Christians of the old type the cross of Christ
meant only an expedient in the scheme of redemption,
not a law of life for themselves.   A man can be an exponent of "the higher life" and never suffer any persecution whatever from the powers that control our sin-

ridden social life. On the other hand, if any man takes social Christianity at all seriously, he will certainly encounter opposition and be bruised somehow. Such an experience will throw him back on the comforts of God and make his prayers more than words. When he bears on his own body and soul the marks of the Lord Jesus, the cross will be more than a doctrine to him. It will be a bond uniting him with Christ in a fellowship of redemptive love.

The personal religion created by social Christianity will stand one practical test of true religion which exceeds in value most of the proofs offered by theology: it creates a larger life and the power of growth. Dead religion narrows our freedom, contracts our horizon, limits our sympathies, and dwarfs our stature. Live religion brings a sense of emancipation, the exhilaration of spiritual health, a tenderer affection for all living things, widening thoughts and aims, and a sure conviction of the reality and righteousness of God. Devotion to the Reign of God on earth will do that for a man, and will do it continuously. A self-centered religion reaches the dead line soon. Men get to know the whole scheme of salvation, and henceforth they march up the hill only to march down again. On the contrary, when a man's prime object is not his soul, but the Kingdom of God, he has set his hands to a task that will never end and will always expand. It will make ever larger demands on his intellect, his sympathy, and his practical efficiency. It will work him to the last ounce of his strength. But it will keep him growing.

It is charged that those who become interested in "social work" lose interest in "personal work." Doubtless there is truth in that, and it is a regrettable one-sidedness. It is only fair to remember, however, that they share this loss of interest with the entire American Church. Evangelism itself had long become so one-sided, mechanical, and superficial in its gospel and methods that the present apathy

I

can be explained only as a reaction from it. Precisely those who have themselves gone through its experiences are now reluctant to submit young people to it. The social gospel will gradually develop its own evangelistic methods and its own personal appeals. What was called "personal work" was often not personal at all, but a wholesale regimentation of souls. It offered the same prescription, the same formula of doctrine, the same spiritual exercises and emotions for all. Those who add the new social intelligence to the old religious love of man's soul will take every man in his own social place and his own human connections, will try to understand his peculiar sin and failure from his own point of view, and see by what means salvation can effectively be brought to him. Such an evangelism would be more truly personal than the old; it would have more sense of the individuality of each man. As Robert A. Woods finely says, "It calls each man by his own name."

Christianity must offer every man a full salvation. The individualistic gospel never did this. Its evangelism never recognized more than a fractional part of the saving forces at work in God's world. Salvation was often whittled down to a mere doctrinal proposition; assent to that, and you were saved. Social Christianity holds to all the real values in the old methods, but rounds them out to meet all the needs of human life.

Salvation is always a social process. It comes by human contact. The word must become flesh if it is to save. Some man or woman, or some group of people, in whom the saving love of Jesus Christ has found a new incarnation, lays hold of an enfeebled, blinded human atom and infuses new hope and courage and insight, new warmth of love and strength of will, and there is a new breathing of the soul and an opening of the inner eye. Salvation has begun. That man or group of men was a fragment of the Kingdom of God in humanity; God dwelt in them and therefore power could go out from them. When a lost soul is infolded in a new society, a true humanity, then there is a chance of salvation.[1] No matter what set of opinions they hold, such men and women have been one of the most precious assets of our American life, and a social theorist who scoffs at them is blind with dogmatic prejudice.

When the Church insisted that it is the indispensable organ of salvation, it insisted on the social factor in redemption. The Church stands for the assimilating power exerted by the social group over its members. The same influence which a semicriminal gang exerts over a boy for evil is exerted by the Church for good. The advice in the Gospel to win an offending brother back by pleading with him first alone, then drawing two or three others into it, and finally bringing the matter before the Church, shows a keen insight into the powers of the social group over its members. More and more units of power are switched on until the current is overpowering.[2]

In a small and simple country or village community the Church could follow a man in all his relations. In our modern society the social contact of the Church covers only a small part of life, and the question is whether the influence it exerts on the saved man is strong and continuous enough to keep him saved. Suppose a poor "bum" leaves the Salvation Army barracks with a new light of hope in his eyes. He passes out on the streets among saloons and gambling dens, among sights and sounds and smells that call to his passions, among men and women who are not part of the saving Kingdom of God, but of the carnivorous kingdom of the devil. So the poor fellow backslides. Suppose a millionaire has been at a meeting where he has caught a vision of a new order of business, in which

---

[1] Begbie's "Twice-Born Men," which has been a summons to personal work, proves throughout that salvation comes by social contact with religious groups. [2] Matt. xviii. 15–20.

men are not boozy with profits, but in which such as he might be brothers to all. Next morning stocks are tumbling on 'Change, and profit is calling to him. So the poor fellow backslides. The churches do save men, but so many of them do not stay saved. Even in very active churches an enormous percentage of members are in the long run swept back so that all can see the failure, and if love of money and the hardness of social pride were properly reckoned as a religious collapse, the percentage of waste would be still greater.[1] The social organism of the Church becomes increasingly unable in modern life to supply the social forces of salvation single-handed. It may save, but its salvation is neither complete nor durable.

Sin is a social force. It runs from man to man along the lines of social contact. Its impact on the individual becomes most overwhelming when sin is most completely socialized. Salvation, too, is a social force. It is exerted by groups that are charged with divine will and love. It becomes durable and complete in the measure in which the individual is built into a social organism that is ruled by justice, cleanness, and love. A full salvation demands a Christian social order which will serve as the spiritual environment of the individual. In the little catechism which Luther wrote for the common people he has a charmingly true reply to the question: "What is 'our daily bread'?" He says: "All that belongs to the nourishment and need of our body, meat and drink, clothes and shoes, house and home, field and cattle, money and property, a good wife and good children, good servants and good rulers, good government, good weather, peace, health, education, honor, good friends, trusty neighbors, and such like." Yes, especially "such like." In the same way

[1] The General Conference of the Methodist Church and the General Assembly of the Presbyterian Church in 1912 confronted the tremendous losses by the "dropping" of members as one of the most serious questions of church life.

"salvation" involves a saved environment. For a baby it means the breast and heart and love of a mother, and a father who can keep the mother in proper condition. For a workingman salvation includes a happy home, clean neighbors, a steady job, eight hours a day, a boss that treats him as a man, a labor union that is well led, the sense of doing his own best work and not being used up to give others money to burn, faith in God and in the final triumph and present power of the right, a sense of being part of a movement that is lifting his class and all mankind, "and such like." Therefore the conception of salvation which is contained in the word "the Kingdom of God" is a truer and completer conception than that which is contained in the word "justification by faith," as surely as the whole is better than a part.

I set out with the proposition that social Christianity, which makes the Reign of God on earth its object, is a distinct type of personal religion, and that in its best manifestations it involves the possibility of a purer spirituality, a keener recognition of sin, more durable powers of growth, a more personal evangelism, and a more all-around salvation than the individualistic type of religion which makes the salvation of the soul its object. I want to add that this new type of religion is especially adapted to win and inspire modern men.[1]

It must be plain to any thoughtful observer that immense numbers of men are turning away from traditional religion, not because they have lapsed into sin, but because they have become modernized in their knowledge and points of

[1] In the following pages I am deeply indebted to the inaugural address of Leonhard Ragaz, "Zur gegenwärtigen Umgestaltung des Christentums," published in *Neue Wege*, Basel, October, 1909. Professor Ragaz is one of the most brilliant preachers of Switzerland, professor of systematic theology in the University of Zurich, together with Kutter one of the most eminent leaders of Christian Socialism in Switzerland, and altogether one of the finest examples of the new type of Social Christianity that I have met.

view.   Religion itself is an eternal need of humanity, but
any given form of religion may become antiquated and inadequate, leaving the youngest and livest minds unsatisfied,
or even repelling where it ought to attract.   The real
religious leaders of this generation must face the problem
how they can give to modern men the inestimable boon of
experiencing God as a joy and a power, and of living in
him as their fathers did.   I claim that social Christianity
is by all tokens the great highway by which this present
generation can come to God.

For one thing, it puts an end to most of the old conflicts
between religion and science.   The building of the Kingdom of God on earth requires surprisingly little dogma
and speculative theology, and a tremendous quantity of
holy will and scientific good sense.   It does not set up a
series of propositions which need constant modernizing
and which repel the most active intellects, but it summons
all to help in transforming the world into a reign of righteousness, and men of good will are not very far apart on
that.   That kind of religion has no quarrel with science.
It needs science to interpret the universe which Christianity wants to transform.   Social Christianity sets up
fewer obstacles for the intellect and puts far heavier tasks
on the will, and all that is sound in modern life will accept
that change with profound relief.

Social Christianity would also remove one other obstacle which bars even more men out of religion than the
scientific difficulties of belief.   The most effective argument against religion to-day is that religion has been
"against the people."   The people are coming to their own
at last.   For a century and a half at least they have been on
the upgrade, climbing with inexpressible toil and suffering
toward freedom, equality, and brotherhood.   The spirit
of Christ has been their most powerful ally, but the official
Church, taking Christendom as a whole, has thrown the

bulk of its great resources to the side of those who are in possession, and against those who were in such deadly need of its aid.   This is the great scandal which will not down.   Scientific doubt may alienate thousands, but the resentment against the Church for going over to the enemy has alienated entire nations.   Nothing would so expiate that guilt and win back the lost respect for religion, as determined coöperation on the part of the Church in creating a social order in which the just aspirations of the working class will be satisfied.   Those Christian men who are the outstanding and bold friends of the people's cause are to-day the most effective apologists of Christianity.

The Christian demand for the Kingdom of God on earth responds to the passionate desire for liberty which pervades and inspires the modern world.   That desire is really a longing for redemption.   Just as an individual may long to be free from vicious habits that enslave him and rob him of his manhood and self-respect, so great social classes now want freedom from the social unfreedom and degradation which denies their human worth and submerges their higher nature in coarseness, ignorance, and animal brutality.   The theological word "redemption" originally meant the ransoming of slaves and prisoners.   Christ is the great emancipator.   Every advance in true Christianity has meant a broadening path for liberty.   The highest Christian quality is love; but love is supreme freedom, a state in which even moral compulsion ceases because goodness has become spontaneous.   This world-wide desire for freedom is the breath of God in the soul of humanity.   Men instinctively know it as such, and they hate a Church that would rob them of it.   Social Christianity would rally that desire in the name of the Kingdom of God, and help the people to a consciousness that they are really moved by religion when they love freedom.   On the other hand, by its strong emphasis on social solidarity and the law of service, it will counteract that exaggerated assertion of individual rights and that selfish soul-culture which dog the steps of Freedom.

Every individual reconstructs his comprehension of life and duty, of the world and of God, as he passes from one period of his development to the next. If he fails to do so, his religion will lose its grasp and control. In the same way humanity must reconstruct its moral and religious synthesis whenever it passes from one era to another. When all other departments of life and thought are silently changing, it is impossible for religion to remain unaffected. Other-worldly religion was the full expression of the highest aspirations of ancient and medieval life. Contemporary philosophy supported it. The Ptolemaic astronomy made it easy to conceive of a heaven localized above the starry firmament, which was only a few miles up. But to-day the whole *Weltanschauung* which supported those religious conceptions has melted away irretrievably. Copernican astronomy, the conviction of the universal and majestic reign of law, the evolutionary conception of the history of this earth and of the race, have made the religious ideas that were the natural denizens of the old world of thought seem like antique survivals to-day, as if a company of Athenians should walk down Broadway in their ancient dress. When Christianity invaded the ancient world, it was a modernist religion contemptuously elbowing aside the worn-out superstitions of heathenism, and the live intellects seized it as an adequate expression of their religious consciousness. To-day the livest intellects have the greatest difficulty in maintaining their connection with it. Many of its defenders are querulously lamenting the growth of unbelief. They stand on a narrowing island amid a growing flood, saving what they can of the wreckage of faith. Is religion dying? Is the giant faith of Christianity tottering to its grave?

Religion is not dying. It is only molting its feathers, as every winged thing must at times. A new springtide is coming. Even now the air is full of mating calls and love songs. Soon there will be a nest in every tree.

As the modern world is finding itself, religion is returning to it in new ways. Philosophy in its most modern forms is tending toward an idealistic conception of the universe, even when it calls itself materialistic. It realizes spirit behind all reality. The new psychology is full of the powers and mysteries of the soul. It is no slight achievement of faith to think of God immanent in the whole vast universe, but those who accomplish that act of faith feel him very near and mysteriously present, pulsating in their own souls in every yearning for truth and love and right. Life once more becomes miraculous; for every event in which we realize God and our soul is a miracle. All history becomes the unfolding of the purpose of the immanent God who is working in the race toward the commonwealth of spiritual liberty and righteousness. History is the sacred workshop of God. There is a presentiment abroad in modern thought that humanity is on the verge of a profound change, and that feeling heralds the fact. We feel that all this wonderful liberation of redemptive energy is working out a true and divine order in which our race will rise to a new level of existence. But such a higher order can rise out of the present only if superior spiritual forces build and weave it. Thousands of young minds who thought a few years ago that they had turned their back on religion forever are full of awe and a sense of mystery as they watch the actualities of life in this process of upbuilding.[1] By coöperating with God in his work they are realizing God. Religion is insuppressible.

[1] This line of thought was worked out more fully by me in a sermon preached before the National Conference of Charities and Corrections, 1912, and in a little book, "Unto Me," published by the Pilgrim Press, Boston, 1912.

It is true that the social enthusiasm is an unsettling force which may unbalance for a time, break old religious habits and connections, and establish new contacts that are a permanent danger to personal religion. But the way to meet this danger is not to fence out the new social spirit, but to let it fuse with the old religious faith and create a new total that will be completer and more Christian than the old religious individualism at its best. Such a combination brings a triumphant enlargement of life which proves its own value and which none would give up again who has once experienced it. There is so much religion even in nonreligious social work that some who had lost their conscious religion irretrievably have found it again by this new avenue. God has met them while they were at work with him in social redemption, and they have a religion again and a call to a divine ministry. Faith in a new social order is so powerful a breeder of religion that great bodies of men who in theory scorn and repudiate the name of religion, in practice show evidence of possessing some of the most powerful instincts and motives of religion.[1] One of the most valuable achievements in the domain of personal religion which is now open to any man is to build up a rounded and harmonious Christian personality in which all the sweetness and intensity of the old religious life shall combine with the breadth, intelligence, and fighting vigor of the social spirit. Every such individuality will reproduce itself in others who are less mature, and so multiply this new species of the genus "Christian."

[1] This is the message of the brilliant book of Kutter of Zurich, "Sie müssen," which has been edited in English by Rufus W. Weeks, and published by the Coöperative Printing Company, Chicago. Richard Heath has summed up all the teachings of Kutter in "Social Democracy : Does it Mean Darkness or Light?" Letchworth, England, 1910.

PART III

OUR SEMI-CHRISTIAN SOCIAL ORDER

CHAPTER I

WHAT DO WE MEAN BY "CHRISTIANIZING" THE SOCIAL ORDER?

WE often hear the assertion that no one can tell whether Christianity would work, because Christianity has never been tried.

I deny it. Christianity has been tried, both in private and in social life, and the question is in order whether anything in the history of humanity has succeeded except Christianity.

It is true enough that there has never been a social order which was Christian from top to bottom. But large domains of our social life have come under the sway of Christ's law in their spirit and in their fundamental structure, and these are by common consent the source of our happiness and the objects of our pride, while those portions of the social order which are still unchristianized are the source of our misery and the cause of our shame.

It is unjust to Christianity to call our civilization Christian; it is unjust to our civilization to call it unchristian. It is semi-christian. Its regeneration is in process, but it has run in streaks and strata, with baffling inconsistencies and hypocrisies, even as with you and me. But so far as the process has gone, it will warrant us in taking the completion of the job in hand with serene confidence that it will work. Christian history is not a dismal failure to date. The largest and hardest part of the work of christianizing the social order has been done.

In the next chapter I shall try to show how the Christian portions of our social order were christianized. This will furnish us a working conception of the means by which the unregenerate parts can be put through the same saving process. In several subsequent chapters I shall then analyze the unchristianized portions of the social order in order to make clear why and in what respects they are still unchristian.

But first we shall have to define what we mean by "christianizing" the social order or any part of it.

I do not mean putting the name of Christ into the Constitution of the United States. Some descendants of the Scotch Covenanters still refuse to vote or hold office under our government because Jesus Christ is not formally acknowledged as the head of our nation. But in the present stage of our life that would only be one more act of national hypocrisy. Moreover Jesus himself does not seem to have cared much about being called "Lord, Lord," unless there was substance to the word. To put a stop to child labor in our country would be a more effective way of doing homage to his sovereignty than any business of words and names.

Neither do we want to renew the attempts made in the past by both Catholicism and Protestantism to set up a theocracy ruled by the Church and making Christian belief and worship a compulsory duty of citizenship. All the experience of history protests against coercion in religion. The small amount of compulsion still surviving in the established churches of Europe and South America is felt by outsiders to be a relic of past evil and a present-day scandal.

Christianizing the social order means bringing it into harmony with the ethical convictions which we identify with Christ. A fairly definite body of moral convictions has taken shape in modern humanity. They express our collective conscience, our working religion. The present social order denies and flouts many of these principles of our ethical life and compels us in practice to outrage our better self. We demand therefore that the moral sense of humanity shall be put in control and shall be allowed to reshape the institutions of social life.

We call this "christianizing" the social order because these moral principles find their highest expression in the teachings, the life, and the spirit of Jesus Christ. Their present power in Western civilization is in large part directly traceable to his influence over its history. To the great majority of our nation, both inside and outside of the churches, he has become the incarnate moral law and his name is synonymous with the ideal of human goodness. To us who regard him as the unique revelation of God, the unfolding of the divine life under human forms, he is the ultimate standard of moral and spiritual life, the perfect expression of the will of God for humanity, the categorical imperative with a human heart. But very many who do not hold this belief in a formulated way or who feel compelled to deny it, including an increasing portion of our Jewish fellow-citizens, will still consent that in Jesus our race has reached one of its highest points, if not its crowning summit thus far, so that Jesus Christ is a prophecy of the future glory of humanity, the type of Man as he is to be. Christianizing means humanizing in the highest sense. I ask the consent of both classes to use his name for the undertaking which he initiated for us. To say that we want to moralize the social order would be both vague and powerless to most men. To say that we want to christianize it is both concrete and compelling. Christ's spirit is the force that drives us. His mind is the square and plumb line that must guide us in our building.

The danger in using so high a word is that we shall be led to expect too much. Even a Christian social order cannot mean perfection. As long as men are flesh and blood the world can be neither sinless nor painless. For instance, how can any form of social organization keep the tremendous electric current of sex desire from going astray and dealing misery and shame? The law of growth, which is essential to human life, itself makes any static perfection impossible. Every child is born a kicking little egotist and has to learn by its own mistakes and sins to coördinate itself with the social life of every successive group which it enters. If perfection were reached to-day, new adjustments would be demanded to-morrow by the growth of new powers. The justest and most sympathetic human society conceivable would unknowingly inflict injury and wrong, and only slowly realize it when it heard the insistent cry of pain. The structure of society can never be up to date. It is necessarily a slow historical growth, and men will always have to labor hard to rid it of antiquated and harmful customs and institutions brought down from a worse past.

I must ask my readers to keep these limitations of human life in mind as axioms in all the discussion that follows, even when they are not stated, and to assume that we are keeping within hailing distance of common sense. We shall demand perfection and never expect to get it. But by demanding it we shall get more than we now have. Straight-cut insistence on moral duty is quite compatible with the largest patience, as human frailty limps up to God's judgment seat and pleads guilty for a thousand sins. Jesus is the classical example of the combination between high-voltage moral demand and the tenderest understanding.

But within the limitations of human nature I believe that the constitutional structure of the social order can be squared with the demands of Christian morality. At every new step of moral progress the clamor has gone up that fairness and decency were utopian fanaticism and would ruin society, but instead of making the social machinery unworkable, every step toward collective Christian ethics proved an immense relief to society.

An unchristian social order can be known by the fact that it makes good men do bad things. It tempts, defeats, drains, and degrades, and leaves men stunted, cowed, and shamed in their manhood. A Christian social order makes bad men do good things. It sets high aims, steadies the vagrant impulses of the weak, trains the powers of the young, and is felt by all as an uplifting force which leaves them with the consciousness of a broader and nobler humanity as their years go on.

Having now explained what we mean by christianizing the social order, we might draw from the Gospels a list of the Christian principles of social life and test the existing social order by them. But we shall find it more fruitful to trace the moral evolution of those social institutions which have to some degree been christianized and in this way amplify our conceptions of the christianizing process. History will give us a better comprehension of the problem than the closest definition of terms. If we know how a thing has been done, we see how it can and ought to be done.

CHAPTER II

THE simplest and most familiar social organization is the family. It is also the most Christian. It is so Christian that the word "Father" has become the most satisfactory symbol of a loving God, and the word "child" the most trustful expression of our relation to him. When Jesus substituted these family terms for the old royal conceptions with their connotations of despotism, the change meant a redemption of religion.[1] Wherever the members of a social organization have taken to calling one another "brother," it has stood for higher social ideals. "The fatherhood of God and the brotherhood of man" is one of the cherished phrases of our time; it expresses the faith that the same solidarity and tenderness which we know in family life will yet become common in our wider social relations. As for the word "mother" — that carries a mystic breath of religious sweetness to which we all do homage. Thus the social institution of the family is so Christian that we can use all its terms freely as symbols and vehicles of spiritual thought and feeling. Could we do the same with the terms of business life, "boss," "hands," "foreman," "clerk"?

The cheering fact about this is that the family did not set out with so much love and beauty, but had to go through

---

[1] Note Paul's sense of relief when he contrasted the spirit of the old religions with the spirit prevailing in Christianity. When you became Christians, "you did not receive a slavish spirit so that you had to be afraid again, but you received a filial spirit which impels us to cry out, Abba, Father!" Romans viii. 15.

a long, sanctifying process. In its early stages the patriarchal family from which our own family organization is
derived was held together by stern force and selfishness,
quite as much as by love and kinship. The slaves and servants were worked and ruled for the good of the owner and
master, and however kind a man he might be, the whip was
a matter of course and the infliction of death was his right.
Wives were dragged off as the booty of war, or purchased.
They represented sex desire and love, but also labor force
and the breeding of children. A patriarch with a lot of
wives was a capitalist and became rich on the "surplus
value" they created for him. His sons were his fighting
outfit with which he gained and protected his wealth and
power. Around the hall of Priam were fifty apartments
for his sons and their wives, and the prowess of the young
men was the constitutional basis of his kingship.
Daughters too were capital, and beauty might prove a
bonanza. When Jacob fled from Esau and fell in love with
Rachel at the well, he had no cattle or jewelry to buy her,
so he bound himself to work for Laban seven years. Since
his children were born in Laban's family, that excellent
business man claimed them as his unearned increment,
and felt as sore as an outraged landlord when Jacob finally
made off with them all. The old gentleman felt a conscious glow of virtue when he let them go unscathed.[1]

The life and welfare of every member of the patriarchal
family were controlled by its head. He was their economic
manager, directing their work, allotting their goods, and
selling the common product to his own advantage. They
took their religion from him as the household priest. He
was ruler and judge over his own, and law and custom upheld his despotic power, for the law was made and the precedents were set by him and his peers. He could divorce his

[1] Genesis xxxi. The whole story is very interesting material for the early
history of the family.

K

wife or bring in other women to share her most precious rights. If she was unfaithful, he could kill her. She had no corresponding claim on his fidelity, for it was his right to do as he liked. Over his children too he held the power of life and death. The practice of exposing crippled or female children, which still exists in some nonchristian nations, is merely a remnant of larger powers in the past. The Romans were proud that the *patria potestas* was nowhere more absolute than with them.

This despotic family organization contained very large ingredients of good. It furnished the weak protection against enslavement and death. It coerced the savage to work, sweated the idleness out of him, and made his labor more productive by forcing him into coöperation with others. It placed the capable in the position of leadership, and killed them off when they failed. To expand a family of two into a patriarchal tribe of fifty or five hundred, to keep sons and slaves together, to beat off hostile competition and attack, and beat down domestic intrigues and conspiracies, was quite as great a feat of leadership then as to organize a department store or a trust nowadays. The patriarchal family in its tyrannous beginnings can claim the gratitude of posterity with the same right as our present industrial organization. For thousands of years it was the social system within which the larger part of the race found food and protection, education and religion.

Nevertheless the fact remains that the family as an institution was based on despotism and exploitation. The relation of husband and wives, of father and children, of master and slaves, could be made fine and noble by personal goodness, but the personal virtue was constantly vitiated by the wrong inhering in the social order in which they lived. The Old Testament gives us an intimate insight into a number of families, either as they actually lived, or as the admiring and idealizing tradition of later times imagined them, and not one of them shows us a good home from a modern point of view. Abraham was a true gentleman, whose acquaintance would be a benediction in any civilization; Jacob would surely be a millionaire and church elder if he lived to-day; David is one of the most brilliant and spiritual figures in history. Yet the family relations of these men were such that no self-respecting church could retain them as members if they did the same to-day. An unregenerate social institution put these good men into positions where they did wrong. We see them now as posterity will see our Christian business men.

The history of the family tells of a slow decrease of despotism and exploitation. Gradually wives were no longer bought outright. The right of divorce was hedged about. The wife gained an assured legal status and some property rights. When polygamy ceased and adultery was considered a crime in man as well as in woman, the basis was laid for equality between man and wife. But only within the last hundred years has woman risen toward acknowledged equality with swift and decisive steps. Most other countries are still far from conceding what our American women have now learned to take as a matter of course. The present agitation for woman's suffrage is one of the final steps of this ascent. The suffrage will abolish one of the last remnants of patriarchal autocracy by giving woman a direct relation to the political organism of society, instead of allowing man to exercise her political rights for her.

In the same way the relation of the father to the children became less autocratic and more loving. The killing of a child by the father became rare, then illegal, and finally a crime. Marrying off his daughters has ceased to be a lucrative business and has become an expensive joy. Instead of exploiting the children for his own enrichment the father has learned to sacrifice himself for their education

and advancement.   Changes in the legal status of children
have followed the change in family feeling.   Here again
the course of evolution has come to a swift culmination.
Our own generation has witnessed a remarkable advance
toward democracy in the relation between parents and
children.

Imagine that a Syrian village had fallen asleep in the
year 4000 B.C., like the palace of the Sleeping Beauty in
the old fairy tale, and were waked to life to-day.   The
elders in the village gate resume their discussion of current
affairs, — of the slave who has run away to escape a beat-
ing; of the ten sons of a neighboring sheik who conspired
to kill their father and take his slaves and harem to set up
for themselves; and of the sad poisoning of a favorite
wife's son by some other wife "to this jury unknown."
The elders agree that a pernicious social unrest is abroad
which makes their life a burden and threatens the foundations of civilization.   To them enters a modern tourist,
pastor in a staid Pennsylvania town, a man who prides
himself on being untainted by radical social notions.   As he
listens to their woes, he promptly sees the cause and expounds the orthodox American conception of the family,
advising them to treat their wives as their equals, to live
for their children, and to give their servants one night off
per week.   They listen to the stranger with patient courtesy
at first, explaining that his views are utopian; that all
authority would be undermined if a man could not beat his
wife; that the women like being beaten, and would take
it as a sign of diminishing affection if they were no longer
chastised; that polygamy is an index of high morality,
since the best citizens have most wives, and you would
have to change human nature to make monogamy compulsory; that slaves would have nothing to eat if they
had no masters to feed and employ them; that theology
rightly teaches that a father, being the author of a child's

life, has a right to take its life if he considers it superfluous. The American, aglow with Christian indignation, describes how wisely his wife manages the common finances and selects his neck-ties; how he sends his girls to Vassar, though it ruins his bank account; how fond the girls are of their dad, and how he would hate himself if he thought that his family regarded him as a tyrant. But he sees dark frowns gathering on their faces and ominous whispers running about. He pales as he hears the ancient Hittite equivalent for "socialist and anarchist" applied to himself. The scene is full of tragic possibilities, and we abandon the unhappy extremist to the imagination of the reader.

Doubtless the head of a patriarchal family, if he could have foreseen the later democratizing of the institution, would have felt that while wife and child might gain, the father would certainly lose by the change. Yet in fact the father too has gained. He has lost in power, but gained in love. In the beginning children seem to have formed a permanent attachment only for the mother. When the father ceased to be a tyrant, he won his share of love.

Thus the constitutional structure of the family has passed through an ethical transformation by slow historical processes. The despotism of the man, fortified by law, custom, and economic possession, has passed into approximate equality between husband and wife. The children have become the free companions of their parents, and selfish parental authority has come under the law of unselfish service. Economic exploitation by the head of the family has been superseded by economic coöperation and a satisfactory communism of the family equipment. Based on equal rights, bound together by love and respect for individuality, governed under the law of mutual helpfulness, the family to-day furnishes the natural habitation for a Christian life and fellowship. There is no conflict of the Christian spirit with the accepted laws of family life; only with the transgressions of those laws. We can therefore say that the family has been assimilated to Christianity. As an institution it has been christianized.

That does not, however, mean that Christian living has become automatic in the family and requires no religious effort. To make the family a place of permanent love, peace, and spiritual beauty is now, and always will be, a great moral achievement and one of the highest triumphs of personality. The number of really beautiful families is still small. Yet the traditions of the institution, as religion, custom, public opinion, law, and neighborhood example have shaped it, make it an ennobling and restraining force in the life of all. The despotic and polygamous family life of the past caused saints to do shameful things. The christianized family holds even selfish and wayward individuals to some measure of decency, serviceableness, and love. The fact that the institution as such has been christianized predisposes the individuals living in it to be Christians. If they are personally temperate, reasonable, loving, and swayed by religious convictions and duties, they will find the family responsive to their highest desires; if they are not, they will at least find it a restraining, educational, and disciplinary influence.

The process through which the family has been transformed can justly be called a christianizing process, not only in view of the results achieved, but of the forces that accomplished the results. So far as the Græco-Roman world is concerned, Christianity saved and regenerated the institution of the family just as much as it ever saved any sinner. Among the wealthy classes of the ancient world marriage had reached a stage of decomposition compared with which the divorce scandals of some of our millionaires seem decorous, and, as usual, the upper classes infected the lower with their bacteria. The young Christian Church attacked the sexual evils of heathen society, its prostitution, concubinage, ease of divorce, and unnatural vices with the same convinced ardor with which socialists smite our industrial vices, and in the degree in which the Church gained spiritual control, it cemented the family with new religious sanctions, made it once more permanent, and filled it with higher meanings and values. However derelict the Church has been about other social relations, it has always been deeply concerned in the family. It has often taken reactionary positions, for instance, about the public activities and the emancipation of women, but it has always stood for fidelity, cleanness, and tenderness.

Moreover, the influence of the Christian spirit on the home life has been more searching and intimate than mere church influence. It did its work within the four walls of innumerable homes, unrecorded by public observation, and the actors in the readjustments were not aware that they were sharing in a great social transformation. If any one will pass in review the families he has known intimately, he will realize that religion is often the decisive factor in the character of a home. If we go through a tenement house full of slovenly, quarrelsome, and discouraged families, and find one home which seems an oasis of cleanliness, order, and peace, we shall be safe in assuming that we have struck a religious family. But every christianized family leaves traditions in the hearts of its children which they will seek to realize in their own homes, and it sets the standard a little higher for all who come in contact with it. By such precedents public opinion and custom are formed, and ultimately law follows custom. So the ethical transformation of the family becomes comprehensible only through the persistent atmospheric pressure of Christianity exerted on countless families through many generations. We can watch its swift decay to-day wherever the influence of Christianity has lapsed.

On the other hand, religion did not do the work single-handed. Social and economic changes did their part. For instance, the suppression of polygamy was helped by the cessation of slavery. The home became a place of rest and love when household production changed to joint labor in the shop and factory, relieving the family of the coercion of productive toil. Religion always does its most powerful and permanent social work when it supports and invigorates the wholesome tendencies in the common life of men.

To-day this christianized family is being attacked by new disintegrating forces against which it is all the more defenseless because it now rests so exclusively on the finer and more fragile moral instincts. High rents in the cities narrow the home and crush its charms. High prices and high standards of living combine to make family life expensive and to suppress child life. Industrialism is emptying the home of its women folk. A theory of education which imposes no law except the law of pleasurableness on the young is sapping the virtues of self-restraint and patience. The materialistic spirit developed by modern commercialism is weakening the organization of the spiritual life, the Church, and therewith the power of organized religion over the home is failing. Unless these destructive forces are checked in this generation, the institution of the family will have been christianized only to perish like a flower in full bloom bitten by frost. Unless the rest of society is christianized, the christianized family cannot survive in it.[1]

A similar christianizing process has taken place in the Church, which is the social organization of the religious life of humanity.

At the beginning of the modern era the Church was a despotic and exploiting organization. Instead of being the great exemplar of fraternity, it was ruled by a monar-

---

[1] Some of these causes of decadence have been discussed more fully in "Christianity and the Social Crisis," pp. 271-279.

chical and aristocratic hierarchy, which used its immense powers to lord it over the people and to enrich itself. Though founded on the principle of love and freedom, it coerced belief and terrorized men into uniformity by physical constraint. But coercion is in religion what rape is in love. The Church owned nearly a third of the landed wealth of Europe, and in addition to its rents extorted tithes and fees by civil process. It had commercialized heaven, hell, and purgatory, and did a thriving business in assorted religious commodities. Because many of its positions were rich sinecures, they were bestowed on favorites, granted for a rake-off, and often held by absentees, while hungry vicars did the actual work. Every effort to reform the Church before the Reformation turned, not, as we would suppose, on the restoration of evangelical doctrine, but on the abatement of simony, which was the ecclesiastical term for what we call "graft." A hundred years before Luther all the best minds of Europe were exerting themselves to reform the Church "in head and members," an equivalent of our efforts to get at "those higher up" in political corruption. Three international councils were convened in rapid succession and sat for years, but the net outcome for decency was slight. The ecclesiastical Tammany Hall was able to counter every move. The forces of corruption were so solidly intrenched and the forces of moral indignation were so carefully gagged, that even the almost universal condemnation of all honorable men was unable to work a permanent change. Instead of being a great, free, mobile force available to work righteousness, the Church was itself the chief object of contempt and reform. Scientific Catholic historians to-day agree in confessing the practical abuses prevailing, and they would be less guarded in their condemnation of them if Protestants did not point to this degradation of the Church to justify the terrible split of the Reformation.

If any one in the year 1500 had prophesied that the time would come when the type of the lazy and fat-bellied priest would disappear from literature and the stage, and when the ministry of the Church would be wholly free from any charge of general sexual impurity; when the Church itself would be without governmental powers, without legal privileges, without power to collect its tithes and execute its verdicts by the aid of the State, without endowed wealth, and depending entirely for support on the free gifts of those who loved her; when corruption and graft would be unknown and impossible in church life, and ministers, with few exceptions, would be sincere and hard-working men; when any attempt to repress or force religious belief would arouse general condemnation and every man would be free to follow the inner light, — if any one had prophesied all this, it would have been read as a delightful utopian dream, and very likely the Church would have suppressed the book.

Yet that is the condition actually attained in our country. Our ministers as a class are a clean, laborious, and honorable profession. They are anxious to serve the community, and do so according to their best light, even when they derive no tangible benefit whatever. If there is any graft in the ministry, it is the graft practiced by the churches in underpaying their pastors, using their wives as unpaid workers, and turning them off on a pittance or on nothing when the magnetism of youth has been worked out of them. That is graft, but the old graft reversed. The Church itself is almost without special privilege except the tax exemption which it shares with other benevolent organizations. Very few churches have any endowment; they all live from hand to mouth, and rejoice when they end a year without debt. In all the criticism of the Church to-day is there any charge that the Church is doing conscious and positive wrong? The substance of all charges is that it fails to rise to its highest opportunities. May none of us have a blacker mark than that when we stand at the judgment bar!

All this means that the Church has become a Christian. It was christianized when it got rid of its elaborate and profitable superstitions, and made salvation both simple and free. It was christianized when it lost its power and its will to tyrannize. Some Protestant churches have entirely democratized their organization; others, which have retained a monarchical or aristocratic form of organization in our country, have at least been steeped in the democratic spirit. The clergy was christianized when it lost the opportunity to live on easy money and learned to do hard work for plain pay. The Church is hated to-day only in countries where it suppresses religious and intellectual freedom and resists the moral aspirations of the people. It is loved where it is a coöperative organization, resting on a basis of liberty and equality, held together by good will, and serving the highest ends known to the people. Let no one say that the churches of our country are not loved. What other nation-wide organization is there which is supported freely by the people with such an output of money and of voluntary service, and which can offer them so little in return in the way of financial help or of pleasurable excitement? Why do the people do it if they do not love their churches?

For centuries before the Reformation the instinct of Christian men had located the fundamental cause for the corruption of the Church. It was a common conviction that the debasement of the Church had set in with the "Donation of Constantine," by which the Emperor Constantine was supposed to have conferred large territories and sovereign rights on Pope Sylvester in the fourth century. That had been "the poisoned bone which the devil had thrown and which the Church had swallowed." Since then the Church had become an antichristian power.

Constantly the bolder reformatory spirits taught that the Church could be saved only by surrendering its wealth and political power and returning to apostolic poverty, supported only by the free gifts of those who loved her. And that has, in fact, been the way by which the salvation of the Church has come. Church historians have overestimated the purifying influence of Luther's and Calvin's doctrine, and underestimated the tremendous fact that in consequence of the terrible punishment of the social and political changes accompanying the Reformation, the power of the Church to tyrannize and exploit was stopped, and rent and profit began to disappear from church life. That took the Church out of the captivity of Mammon, and brought her back to God and the people.

The Church did not welcome its salvation. When the princes of the Church lost their temporal sovereignty; when the property of the Church was "secularized"; when the constitutionalized "pull" and graft of the clerical aristocracy was canceled; the classes affected always felt that the cause of religion had received its death blow. Even to-day the papacy is not reconciled to the loss of the little State which had given the Pope the status of a sovereign prince, and even American Catholics feel compelled to demand the restoration of the papal sovereignty in order to enable the papacy to get back into the game of international politics which has always been so ruinous to the spiritual power of the papal institution. The process by which the Church was stripped of power and wealth was no beautiful act of self-renunciation, but a shameless hold-up by the powers that be. The ruling classes, the princes and aristocracy, found the Church ditched with punctured tires on the road from Jerusalem to Jericho and proceeded to help themselves to what Providence had provided, being careful to show their governmental badge of authority to prove that it was all done legally. Some fractional part was usually devoted to endow education and charity, but the bulk of the landed wealth of the Church made the everlasting fortune of those who were "on the inside" at the time. The despotic power of the Protestant princes was also greatly augmented by seizing the ecclesiastical powers hitherto exercised by the bishops and the Pope, so that the Reformation helped to create the era of absolutism to which the French Revolution began to make an end. Yet, in spite of its evil side effects, the revolution by which the political power and the unearned wealth of the Church were fatally broken and started on the way toward extinction proved to be the moral salvation of the Church. Wherever remnants of the old conditions survive, the Church is under the challenge of the modern spirit, and wherever that spirit becomes conscious and militant, the Church is distrusted and hated as a constitutional foe of truth and liberty. On the other hand, wherever the Church has been set free from even the chance to tyrannize, it has become a powerful member in the alliance of forces that are redeeming the social order.

Here, then, we have another great section of the social order which has passed through a moral transformation and redemption, still incomplete, but far-reaching and tremendous. Like the family, the Church was christianized by unlearning despotism and exploitation, and coming under the law of love and service. Its salvation came, not merely by multiplying the number of good men in it, while leaving the social invitations to tyranny intact; not merely by purifying the Gospel preached, while the clergy continued to live abnormal and parasitic lives; but by stripping the Church of its unearned wealth, depriving its leaders of special privilege and the food of arrogance, wresting from their hands the means of coercion, and making them answerable to those whom they served and from whom they got their living. When coercion ceased, a purer gospel followed. When the ministry was democratized, Christian ethics had a chance. When the official servants of the Church stepped out of the classes that fatten on rent and profit, and entered the honorable poverty of the wage earners, the lust of rule passed into the will to serve. Because evil had intrenched itself in the Church and fought against betterment, salvation had to come by a disastrous revolution which created new evils in place of those which it abolished. It took several centuries of organic development to complete the process, and even now it is not completed. But a constitutional change has been wrought which amounts to a christianizing of the Church.

This christianized Church is now, like the christianized family, in danger for its very existence. Its financial needs, the supply and hopefulness of its ministry, its hold on the mass of the working people, its stability in the rural districts, are all threatened by modern conditions.[1] Its very value is called in question by the materialistic spirit created by our commercialism. The poor who are reduced to barbarism by poverty, and the rich whose higher life is drowned out by excess, alike stare at the Church with dull and apathetic eyes. If the income of the Church were big enough for graft, there would be solid "interests" to fight for it. If it could still terrorize the people, it could coerce them into attendance, support, and obedience. Because it appeals only to the free impulses of a mature spiritual life, it languishes where the spiritual life of the nation is atrophied. Unless it helps to save and christianize the national life, large sections of the Church will wither away, and it will survive only in those lower forms which still appeal to superstition, dogmatism, and emotionalism.

A third section of the social order which has gone through a christianizing process is the organization which serves the purposes of education.

[1] These points are fully discussed in Chapter VI of "Christianity and the Social Crisis."

In its unregenerate days education was a perquisite of
the secular and religious aristocracy. Those families and
classes which had gained leisure and taste for the intellectual life cultivated and refined it further. But instead of
being a missionary force which impelled the cultured minds
to put themselves at the service of the ignorant, it was an
added influence to put the upper classes out of sympathetic
contact with the lower. In every aristocratic society the
possessing class has watched the spread of education downward with jealousy and has yielded the means for it grudg-
ingly, realizing that education breeds unrest and discontent
and makes the servile and laboring class less respectful
and dependent. Governor Berkeley voiced the attitude of
the Cavaliers in England and Virginia in his famous report
of 1670: "I thank God there are no free schools, nor printing, and I hope we shall not have them these hundred years;
for learning has brought disobedience and heresy and sects
into the world, and printing has divulged them, and libels
against the best government. God keep us from both!"
The prohibition of negro education in some of our slave
states before the war was simply an extreme expression of
the unregenerate spirit in education. Even when popular
education becomes common, the upper classes maintain
special educational privileges for their children. In Germany, for instance, there are two sets of government
schools, even for the very young: one for the children of the
common people, who expect to go to work as soon as they
have reached adolescence; the other for the children of
parents who can afford to give them a higher and longer
education. As long as the social order is divided into these
classes, this is a very practical system, but it neither expresses nor creates democracy.

The spirit in which education was imparted was also
autocratic and even tyrannous. The novels and biogra-
phies of the early Victorian era are full of the flogging of

schoolboys.   Corporal punishment was so constant that children were under a reign of fear, witness Shakespeare's "whining schoolboy, with his satchel and shining morning face, creeping like snail unwillingly to school." The final escape from school life was often marked by a wild bound for liberty.   Maturer students too were mentally coerced by the authority of the teacher and the great names of learning.   Freedom and originality in the student were regarded with suspicion, and a purely receptive attitude was encouraged.   In the higher walks of intellectual life freedom of investigation and teaching was always an individual conquest, and the yoke of orthodoxy, religious, political, and social, lay heavily on the neck of teachers.

It would be idle to claim that even a single one of these evils has been fully outgrown by education.   But there has been a revolutionary change.   Corporal punishment has fallen into disuse, and within one generation the reign of fear has so far ceased that the majority of children now seem to love school.   In the higher schools habits of intellectual freedom are encouraged.   Scientific investigation in the universities has become almost autonomous.

Except in private schools patronized by the wealthy, manifestations of social exclusiveness call for apology, and every advance in democracy is proclaimed with pride. The Christian missionary impulse has taken possession of the teaching profession and the great organization of education.   Institutions eagerly create extension courses and implore the intellectually lost to come in and be saved.   The presence of even a fraction of one per cent of persons who cannot read and write is felt as a reproach by civilized nations. Individual teachers may be lazy and stale, but the teaching profession as a whole is under the law of Christ.   It seeks to serve, and the road to greatness in it is by preëminent service.

Profit making is not unknown in educational life, but

it is limited in scope and always felt to be a degradation. Medical schools run for profit, for instance, are inferior institutions and often a disgrace to the profession. Compared with the prizes of business life even the highest incomes of teachers are modest. Yet for plain pay men and women give faithful and efficient work and take satisfaction in doing it.

The financial support of the public school system is always niggardly compared with the real needs, and it has often been the nesting place of graft. Nevertheless it is on an essentially Christian basis. Louis Blanc's maxim, "From every one according to his ability, and to every one according to his need," is so lofty and unselfish that even socialists think it would not work in a society just emerging from capitalism. Yet that is the principle on which our schools are maintained. Every family is taxed for their support according to its financial ability, and it gets the benefits of the schools according to its needs. A rich man contributes heavily to the school tax though he may have neither child nor grandchild to profit by them. A man with ten children gets ten times as much good from the schools as the man with one child, and—other things being equal —pays no more for their maintenance. Every enlargement of the functions of the schools makes this Christian principle more striking.

Thus our educational system has passed through a regenerating process. As with the family and the Church the line of progress ran from tyranny to freedom, from aristocratic privilege to democracy of opportunity, from self-seeking to the enthusiasm of service. In detail the bigger part of the change is still before us, but here too a constitutional change has taken place which may justly be called a christianizing of the educational organization. The love of the people has put its approval on the result. It works. The support of the common schools is the

L

largest item in the tax bills of our communities. We have learned to be ashamed of some powerful elements of our national life, but we are proud of our schools. When we annexed the Philippines, and our astonished American conscience inquired how we could create foreign dependencies and subject peoples by conquest and purchase like any other bloody tyrant, we hugged the consolation that at any rate the school would follow the flag. In sizing up the future for our Filipino brothers, the commercial corporation was our biggest anxiety, the public school our best justification. The school is Christian; the corporation — not yet.

In the case of the school, as in the case of the family, organized Christianity contributed a large part of the forces which worked the change. Before the educational appetite had pervaded the people sufficiently to run on its own strength, and before the democratized State had bent its larger resources to the task of popular education, the Church was the chief agency that fostered it. Wherever in its earlier stages the school sought out the poor and neglected classes, the missionary impulse was furnished by religion. That pioneering service of the Church is in danger of being obscured to-day in some countries because the Church is so reluctant to be superseded by the State, and because it has often blocked the emancipation of the intellect. But taking the whole history of education in the Christian nations, a fair judgment will allow the Church a large balance to its credit.

In our own country education certainly owes an immense debt to Christianity. Most of our American colonies were organized and developed by financial corporations that were in the colonizing business for the profits they hoped to make out of the colonists. I fail to remember any noteworthy efforts by these dividend makers to put education on its feet in the new country. The high standards set by the New England colonies were set by religious men and under religious motives. In the westward march of our population, when the life of the frontier absorbed the energies of the settlers in a hard struggle to get a footing, and reduced even the educated individuals to the monotony and the fierce passions of primitive civilization, the churches stood almost single-handed for the higher interests of mankind. They were always hard-pushed to build their simple edifices and support their ministers, yet they founded academies and colleges and encouraged their young people to deny themselves for years and "get an education." The educators who molded the earlier generations of American manhood by their earnestness and heroic devotion, and to whom we look back now wistfully as an almost extinct race of life-givers, simply embodied the spirit of Christianity applied to the intellectual life. That enthusiasm for education, which is one of the finest characteristics of our country and has gone far to redeem us from the charge of gross mammonism, was kindled and fed by the churches and ministers, by the denominational academies and colleges, and by the men and women who were bred in both. These forces have infused that missionary spirit into our educational system which reaches out a summoning hand to the needy and aspiring. Our country has been distinguished for the immense gifts to the cause of education. How many were directly prompted by religion? How many at least indirectly by the moral impulses surviving in the children of religious families? The friendly helpfulness of churches and ministers toward the public schools and high schools has been all the more creditable because there has been no organic connection to call out the sense of responsibility.

A fourth great section of our social order which has been christianized is the political life. To Americans this may seem a staggering assertion, for of all corrupt things surely our politics is the corruptest. I confess to some misgivings in moving that this brother be received among the regenerate, but I plead on his behalf that he is a newly saved sinner. Politics has been on the thorny path of sanctification only about a century and a half, and the tattered clothes and questionable smells of the far country still cling to the prodigal.

The fundamental redemption of the State took place when special privilege was thrust out of the constitution and theory of our government and it was based on the principle of personal liberty and equal rights.

When the rich and the poor have justice meted to them in our courts with an uneven hand, and the fact is made plain and comprehensible, it is felt to be an outrage and a betrayal of the spirit of our institutions. When powerful interests receive special consideration and benefits from Congress or the State legislatures, all concerned are careful to mask the fact and disguise the action as if it were done for the public interest. When the property of the rich is partly exempted from taxation by unequal methods of assessment, and the burden of public expenditure is thrown on the poorer classes, we feel free to protest against it as a departure from the clear intent of our fundamental laws. In short, inequality and oppression, the denial of equal rights and of the equal humanity of all is felt to be a backsliding and disgrace.

But the time was when these things were sanctioned as just and honorable by law and public opinion. Inequality and privilege were part of the constitution of States. Feudalism shaped the social order of the Middle Ages, just as democracy and capitalism make up the social order of our own age. But in feudalism class differences and class privileges were essential to the very theory of government. The nobleman was on a wholly different footing before the law from the common man. He had to be tried by men of his own class, who were disposed by class feeling to side with him, and the baser forms of punishment did not exist for him. Some remnants of this inequality still linger wherever feudal rank survives. A Russian noble and a moujik who commit the same offense do not receive the same punishment. In Germany two workmen who cut each other up with knives and two army officers who cut each other up with swords in a duel are treated in a very different manner by the law. In Italy two cardinals recently claimed their right as Italian princes to have their deposition as witnesses taken in their own houses instead of coming into a public court like common people. Within certain limits the feudal nobles usually had the right of judicature in their territories; when a peasant was oppressed by the servants of the baron and claimed justice in the court, he found the baron or his appointee sitting in the court to decide the case. Imagine that the constitution of Illinois provided that a director of a corporation could be tried only by a jury of corporation officers, and that every public service corporation had the right to operate its own court of justice to settle all difficulties with its employees and the ordinary public, and could put the offensive citizen who protested against the size of his gas bill into the corporation jail! In the feudal age landed property was almost the only form of property, and the landed nobility corresponded very fully to what we call "the Interests," so that the illustration is not at all fanciful.

A hundred other special privileges were claimed and exercised by the nobility, not "on the side," but frankly as their natural right. Even a petty noble could declare and wage war, a right of such momentous importance for the people that in our vast nation only a single public body is vested with that power. At one time about a hundred and fifty peers and barons of France could coin and circulate money, another right of profound importance to public welfare. The higher civil and military careers were open only to nobles and churchmen. Political rights were restricted to landowners; consequently it was made hard for the baseborn to acquire land at all. The system of restricting the suffrage on property lines is a remnant of the feudal system of granting political power to those who already had economic power, and of depriving the economically helpless of the political means of asserting their rights. Even in so enlightened a country as Prussia a three-class system of suffrage prevails by which one heavy taxpayer in the first class may count for as much as a hundred workingmen in the third class.

Only by comparison with the past do we realize that our political system has really entered on a decisive moral change. The foundations of our commonwealth were fortunately laid when the democratic idealism of the eighteenth century was gathering strength. Soon afterward it got its tremendous utterance in the French Revolution. In every revolutionary movement the highest political and social conceptions of that age are seized by the revolutionary party, and put forward in order to enlist moral support and enthusiasm. When the plowshare tears open the soil, new seeds can gain lodgment. The American Revolution, like the French, was essentially a movement of the capitalist class and was impelled by their economic interests, but as long as the struggle lasted the leaders were inspired by higher enthusiasms, and the necessity of rallying all available spiritual forces gave the convinced radicals and idealists a comparatively free hand for the moment. Between 1776 and 1786 the ardent sentiments of the Declaration of Independence had cooled down into very calculating class interest, and the fundamental law of our country was by no means framed to promote and extend democracy in coming days. But at least we had no king, and no landed and hereditary nobility. The young capitalist class still had its milk teeth. So by the favor of Providence and by our political and economic babyhood the principles of liberty and equality got a solid footing in our traditions. Some of the inherited immoralities, such as the restrictions of the suffrage under which the Constitution was adopted,[1] were overcome, and even when immense inequalities of possession grew up, appeal still lay to the primitive decalogue of our liberties.

In practice we are a nation of backsliders. The whisper of awe and surprise that runs through the country when a powerful malefactor is actually brought to justice is proof that the rich and the poor are not equal before our courts. The real decisions in politics are made by small cliques, and except in seasons of popular revolt the votes of great numbers of citizens count for almost nothing. In actual practice the administration of public affairs is full of favoritism to the powerful, and even more full of damnable neglect for those things which are really vital to the common people.

Yet all these things are in the nature of a derailment of justice; the roadbed and the trackage are still there, even when the train is ditched. These apostasies from the American standards of right have to cloak their real nature in order to exist at all. The means of dethroning the usurpers of public power are always within reach. Graft is at least not embodied in the Constitution, nor declared to be the hallowed foundation of the commonwealth. When some of our States concluded to curb the extralegal power of the bosses by direct primaries, uniform accounting, direct legislation, and the recall, these enormous changes were secured by only a few years of moderately vigorous agitation. On the other hand, when great bodies of voters in Berlin in 1908 tried to make a peaceful protest against the iniquitous Prussian three-class system of suffrage, by parading in the streets, they were dispersed and cut down with sabers. Slavery was the one great social institution contradicting the democratic principle which was able to secure

[1] Of 3,000,000 inhabitants about 120,000 had the suffrage.

recognition and protection in the federal Constitution. It long jutted into our American life as a disturbing remnant from an earlier and evil age. From the terrible sacrifice which it cost our nation to get rid of it we can learn the difference between a suppression of .human rights that is supported by the fundamental law, and a frustration of human rights that circumvents the law.

The backslidings of our politics are partly due to the youth of democracy. It is still in its adolescence. For ages government was managed for the people by a select group and all the expedients and theories of government were evolved to suit that condition. The people have to learn how to do it. The running of coöperative stores and factories is a new art which has to be learned with losses and suffering, whereas management by corporations is well understood and effective. Democracy stands for the coöperative idea applied to politics; monarchy and aristocracy represent in statecraft the same ideals and methods which corporations represent in business.

Another cause for the frequent breakdown of popular government is the fact that the State very directly affects the property interests of the country. But these interests do not in the least acknowledge the principle of equal human rights, and balk at every attempt to conform them to that doctrine. Consequently politics is the battleground of two opposing forces, of the Christian principle of liberty and equality lodged in our democracy, and of the mammonistic principle lodged in our business life. The family, the Church, and the school are only indirectly affected by this struggle; politics is involved directly. The State is like a breakwater, pounded by hungry seas. As long as it holds, let us thank God and not wonder if it is wet and slippery with ooze. When our business life is christianized, the fundamental Christianity of our political structure will become clearer and more effective.

In spite of all failures we can assert that our political communities are constitutionally on a Christian footing. Instead of legalizing class inequality, they at least try to be an organized expression of the equal rights of all. Instead of being a firmly wrought system for holding down the weak and depriving them of the natural means of self-help and even of a voice to utter their wrongs, our government tries to be a guarantee of freedom and a protection to the helpless. Instead of being constitutionally an organization of a clique for their private advantage, it is planned as an organization of all for the common good, and only falls into the hands of marauding interests through the ignorance and laziness of the citizens. Democracy is not equivalent to Christianity, but in politics democracy is the expression and method of the Christian spirit. It has made the most permanent achievements in the younger communities of the Anglo-Saxon group, but it is making headway throughout the world, and is the conquering tendency in modern political life.

If politics has been christianized, how much did Christianity help in converting it? It is possible to make out a strong case for the proposition that democracy has come in spite of the Church and that its best champions were avowed infidels. But Christianity is more than the Church. The reactionary doings of ecclesiastical machines can be put down in black and white and quoted by scoffers to the end of time. But the decisive movements of the Christian spirit are subtle and hard to record; like the wind it bloweth where it listeth, and few listen to it even while it is blowing; fewer still can trace its effect after the wind has hushed. The struggle for political democracy in its infancy was so closely connected with the struggle for religious toleration and freedom that it is impossible to disentangle the two and decide how much strength each factor would have had by itself. Certainly the success of political democracy was most early and durable where radical and pure types of Christianity had gained a footing and influence. The sense of human worth, the sensitive response to the rights of the poor and helpless, the fighting courage bred by bold religion, are pervasive ingredients in the national life which silently coöperate with all efforts to christianize public life. Democracy has been best led in Protestant countries where a free type of religion ranged men of distinctively Christian character on the side of popular liberty. On the other hand, where free Christianity was suppressed by Church and State, the lovers of liberty were ranged against both Church and State and the hatred of tyranny took on the colors of irreligion. In that case the infidels really voiced the spirit of Christianity better than the Church; Christ once more found better friends among the publicans than among the Pharisees. Voltaire, for instance, was a destroying angel who mocked and lashed an apostate and unbelieving Church with the Christian weapons of humanity, charity, and fraternity. But the fact that such cases are abnormal impress them on the public notice and memory. The more broadly and justly we view the history of the last eight centuries, the more influence will we attribute to Christianity in the rise of modern democracy. In the Anglo-Saxon communities especially the spirit of religion has blended with the spirit of freedom; or rather, here the spirit of Christianity has been set free sufficiently to do its work in the field of political life, and has found one great outlet for its power in creating a passionate love for freedom and equality.

Four great sections of our social order — the family, the organized religious life, the institutions of education, and the political organization of our nation — have passed through constitutional changes which have made them to some degree part of the organism through which the spirit of Christ can do its work in humanity. The analysis of these redeemed parts of our social order has explained by historical object lessons in what sense we can speak of christianizing the social order, and has also brought home to us with what gradualness and through what complex forces such a process has to work its way. The presumption is that other portions of the social order will have to submit to similar changes if they are to be christianized.

If this analysis is even approximately correct, it ought to create an immense hopefulness in all Christian minds. Social Christianity is not, then, an untried venture. The larger part of the work of christianizing our social order is already accomplished, and the success which has attended it ought to create a victorious self-assertion in all who stake their faith on its effectiveness. These redeemed portions of our social life are the portions to which our hearts go out in loving pride and loyalty. Christianity works. Moreover every part of the social order which has come even a little under the law of Christ has immediately served as a vantage ground for further progress. There has been a speeding up of redemption. When a man is gagged, bound, and tied to a stake, the hardest part is to get one hand free : every further gain is easier and makes ultimate freedom surer.

What is next ?

CHAPTER III

THE next thing is Business.

Our business life is the seat and source of our present troubles. So much ought to be plain to all who care to see. It is in commerce and industry that we encounter the great collective inhumanities that shame our Christian feeling, such as child labor and the bloody total of industrial accidents. Here we find the friction between great classes of men which makes whole communities hot with smoldering hate or sets them ablaze with lawlessness. To commerce and industry we are learning to trace the foul stream of sex prostitution, poverty, and political corruption. Just as an epidemic of typhoid fever would call for an analysis of the water supply, so these chronic conditions call for a moral analysis of the economic order and justify the presumption that it is fundamentally unchristian. Business men themselves concede that it is; some by calmly denying that Christian principles have anything to do with business; others by sadly confessing that Christianity ought to govern business, but that it would mean loss or ruin to put Christian ethics in practice.

Business life is the unregenerate section of our social order. If by some magic it could be plucked out of our total social life in all its raw selfishness, and isolated on an island, unmitigated by any other factors of our life, that island would immediately become the object of a great foreign mission crusade for all Christendom. Our argument, therefore, will now concentrate on this unredeemed portion of the social order.

Our first need is to analyze our economic system so that we may understand wherein and why it is fundamentally unchristian. Most of us have accepted our economic system as we accept our stomach, without understanding its workings. Nor is it easy to understand the moral essentials of this huge and complicated social machinery. We have no such historical perspective of it as our great-grandchildren will have when they study the Great Industrial Transition of the Twentieth Century in college. We are like a swimmer in a stormy sea. To negotiate the next wave is the great object of his concern, but whether that wave is part of a tidal current sweeping him toward shore or out to sea, his narrow horizon does not tell him. So amid the swift changes of our age we find it hard to distinguish between incidental troubles and the essential drifts of our economic system.

We stumble along untraveled trails when we attempt an analysis of our economic system from a Christian point of view. The collective intelligence of the Christian Church has not really come to any clearness about the fundamental moral relations involved in modern economic life. It instinctively condemns some of its worst excrescences, but even among its leaders many have no clear grasp of the moral nature and genius of our industrial and commercial world. We have been neglecting the Doctrine of Sin in our theology. We might look to Christian business men for an incisive comprehension of the moral conditions amid which they work, but most of them are so driven by business that they have no time to consider their situation broadly and with historical insight. They see keenly what is immediately necessary, but in the broader tendencies of their life a vast collective will bids them go, and they go. They are slaves of the lamp. Business imposes its point of view on them, just as the Catholic Church molds the ideas of the priests who labor in it. When "practical men" do theorize, they are often the dizziest theorizers of all.

Nevertheless, a moral analysis of our economic life is now in the process of making. Our whole nation has of late constituted itself a commission of investigation and is engaged in a profoundly earnest attempt to understand the morals of business. Nothing calls out such serious thought and discussion at present as the unsatisfactory relation of the economic life to the higher laws and values of humanity. This book is part of this collective effort to understand. I propose throughout to think from the point of view of a Christian man. The tests that I shall apply are not technical but moral. Does our business system create sound and noble manhood ? Does it make it fairly easy to do right and hard to do wrong ? Does it call men upward or tempt them downward ? Does it reward or penalize fraternal action ? Does it furnish the material basis for the Reign of God on earth ? As a Christian man I shall have to judge more patiently and forbearingly than if I were inquiring why high prices are making it hard for me to feed my family and rear my children. I shall also have to probe more incisively and condemn more sweepingly than if I were arguing as a lawyer or an economist. Christ would pardon many of those whom we send to cruel years in prison, and would consign to the Gehenna of wrath some of those who sit in our seats of judgment and respectability.

We should get the most enlightening comments on our economic life if we could bring to life some able mind that went to sleep in A.D. 1700, or if some one could live in the year 2000 like the hero of "Looking Backward" and come back to us. By comparing our present system backward with the order out of which it has developed, or forward with the order into which it is silently passing, we should get a realization of the distinctive qualities of the life in the midst of which we are moving. But even if the range of our experience is short, yet the movement of society has been so rapid that even twenty or thirty years of observation allow us to measure the curve of the road along which we are all swinging.

When I was a boy in the seventies, I spent several happy summers working on the farm in a German community in Lycoming County, Pennsylvania. The tools of our work were very simple. There was a horserake and a mowing machine, but the sheaves of grain were raked and bound by hand, and the hoe was the pillar of agriculture. Except for the buzz saw in the old sawmill by the creek there was no power machine in sight. Most of the products of the farm were consumed by those who raised them. We took the grain to the mill and waited till it was ground. The miller took his pay in grain. Occasionally we butchered a sheep and had fresh meat to eat. The spinning wheel still buzzed in the kitchen, and a hand loom pounded in the "shop." On market days we took butter, eggs, and berries to Williamsport and sold them to the housewives on the street curb, or we went from house to house offering what we had. The old farmer liked to have me along because multiplying pounds by cents was a confusing operation for which a city boy came in handy. The calculating age had not yet struck him. There was little money to handle.

On that farm we lived the economic life of the pre-capitalistic era. All who have ever worked on an old-fashioned farm can have a living comprehension of the industrial era that is slowly sinking out of sight.

Since that time modern methods have invaded and revolutionized farming at some points. Think of the great wheat farms where gasoline engines and power machines have become the farmer's pets; or the truck farms where they raise asparagus, cranberries, or peaches in quantities that make the digestive apparatus of the onlooker seem puny and behind the times. In the busy season these farmers become employers of gang labor. They have learned to figure and to calculate their expenses and profits in fractional percentage. Their produce is raised "for the market" and not for their home. The farmer's family eats flour milled in Minneapolis and canned stuff that he buys in town. He ships his produce to commission merchants in a distant city, who sell it to dealers, who sell it to hotel men and housekeepers whom the farmer never sees. He has become a cog in the vast machinery of modern production. He feeds the world, and the world feeds him. On these modernized farms we can watch the industrial revolution invading the backward domain of agriculture. Farming has begun to travel the same road which industry began to travel a century earlier.

My own boyhood has also supplied me with a lively impression of the patriarchal régime of the old handicraft system. On a visit to Germany I spent some days in the home of a master tailor in the ancient town of Altena in Westphalia, where my father and grandfather had been Lutheran pastors. His shop was upstairs in his home. Half a dozen journeymen and a couple of apprentices squatted cross-legged on tables, plying the needle. The master worked with them and shared their talk. At noon all ate at his table and he cut the bread and served the soup to them with due respect to seniority. When he said grace before and after meat, all bowed their heads with him. Downstairs in a tiny store, like a hall bedroom, he kept a few bolts of stuff. From these his customers selected their cloth, or they brought him their own goods to make up. A stock of ready-made clothing, made for potential and invisible buyers, probably never entered his mind.

This is a miniature picture of industry in the precapitalistic era, of its narrow market, its simple methods, and its direct relations between men. Such little shops continue to supply the bulk of economic products throughout the Orient and to a large extent in continental Europe. Very recently I found only one small shoe store selling factory-made shoes in a German city of twenty thousand inhabitants, but more than a hundred small shops ready and able to take any order that dealt with leather and feet.

Contrast with this simple form of industry the great centers of the shoe or clothing trade in America. Huge factories whirr with specialized machinery. Every turn of the process has its machine; every man has his trick. Thousands of men coöperate under centralized direction. The old patriarchal relations between master and men are gone; they no longer work together, nor talk together, nor eat together, nor pray together. The most competent manager of a shoe factory may not be able to make a shoe, to save his life. But he is an expert in organization. The men who own the factory may be still farther remote from its actual work. Some of them may never have seen the place; they have bought stock because it is earning 8 per cent and has a good rating. While the goods are being made, no one knows who will wear this coat or those shoes. They are made for the market, seized by the roaring wheels of commerce, and carried to the ends of the earth.

In the old order the aim was to make a living, to give the children an education and a start in life, to lay something by for a rainy day, and to rise a step in life if possible. The range of possibilities and the range of ambition were both narrow. There was always a big difference between the thrifty man and the shiftless man; between the mechanic who sent his boy to college, and his cousin who went fishing and let his job wait for him. But the richest and the poorest in our old-time village communities were only a few thousand dollars apart. In the cities men of business sagacity equal to any that we now have were content if a lifetime of success won them a few hundred thousand dollars.

To-day the range of possibilities is enormous, and the unsatisfied thirst for wealth has grown correspondingly.

M

The poorest and the richest are as far apart as the mole-hill and the peaks of the Sierras. In the higher reaches of business getting a living drops out of sight. The dominant concern is to get profit, and to invest it to get more profit. In its main river bed the current of business has become a torrent.

Thus the modern economic order is developing right before our eyes. We younger men and women have seen the revolution proceed in American industry and commerce. We have seen the great department stores, the manufacturing centers, and the trusts sprout and shoot up like magic. Our children will see similar transitions in farming. Within one generation our country has become the classical demonstration of capitalistic industry. A similar transition took place a century earlier in England, and more slowly on the continent of Europe.

This modernizing of industry has largely been a simple expansion in size, a sort of adolescence of the industry previously existing. The essential thing in it was not the application of steam power, but the utilizing of human association on a large scale. More men were coördinated under one management, more wealth combined in joint-stock enterprises. A vaster market was opened up. Organization became a science and the chief of all crafts. The tendency to combine and mass human labor was in full swing before the invention of the steam engine, and would have gone on without it, but the power machine immeasurably intensified it and furnished the technical basis for the combination and division of labor. Gradually the machine has become a sort of new partner in production. The old hand tools merely aided the hand that plied them and never made that hand unnecessary. The new machine tools tend to become the real workers. They supplant some men entirely, and reduce others to the position of feeding and tending the machine.

Now, in so far as our present economic order is simply the perfecting of human association, Christianity can have no quarrel with it. The massing of industrial units, the specializing of functions, the mastery of natural forces by science and technical skill, are henceforth part and parcel of every social order that will develop on this planet unless the race reverts to barbarism. The attempts to check this process by prohibiting department stores or enforcing the Sherman Antitrust Law have bucked against manifest destiny and the law of evolution. An ideal social order would have the serious problem of counteracting the monotony and one-sidedness which are inseparable from machine work, and of protecting the freedom and individuality of the single worker in the centralized pressure of industrial organization, but it could not turn its face back to patriarchal simplicity. An enlarged and diversified industrial organization is not an evil, but a good.

The moral objection lies, not against the size and complexity of the modern system, but against the fact that this wonderful product of human ability and toil with its immense powers of production has gravitated into the ownership and control of a relatively small class of men. This group is always changing; some drop out, others enter. But these personal changes are of little importance for the make-up of society. The group is permanent, and the men in it have acquired a proportion of power over their fellows which — human nature being what it is — must lead to injustice, to inequality, and to the frustration of the Christian conception of human fellowship.

In the old handicraft system ownership and power were widely distributed. Every little shop was an industrial unit, and every master mechanic was an independent power. Every apprentice could hope in time to become the owner of so simple a plant. This is the condition still prevailing generally in our farm life in America. Our farmers are workmen who own their instruments of production. They are workmen and capitalists combined in one. That makes them strong, and it is no wonder that they work like grim death before they will let a mortgage force them from the hold which their farm gives them on God's universe. On the other hand, our factory operatives have no right nor claim in the place, the tools, or the output of their work. They are propertyless men who own only their body and its working force. Even if they own a home and have a savings-bank account, that property does not aid them in their work and gives them no share in the control of their shop. In such cases they have property, but no capital.

In the modern industrial order ownership and control are not vested in the workers, but in an entirely different social group which stands apart from them by its interests, social status, habits of life, and modes of thought, — the group of investors or capitalists. A man may work twenty years for a corporation and contribute the most valuable service in building it up, yet have no part nor lot in it at the end, and be liable to dismissal at any time. Another man who has never contributed a hard day's work to it either of body or mind is a part owner of it and shares in its control because he has invested money in it. It is true that in most cases the two groups overlap. A number of individuals are usually both owners and active intellectual workers in the concern, and this is the redeeming feature in the situation. But even that is not essential. The managing officers of a corporation may all be salaried men. And in any case the power which the managers wield comes to them from the owners and not from the workers. The capitalist group is in control.

It is the extent and thoroughness of this two-class adjustment which differentiates the modern industrial order from the old. It is this also which creates its chief moral dangers. No one will understand the moral side of our economic relations unless he comprehends this two-group system. Wherever any industrial undertaking is really modernized, the separation of these two groups becomes clearly marked. On the one side, we have a growing body of workers to whom possession of the plant in which they work becomes a more and more remote possibility; on the other side, a scattered group of owners, of whom only a few share in the productive labor of the concern. But the former group is under the control of the latter. For this reason our modern system is called the capitalistic system.

Divergent points of view and a conflict of interests follow with absolute necessity from this two-class system. The interests of the worker revolve around his job, for a job is his only chance to apply his working force, and his working force is all he has. So the job is his sole hold on life. His entire system of ethics becomes job-centric. To get a job, to hold it against those who might take it from him, and to make it yield him as much as possible of pay, leisure, and comfort is the absorbing concern of his soul. As the sun is the source of warmth and life to the earth, so is the job to the worker.

On the other hand, the economic interests of the capitalist revolve around his profits, and since the capitalist class is the controlling and dominant class, the desire for profit dominates our whole industrial organization. All its efforts converge on one end, to make dividends. All the parts of the great organism of production move toward profit with an overwhelming singleness of purpose. Whenever profit has collided with the higher interests of humanity, the latter have hitherto gone down with sickening regularity. This triumphant sway of profit as the end of work and existence puts the stamp of mammonism on our modern life.

Another essential feature of our modern business life

is its speculative method. In large sections of industry production is not in response to an actual demand, but in anticipation of a possible demand. Business has to forecast the future, not only in the size and quality of a season's output, but in the erection of great plants. This means risk and venture. Now there is an element of risk in any productive labor, even in baiting your hook for a fish or planting cabbages in your back yard. But when production is on so vast a scale as to-day, when competition is so keen, and when the lure of possible profit is so dazzling, the wholesome natural tingle of daring becomes a consuming fever. The speculative character of business causes enormous waste and to that extent stamps business as technically inefficient. But what concerns us here is that it creates a feverish heat of desire in which the higher qualities of life are melted and burned. If covetousness is a valuable quality in human nature, business is a superb institution to stimulate and educate it. But if "the love of money is the root of evil," what is business?

When we try to judge our economic system from the point of view of Christian morals, we must not forget that it has biased the moral judgment by which it is to be measured. Recent as the capitalistic system is in human history, it has been in operation long enough to mold the laws and policies of all industrial nations, and to put a deep impress on the ethical and religious ideas of the modern world. On the cut-stone front of a skyscraper are mighty caryatids that seem to hold up its vast weight on their bent shoulders. But we know that it is really supported by the steel girders and trusses of the framework, and all other features of the building must adjust themselves to the mechanical necessities of this essential structure. So in every social order that has ever existed, the economic system then in force was one of the determining influences. Dogmatic socialists often run the theory of "economic determinism" into the ground, but no student of history can question the tremendous importance of the economic factor. In the old handicraft order generations of small producers had built up a system of municipal laws and guild regulations which sheltered them and their interests against powerful and greedy competitors. The aim of Christian legislation at that time was to secure to every business man a moderate circle of customers and a decent living, and to shackle those who would try to secure inordinate wealth by snatching the bread of their fellows. When the capitalistic method gathered force and headway, it swept away these protective laws which hampered free competition and the massing of capital and labor. It created a new philosophy of economics. It secured control of political power, and enacted laws that threw the field open to those who were strong enough to seize the vantage points. If anything, it favored the strong against the weak, and gave to him that hath. The fierce struggle which followed speeded up the machinery of production, increased the material wealth of the industrial nations boundlessly, and put a generation of strong executive intellects in the saddle. But it trampled down the humane considerations of mercy and fraternity which had to some extent prevailed, and created a general temper of lawlessness and ruthlessness which has now become second nature to us all, so that we hardly realize how hard and inhuman it all is. To limit female labor to ten hours a day in the interest of humanity is to-day a great moral achievement, and the idea of a legal living wage is a startling innovation to a generation that has inherited the moral point of view of the competitive era.

In a rough and preliminary way we have now sketched the chief moral features of our economic system. We have found the business man in the seat of power. He and his class own and control the immense enginery of modern production. All moral relations run back to him. In the chapters that now follow, we shall take up the various relations which he sustains to his fellows in the organism of business life: first, his relation to other men of his own class with whom he competes or associates; second, his relation to the workers whom he employs; third, his relation to the consumers whom he supplies.

CHAPTER IV

WHEN a number of men in the same community engage in the same line of productive labor, what is the normal and desirable relation between them? Isolation, if the nature of their work compels it; coöperation, if the nature of their work permits it. A coöperating group, in which all have a common end, each man contributing his share and depending on his fellows for their part, brings men into the most efficient, the most happy, and the most moral relation to one another. Wherever teamwork is done, on the baseball field, in war, in gang labor, in the faculty of a college, or in political groups, work has zest, and the nobler qualities of men are brought out. The loyalties called out by teamwork are so great that even when a team unites for immoral ends, as in the case of a gang of toughs, a marauding clan, or a ring of corrupt politicians, the men feel that their faithfulness to their comrades excuses any evil they do and casts a glamour of nobility over their organization. War has been made splendid in all its red-handedness chiefly because it trains to teamwork and develops devotion to the group.

The instinct and capacity for coöperation among workmates is one form of the great social instinct of love in man. The same pervasive force which draws man to woman, friend to friend, and countryman to countryman expresses itself in economic labor by the pleasure and stimulus of combined work. Wherever men work out a smooth and effective system of coöperating in their labor, love has found an organized social expression, and as such a group works in common, the capacity for mutual understanding and good will is strengthened.   But to increase the strength of love and to make it effective in all human relations is also the great aim of Christianity.   "Love is the fulfillment of the law."   Therefore an effective coöperative group is a christianized segment of humanity.

Coöperation is not only morally beautiful, but economically effective.   The great achievements of modern life are almost wholly due to the application of this principle. Progress consisted in learning to expand the size of our coöperating groups and to make all the parts interlock more smoothly.   The triumphs of applied science are due to the sharing of intellectual results and methods.   The modern means of traffic and communication have turned entire nations and groups of nations into semiorganized coöperating groups.   Individually we are neither stronger nor wiser than our fathers, but we have learned to work together, and that has created our wonderful age.   The old saying that "competition is the life of trade" is a lie.[1]   Competition may be a stimulant of sales, but coöperation is the life of the whole economic process.   Capitalism itself gets its strength and value not from its competitive element, but from the fact that it furnishes the means of combining many units of capital in the financing of an industrial undertaking, and many units of labor in the operation of it. Thus coöperation is both moral and efficient.   If it were not economically efficient, it would not be moral; if it were not moral, it would not be permanently efficient.

In so far as modern business life has wrought out effective methods of associating many workers in friendly coöpera-

---

[1] The economic inefficiency of competition is another story.   In Rochester 28 milk peddlers travel up and down one street to serve 79 homes.   On another route 57 milkmen travel 30 miles to serve 363 homes; one man would travel two miles to serve them all.   As a consequence of this waste of labor milk is dear and its quality uncertain.

tion, it is good. But the application of this principle of coöperation is still limited to small areas and territories, and at the border line of these territories we have antagonism and war. In the sixteenth century Germany was cut up into something like a thousand political units, crazier than any jig-saw puzzle, each with its own government, its own taxes, its own loyalty, and its own right to go to war. While France and England were growing into compact political organisms, Germany remained disunited, torn by internal dissensions and wars, mocking the patriotism of its sons by its petty fatherlands. The Franco-German War at last welded the surviving States into an empire, and the wonderful rise of German commerce and wealth since 1870 is another demonstration of the power of teamwork. The industrial and commercial map of our nation is still cut up into hundreds of thousands of economic units. Inside of each firm or corporation coöperation and efficiency prevail, but where one business concern collides with another of the same kind, we find either war or a truce. All the virtues and the vices of war are developed. Most competitors conceal their methods, their markets, their prices, their plans, like the generals of contending armies. Some department stores have an organized spy system to see that their rivals offer no special bargains without being followed and countered. The secretiveness made necessary by competition is one chief reason why our government has found it so hard to secure publicity, or even to get at the inside facts of business life for its own purposes. Some of the investigating commissions have had to drill and blast like burglars trying to get into a bank vault. In many lines of business a truce has been called in the competitive war by tacit or express agreements to maintain prices and respect trade areas, but where competition is in full swing, it is a war that aims to capture the other man's trade, and does not end until he goes out of business. Then he may come in as a partner or employee, and therewith the whole attitude to him changes.

What is the moral effect of such a collision of interests? Coöperative action calls out instincts of good will and solidarity; competition represses good will, and calls out selfishness and jealousy. Men who are doing the same kind of work and who ought to be workmates are set into an antagonism which makes Christian love heroic instead of natural and spontaneous. Imagine a Methodist grocer who has built up a good trade on a suburban street corner. The trade is not large enough to support two stores, but a Baptist, surveying the situation and having come into a little money from his mother-in-law, stocks up a place on the opposite corner, and proposes to open his store to-morrow morning. The Christian law bids us love our neighbor as ourselves. Will the Methodist kneel down to-night and pray God to bless his Baptist brother and give him success in his new business? Will the Baptist pray that his fellow-Christian may continue to prosper? If they do it and mean it, they are both so saintly that the Pope ought to overlook any little heresies and canonize them. A man who is secure in his business success may feel genuine good will toward a young man starting out for himself in the same line, but in that case he is like a champion chess player who gives both bishops to a beginner; he is not really playing the game of competition, but lapsing into the happier game of human brotherhood.

The moral instinct of men has always condemned competitive selfishness, just as it has always admired the moral beauty of teamwork. Our hearts thrill when we see any one throwing himself heart and soul into a common task and risking his own safety to insure the common success. By the same token we fail to thrill when any one haggles for himself and seeks to get the better of his fellows. The child that "won't play," the soldier that deserts in time of danger, the workman that helps to break a strike, the boy that "snitches" on his pals, are not objects of admiration to their mates, nor to wise outsiders. The trader has always been the outstanding case of the man who plays his own hand and sacrifices social solidarity for private gain. Consequently the trading class has never ranked high among the social classes in older civilizations, like that of Japan. He was not expected to limit himself by the law of honor, but neither did he receive honor. On the other hand, in our modern era the trading class has become the ruling class, and consequently the selfishness of trade has been exalted to the dignity of an ethical principle. Every man is taught to seek his own advantage, and then we wonder that there is so little public spirit. We have allowed workmates to be pitted against each other in the competitive struggle and then are astonished that Christianity has a hard time of it.

The reign of competition is a reign of fear. The rate of mortality for small business concerns is higher than infant mortality. If all the leaden weight of fear of all business men who watch a vanishing margin of profit through the year could be gathered up and set before us in some dramatic form, it would palsy our joy in life. Business panics merely render this chronic condition acute and make men high up who have been secure in prosperity feel the same sufferings which others have felt who went down before them. A reign of fear is never a reign of God. Fear makes children lie and business men cheat. In competition the worst man sets the pace, and good men follow because they are afraid. A capable mind with no bowels of mercy to hinder, who can wring the last ounce of strength from his men, and who puts women and children to work wherever men can be displaced, can outbid a morally sensitive man unless the latter has some counterbalancing advantage elsewhere. In a coöperating group the efficiency and courage of the best members of the team hold the rest up to their level; in commercial competition the greed and inhumanity of the worst infect the rest through the medium of fear. For this reason considerations of humanity have often had so little response from communities of business men composed largely of Christian persons. Individually they are kind-hearted men; but as members of a competitive social order they are driven by fear and forgetful of mercy. Workmen complain when their employers speed up the machinery, which compels them to keep up with its pace or be hurt. But their employers are also slaves of a huger machine, and many of them are seeking with laboring breath to keep up with a treadmill that will mangle them if they do not.

The objection will be raised that the instinct of competition is inherent in human life and that its free play is a necessary factor in the evolution of the race. That is quite true. Life would lose much of its zest and of its educational value if competition were eliminated from it. But there is no danger whatever that it will be. Young men will always compete for the love of woman (and sometimes that game is reversed); students will compete for educational honors; workmen will compete for leadership within their group; statesmen will compete for popularity and power. When the ablest are honored and promoted, it benefits all. A superior type is thereby placed in a conspicuous position, and the rest are more or less modeled after it. The unsuccessful competitors may suffer all the pangs of disappointed ambition, but they are not usually impoverished or disgraced. A college boy who fails to win a prize is not on that account reduced to high school rank. A workman who fails to be promoted to the position of foreman does not lose his old job. Such emulation advances some without ruining the rest. For that kind of competition an economic system founded wholly on co-operation would offer splendid chances, with more publicity and fame for the winners than is now offered in business life.

But commercial competition differs in important ways from these salutary forms of human competition, and we ought to understand the difference.

In the first place, the stakes are too large for safety. Any blessing may become a curse by growing excessive. A baby is a benediction; triplets are a calamity. We are glad when the temperature of a room rises from forty to seventy degrees, but we object to a hundred and seventy. A pinch of salt and pepper is pleasant as a condiment, but a handful makes wry faces. So there is no great harm when boys play marbles "for keeps" or old ladies play piquet for small stakes, but when clerks stake a week's wages on roulette or the races, it creates a moral situation about which great States enact laws. In business the stakes are enormous. They are larger absolutely, reckoned in money values, than ever before, because business is done on a larger scale. It is no longer a question of a few hundred dollars on a single deal, but of hundreds of thousands, and even millions of dollars on a single transaction. The stakes are also excessive relatively, measured by their importance to the man who plays the game. The terrible game of competition always involves the possibility of business failure as the ending for one party. Therewith a man drops from the position of an independent man to that of a subordinate, from participation in profits to a mere salary, from large hopes to a contracted outlook. If he is past his youth, the drop may be final. It involves the social standing of his family, the prospects of his children, even their health and length of life. If men gambled at faro for their fortunes, or bartered away their wives and children into peonage, the police would intervene. Yet any stringency of the market witnesses situations which are morally much like that. No human character ought to be submitted to such cruel tension and strain. Is it strange that men under such conditions cut wages in order to be able to lower prices, and submerge the men dependent on them in poverty and the women in prostitution?

In the second place, in so far as emulation is valuable, its object is to gain human affection or honor. As soon as money enters, danger begins. For this reason money prizes are barred in amateur sportsmanship. In education, too, we have learned to dread the stimulation of prizes having money value. A race to the North Pole puts nations in a quiver as long as it is a contest for personal and national honor, but if the claimants exploit it as a business monopoly, it becomes sordid and humiliating. But in commercial competition money dominates the situation; honor is secondary; in many cases self-respect and the sense of honor have to be drugged temporarily in order to put a deal through. Success wins notoriety, but not honor. Are there any admiring plaudits in a city when two department stores put a third out of business and the old sign is taken down? Do men feel that they have witnessed a big, splendid human event when a large corporation swallows a smaller one? Unusual business success in our country actually seems to cloud a man's reputation and put him on the defensive for his honor. Surely it is possible to conceive of a situation where men of organizing ability would be the captains of great industrial teams comprising all the workers of a given industry in the community, and where they would be rewarded for their achievements with little money and great honor, instead of big money and little honor.

In the third place, commercial competition is not good sport. When competition is defended as a social principle, it is usually treated as a great game which braces and invigorates human nature and gives the prize to the best. Men say they do not care merely for money; they

are "playing the game." Then let them quit marking
the cards and loading the dice. Competitors in the game
of business do not start even. Some have enormous
special privilege which the others cannot possibly share.
Is it a fair race to all when an electric company owns all
the available water power in the State? Is the Steel Trust,
with its enormous capital and good will and its mineral
holdings, running on a level with any young concern that
wants to enter the race? Our economic system is based
on a mass of special privilege. Private property in mines
and real estate locations have institutionalized inequality.
And then we invite men to play the game on the theory that
it is fair competition between equals. Some have been
through the pack and have taken all the cards that looked
good to them, and then invite the rest to play the great
game for the prizes of life with strict regard to the rules.
In honorable athletics the man who has shown speed in one
race is handicapped in the next, and so reduced to equality
once more; or he is put into another class where he will
once more be pitted against equals only. That system
favors the young and seeks to develop new ability. On the
other hand, in commercial competition it is the beginner
who is handicapped in every way, and the star racers are
furnished with motor cycles to make sure that they will
henceforth always distance the crowd that runs on foot.
Where is the educational value and the moral stimulus of
that sort of sport?

For a century the doctrine of salvation by competition
was the fundamental article in the working creed of the
capitalistic nations. It was the "natural theology" of
industry, and no political economy was orthodox that did
not preach it. Governments felt it would be a sin to interfere while competitors were having a Donnybrook Fair.
In theory it is still in effect in our country. Business men
are indignant when workingmen refuse to permit unre-

N

strained competition among themselves. Government is supposed to punish combinations "in restraint of trade." But in practice competition is being hemmed in and tied up on all hands. None of the big leaders of business believe in it. If they do, their faith is even farther removed from their works than usually. The doctrine of competition was once historically useful because it helped to clear away an outgrown economic system and to substitute larger coöperating groups for the little groups of the handicraft system. But that work has been done, and to-day competition has itself become an antiquated method which ties us down to petty and inefficient forms of teamwork. The polliwog is through with its tail and gills, and is anxious to grow legs and lungs, and sit on a stone in the pride of its froghood. But legislators, lawyers, and old gentlemen generally are anxiously trying to coax back the vanishing tail. The only valid defense for the wastefulness and inefficiency of the competitive system is that it protects the consumer against the voracity of the monopolist. That end is wholly laudable, but we shall have to find more effective means of attaining it than moving back the clockhands that destiny is driving forward.

Business is abandoning competition because it is inefficient, and larger and more powerful forms of association and teamwork are being wrought out. Christianity should help to end competition because it is immoral. Its murderous effect in England at the beginning of the capitalistic era is a matter of record. It has had much the same effect every time it invaded a new country or community. It is a short-sighted and suicidal policy. One nation after the other has had to hog-tie competition by government interference, inspection, and paternalism in the interests of safety and humanity. Competition as a principle is a denial of fraternity. In so far as it is allowed to do its unrestrained work, it establishes the law of tooth and nail, and brings back the age of savage warfare where every man's hand is against every man. It dechristianizes the social order. Whatever progress was achieved under the competitive system was secured, not by the competitive element in it, but by the fact that it allowed so large an application of the forces of association and teamwork. It behooves us to find forms of organization that will expand the present narrow areas of coöperation and make them nation wide. Men who are in the same line of work must be so organized that they can emulate while they coöperate. Commercial competition has developed in our commercial communities the lower instincts of selfishness, covetousness, and craft. A Christian social order must be such that it will develop and educate mutual interest and good will, and equip workmates with that sense of comradeship and solidarity to which they are entitled.

CHAPTER V

"THIS is the essence of Capitalism, that two distinct social classes coöperate in the creation of goods; on the one side the capitalist class, which owns the necessary material factors of production, the machinery, the factories, the raw material, etc.; on the other side the class of free wage workers, who own the personal factor of production, their working ability, and nothing else. Now, all human production consists in applying this personal factor to the material factors. Therefore, what differentiates the capitalistic system from all other methods of production is the fact that these two essential factors are represented by two distinct social classes." [1]

Wherever our social order has been modernized and industrialized, these two classes confront each other in clear formation, and the relation between the two is the overshadowing moral problem of our age.

The capitalist class holds the position of industrial leadership. The capitalist is either himself the employer of labor and the manager of industry, or else he directly or indirectly appoints the managers, superintendents, and foremen who organize and command the industrial army. All power is exercised by his authority.

Now, leadership is one of the indispensable forces and assets of human society. Humanity will never get beyond the need of it. The efficiency of any social organization

[1] Werner Sombart, professor at the University of Breslau, " Sozialismus und soziale Bewegung im 19. Jahrhundert," p. 4.

depends on its success in dethroning the incapable, putting the able individuals in positions of leadership, and properly harnessing them to the common service. In times of danger, or in occupations demanding swift decision and action, men have always invested their leaders with dictatorial power and accepted stern discipline as part of the day's work. If the regimentation of the workers in modern industry is simply leadership which aims at their maximum efficiency, comfort, health, and prosperity, the workers must submit to the limitations of freedom imposed by modern industrial necessities.

Even in that case leadership has potencies of evil. Power is the most subtle intoxicant known. Leadership easily verges into tyranny. Even if there is no motive of economic exploitation, men and women love to exercise power simply to see others yield to their superior force, and when they have grown wonted to power, they resent resistance even if it is just. For that reason all free States have watched jealously against any perpetuation of power on the part of temporary leaders. In politics we provide short terms of office in order to give opportunity for a new verdict of the people and a fresh grant of power. We have never allowed any President more than eight successive years of authority and are considering the advisability of limiting the presidency to a single term of six years. Hard experience has developed the device of the Recall. Therefore if our industrial organization embodied nothing but the leadership of the capable, there would still be need of checks and safeguards against the growth of tyranny. But what protection has industry developed analogous to the checks of political democracy? Do miners have any voice in the selection of the mine bosses? Can the cotton spinners of a mill recall the superintendent who speeds up the machinery beyond the limit of safety and endurance?

Despotism is the permanent temptation of the strong,

even when their power is delegated and representative power. But in industry the master class are not representatives of labor; they hold their power *suo jure* and *Dei gratia*. They own the property without which industry cannot go on. Without them Labor holds a lever without a fulcrum on which to rest it. Without the material factors of production Labor, physical and mental, would be like a paddle wheel revolving in a vacuum. This puts the adjustment of power between the two great classes on a different footing than mere ability of leadership.

By right of property capital is on the inside. It holds the buying public at its mercy and plays tag with the omnipotent State. The rest of us draw no rent from our castles in the air; our great corporations capitalize even their hopes and turn them into present profit. They perform the miracle of Cana every day, changing water into the wine of dividend-earning securities. They are so much master of the economic situation that they can turn their defeats into victories. As a result of the great anthracite coal strike of 1902 the coal barons were induced to pay the miners an advance of sixteen cents per ton, but my coal has since advanced by $1.30 per ton. Even dissolution and death seem to be good for the health of a Trust.

Now if Capital can play with the Consumer who holds the purse and from whom its profits come, what will it do with Labor, which is dependent on it, not only for bread, but for the very chance to work for bread? Capital turns its defeats into victory; Labor sees its hard-won victories slip away and turn into defeat. If the workers by organization, sacrifice, and good leadership win higher wages, they must pay them out again in higher prices for what they consume. If any hold a safe and highly paid position by virtue of special skill, the best technical talent that can be hired is busy devising machinery that will turn their work over to women or boys. If for once there are more jobs than men, steamship companies and other mysterious agencies bring cheap foreigners from the ends of the earth who seep through the levees of organized labor like a Mississippi flood and drive the native population from their jobs and their homes.

Such power on one side and such weakness on the other constitute a solicitation to sin to which human nature ought never to be subjected. None of us is good enough to hold the lives of his fellow-men in the hollow of his hands and see them quiver at his smile or frown. Watch a file of men asking for work, and you will see men begging for a boon from a human god.[1] If such power is habitually exercised by one social class over another, it will inevitably sap the sense of common humanity and create the feeling that a sort of semimorality is right and sufficient toward the subject class. If any difference of race, nationality, language, or religion is added to the economic chasm, as in the case of the negroes and immigrants, moral responsibility is further lessened. Looking back across the ages, we can see these two classes always confronting each other, as master and slave, as lord and serf, as employer and workman. Their relation was never without human warmth and moral nobility. It was probably always better than it looks in the retrospect. And yet, taking it all together, it is a record of sin. Theology tells us of a sin of origin, derived from Adam and transmitted from generation to generation. History too might teach a doctrine of hereditary sin, running by social tradition down the sin-cursed

[1] Here is the substance of a newspaper clipping, dated New York, Aug. 18, 1911. The Interborough Rapid Transit Company advertised for fifteen laborers. About 600 men formed in line in front of the yards at 98th Street and Third Avenue. William Swacott was one of the first. When the gates were opened to admit the applicants for work, there was a rush from the rear. Swacott lost his footing, fell on the pavement, and was stepped on by several hundred men before the police rescued him. At Harlem Hospital the doctors said he was injured internally.

generations of man, the original sin of oppression and exploitation.

Our own age has given a peculiar new twist to this ancient temptation to inhumanity that has always dogged the relation between master and man. It has depersonalized the master. The redeeming feature of the relation in all its historic forms has been the human contact between the individuals of the two classes. No matter if one man was black and the other white, the one a slave and the other a Virginia gentleman, if the two worked and hunted, laughed and mourned together, their common humanity often got the better of the law and made them friends. Perhaps Satan foresaw that Christianity and democracy if once united would put a new heart into mankind which would no longer tolerate the old oppression. But if fraternity arrived, the jig was up for the Devil. So he invented the corporation.

A corporation, as every lawyer knows, is an artificial person, begotten by the Law, a vast being composed of many individuals, with powers both greater and less than the sum of all its parts; invisible and without the imbecilities of the body, immortal and yet without a soul. It is not tempted by wine, woman, or song like the rest of us, but its whole life is ruled and directed by one desire and passion which is never quenched nor satisfied, the lust for profits. It is created for profit; it gets its life breath, its muscles and thews, its intellect, and its size by profit. It has a vast acquisitive mind, but no heart of pity nor bowels of compassion. This uncanny race of incorporeal but corporate persons has begun to multiply among us of late and to grow to unearthly size, towering among us mortals as the skyscraper towers among the plain old homes of our cities. It is doing our work for us with giant hands and doing it well, but it demands to be fed with profit, and its hunger is insatiable.

The corporation, which is fast becoming the agency through which we manage all our large affairs, interposes between the individuals of the owning class and the individuals of the working class in such a way that human kindness and good will get in a minimum of influence. The stockholders are scattered absentee owners. A corporation might be composed of retired missionaries, peace advocates, and dear old ladies, but their philanthropy would cause no vibrations in the business end of the concern. On the other hand, the directors would never be in doubt that 4 per cent is a more acceptable rate of semiannual dividend than 3 per cent, and by the time that desire for substantial profit reached the manager and superintendents, it might be transformed into a cut in wages, a speeding up of the machinery, a cruel system of fines, or any other form of heartlessness.[1] Ruskin mockingly called the "economic man" that did business in the orthodox political economies "a covetous machine." The corporation is that thing. It does not smart under public disapprobation like a business man. Like the judge in the parable, it feareth not God and regardeth not man. It doesn't have to have religion, for even God cannot put a corporation in hell.

A civil engineer can calculate with fair accuracy the amount of water pressure which a certain dam can safely stand. He may be a little out of the way; he may say ten feet of water, when really it will stand eleven; but he could predict with absolute certainty that it would collapse if twenty feet of water were piled behind it. Human nature is wonderfully variable in its individual expressions, but fairly constant in the bulk, when taken by the million. Statistics flow on as evenly as a great river with periodical rises and falls; so many births, deaths, marriages, murders, and suicides year in and year out. A moral engineer can

---

[1] See the chapter on "Sinning by Syndicate" in Professor E. A. Ross's brilliant little book, "Sin and Society."

never predict how much pressure of temptation a given individual will stand, but he can predict with absolute certainty that human nature in the mass will collapse under such temptations as our economic system puts upon it.   A given employer may regard his workmen with genuine human affection, while all his business interests bid him regard them as mere units of labor making money for him.   But the mass of human nature in the business world has followed the line of least resistance and acted as the situation prompted.

As one looks across the industrial nations to observe the condition of the working class, he sees considerable diversity of income and independence in different nations and trades, and yet withal there is a certain uniformity of impression throughout.   It is always a class under pressure. Even where Labor is strong and well organized, it is like a man holding up a heavy piece of timber with his hands, with every muscle tense and the sweat running down his body.   All the costly organization of labor, the privations borne during strikes often extending for many months, the fury of occasional riots, the secret violence, the slugging of strike breakers, the magnificent sacrifices of great bodies of workers for those who are out on strike in some notable cause, the patient and wise efforts of leaders to secure some slight improvement in the conditions of labor, are overwhelming evidence that a weak class is struggling against a strong class, and that the odds are against the workers. The great strikes that get notoriety, like the shirt waist strike in New York, the garment workers' strike in Chicago, the strike of the steel workers at South Bethlehem, the strike of the miners in Westmoreland (which lasted for sixteen months and finally failed), simply heave up and turn to the daylight conditions that had long existed and which continue to exist elsewhere.

Take the strike at South Bethlehem in 1910 as an instance.   Here were nine thousand men making steel for a

wealthy corporation in one of the great protected industries
of Pennsylvania.   More than half of them worked twelve
hours a day, and nearly all the others between ten and
eleven hours, with frequent overtime.   By the device of a
time bonus system the work was speeded up and men had
to earn the bonus to get the wages prevailing elsewhere.
The foremen got large bonuses for big outputs, and that
made some of them drivers of the men.   In addition, between 28 per cent and 43 per cent of the men worked seven
days in the week.   Furthermore, whenever the day and
night shift turned about, the seven-day workers had to
work a shift of twenty-four hours of labor without rest.
Sixty-one per cent earned \$2.16 for a twelve-hour day;
31.9 per cent earned less than \$1.68 in twelve hours.   This
is a wage scale that leaves no option to the common laborers but the boarding-boss method of living, with many
men to the room.   (Let those who know ponder that.)
In return for these wages the workers incurred some risk.
In 1909 there were 927 injuries in the Bethlehem plant;
twenty-one men lost their lives.   When the strike began,
none of the men were members of any labor organization.
The union to which the men would naturally belong had
been systematically forced out of the works in 1883.   In
the course of the strike the men organized, but "it is probably only a short time when these organizations will lapse, as
it is one of the avowed principles of the Steel Company to
discourage the organization of its employees."   The men
did not demand the recognition of their union, and that
question played no part in the strike.   It began when three
machinists on behalf of their fellows protested against the
Sunday labor exacted of so many.   They were discharged for
standing up for the Decalogue and the common welfare.[1]

[1] We have two trustworthy reports on the Bethlehem st⁻ʻke : one by the
U. S. Bureau of Labor, the other by a special committee (Charles Stelzle,
Josiah Strong, and Paul U. Kellogg) of the Social Service Commission of the
Federal Council of the Churches.

This strike laid bare the chronic conditions of one important group of industrial workers, but it is fairly symptomatic of the whole situation. The Autocrat of the Breakfast Table thought an archangel could pick up a pebble on the beach and deduce the laws of the universe from it. It requires no angelic wisdom to read the situation of industrial labor from one such record. When the clinical thermometer registers 102 degrees under the tongue, the doctor does not have to measure the temperature of the toes; he knows that the whole body is at fever heat. In the social body there is no such equilibrium as in the human body. Cleanliness and good will may reign next door to tyranny and dirt. But if this "little town of Bethlehem" was wholly exceptional, why did not the men get out and go elsewhere? Labor to-day is at least not bound to the mill as the agricultural serf was bound to the soil. It is because the workers are pent up by approximately similar conditions elsewhere, and only the strongest can climb out of the blind alley in which they are jammed. A corporation paying 40 per cent dividends would not reduce its male employees to an average of $10 a week if they could easily get more elsewhere. The men then have to figure out if they can support a wife and a home on that amount. One sociological expert will tell them that it takes $10.38 to do it; another thinks it can be done for $9.67, and they would be 33 cents to the good if they look sharp. It seems a close gamble. The report of the Chicago Vice Commission revealed conditions that staggered even those of us who thought they knew something of vice, and was fit to plunge any one who loves his kind in days of gloom. The first thought is of the girls who are pushed by poverty, physical weariness, loneliness, the feminine love of finery and pleasure, or faithfulness to their dependent relatives, into the mantraps of commercialized vice and are speeded up in their degrading services as in a factory. But I pity also the thousands of men for whom fifty cents purchases a brief and ghastly approximation to the love of wife and home. O Christ in heaven, who brought thy brothers to that point?

In a single issue of a weekly paper that has just come to hand[1] I find the following items as part of the general news: 125,000 transport workers had tied up the port of London, and orders had been telegraphed for a national strike in all the British ports. Post-election riots had broken out throughout Belgium, accompanied by violent strikes on a large scale in which socialist orators were hissed because they counseled moderation and return to work; the riots were a protest against the victory of the clerical and conservative parties which involved that the Catholic schools were still to draw support from the public funds, and that the upper classes were still to be armed with a plural ballot to vote down the more numerous lower classes.[2] In the Hungarian Diet eighty-two members of the Opposition Party had been violently ejected from the Chamber for obstructing the proceedings; their action was part of an effort to win the suffrage for the working class; a great labor strike at Budapest for the same end had just subsided. The police in Newark, N.J., had fought a street battle with strikers, women fighting with the strikers, and many persons were injured with gunshot wounds by the police. A referendum in nine craft unions of shop employees on railroads running west of Chicago had resulted in a two-thirds or three-fourths vote in eight of them to strike in sympathy with the industrial union strike on the Illinois Central and Harriman Lines; another effort was to be made to get a conference with the general managers of

[1] *The Public*, June 14, 1912.
[2] Men of property have two votes; professional men and high officials have three: 993,070 citizens have one vote each; 395,866 have 791,732 votes; 308,683 have 926,049.

the united roads; a previous request had been denied. The employees of the Boston Elevated had voted 1398 to 8 to strike; riotous attacks on cars followed; traffic on all the electric lines in and around Boston was suspended partly or completely; 100 Wellesley girls were said to have agreed not to ride on the Elevated and to give the money saved to the strike fund. A riot between strikers and strike breakers had occurred at the freight yards of the C.B. & Q. in Chicago in connection with the freight handlers' strike; 500 men were engaged in the riot; one striker was desperately wounded, another killed. The Illinois Central was preparing to "cut a melon" regarding Lakeshore real estate at Chicago, but it was not yet clear who was to get a slice. The manager of the New York Clearing House had testified before the Pujo Congressional Committee that five men control the Clearing House, and the Clearing House controls the financial interests of the whole country. (Perhaps these two last items have some remote bearing on the others.)

    This is the casual grist of a single week. If such a survey says nothing to us, let us hunt up Pharaoh in his own place and call him brother. He thought the social unrest in Egypt was due to the excess of leisure among the Israelite Bricklayers' Union and to the mischievous agitation of two walking delegates, Moses and Aaron. Our government rests on the assumption that the common man on the whole judges sensibly on affairs that concern him. But how can he be trusted to govern a nation if in his own trade he strikes madly at mere shadows? The class of men who are now chafing in the world-wide struggles between capital and labor is the same class and breed of men who settled our country and built up our nation. Our continent from ocean to ocean bears eloquent testimony to the willingness and capacity of the plain man, provided he has a chance and a motive to work. Dissatisfaction among the working

class is not confined to the disgruntled incapables. The
entire trades-union movement is an institutionalized expression of dissatisfaction, and the members of the unions
are the élite of their class.   The world-wide socialist movement is nothing if not a protest of the working class.   The
growing unrest has kept step with the growing intelligence
and self-respect of the workers.   Time was when they
were so stupid and cowed that they accepted poverty and
inequality as their inevitable lot.   Democracy has brought
them a great spiritual awakening.   Education has performed for the torpid classes of society the miracle Elisha
performed on the Shunamite's son when he stretched his
body over the body of the boy, eye to eye and mouth to
mouth, until the flesh of the child waxed warm, "and the
child sneezed seven times, and the child opened his eyes."
The working class has sneezed seventy times seven times.
It looks like convulsions, but it means the awakening of life.

It is not true that the working class as a whole is needlessly prone to use violent means to right their grievances.
"The endurance of the inequalities of life by the poor is the
marvel of human society." [1]   I read of the increasing inclination to use "direct action" and sabotage with a sinking of the heart, not only on account of the immediate
damage that will be done and the spread of lawlessness,
but because of the harm it will do to the cause of labor.
I am Christian enough to believe that evil cannot be overcome with evil, and that the recoil of violence will usually
more than offset any immediate advantage gained by it.
But I do not wonder that men resort to physical force.
My wonder is that men whose physical force is the only
force they know how to handle have used it so little.   They
have been slower to resort to violence than women in the
agitation for the suffrage.   If we could pick out a thousand
employers who in some way have been conspicuous for their

[1] James A. Froude.

opposition against organized labor, put them all in one mill town together, subject them to the average conditions of industrial workers, leave them just as able and energetic as they are now, but somehow deprive them of the hope of escaping from this condition and lot, they would have a rampant labor organization in running order inside of a week, and the world would listen to an explosion before a month was up. If they could no longer use the physical force of constabulary, deputy sheriffs, Pinkertons, and militia, they would fall back on their own physical force, and organizers of the Federation of Labor would come in to counsel steadiness and peaceable methods.

If we found in the reading of history that a given nation or class through a long term of years was rising again and again in some form of forcible revolt, we should be justified in assuming that it must have been without orderly means of redress and that peaceable agitation was suppressed. Further study would surely prove the truth of the assumption. If any one doubts whether the violence of the working class is due to repression, let him read the history of trades-unionism and of socialism. These two are the organized forms of orderly protest, the one industrial, the other political. Both have been met with persistent efforts of repression by the employing class and by governments. The industrial workers have long ago discovered that the lone worker is helpless when he confronts the employer of hundreds. The best and ablest among them have worked hard to overcome the short-sighted selfishness of their fellows and to create effective organizations. How profoundly they feel the need of their unions is shown by the fact that the demand for the recognition of the union comes up persistently in nearly every labor conflict, like the bell buoy in a dangerous channel rising again with tireless peal whenever a wave has submerged it. If the labor struggle were all on the other side of the globe, and

we learned that these men are merely demanding the right
to deal with their employers as a body by orderly representation, we Americans would hold that of course they had a
right to organize if they wanted to.   Yet that right has
been denied them.   Laws passed against political conspiracy
were applied if several workmen quit work together.   In
our own country powerful associations of employers have
united to cripple and suppress the organizations of labor.
Employers have refused audience to the business agents
empowered and paid by the unions, on the ground that
these persons were outsiders and that they would deal only
with a committee of their own men.   But the individuals
of such a committee would be dependent on the employers
for their bread; the more ably and fearlessly they would
conduct the negotiations on behalf of their fellows, the more
liable would they be to make themselves obnoxious to their
employers and to be dismissed later as trouble makers.
If the United States were negotiating a treaty with Russia,
would Russia demand that the American plenipotentiary
must be a Russian subject and in Russian pay before she
would consent to negotiate?   If Russia even suggested
such a thing, it would serve notice on all the world that
America had become a subject nation.

This chapter set out with the proposition that the relation between the two great industrial classes, the class of
the owners and managers on the one side and the class of
the industrial workers on the other, is the great moral
problem of our age.   Our discussion has reminded us of
the fact, which every intelligent man knows, that this relation is one of unrest and increasing dissatisfaction to both
sides.   An unrest so universal and so durable cannot be
set down to mere personal and local causes, but must be
due to some constitutional maladjustment in the moral
relation of these two great classes.   The grievances of the
working class are mainly two.   They feel that they are

o

being deprived by the more powerful class of part of their just share in the proceeds of their joint labor, and in many cases are being compelled to labor too fast, too long, and under conditions harmful to their physical and mental health. Therefore they raise the charge of injustice and exploitation. They also feel that they are not being treated as free men and of equal worth with the other class. Therefore they raise the charge of oppression. The two things are closely related. The weak have always been kept unfree in order that they might be exploited. The demand for manhood suffrage in Hungary, the protest against plural suffrage in Belgium, and the demand for recognition of the union in America are demands for freedom, but if granted, these rights will serve as a protection against exploitation.

Back of all material demands in the labor movement is the spiritual demand for a fuller and freer manhood. If the wages of the workmen were doubled, but were given them in a spirit of condescension or contempt, as we throw a bone to a dog, would they be content? The unrest of our American workingmen is in part at least the unrest of men who know liberty and are forced to live in unfreedom. Most of our relations in America are on a footing of democracy. When men meet on the street, in the cars, in the lodge, in church, in the college class room, at the polls, they meet on a footing of equality, however widely they differ in wealth or ability. On the other hand, the relation of employer and employee is still frankly undemocratic. Every business concern is a little monarchy. It may be a just and benevolent monarchy, better and happier than most democracies, but it is not based on freedom and equal rights. In our economic relations we stand now where we stood in our political relations before the advent of democracy. Everywhere else autocracy is on the retreat, or creeping back under cover to regain its lost fortifications. In business the autocratic principle is still in full possession, unshaken and unterrified, with its flag flying from every battlement. Business is the last intrenchment of autocracy, and wherever democracy is being beaten back, the sally is made from that citadel.

The industrial unrest is not due to the badness of men, but to their relish and hunger for applied Christianity. They have tasted democracy and found it good, and they can never again be content with any relation that denies them freedom and equality. They refuse to live a double life, "half slave and half free," and the refusal is wholly to the credit of their morals. We must either deprive them of their other liberties, deny them education, and cow them into contentment, or else democratize the industrial life too.

Fortunately, prudence runs with righteousness in this matter. It always takes faith to believe in freedom, but in the long run freedom always justifies our faith in her. To a shortsighted profit maker prison labor might seem the ideal form of production. No labor agitators, no strikes, no nonsense, allowed, and a minimum of expense to eat into your balance — what a paradise of succulent profits ! Corporations having prison labor contracts set forth these advantages in suggestive terms. Yet in fact prison labor is the dearest of all labor, and if all workmen were reduced to that condition, the decrease of output and increase of expense would bankrupt the nation in six months. The cheapest labor is highly intelligent and free labor. Slavery has disappeared, not simply because it contradicted the moral convictions of mankind, but because it was inefficient labor and unable to stand against the competition of the free man working for his own good. The slave could be trusted only with the crudest tools and employed at the coarsest forms of agriculture, and the expense of overseers, man hunts, and assassinations had to be figured into his keep. The only motive that wrought on him with full force was the fear of punishment. The higher motives that give the perpetual spring and keenness of edge to our work — the hope of economic advancement, the desire for honor, the sense of duty, and the love of work for its own sake — scarcely touched him.

Our own industrial workers are only semiefficient because they are still but semifree. They are not partners, but hirelings, and have the indifference of the hireling shepherd to whom Jesus alluded. They too are impelled only by the lower motives and therefore have to be driven by overseers. As long as they can hold their job and draw their pay, why should they exert themselves to increase the dividends of the company, of which they get nothing? The leakages in the efficiency of wage labor are precisely at those points where it most resembles slave labor. As soon as a man gets a chance to be his own master and work for his own good, there is almost always an increase in interest and efficiency. There will be a bound upward in efficiency when we have found the way of making our wageworkers labor copartners. In the industrial rivalry of nations that nation will finally come out ahead which gives its workers the largest amount of physical health and security, of intellectual initiative, and of social freedom. One reason why the South broke down in our Civil War was that its slave labor had kept it industrially incompetent. Wars are fought with iron, and the South did not know how to work the iron that lay in mass under its soil. Unfreedom means imbecility. Freedom works because it is essentially moral and founded on the will of God. Unfreedom is the favorite device of greed, but it frustrates its own purposes because it is fundamentally immoral.

All higher philosophical thought agrees in the conviction that freedom is an essential condition of real manhood. There is no true individuality without it. Gladstone said that one of the chief lessons which life had taught him was that freedom is a good for its own sake, apart from anything that might be attained through freedom. The unsatisfied longing for liberty in past history is one of the great tragic facts of human life. The spread of liberty is the glory of the modern world. Our own nation was dedicated to the principle of freedom at its birth, and rededicated to it by a baptism of blood. Whenever any other nation is stirring uneasily under despotism or is trying to break the strangle-hold of ancient tyranny, an instinctive thrill of sympathy runs through our American people, showing that we have not forgotten our divine calling. As for our religion, — the passion for, freedom is a distinctive mark of genuine Christianity. Paul summed up the genius of the new religion in contrast to the old : "Where the spirit of the Lord is there is liberty." Jesus has been the great emancipator of humanity. Wherever his spirit has really touched any human soul, it has been made free in some way. Wherever it has touched any prostrate and shackled nation, there has been a stir of fresh life and manhood.

These things we know, yet we have allowed a great and growing class of our people to be submerged in economic unfreedom so deep that "liberty of contract" has become an instrument of enslavement for them, and the State is compelled to limit their liberty in order to save them from being utterly ground up. Economic freedom is an essential part of human freedom. Without economic independence political and religious liberty become hollow and fragile, a reminiscence and a mocking sham. A woman has a right to herself. When she gives herself freely, it is the highest gift she can make. If she is compelled by force or need to submit to the will of another, and yields to necessity what should be yielded to love alone, it makes her a tool and degrades her womanhood. A man likewise has a right to himself. He must be free to develop his own personality and to contribute his work to the common good in free exchange and interaction with his fellows. If he becomes a mere tool to serve the will of another and exists for the other man's profit, his freedom is gone and his manhood degraded. Whoever of us can bear to see his fellow-men so used without shame or protest, sins against the manhood in himself and against God. We have accepted the Statue of Liberty from a younger sister republic and have set it at the gateway of our land for all the world to see. Therewith we have pawned our honor to the nations that this country shall be a home of freedom. Yet in the great city behind the statue thousands of men nightly sleep in the fetid air and amid the vermin of cheap lodging houses for five and even for two cents a night. Those men may be American citizens, but they are not free men. They are galley slaves of poverty.

A subject working class, without property rights in the instruments of their labor, without a voice in the management of the shops in which they work, without jurisdiction over the output of their production is a contradiction of American ideals and a menace to American institutions. As long as such a class exists in our country, our social order is not christianized. Civilization has now reached the point where power must shift from the ruling class to the people in industry as it has shifted in the political constitution of States. We need industrial democracy.

With all its imperfections democracy has caused a tremendous improvement in political morality. Theorists sometimes doubt the value of political democracy; the common sense of the people never wavers about it. When the people have the right of free speech, free assembly, and a free press; when they have an orderly expression of their will through a parliament; when the monarch no longer has the right to tax the people at will and to spend their hard-earned money on his favorites and prostitutes, —

then bad kings begin to behave themselves, good kings remain good, and in any case the character of the king is no longer of such fatal importance, because the people can take care of themselves.   Under an absolute monarchy like that of Russia Christian people may feel that the greatest thing they can pray for is that Providence may make the oldest boy baby of the Romanoff family a good baby. But most of us will agree that a Douma with powerful elbows would be worth more to Russia than a good little prince.

So in industry we need a constitutional increase of freedom and power for the working class even more than we need good and kind employers.   The generous, old-fashioned employer is apt to die or he has to sell out to a trust. The clean-handed manager of a corporation may be dismissed by the directors because he "does not get results." As long as the happiness of the workers rests on the personal character of employers, it is insecure.   What is granted as a favor when the directors feel cheerful may be canceled when they feel hard up.   We must set our faces toward a thoroughgoing change in the relation between the two great economic classes.   Nothing else will serve.

This is perhaps the most searching test that can be applied to the Christian character of a business man to-day: Is he willing to aid and speed the transition to industrial democracy?   No man is moral unless his heart is set on a reign of freedom and justice.   No man is a mature Christian unless he is willing to suffer personal loss to bring in freedom and justice.

Business men often feel that radical social thought is cruelly unfair to them in charging them with wrong in all their relations.   Individuals certainly have been hit most unfairly.   But really those who have learned to take the social point of view are far more patient and lenient judges than those who have only individualistic morality to guide their judgment.   The latter see nothing but personal wrong-doings behind the miseries of industrial life.   They thunder against the "malefactors of great wealth" and are eager to get the grip of the criminal law on the officers of corporations.   On the other hand, those who have learned to understand the organic unity of society know how profoundly the individual is conditioned in all his acts and thoughts by the social life that makes and molds him, and sets his goal and his limits.[1]   They see more evil than others see, but they can feel compassion for the man who does it.   And when they see a man in the midst of the autocratic temper and customs of his class sincerely reaching out for justice and fraternity, they can appreciate his moral quality at its proper value.   Socialists are bound by their own doctrine of "economic determinism" to regard every man who overcomes the pressure of his material interests even by a little as a sort of spiritual miracle.   If he is a member of the master class, and yet treats his workers with real human fellow-feeling; if law and the traditions of his class allow him to exploit them, and he willingly pays union wages or a little more; if competition presses him and he protects them against its effects as long as he can, — then he deserves the lasting respect of all intelligent socialists.

Christianity will not let him off so easily.   It lays down the doctrine of moral freedom and personal accountability. For whatever freedom and power a man has, he must answer to God.   "To whom much is given, from him much is required."   That certainly applies to modern business men.   The evolution of industry has thrown all power their way, and they have eagerly taken all that was offered, and more.   Then they cannot complain if much is required of them.   The case is up to the business community at

[1] John Spargo explains the mercifulness of socialist criticism in his "Substance of Socialism," pp. 138–162.

present. They are in charge of the vineyard, and God is sending frequent and urgent word to inquire for his share of the output under their management. If they cannot cleanse our industry of despotism and exploitation, they must not be surprised if he terminates their lease of power. To make wages small in order to make dividends large may be common practice, but perhaps the Almighty takes a more serious view of it. Of three sins the Bible says that they cried to heaven. The first was the sin of Cain: "The voice of thy brother's blood crieth unto me from the ground." The second was the sin of Sodom: the cry of it "came up to God." The third is the exploitation of the working class in their weakness: "Behold the hire of the laborers who mowed your fields, which has been withheld by you, crieth out, and the cries of them that have reaped have entered into the ears of the Lord of hosts."

CHAPTER VI

THE REIGN OF THE MIDDLEMAN

WHEN Adam delved and Eve span,
Where was then the middleman?

With the exception of one questionable personage who persuaded them to try a new kind of fruit, there wasn't any. They produced for their own needs, and some of us feel that we are camping near the gate of Edenland when we can bring in food we have raised by our own labor, and see our wife prepare it and our children eat it with us.

Nor was there any one to intervene between producer and consumer in the old-fashioned village life when the smith and the weaver exchanged their products as each had need of the other's skill. With the appearance of the middleman a new moral factor entered the situation. The trader has always been the advance agent of civilization. He awakened new desires in the breast of the lazy savage and made him work. He sharpened the wits of all he dealt with in the dear school kept by experience. But his name has never been a synonym for honesty,[1] and the admiration we all feel for his cleverness has often been embroidered with maledictions. Will the trader ever be Christianized? Will the biggest strawberries ever be at the bottom of the box?

---

[1] "A merchant shall hardly keep himself from doing wrong,
    And a trader shall not be judged free from sin."
"As a nail sticketh fast between the joinings of the stones,
    So doth sin press in between buying and selling."
Ecclesiasticus xxvi. 29, and xxvii. 2.

In primitive communities the trader was a more or less happy accident that occasionally lent a new flavor and tang to life. To-day he sits at the center of things and all things revolve around him except the solar system. For our business men are all middlemen; they stand between social groups and mediate between them. The farmer, the miner, the fisherman, the trapper come to the business man with their products, and he buys them. He turns to us who need bread, coal, fish, or fur and sells them to us — at a profit. He organizes the workers in factories and buys their work — at a profit. He organizes the buyers in stores, routes, and mail-order systems, and sells them the product of that work — at a profit. He organizes the small savings of the people in banks and sells the use of their money to others — at a profit. He looms up huge and wonderful as the real master of modern life. Of him, and through him, and unto him are all things. If all business men could be rolled up and compounded in one huge person, he would be the god of this world. Our present economic system is the apotheosis of the middleman.

The business man is the steward of our national household. Is his work efficient and honest? We can say heartily that it is done more efficiently than any ruling class has ever done it before. Compared with the feudal lords who used to own the means of production and boss the workers in the agricultural age, our modern lords of industry are a wonderfully intelligent and serviceable class of men. Since they have taken charge of our civilization, a square mile of land sustains more men, a human life lasts longer, and a day's work turns out more goods than ever before. And our business in the main is honest business. If it were not so, the bottom would have dropped out of our social order before this, for our business rests on good faith and confidence more than ever before. As a suspension bridge hangs by cables, so business hangs on a network of fiduciary relations. Innumerable business men have managed their business in such a way that after years of buying and selling, they have the sincere liking and esteem of their customers. Even those who slip over into tricky methods or sell shoddy goods would prefer to do clean business if only their competitors or customers would let them.

If the sins committed in the relation between business men and their customers are simply the inevitable slips of weak human nature, we can afford to be patient and must try to increase the efficiency of the Sunday schools in teaching the Ten Commandments. In handling crockery we must allow for some breakage. Even in the strictest socialist State boys will presumably swap knives and men will trade horses, and one will take and the other will get left.

But is dishonesty merely an accident in business? Or is business of such a nature that it invites to unfraternal dealings? Is good Business always being corrupted by wicked human nature, or is human nature the saving element in a system of business that ought by its own laws to turn out a far larger percentage of immoral action? Are business men in need of personal improvement, or is Business as such in need of constitutional readjustments? Or both?

When seller meets buyer, their relation calls out the selfish motives in both and leaves the finer social motives quiescent.

Parents would have the best possible chance to overreach their children and palm off adulterated food on them if they were so inclined, for the children are trustful and ignorant. Yet we are assured on good authority that even a poor sort of father is not apt to give a stone when his son asks for a loaf of bread. He loves his child. There is no such love of kinship between buyer and seller, and so there may be chalk in the bread and terra alba in the little boy's candy when he comes out of the store. Neither has the seller that sense of official responsibility which constrains the pastor to care for his people, the ship captain for his passengers, the physician for his patient, and the lawyer for his client. The members of a group often develop a powerful sense of solidarity which forbids overreaching one of their fellows. For instance, to a company of starving Arctic explorers it came as a terrible shock that one of their number had been secretly taking more than his share of the rations. There is no such solidarity between buyer and seller. The Law also touches the little fraudulent tricks of trade lightly. The municipal regulations developed under the influence of the medieval guilds dealt very severely with bad workmanship. A baker or cobbler was liable to be drawn through the streets of the town on a tumbril or exposed in the pillory with his defective loaf or boots hung round his neck for all to see. Capitalism promptly abolished these restrictions on the freedom of trade, so that fear of the law is no strong motive to help the weak in resisting temptation. The unwritten law of custom likewise leaves the seller ample room to operate. *Caveat emptor!* Let the buyer look out for himself. Thus love, duty, fellowship, law, and custom stand to one side when buyer and seller have it out between them.

On the other hand, the selfish motives are hard at work. Business is under the one great law of Profit. It is not carried on primarily to supply men with wholesome goods but to make a profit for the dealer. Almost all business men would prefer to sell good and wholesome things, but if they had the alternative between selling solid goods at slight profit, or flashy goods at a heavy profit, they would probably console themselves that the public demands the latter, and sell them. Their natural desire for profitable business is stimulated by the prod of competition, and by the general spirit and pace of profit-making business all around them. If the margin of profit is being cut down by competitors, it can be widened by tampering a little with the goods furnished. The only restraint is that of prudence; the tricks of the trade must not injure sales or anger customers. Thou shalt not kill the goose that lays the golden eggs.

Under such conditions ordinary integrity becomes an heroic virtue. A business man who never overreaches a customer is mentioned with a hush of respect. It is wholly to the credit of the characters bred in American life that a large, and probably an increasing volume of business is done above board and honestly. But it would be idle to assert that the temptation to overreach is not a persistent pressure in the life of a large percentage of business men.

The temptation to overreach is all the more insinuating nowadays because it is harder for the buyer to protect himself than in former times. The ignorance of the buyer has always been the opportunity of the trader. Fortunes used to be made in the African trade when negro kings eagerly traded an elephant tusk for six yards of red cotton and an entrancing string of glass beads. But in the good old times people used to have a fair knowledge of the few staples sold in their community. On the other hand, how helpless we are when we finger woolen or silk goods and wonder how much wool there is in the wool and how heavily the silk is loaded. It is so infernally well done. The modern dealer has all the resources of chemistry and applied science to aid him in meeting the customer's suspicions. We have heard the fame of the wooden nutmegs sold by the Yankee peddler long ago. What a crude scheme! They had no taste of nutmeg and would be detected as soon as they touched the grater. That peddler could never travel that route again. Your modern Yankee would make up an elegant nutmeg that would taste and grate like the genuine article, and he could sell the same thing to the same woman over and over, even if Dr. Wiley told her not to buy it. Why not? We make up a very salable sort of coffee that hasn't a genuine coffee bean in it; only dry peas and cocoa shells. Our mothers could tell when milk was old because it was sour. To-day the refrigerator and a dose of formalin or formaldehyde will take care of the bacillus that curdles the milk, and the ptomaine cannot be detected by any test of taste or smell with which the Lord has equipped a housewife.

Weights plugged with putty, falsely adjusted scales, measures with false bottoms or dented sides are ancient but ever youthful devices. Our cities employ officers especially to hunt them down, but they thrive like English sparrows. The inspectors in New York City confiscated 3906 of them in three months of 1910, and Indianapolis totaled over 13,000 of them in four and a half years. The modern factory packs goods in packages and bottles ready for retailing, and that gives a chance for many slight subtractions that make a large aggregate. Pails of paint and boxes of ice cream, pints of whisky and rolls of ribbon, may all be a trifle short. During a special investigation in 1910 the city sealer in Harrisburg, Pa., could not find a single wooden berry box in the city that would hold a quart. Prints of butter are often short weight. The creamery people say they shrink by the evaporation of the water in the butter, but when the New York State Superintendent visited 30 creameries throughout the State and weighed 252 prints dripping wet from the molds, he found 124 short. Those intended for sale in Massachusetts seemed to evaporate least; that State has stringent laws.

Tampering with the quality of goods is only another form of the same game. Manufacturers of turpentine have found that five gallons of kerosene in a forty-gallon barrel of turpentine cannot be detected. Kerosene will cost them five cents a gallon and turpentine recently ran up to eighty-six cents, so that this makes a neat profit. But retail dealers and painters probably know the same trick and baptize the turpentine further as it passes down the line. The commercial value of oleomargarine was chiefly that it could be made to look and taste like butter. The law got after it, not because it fooled the consumer, but because it undersold butter and interfered with the market of the farmers and creameries. In this case the hostility of two classes of dealers protected the consumer. Ice cream is thickened with starch or gelatine to make it keep its shape, and made of skim milk, condensed milk, or no milk at all. A new process makes an emulsion of skim milk for ice cream that looks like the richest kind of cream. That ought to be a great saving to the country. But this is a hymn of many verses. We must chant the rest on the day of judgment.

Another mild method of defrauding is to awaken false expectations and so lure the buyer on. Fire sales and bankrupt stocks are advertised to unload old stuff. At mark-down sales the tags are marked up before the old price is crossed off. In the dressing of show windows a few articles of special value are placed close to the window to give respectability to the lot. At bargain sales a few high-priced pieces are mixed in. Trading stamps give the customer the impression that he is getting something to boot, while he pays for it just the same. The lies told in advertising are like the sands of the sea which no man can number. One of the most wonderful symptoms of the moral uplift is the fact that the publicity men of the country under the leadership of an unusual kind of Christian have undertaken to make advertising tell the truth.

Any really fraternal action in business dealings comes to us with a happy shock of surprise. If a druggist told us that some high-priced patent medicine was of no use and that we could get the same ingredients for five cents;

or if a painter advised us that the house does not need paint, but a rubdown with soap and water, — would not our heart warm to these men as if we had met a friend in a foreign land ?

The low morality of commercial life has even affected the language spoken and made words lose their integrity. The most honest merchant who calls goods "all wool" or "all linen" uses these words in a qualified sense. A New York law provides that collars marked "pure linen" or "all linen" must contain at least one thickness or ply of pure linen. The names used in the fur trade have no relation to zoölogy. Two bunnies that wiggled their noses over the same head of cabbage in France turn up in an American fur store, the one as an electric seal, the other as a Hudson lynx. When even words become so slippery, there must be a good deal of oiliness.

The selfish nature of business comes out in its ugliest form when the goods sold are actually harmful to the buyers. The Pure Food and Drug Act transformed the labels of patent medicines, and the 40 per cent of alcohol or 5 per cent of opium, about which they had been so discreetly silent, leered out at last. In the Middle Ages the poisoning of rich men was one road to wealth; to-day it is the poisoning of the poor; but it must be done on a large scale or it doesn't pay. The entire liquor trade is an example of a harmful industry maintained by hook or crook because it is profitable. The men engaged in it save their self-respect by persuading themselves that they too serve human welfare, but they all know that the percentage of harm inflicted by their business is fearfully great. Yet the immense profits in it bear down all considerations of humanity. Alcohol is a spirit born of hell, but he is merely a satellite and tool of a far greater devil, and that is Mammon. The liquor trade is a clear demonstration what business conducted for profit will do when it happens to

P

get behind a product that is harmful instead of wholesome in its nature.

If commerce existed to satisfy the economic needs of the consumers, it would seek to keep pace with their needs. Since its guiding purpose is to make profits for the dealer, it outruns the actual needs. Speculative commerce is always creating a stock which it hopes to sell. A good business man discovers new markets; a great business man creates new markets by creating new desires. The persuasiveness of business may be valuable as well as charming. Vacuum cleaners, fireless cookers, and life insurance policies would not have gone on their beneficent mission so swiftly if the hope of profits and commissions had not urged them on. To awaken dormant desires may be a supreme social service. Education and religion are tremendous stimulators of new wants. The teacher and preacher are rivals of the drummer in seeking to open new markets for their goods. But with them, we hope, the dominant motive is to build up nobler lives. Their self-interest is bound up with their success, but they get no financial commission on the souls they save or the boys they attract to college. On the other hand, the motive of the drummer is not to help men, but to sell goods and make a profit for himself and his firm. A man is a creature to whom, with proper skill, we may be able to sell something. After he has bought the oil painting for $7.89, or has paid the first dollar down on the installment plan, we lose interest in him. Formerly it was common to lubricate the path of persuasiveness by alcoholizing prospective buyers. There is less of that now, but we still hypnotize them with æsthetic surroundings and "sympathetic" saleswomen.

There are large social values in all this and we blame no one for any charm of persuasiveness that he may possess or use, but the total effect on our national character is serious. Christianity and education have combined to build up in our race some measure of self-restraint by teaching us to fix our eyes on some larger purpose far ahead, and for love of that to refuse gratification to our passing whims. The savage, the child, the imbecile, and the criminal yield to the lust of the flesh and the eye. The Indian sold his pack of furs, the product of a winter's work, to get a few glittering trinkets. Does not business, even in its respectable forms, seek to batter down our self-restraint and power of inhibition, and reduce us to the same level? The show windows of our shopping districts and all display advertising do not simply try to inform our intelligence, but seek to break down our capacity for saying No. The present craze for automobiles is not a spontaneous folly of the people. It is carefully worked up by commercial interests. The actual cost of manufacturing is said to be only a third or fourth of the retail price of a machine; the rest goes into persuasion of eye and ear. The automobile is a highly valuable invention, but when men and women mortgage their homes, surrender the chances of educating their children, or perhaps forego the possibility of having children in the coming years, in order to buy an automobile, they inflict a spiritual damage on themselves and the whole nation which will reach down into coming generations.

All serious observers agree that the generation now growing up in our country is lacking in that stern faculty of self-restraint which was ground into their fathers and mothers by their religion and education. The home and the school are held responsible. They are surely to blame for not resisting the decline more effectively, but the active agent in breaking down the old frugality is profit-making business, which surrounds the young with lures and stimulates their desires. Capitalism is sapping its own foundations. It got its first start in the Calvinistic countries, because Calvinistic religion induced saving and the accumulation of reserve capital. All the merry saints' days on which people had stopped work and spent money for pleasure were cut out of the calendar. Sunday was the only rest day left, and all spending and dissipation on that day was forbidden. Calvinism taught sobriety of dress and made conscientious work a fundamental Christian duty. By thus increasing earnings and decreasing expenditures it helped to create the economic reserves which financed the new industry created by the power machine. So religious frugality laid the foundations for capitalism and put civilization on its legs financially. Now capitalism is disintegrating that virtue in the descendants of the Calvinists and persuading them to buy baubles that capital may make profit.

How deeply our standards of morality are affected by commercialism probably no man can estimate. Not only the practice, but the theory of honesty is weakened. Single Taxers in their educational campaign find it exceedingly hard to persuade business men that wealth made out of the unearned increment in land values is morally questionable at all. "A man has a right to a profit on his investments." Stock gambling is defended by good men. To make a profit has so long seemed the essence of business that the demand for any other end and aim is greeted with a smile as the amiable hobby of an idealist. I once put this case to a group of young men in a Bible class: Suppose a furniture dealer had a whitewood bookcase, stained cherry, and valued at $10; a customer shows by his questions that he thinks it is genuine cherry-wood; would the dealer be justified in charging him $15 for it? To my astonishment the majority of the young men thought that was quite right. When I was pastor in New York, I spoke to a fine young man about his religious life and urged him to join the Church. He replied: "I can't become a Christian; I have to lie too much." He explained that he was a salesman and was under instructions to misrepresent the goods. I approved of his refusal to live a double life and urged him to get out of that job. Some time later he came to me with evident satisfaction, said he had found another position, and wanted to join the Church. Later he told me incidentally that he had secured his former job for his brother.

Business men often defend the shady aspects of commerce, the shoddy goods and the bargain counters, on the ground that the public will have it so. The people tempted them and they fell. It is indeed hard to say if the angler tempts the fish or the fish the angler. The bargain-hunting public has been trained by business and then turns on its trainer. It, too, is after profits, and the business man can see the spirit of business reduced to a caricature when he watches a mob of women at his bargain counter.

But if dishonesty is forced on business by the public, why does business fight for the right to be dishonest? The Pure Food and Drug Act was bitterly fought by some of the interests concerned. The officials enforcing its provisions have been attacked and circumvented. The Department of Agriculture and eminent names in it and even above it have been embroiled and besmirched. Every effort to secure publicity in business life has met with opposition.

Our moral diagnosis of Business has given us fairly clear results. The economic wants of society are supplied by a system in which the middleman is the controlling factor. The dominant motive is not to supply human needs, but to make a profit for those who operate the system. The higher motives of human nature are not evoked and educated. The selfish motives are stimulated by fear and covetousness. Whatever moral goodness there is in business — and there is a great deal of it — comes through the fundamental soundness of human nature that insists on being kindly and fraternal; also through the fact that the main economic needs are clean and wholesome, and give moral worth to the work that supplies them. But the one law that pervades business, as completely as the law of gravitation pervades physics, is the law of profit. Profit means success, ease, safety, and opportunity for more profit. No profit means death. Therefore profit must be made; if possible, by respectable methods; but if the vice or ignorance of the buying public, the nature of goods to be marketed, the pressure of competition, or any exigencies of the market force profit to part company with ethics, then the ruling passion of Business will put the personal character of the business man to a test from which it does not always emerge undamaged. The manifold forms of dishonesty and overreaching that we meet in business are the natural result of a relation that is based almost wholly on individual selfishness, and hardly at all on fraternity or solidarity.

That selfishness takes new forms when business passes from competitive to monopolistic conditions. A railway or a trust no longer clings to the ledges of the economic precipice. The monopoly element in their business lends security, and security can afford good manners. They no longer need to lure their customers because their customers have to come to them anyway. They can assume the dignified manner of the Grand Seigneur who despises the tricks of the petty tradesman. Just as a great consolidated industry can afford to plan pension and insurance systems for its employees, so it can afford to treat its customers without resorting to adulteration or false measure.

But while the manners of business may change when it reaches the security of a partial or total monopoly, its spirit and essential nature do not change in the least. More than ever the real end of its existence is profit. A small business is glad of small profit; Big Business wants big profit. Profit is gross income minus expenses. Consequently it can be increased either by raising the gross income or by lowering the expenses. The former may mean higher prices; the latter may mean poorer service. Both are familiar enough.

Generally speaking, income depends on rendering valuable service. But if profit can be made best by neglecting the needs of the public or even by damaging the life and health of the public, then that becomes the policy of business. Stupid corporations have often been so greedy for immediate gain that they have allowed their plant and rolling stock to run down, and the good will of the public, which is an important spiritual asset, to be turned into ill will. Intelligent corporations are ready to improve their service, but only so far as the improvement will directly or indirectly increase dividends. Under monopoly conditions improvement stops at the line of maximum profit. A railway may be keen to buy an improved type of locomotive which economizes fuel, but crowd its patrons in dingy depots and ruin their eyes by poorly lighted cars. Street railways may be ready to introduce pay-as-you-enter cars, because they insure a thorough collection of fares, but allow passengers to hang from straps in indecent crowding because one car with eighty passengers is cheaper to run than two cars with forty each. If improvements are to be made which increase the comfort of the public, but decrease the dividends of a public service corporation, public opinion and the Law have a hard time holding the kicking corporation while its tail is being docked.

Decreasing the expense of service is one way of increasing profits; charging more for the service rendered is the other; the ideal is the maximum price combined with the minimum service. The beauty of any business that contains a monopoly feature is that prices can be raised with more safety. In competitive business new capital rushes in when the price of an article gets too far away from its actual cost. A monopoly can charge what the market will stand. Of course, even aside from legal restrictions, a gas company could not prudently charge $5 per thousand, for people would take to kerosene or candles. But there is a wide margin between the cost of gas and the price of it. For instance, a legislative committee in New York in 1905 found that the Consolidated Gas Company had supplemented its own supply of gas by buying of other companies. The New Amsterdam Gas Company charged the Consolidated 32 cents per thousand for $3\frac{1}{2}$ billion feet; other companies charged prices ranging from 40 down to 28 cents per thousand; presumably they made a profit on the sale at that wholesale price. But the Consolidated retailed this gas to the consumer at $1. Just at present the valorization (fine word!) scheme in the Brazilian coffee trade is occupying public attention. An international syndicate has limited the supply, fixed the prices, prevented them from being cut, and raised the price of coffee from $7\frac{1}{2}$ cents in 1906 to $14\frac{3}{4}$ cents in 1912. The novel feature of this business arrangement is that the Brazilian government has frankly and openly taken part in the hold-up. The meat packers have tried to persuade the public that the high prices of meat are due to a growing scarcity of meat, which in turn is due to the quantity of corn converted into whisky instead of hogs, and the amount of breakfast food consumed by a lavish nation. But the Department of Commerce and Labor replies that the seven principal Western markets received far more livestock in the first four months of 1912 than in the same four months of any year in the last decade. American beef has not risen in price in London as it has in New York. The untrained instinct of the people persists in suspecting some connection between the permanence of high prices and the other permanent fact that all the great staples are now sold to us by consolidations of business which are able to limit output and unlimit prices.

The Pullman Company is an example of business under monopoly conditions. It performs a service which the various railways ought themselves to perform, but the ownership of Pullman stock is so distributed among high officials of the railways and so profitable, that the company has been able to maintain an approximate monopoly. Though the charges are out of all proportion to the service performed, there was no motion by the Company to lower them until the Interstate Commerce Commission compelled lower rates for the upper berths. In consequence the profits have been enormous. The company has paid large annual dividends on its stock, only a fraction of which represents money paid in by stockholders, yet these regular dividends left a constantly accumulating surplus. In 1898 the surplus was divided in an extra cash dividend of 20 per cent and an extra stock dividend of 50 per cent; the latter was worth $45,000,000 at current prices. By 1905 another surplus of $20,000,000 had accumulated. The net earnings of the stockholders increased 50 per cent from 1900 to 1905; the average wages to its employees increased 5 per cent; if the service rendered to travelers has improved, we should be glad to know it. The company pays its porters the pittance of $25 a month, and leaves the rest of their wages to be paid by the generosity of the public. This is the insolence of the middleman when he has a monopoly.

The Express Companies are an excellent illustration of the character developed by the middleman when he becomes a monopolist. In European countries the railways themselves furnish express service at a slight advance over their freight rates; local forwarders attend to the collection and delivery. In the United States alone have subsidiary carriers grown up as middlemen between the railways and the public to care for the rapid carriage of small parcels. The thorough investigation given to the express business by the Interstate Commerce Commission in 1912 has revealed their rank growth. The time when the stockholders ever put any money into the business has dropped out of human memory and record; the Commission feels sure that the original capital never amounted to more than a million dollars, and that the railways could supply the necessary plant to carry on the business themselves for a million. The competitive outfit of all the thirteen companies now doing business in the country is only $27,153,869. Their real asset consists in the monopoly given them by their contracts with the railways. On this slender basis they have made profits so enormous that they have blushed to distribute them outright, and now have $150,000,000 on their hands. They have therefore been in a position to furnish the public excellent service in return for their large profits, if good service follows prosperity at all with profit-making monopolies.

Instead of that, the public has long been in a state of indignation and revolt against them. During the investigation Commissioner Lane said that "if prosecutions were brought on every complaint that has been made to the Commission, all the express companies would be made bankrupt by the fines imposed." The purpose of the express service is to furnish rapid carriage; the companies have often defeated the purpose of their existence by routing packages in circuitous ways in order to give the haul to the railways on which they had their favorable contracts. The express service exists to carry small parcels; the companies have put the heaviest rates on the small parcel and the common man, and favored the big shippers. They have exercised the tyranny of a profit-making monopoly by frequent overcharges and collection of charges at both ends; by excessive insurance and delay in the settlement of claims; by arbitrarily limiting the free delivery zones; by issuing complicated rules and obscure statements which left the public helpless; by doing their patrons out of their rights through craftily worded contracts on the receipts given; and by charging rates which they now confess to have been excessive and extortionate.

Being powerful middlemen between the railways and the public they have used their power to exploit both parties. In times of emergency they have secured favorable contracts from the railways by pressure through financial interests allied to them, or through the directors of the railways whom they had corrupted by ownership of their profitable stock, so that they have become parasites of the railways instead of an arm of the railways. They have been insidious competitors of the postal system by attracting the profitable business to themselves by special rates and throwing the unprofitable business on the government. They have for all these years stood in the way of a parcels post, and have done our people out of untold conveniences and pleasures which we should have enjoyed through the parcels post system. For fifty years they have staved off government control. They themselves were unable to extricate themselves from the complications and tangles in which they had involved themselves, in spite of the fact that the express business had become a family affair, handled in the main by three groups of interests.

Here, then, we have the middleman under monopoly conditions. The telegraph business is another instance. Practically every civilized nation has applied public ownership to the telegraph; we have left it to middlemen. Consequently our tolls are exorbitant and the service is poor. Until the Bell interests secured control of the Western Union and introduced telephone delivery and the night letter, there was no notable improvement in the service for years. It is claimed that inventions have been bought up by the Western Union Company and suppressed, lest the service would have to be improved. The Company hires little boys to deliver its messages, turning their early years into an employment that teaches them nothing for their future career, and sending them into saloons and houses of prostitution to get their education. If the mails were under corporation management, we should presumably have child letter carriers.

Thus the consumer is between the Scylla of competition and the Charybdis of monopoly. If he is under competition, he is bitten by fraud; if under monopoly, he is devoured by extortion. Against fraud and adulteration he may be able to protect himself by using his wits and by going to a competitor; against the extortion of monopoly the individual is helpless. As industrial mechanisms the trusts are far superior to a competitive mob of small concerns, but their efficiency is so little tempered by morality that the great mass of our nation, with the exception of the monopolists and the socialists, is anxious to get back from the fire of monopoly into the cool and refreshing frying-pan of competition. Yet the era of monopoly has only begun, and our masters are wise enough to raise prices slowly. But the Lord have mercy on our children!

Human society tends to become constantly more interdependent. It used to be like a colony of mollusks; it is becoming like the body of a man. We live by faith in one another. We have to trust our health officers to test our water supply and the milk brought into the city, for we cannot do it. We have to trust our newspapers to report the facts correctly to us, or a whole city will be misled in its judgment, and will crucify its Christ and elect Barabbas mayor. Our business men hold a fiduciary relation to the whole community. Through them God answers our prayer: "Give us this day our daily bread." As a class they hold the supreme power in modern society.

Taking business as a whole is the relation of this class to the community on a satisfactory moral basis?

Ruskin says that five great intellectual professions have existed in every civilized nation. "The Soldier's profession is to defend it; the Pastor's to teach it; the Physician's to keep it in health; the Lawyer's to enforce justice in it; the Merchant's to provide for it." Like a true Christian, Ruskin sees that the roots of honor for every profession lie in its capacity of self-sacrifice for the good of all. The honor which each profession gets is proportioned to its readiness to die in the service of the nation. "The duty of all these men is, on due occasion, to die for it. 'On due occasion,' namely: the Soldier, rather than leave his post in battle; the Physician, rather than leave his post in plague; the Pastor, rather than teach falsehood; the Lawyer, rather than countenance injustice; the Merchant — what is *his* 'due occasion' of death? It is the main question for the merchant. For, truly, the man who does not know when to die, does not know how to live." [1]

If the relation of the Merchant to the nation is founded altogether on selfishness, and has no sacrificial qualities in it, he may get money, but he will not get honor and love, and the Business which he fashions and rules will remain an unchristianized portion of the social order.

[1] Ruskin, "Unto this Last," Chapter I.

CHAPTER VII

THE dominant thing in the life of almost every man is the way he gets his living. The dominant thing in every social order are its economic processes. Modern society is dominated by the owners and organizers of industry and commerce, by the class of the business men. And the business men are dominated by Profit. They are the masters of Business but the servants of Profit. Profit is the end and motive of their work, the basis of their power, and the law of their business life.

The thoroughness with which Profit dominates the capitalistic system differentiates it from all other forms of economic organization. In the handicraft system which preceded capitalism, the aim was to fix a price that would be fair and reasonable for producer and consumer, and to curb any hankering for excess profit. The work of the old-fashioned farmer was done for the support of his family and with little commercial profit in sight. All the millions of housewives, who run that important economic organization called the family, are cooking and sewing to keep their folks well fed and dressed, and not to make profit out of them. When the city or the State undertake economic functions, such as road building or the marketing of water, they are not after a maximum income; they are planning to satisfy the needs of the citizens. As soon as our postal system shows a surplus, plans are made to cut it down by lowering the postage or extending the rural delivery system, in order to make it still more serviceable.

On the other hand, in capitalistic industry and commerce the leaders do not focus use and service; they focus profit. If their business is also useful to humanity, so much the better; but first and chiefly it must earn a profit for themselves. In the larger forms of business profit becomes an end in itself; men want profit in order to gain more profit. Business can say with Paul: "This one thing I do." That directness and single-mindedness gives capitalistic commercialism its driving power and efficiency. It wants profit, and it goes for it, untroubled by humane considerations or moral scruples. It gets the best of the State in their common dealings, just as the selfish little girl takes the best apples and leaves the nubbins and cores to her conscientious brother.

If Profit is so much the dominant force in our economic life and in our whole social order, it becomes of the highest importance to every religious man, and especially to every teacher and leader, to understand the moral nature of Profit. A man might be pardoned for having hazy notions about Luther's doctrine of justification by faith, or about the Pharisees and Sadducees, but as for Profit — ought he not to know the god of this world?

"Profit" is a shifty word, used in various meanings. In a broad, popular way it means what is left to a business man after he has paid his expenses. A cripple keeping a newstand can talk about his profits in this sense just as proudly as a railway company. But this total "profit" is like an onion, having many layers that can be peeled away and getting more succulent and odoriferous when you get inside. Rent must be deducted; also interest; even if the business man is his own landlord and his own financial backer. The narrower "profit" which then remains still includes the reward which is due to the business man as an active and intelligent worker. If he had to employ a man of like ability, with the same devotion to business and the same capacity for hustling, he would have to pay a stiff salary. He owes himself this salary, and an able business head is so rare and so essential to success that no fair judgment will grudge him the liberal estimate that he is likely to put on his own abilities. In so far as Profit is a high wage for able work, it has moral quality, and those who defend the justice of the present economic system are apt to put the whole emphasis on this honorable element of profit. Averaging their income through their life, many business men get nothing more than a comfortable maintenance for their family, such as a salaried man also gets, and while the amount appropriated by them may not square with absolute justice, there would probably be no world-wide social unrest if our social order showed no deeper cracks and fissures.

We can also allow the claim — though not with equal confidence — that the profit of the business man ought in justice to contain some compensation for the risk he runs. Competitive business life might be classed as an extra-hazardous occupation which demands high insurance rates. At least for infant businesses the rate of mortality is frightful, and most of them die the violent death of bankruptcy sooner or later. A business man has to suffer so many hard knocks, and is so exposed to "the slings and arrows of outrageous fortune," that we shall be glad in Christian generosity to allow him an extra slice of profit for his risks, provided he will henceforth do the same in calculating the wages of his employees, who run the terrible risk of being out of work for weeks or months at a time, and especially of the miners, sailors, brakemen, lumber-jacks, and mill-hands, who incur the risk, not merely of financial loss, but of bloody mutilation and stark death, and whose pay does not seem to rise with the amount of risk involved.

But the interest on capital, the reward for ability, and the insurance against risk do not yet account for the whole

of profit, at least not for that soft, round profit which sometimes invites inspection like the rotundity of a little boy's
pocket when he comes out of the pantry. Profit is $(a + b + c) + x$. What is the x? Sometimes the ingredients
are clearly separable. Old Grimes used to manage his
business himself and furnished his own capital. To-day
the business is incorporated and managed by MacGregor,
a capable Scotchman, who gets $3500 a year. Young
Grimes, who has the intellect of a third-rate clerk, is more
interested in managing dances, but he is still a heavy
stockholder in the business. Now, when the banks lend
money at 5 per cent, why does young Grimes get 12 per cent
on his stock! It is the great ambition of MacGregor to
be admitted to "a share in the business." He could hardly
work harder then than he does now. He is presumably
getting the "wages of ability and superintendence" now.
Why, then, would his outlook and financial position be so
much changed if he were admitted to a share in the profit?
It seems that an idle and incompetent man may draw
"profit," and a man who has all the qualities and does all
the work ascribed to the ideal business man in the books
may get no "profit." This inside element of "profit" is not
necessarily connected with work, nor proportioned to the
value of work done. How, then, is it obtained, and what
moral basis has it?

This unearned "profit" is made only in the midst of a
developed social life. If two pioneer settlers locate in the
same valley, and one chooses better soil and farms it with
greater efficiency, his increasing prosperity is not due to
"profit," but to greater ability in using the resources of the
earth and of his own mind and body. Unearned profit is
made by farming men, and the more men are farmed, the
vaster is the possibility of profit. It is made up of small
contributions from many. It arises where production has
become a social process, and it falls to those who are able

Q

to keep back and take for themselves some fractional part of what many others produce. It is essentially a tribute levied by power. In his book on "Great Fortunes" Professor J. W. Jenks points out that the ability to possess great wealth and secure the income from it without active participation in the management of a business is a modern condition. He adds: "All methods of wealth-getting in society can apparently be classified under two heads: first, the rendering of service to others or to society for the sake of an adequate reward in return; and second, the acquirement of gain for one's self at the expense of others with practically no service rendered to society." The latter method used to be practiced by beggars, thieves, lords, courtesans, and princes, but, as Professor Jenks says, it is now practiced with success by stockholders.

In so far as profit is only another name for the fair reward which society owes for useful labor and service, it has a sound moral basis and we have no quarrel with it. But in so far as profit contains an ingredient which is gained without productive labor, at the expense of others, and without their willing consent, it rests on power and not on right, and a Christian man is under no obligation whatever to feel moral respect for it. On the contrary, it is one of his highest Christian duties to aid society in tracing this parasitic tribute to its sources and preventing its further absorption.

Such unearned profit may be drawn from various sources, singly or in combination. It may be taken by an employer from his employees. Not necessarily, however. Where free land is accessible in a new country, or where a certain kind of labor is scarce, or where an employer is unusually just and generous, wages may be so high that the workers get practically the full value of their labor in the form of wages. But where the labor market is crowded, and where the opportunities of labor are in the hands of a limited class, the employers are intrenched in a position of power over

against the workers and can lower wages. Thereby they
exact an additional amount of labor for the same unit of
wages, and this additional, unpaid labor is tribute levied
by power. Under such conditions all employers, tacitly
and unconsciously, combine in a monopoly of the opportunities of labor, for they alone can give a man access to
that most important of all commodities, a job and a living.
The wages system, which may be fair under conditions of
equality, becomes extortionate between the strong and
the weak. For this reason the labor question, which had
always existed, was intensified in the capitalistic era, when
the instruments of production passed out of the control of
the workers more completely than ever before. They
became relatively weaker; the class of the owners and
employers became relatively stronger. Thus additional
profit which is made by employers through this combination of weakness and power is unearned profit. It is a tribute and a tax, levied by those who have no constitutional
or moral right to tax their fellows.

Business may also make an unearned profit by unloading
some of its expenses on the community. For instance, if
a factory installs cheap furnaces and hires cheap and stupid
men to stoke them, its expenses are lessened and its profits
increased. But it vomits its soot into the air, which is a
precious communistic possession of all, and the community
pays in discomfort, laundrybills, additional housework,
and throat diseases what the factory adds to its dividends.
If the same factory disposes of its chemical waste in the
most economical way by draining it into the river, it throws
that part of its legitimate expenses on the public. The
boys who would swim in the river, the men who would fish
in it, and the lovers who would get material for a life-long
romance by it are done out of their right to valuable real
estate, and have to seek less innocent recreation in more
costly ways in dance halls, saloons, or moving picture shows.

If a man is killed in a steel mill and the company settles with the widow for $300, she and her children will almost certainly be thrown on the neighbors, the charitable organizations, or the town for some form of help and support.[1] If men are paid wages which suffice to maintain them only during their working years, the community will have to support them when they are old. If a department store pays a girl $6 and expects her family to furnish the balance of her support, it makes its "profit" at the expense of her father and brothers. If it keeps its saleswomen standing for long hours, and makes no allowance for the physical needs of women, it keeps down the cost of labor, but the husbands and children of ailing women in years to come may pay for the unearned profit a hundred-fold.

Business can get something for nothing, but Society cannot. If Business fails to pay its bills, somebody else farther down the line will have to settle up. What is "easy money" for one man is bound to be hard loss to another, or to hundreds of others. Every get-rich-quick concern is balanced by thousands of get-poor-quick people who are still stupid enough to trust their fellow-men.

The unearned profit which is thus made at the expense of the community is also a form of tribute levied by power. The business men are by far the most powerful group in every industrial community. To grant them favors is political wisdom; to anger them is political death. If they were not so powerful, the community would never permit the liberties they take. Wherever the people get real control of their own government they always register it by compelling business to take care of its material and human waste as part of the running expense of business.

---

[1] The New York Association for Labor Legislation states that in 114 cases of married men killed in Erie County, N.Y., the dependents in 38 cases received nothing, in 9 cases received less than $100, and in 34 cases received between $100 and $500.

Business supports the undemocratic control of the boss system in politics in order to keep or get these favors at the expense of the community.

Private ownership of the natural resources of the earth also confers power to levy tribute. Those who own coal and iron mines, oil wells, gas wells, asphalt, or nitrate beds hold what industrial society needs, and needs ever more urgently. They justly expect a reward for their labor and intelligence in making these natural resources available for society; but they charge an additional price, not by reason of their service, but by reason of their power to compel the rest to pay it. The entire supply of anthracite coal, for instance, is in the hands of a few corporations who act as a unit over against the public; consequently the price of coal is not measured by the cost of mining and hauling it, but by "what the market will stand."

Where population is growing and men crowd one another for a chance to breathe and labor, the mere ownership of space gives power to levy tribute. If one man owned the land on which New York is built, plainly all the people who live and work there would be at his mercy, and they would have to pay for his mercy. If ten people owned the land, the case would be only slightly changed. At present less than 800,000 people own the land on which almost 5,000,000 live, and 1000 people own the larger proportion of the land values of New York. These landlords have never come together to agree on the tribute they will levy on the 4,000,000 landless land animals who creep and crawl on their dominions, but by the silent play of social forces they know how much their tenants are willing to pay rather than give up any more of the precious margin of time they can spend with their families, and this they exact. Political economists distinguish between rent and profit. In so far as both are based on monopoly they are alike. Both are tribute levied by power.

Ours is an age of social consolidation.   California throws oranges at Massachusetts, and Gloucester tosses back codfish balls to Los Angeles.   The very life of society is dependent on its channels of transportation and travel, as surely as my life depends on my heart and arteries.   We transport men along steel rails, gas along underground tubes, electric dots and dashes along wires strung in the air.   If, now, we have put these arteries of communication into the hands of those who love us not, but who love gain, we have put ourselves at their mercy and must pay their price.   And so we do.   For gas that costs fifty cents we pay a dollar.   For a telegram that costs an Englishman sixpence we pay forty cents.   The Lords of Transportation exact their tribute.

Away back in 1892 the *New York Tribune*, being a chief exponent of the doctrine of protection and chafing under the charge that the protective tariff was the cause of the swollen fortunes, compiled a list of 4047 millionaires in order to prove that the great fortunes were due to other causes.[1]   There is a curious absence of the higher intellectual activities in this list of men to whom our social order has given its largest material rewards.   Poets, artists, scientists, and professors apparently had not served their fellow-men sufficiently well to deserve a million.   We hear of thirty who published newspapers and story papers, of twenty-five who published copyright books, and of two who published copyright music; may some gentle author or musician be hiding in these figures !   On the other hand, 468 became millionaires by the advance of real estate values; 981 by the ownership of natural resources, such as mines, forests, plantations, together with the rise of real estate values; 386 by natural monopolies in the distributive industries, such as railways, express companies, tele-

[1] Professor John R. Commons has analyzed the table in his "Distribution of Wealth," Chapter V.

graphs, telephones, and gas; 303 by banking and the control of money; 65 by combining banking, real estate, and securities with the practice of the law; and one by making the same happy combination with the practice of medicine. One "made his'n" through the Tweed Ring; none apparently by preaching the Gospel. 2141 had engaged in some kind of competitive industry, but aided by monopolies or combined with real estate investments and securities; only 354 were reported to have made their money in purely competitive business, and of these some had at least enjoyed tariff protection and railway rebates.

This newspaper compilation was made in defense of protection and not in arraignment of monopoly, but it proves clearly that great wealth is accumulated, not by preeminent service, but by the power to levy tribute through monopoly control. The more closely and intelligently these fortunes would be analyzed, the more monopoly factors would be disclosed. The results would be still more striking if the millionaires were not simply counted, the big and the little alike, but weighed according to the quantity of their millions.

Since 1892 the number of our millionaires, the average size of their fortunes, and the proportion which the aggregate of their property bears to the total wealth of the nation have all increased enormously.[1] Necessarily so; for the more completely the natural resources of the country are occupied and consolidated, and the larger the population is which needs them, the greater is the opportunity to collect tribute. Industries that formerly seemed purely competitive have been able to create durable trusts and to control prices by bracing themselves against genuine

---

[1] In 1855 the *New York Sun* published a list of the "rich men" in New York City. Men began to be "rich" at that time when they had $100,000. The *Sun's* list contains only 28 millionaires. Yet there were very able men doing business in New York in 1855.

monopolies. The United States Steel Corporation, for instance, gets its power largely through its immense mineral holdings, its patent rights, and its control of essential transportation lines, all of which are monopolies. Banking, too, is approaching monopoly conditions, and a small group of bankers can so give or withhold credit that industrial trusts are protected from serious competition and given the security of monopoly.

Monopoly charges are fundamentally like taxes. Government collects taxes from every man according to his ability to pay. A monopoly likewise charges what the market can stand. In each case a superior power levies tribute by compulsion. The State professes to do it for the common good, and in a well-governed community the people get back all they pay in the form of taxes. In fact, our taxes buy more for us than any other money we spend. If the money levied by public taxation is appropriated by private persons or organizations, we call it corruption, and all our democratic system of government is largely a device to keep a jealous eye and a firm grip on those who spend our taxes for us. On the other hand, the taxation by monopoly in its hundred forms is not for the public good, but for private enrichment, and the people who are taxed have no control over the tax rate levied on them and over the money collected from them. It is taxation without representation.

The chief danger of this form of spoliation is its subtlety. It is the most ingratiating and disarming form of theft ever invented. If a man held us up at night and collected a dollar from us, we should clamor to all the world that we had been robbed. When we fill our coal bin for the winter, we are being held up for many times that amount, but the robbery is connected with so much useful service, it is done so peaceably, and the coal dealer who collects the tax from us is so innocent of guilt, that we are in doubt where our thanks should end and our profanity should begin. Even to those whose fortunes are swollen with monopoly profits the real moral character of their extortion is so disguised by the genuine social service they have rendered that they feel proud of their benefactions to humanity, and pained and wronged when an ungrateful world turns against them.

Yet the collection of monopoly profit is immoral, and that's all there is about it. To charge another man more than a thing is worth is unfair. To take advantage of his need to coerce something extra from him is yellow. Even to our muddled judgment it becomes morally intolerable when practiced between friends, or under circumstances where man gets close to man. When Jacob made his tired and hungry brother Esau sell his birthright to get some of the pottage that stood steaming and savory before him, he charged what the market could bear, but he did a shabby thing. It is not to the credit of those who have taught us christian conduct that our judgment still fumbles about the moral nature of unearned profit. If our social order is to be christianized, wealth by extortion must cease; work and service must become the sole title to income. But if our economic order is not christianized but goes on developing on its present basis, then we must bend our head to the winter storm that is upon us. In that case there is nothing ahead for us but a swift increase of unearned fortunes, and a corresponding swift increase in the price of all the joys and necessaries of life. Some men will have power to levy tribute; the rest of us must pay it. We shall pay it in the excess of work exacted from us in return for the right to food and shelter. We shall pay it in the sin and misery thrown back on us by those who create it. We shall pay it in the food we give to our children with stinting hand, and in the price of the little blanket on the baby's crib.

In one of the sublimest of the Psalms the poet describes the all-pervading presence of Jehovah which envelops him with awe and follows him with its comfort wherever he goes. Woe to the generations yet unborn if, instead of the searching but loving presence of the Almighty, they shall find themselves beset behind and before by another Power, equally pervasive, invisible, and intangible, but selfish, merciless, and insatiable! Then the great psalm would be pitched in another key: —

> Whither shall I go from thy hunger,
> Or whither shall I flee from thy greed?
> If I ascend to the mountain forests, thou art there.
> If I swing my pick in the mines, thou art there.
> If I take the wings of the morning,
> And emigrate to the uttermost coasts of the sea,
> Even there shall thy hand seize me,
> And thy right hand shall drain me.

PART IV

THE INVASION OF GOD'S COUNTRY

CHAPTER I

THE MORAL VALUES OF CAPITALISM

CAPITALISM is the most efficient system for the creation of material wealth which the world has ever seen. Wherever it invades an old civilization, the ancient organization of production is doomed and goes down before it. This technical efficiency proves that the system must have powerful moral forces and cohesions in it.

It has put humanity under the law of work as never before. The pace of work has speeded up in all the industrial nations. Its dire compulsion has overcome the primitive laziness and intermittent working habits of undeveloped men, and forced their latent resources of physical and mental energy into use. It has done for society what parental compulsion or hunger has done for countless boys who knew how to work when they wanted to, but usually preferred to go fishing or "hang out with the other fellows."

Capitalism has taught society the laws and habits of association on a large scale. We have seen newly arrived Chinamen shuffling along in Indian file as the narrow streets of their own country had taught them. We have also seen regiments of drilled men in parade sweeping down a street, keeping step to the boom-boom of the big drum. Which shows the higher morality? Association is the result of ethical cohesion, and it is the creator of loyalties and human affections. Many factories even now have a fine spirit of fellowship in them. The development of the factory is a necessary stage in the evolution of any co-operative system which the future may have in store. Some of the harsh and despotic elements of capitalistic organization were doubtless historically justified as peda-gogic necessities. If men were wise, they would combine freely; being stupid as well as selfish, they need to have the beauties of coöperation knocked into their reluctant heads.

In the leaders of commerce and industry the power which they wield under the capitalistic system evokes the same moral qualities which we admire in the great cap-tains and kings of history, the rough directness of aim, the imperious command of social forces by a single will, the self-confidence and driving power of men who are accus-tomed to make decisions and be obeyed. It begets the daring venturesomeness which the old pioneers and ex-plorers had. It demands a wonderful concentration of will and intellect, a perpetual forward reach of the mind. They learn to take the pounding of adversity with cool fortitude, and to rig the last shred of sail to the stump of the mast when all the rigging has gone overboard.

On the other hand, the defenders of capitalism often inflate its stock. They assume that the whole spiritual and material advance of modern civilization is due to the capitalistic system, just as the Roman Catholic Church sets all the moral progress made by Western humanity in fifteen hundred years to its own credit. The increase in moral and intellectual force during the nineteenth century was largely due to the spread of democracy and education. The material triumphs of our era are due to the rise of science. Applied science would have served any social order that might have been in existence during the last century. If socialism succeeds capitalism, it will probably make even larger use of science than the short-sighted haste of economic individualism has been able to do. Capitalism can claim as its virtue and achievement only what its peculiar organization and spirit alone were adapted to accomplish. It has served civilization best in two directions: in developing the application of machine power to production, and in furthering the organization of associated groups of workers on a large scale. Profit could best be made by power machines and by gang work; consequently capitalism developed both. At these points it was in line with human progress and boosted it. It entered into a working partnership with science in so far as science could build machinery, develop the exactness of operation necessary for machine work, analyze and combine material, and in general aid production and the creation of profit. For all aid it gave science in this way it deserves our gratitude.

We have taken the hopeful position that our entire social order, with all its terrible immoralities, is nevertheless woven through with Christian elements, which form the basis of its further regeneration. The same thing is true of our economic order. With all their bitter cruelty and wrong our factories are the cells out of which a christianized industry must be evolved. Even now business men are public servants in embryo. They pride themselves on the community service they are rendering, and many a one of them would serve admirably as Bishop of the Church of Holy Industry, if he had half a chance to put his Christian good will into action.

But the great powers of human goodness that lie latent in our economic life are largely kept down or misdirected through the constitutional maladjustment of social forces in capitalism. The power of association is thwarted or soured by the competitive struggle and the autocratic relation into which the leaders are placed over against the workers. The profit system lures the economic stewards of society into tricking or extorting from those whom they ought to serve. Our economic system in its fundamental structure is still nonmoral or immoral, nonchristian or unchristian. It offends the thoughtless by its excesses, and the thoughtful by its essence and spirit. The more the Christian spirit rises to clear-sighted ascendency in any individual or any social group, the more offensive and intolerable does the ethic of capitalism seem.

We must remember in favor of our economic life that it embodies the material interests, which are naturally least touched by spiritual considerations. Church and school deal with the soul and the intellect, and so call out the higher motives and relations. The home can lean on the powerful instincts of sexual and parental love in holding its members together in helpful relations. The home was relieved of its former despotic and exploiting elements partly by unloading its economic work on the factory. On the other hand, industry and commerce deal with that part of life in which the selfish and animal nature is most interested. Therefore they have lagged behind the other portions of social life in coming under the higher law of fraternity and service.

But it would be fatal to the evolutionary redemption of mankind if we abandoned the great economic domain to the brute laws and tried to live as Christians in our other relations. Neither the individual nor society can live a double life with impunity. To our whole modern world Christ says: "Ye cannot serve two masters. If ye hold to Mammon, ye will learn to despise God." Society is not divided into water-tight bulkheads. The influences flow back and forth incessantly.

On the one hand, the Christian sections of our social organism are sending wholesome human impulses into relations that would otherwise be purely cannibalistic. The good-fellowship with which even competitors often stand by one another; the democracy and human kindness with which some employers and employees regard each other; the genuine courtesy and helpfulness which business men show to their customers; the public spirit with which great business concerns are taking hold of the new social service measures — are qualities bred and educated in the christianized life of the Home, the School, the Church, and the Neighborhood. Business has banked on the moral resources, the honesty and trustworthiness, created by agencies outside of business life. The personal virtues of business men have pulled Business through and made it tolerable and respectable.

The democratic State too has supplied Christian virtues to Business. Usually the State in each case began by letting Capitalism run according to its own laws, but the thing became intolerable, and the State had to pull its teeth and shorten its chain. The State had to step in with its superior Christian ethics and put certain limits to the immoralities of Capitalism. If it had not done so, Capitalism would have mutilated and killed the men, brutalized the women, and drained the children so fast that the human material of civilization would have been rotten in the second generation and the social order would have collapsed.[1] It would have devastated its own feeding ground and killed itself, or, to put it in theological terminology, it would have gone to the devil. The State, in the interests of morality, has so emasculated and domesticated Capitalism that there is hardly a specimen of the untamed variety at large. Foreign observers think we have the nearest approach to the genuine beast in America.

So the redeemed portions of the social order have influenced Business for good. But the influence runs the other way, too. Business is a great institution which incul-

[1] See the story of early English capitalism in F. Engels, "The Condition of the Working Classes in England in 1844."

cates its own laws and spirit, until they get into the blood
of men. All the other institutions of society are affected
by the mere existence of this powerful assimilating force
alongside of them. In addition to that, Business has an
expansive power in it which compels it to reach out and
rule. Like Christianity, it is a missionary force. It is
impatient of any moral restraint that hampers it in making
profit. The Slave Power of the South was a great business
system, and it was not content with being safe from interference in the slave States, but enforced the active coöperation of the free States, and demanded the right of expanding
into the new territory of the West. The liquor interests
are simply a big section of the capitalistic interests of the
country. Like all other business, the liquor business needs
an expanding market for its products. When it collides
with the moral determination of our people to put a stop
to its ravages, it fights. It fights to keep possession of the
wet cities and country districts, and it actively invades the
dry districts. Sovereign States find their laws nullified by
the shipments of liquor from adjoining States, by the aid
given to blind tigers and boot leggers, by systematic business campaigns to keep the desire for liquor active in dry
districts, and by corrupt interference by outside parties in
local political fights. This is not simply an illustration,
but an important sample of the way in which Business in
its necessary pursuit of Profit will break down any barriers
of law or morals that fence it from its pasture grounds.

We shall not understand the problem of christianizing
the Social Order properly as long as we regard unchristianized Business as a passive object to be molded into
finer and nobler lines under our hands. It is alive, vibrant,
strong, assertive, impatient, and full of fight. It will maul,
ride down, and trample any force that interferes with its
profits. It has tried to thrust out of position and income
every public man who has really hurt it, and in many

cases it has succeeded. It will misrepresent and slander, and if necessary imprison and kill. The conflict between the Christian and the unchristian forces in our social order is a real war, a conflict of principalities and powers in high places. If any one has lost faith in the existence of the Devil, of the personal power of malicious evil, he can regain his faith by tackling Big Business hard enough to make it mad. The moral nature of our economic system stands out clearly only when we see the way it deals with the higher ethical values of society. We must test it by the way it treats what is holy. In the following chapters we shall see how Mammon invades God's country.

R

CHAPTER II

"Skin for skin, yea, all that a man hath will he give for his life," was the judgment of the greatest of all experts on human nature.[1] A man who would save his money from a burning house and let his child perish would be regarded with horror. Whenever human life is at stake in some striking, dramatic way, as in the *Titanic* disaster, our calloused dullness gives way, the awe of human life wakes up in us, and a nation holds its breath to know if life has triumphed. If a man's property is injured, the Law lets him sue for redress; if a human life is lost, the State itself with its solemn powers takes up the case. Reverence for human life as such is one of the best products of Christian civilization. The teachings of the Church on the eternal destiny of the soul increased the valuation of life. A passionate tenderness for life was one of the marks of Jesus. His care for "the least" and "the lost" was an expression of love for human life even in its stunted and wrecked remnants.

There is a genuine love for human life in modern society. But alongside of great sympathy for single cases of suffering runs an astounding indifference to suffering and death in the mass. We strain out the gnat of football accidents and swallow the camel of Pittsburgh steel industries without winking. More than 15,000 persons are annually killed in American work accidents, and some 500,000 are injured. Industry is like a guillotine dropping minute by

[1] Job ii. 4.

minute, year in and year out, on some part of a human body. "The total number of casualties suffered by our industrial army is sufficient to carry on perpetually two such wars at the same time as our Civil War and the Russo-Japanese War."[1] To the accidents we must add the unknown total of sickness and death through occupational diseases, such as the poisoning by chemical fumes, or the lung diseases induced through breathing metal dust or cotton fluff.

Now, some accidents are inevitable when men go digging in the bowels of the rocks or turn iron into a blazing torrent, but a large proportion of the suffering inflicted by industry to-day is entirely preventable. "In 1909 few competent authorities dared to assert that more than 50 per cent of the industrial accidents were preventable. To-day we do not hesitate to say that from 75 per cent to 90 per cent are preventable."[2] They have not been prevented because we are all stupid and busy, and because our economic system is not interested in Life, but in Profit.

The two-class system of Capitalism has taken nearly all initiative and authority away from the body of the workers and has reduced them to a mute and passive condition.[3] It has put their comfort and safety at the mercy of the owning and managing class who do not share their dangers in the mines and shops, and many of whom are ignorant of

[1] See the valuable facts and quotations appended to the report of the Committee on Standards of Life and Labor presented at the National Conference of Charities and Corrections, 1912. Section III deals with Safety and Health. [2] Accident Bulletin, No. 3, Minnesota.

[3] *Collier's* for Jan. 15, 1910, quotes the following from former Senator Colby of New Jersey: "A girl working in a certain factory was warned that her machine was defective and that she would lose an arm unless the defect was made right. She plucked up courage to speak to the proprietor about it, but he roughly informed her that she was not employed to tell him how to run his business. She lost her arm and sued for damages. The defense was 'contributory negligence,' which the employer proved by the fact that the girl had known of the defect and had continued working at her own risk."

the conditions under which their money is made. If the sons and daughters of the owners had to work with the employees, accidents would be rarer. The autocracy prevailing in industry by itself accounts for the neglect of safety. Every advance of industrial democracy will help to establish health and safety in the workshops.

In addition to that, the class in control has no direct financial interest in the safety of the workers. If a machine breaks down, the owners must buy another; therefore the machines are kept oiled and burnished. If a man sickens through carbon-monoxide fumes or the heat of the blast furnaces, a new man steps in and it costs the owners nothing. A slave was cared for in sickness, because it would cost $600 to $1200 to replace him; free laborers are replaced gratis. The miners say if a mule is killed in the mines, the superintendent wants to know how it happened; if a man is killed, they take him out of a side door.

Worse yet: in many ways the safety of the one class can be increased only by decreasing the income of the other class, and therewith Profit is pitted against Life. It costs money to install hoods and blowers to suck up the dust while grinding metals. It would cut down profit to substitute adult workers for the child workers. Thirty-one and four tenths per cent of the girls under sixteen employed in the silk weaving industry of Pennsylvania cost their employers less than $2 a week. The capital invested in an industrial plant will return the maximum of profit if the machinery is in operation for the maximum of time and at the maximum speed. But the longer the work day, the more exhaustion and accidents; likewise the faster the speed, the more exhaustion and accidents. The interest of the owners to that extent is against the safety and health of the workers. This is a dangerous condition to set up and institutionalize. Human kindness is not vigorous and durable enough to offset such a strain.

Thus Capitalism, by putting the workers under the control of another class whose interests are not identical with theirs, is directly responsible for a part of the large ratio of industrial accidents and diseases. This indifference to the life of the workers was clearest during the youth of Capitalism, before the State interfered with its workings. In its infancy it impoverished and degraded great strata of the population of England. It devastated the people in the colonies. "We have grown rich because whole races and tribes have died for us and continents have been depopulated for us."[1] The Congo and Peruvian rubber trade are an aftermath of this. State interference has lessened the murderous effects of the system, but every step of interference was resisted by the financial interests affected by it. The railways, for instance, opposed the federal legislation which compelled them to introduce automatic couplers, though hand couplers decimated the trainmen. Even after the law was passed, some of the roads delayed the installation as long as possible. The manufacturing interests have never been friendly to factory inspection. This attitude is more damning than mere indifference, which might be due to ignorance.

Industrial accidents have multiplied with the spread of power machinery. Power hammers and lathes have a very different way of inflicting injury than the old hammer and chisel of the carpenter. Capitalism has shown the most wonderful resourcefulness in mastering all the problems of the machine in so far as it could multiply and economize production and increase profits, but it has been backward and even obstinate about adapting machinery to protect the safety of the workers. The same situation has been duplicated in the industrial communities in general. The interests of the powerful class that lives on profits are not identical with the class that lives on wages; therefore our

[1] Professor Sombart, "Geschichte des modernen Kapitalismus," I, 325.

industrial cities are clean and beautiful at one end and dirty and joyless at the other. The hard and loveless spirit of industrial life spreads to the whole community and tends to brutalize us all.

Industrial accidents represent only one way in which Profit is the enemy of Life. Business sells us death because it is profitable. I have before me a list of proprietary medicines condemned by the United States government because they contain habit-forming drugs, such as cocain, chloroform, and morphine. Some of them are especially intended for little children and are sold as "Children's Comfort," "Kopp's Baby's Friend," "Mrs. Winslow's Soothing Sirup." On the firmness of rubber hose may depend the lives of women and children at a tenement fire, but a test of thirty-two samples of the rubber lining of hose showed only one to be of high grade.[1] After the burning of the steamer *General Slocum* it was found that life preservers were sometimes stuffed with rotten cork or sawdust. The lack of life boats on the *Titanic* was part of the general economy of business management. Two years ago the President of the International Seamen's Union of America said: "There is not sailing to-day on any ocean any passenger vessel carrying the number of boats needed to take care of the passengers and crew, nor a sufficient number of skilled men to handle those boats which are carried. If there were, the seamen's condition would be much better than it is now."[2] When Business adulterates the food of the working people, it lowers their physical efficiency on which they must depend to earn their living, to strike the pace of work required, and to resist disease. Money made by such adulteration is made at the expense of life. The artificial raising of food prices to increase profit has the same effect. If the cold-storage

[1] Report of a committee at the convention of the National Fire Protective Association, 1911. [2] Quoted in the *Survey*, April 27, 1912.

system were in the hands of a community planning wisely for its own welfare, it might make good food cheap all the year. In the hands of profit-making commerce it has to some extent been turned into a means of counteracting the prodigality of God and the summer, and of making food dear all the year. The consideration of Profit may so distort the natural point of view that a large crop is regarded as a disaster. Business bends all its energies to keep up prices and to keep down wages, for either increases profits. Therefore Business, as now constituted, has a constitutional and inevitable interest in raising the value of Things and keeping down the value of Men. That makes property an enemy of Life instead of its support.

Whenever Life is set above Profit in business there is a thrill of admiration which indicates that something unusual has been done. In 1911 the Diamond Match Company allowed its competitors the use of sesquisulphide, on which it holds a patent, in order to put a stop to the terrible phosphorus poisoning among the workers in the match industry. It thereby set the health of the workers above its monopoly profit, and all the country stopped to cheer the action. Doubtless it deserved applause. But what shall we say of the general morality of business when it is reckoned an heroic virtue to set the life of men above an additional fraction of one per cent? It is the surest sign of moral inferiority when ordinary honesty and decency in a given class are praised as noble. We have to add that only two of the competitors accepted the offer because phosphorus was slightly cheaper than the harmless substitute, and Congress in 1912 had to force the whole industry by law to abandon the use of phosphorus.

The economic organization of a civilized nation ought to be able to keep the people in a state of physical efficiency. In fact, that would be the minimum that ought to be required of it. The real test of the national system would lie in the speed and thoroughness with which it would raise the mass of the people to real intellectual culture, to artistic taste, and to refinement of manners. Mere living is not yet Life. The economic organization of our nation does not meet even that minimum requirement. In spite of the wealth of our natural resources and the comparative sparseness of our population, several millions of workers have not enough income to keep themselves at normal physical efficiency.[1] As to real culture and refinement, the effect of capitalistic industrialism is largely the other way. The peasants from southern Europe lose their cheerfulness, their songs, their art, their courtesy, in the somber pressure of our industrial towns. When they are industrialized in their native homes, the result is the same.

The real joy of Life is in its play. Play is anything we do for the joy and love of doing it, apart from any profit, compulsion, or sense of duty. It is the real living of life with the feeling of freedom and self-expression. Play is the business of childhood, and its continuation in later years is the prolongation of youth. Real civilization should increase the margin of time given to play. The advance in science and organization has so increased our power of production that even now it would be possible to supply the average needs of all by four or five hours of daily work by all, and the rest of the day might go to athletics, gardening, handicraft, visiting, music, study, or any other form of play. Instead of that a ten and twelve hour working day is frequent, even in exhausting industries, and an eight-hour day is the ideal of organized Labor. The long hours and the high speed and pressure of industry use up the vitality of all except the most capable. An exhausted body craves rest, change, and stimulus, but it responds only to

[1] See Report of Committee on Standards of Living and Labor, National Conference of Charities and Corrections. Nearing, "Wages in the United States." Hunter, "Poverty."

strong and coarse stimulation. In all mill towns where
the long work day is the rule, the night school, library, and
church languish, and the saloon and house of prostitution
flourish. Drink and sexual vice are the ready pillows of
an exhausted body, the only form of play which degradation knows. Unrestrained capitalism would kill out play
and put even childhood in the yoke. But the killing of
play means taking the life out of Life.

The specific gravity of the human body is almost the
same as that of water. With proper breathing and motion
a man can move about in the water with ease and delight.
But he has only a narrow margin of freedom, and a few
pounds' weight would make his swimming a terrible struggle
against strangulation, and in time convert his playground
into a death trap. The same is true of our life and work.
We have a margin of freedom where the soul can rise and
feel the joy and beauty of living, but there is a limit where
fatigue begins, and where work becomes a strain and grind.
Jane Addams has suggested that our insane asylums ought
to investigate "how many patients become insane because
of black terror lest they lose their work, how many through
malnutrition when they have lost it, and how many because of the sheer monotony of their employment." For
every person who loses his reason through brooding fear or
impoverishment of the blood, there are scores who suffer
some permanent impairment of their spiritual vitality, and
hundreds who lose the bloom of their merriment and enter
a somber world of anxiety. They may live till they are
old, but some of their life has been taken from them, and
their children are "born to hoarded weariness as some to
hoarded gold." Merely to look at the life of the poor from
a window in the House of Plenty darkens the days. "Then
I returned and saw all the oppressions that are done under
the sun: and behold the tears of such as were oppressed
and they had no comforter; on the side of their oppres-

sors there was power, but *they* had no comforter. Wherefore I praised the dead that have been long dead more than the living that are yet alive; yea, better than them both did I esteem him that hath not yet been, who hath not seen the evil work that is done under the sun."[1]

A free soul has reservoirs of life within. If we labor for our children, for our country, or for a cause we love, spiritual forces rise within us and give us a superhuman endurance. But when we are drained by compulsion, it is enslavement and strangulation of the soul. This is the condition in which thoughtful workingmen feel they are placed. They believe that they produce enough to give them a margin of leisure for real life, but one extra hour of toil, one dollar taken from their wage, a little additional speeding of the work, wipes out that margin of time and vitality which makes their life free and livable. That margin is God's country in their life, the soil where all the higher instincts and desires are cultivated. Wipe that out and you leave the brute needs. Their resentment is deepened by the knowledge that the extra strength taken from them is often turned to useless luxury by those who take it. An additional vase or rug in a wealthy woman's drawing room may add nothing to the real comfort of any one; yet it may embody the excess toil of a thousand girls for a week. If each girl had been able to retain that additional fragment of earnings, it might have meant an excursion on Saturday, a concert, some article of womanly adornment, a present to a friend, something to give the feel and joy of life. Instead of that it is bottled up in that vase to which a few satiated ladies may say "Ah!"

When David was a hunted exile in the cave of Adullam, he became homesick for his native town and for the spring from which he drank as a boy, and he said: "Oh that one would give me water to drink of the well of Bethlehem

[1] Ecclesiastes iv. 1-3.

which is by the gate !"   At that time a Philistine war party
was camped at Bethlehem, but three of David's mighty
men, for love of their chief, broke through the lines of the
enemy and brought some of the water to David.   "But
he would not drink thereof, but poured it out unto Jehovah.
And he said, Be it far from me, O Jehovah, that I should
do this !   Shall I drink the blood of the men who went in
jeopardy of their lives?" [1]

Life is the sacred spark of God in us, and the best of
our race have reverenced it most.   Wherever life is held
precious, and restored and redeemed when broken or soiled,
there is God's country, and there the law of Christ prevails.
But in our economic system life is held cheap and wasted
needlessly, and the play and beauty of life are turned into
weariness.   Death rules because love and solidarity do not
rule.   Brothers are set against brothers in two classes, of
which one can flourish in luxury, while the other toils in
want.   The exhaustive toil and the want of the one class
may even be the means to speed and pile up the wealth of
the other.   The Profit of the Few has turned against the
Life of the Many.   God's reign will not come until the
Profit of all shall support the Life of all.

[1] 2 Samuel xxiii. 13–17.

CHAPTER III

GOD's country is the home of beauty. God is not only the all-wise and all-powerful, but the all-beautiful. The connection between religion and beauty, between morality and art, is of the closest. The sense of beauty is the morning portal of the temple of God by which the young best love to enter for worship. Ruskin has taught us that art has its roots in the moral life, and that permanent ugliness is a product of sin and a producer of brutality.

The redeemed portions of our social order all cultivate beauty. There are few homes so poor that you will not find some pathetic attempt at beauty for its own sake. In our churches religion long ago entered into partnership with architecture, music, and color. As our schools outgrow the poverty of "the little red schoolhouse" they are decorating their walls with pictures. Our cities and States are developing beauty in their parks and public buildings in just the measure in which they are struggling free from the clutch of political avarice.

How do capitalistic industry and commerce deal with the æsthetic life?

Human labor beautifies nature. If the soil is well tilled, it becomes more fertile year by year. Science has furnished labor unparalleled powers to fashion nature according to its will and with wonderful results. Arid lands have come to teem with life and verdure; dreary swamps have been redeemed from desolation. But side by side with this fertilizing influence of the hand of man goes an influence of devastation. I have revisited country sides that I knew in wooded glory in my boyhood, and have found the trees slashed out and the mountain looking like a house rifled by burglars. In a lovely university town of Ohio, in which the streets were lined with young and vigorous shade trees, a corporation hacked and butchered the trees to string its wires more cheaply. The trees now stretch out their lopped and dying limbs like deformed beggars in the East that wave their handless arms for alms. If the State had not stepped in to protect them, the palisades on the Hudson would have become a mere quarry. Two governments tried to preserve the falls of Niagara, but the time is coming when we shall stand by the dribbling rocks and try to remember how Samson looked when he wore his locks and before he had learned to grind corn for the Philistines. Nature, our common mother, sits like a captive queen among barbarians who are tearing the jewels from her hair. Beauty that ages have fashioned and that no skill of man can replace is effaced to enrich a few persons whose enrichment is of little use to anybody. In the Middle Ages the degenerate descendants of the Romans knew no other use for the priceless fragments of ancient art that lay scattered among the ruins than to grind up the marble for lime and mortar. We do the same with the inherited beauty of nature. Our trains as we approach a great city begin to move through a lane of sign boards. The fences and barns along the country roads beseech us to pay no attention to the fact that the golden-rod and purple aster are in bloom, but to concentrate our mental efforts on the fact that Levi, Flannigan, and Schmidt will sell us a suit of sweat-shop goods cheaper than any other set of Christians.

These things are done by a form of industry in which immediate profit for a few is the animating force. Consequently the higher needs, the common possessions, and the

longer outlook are sacrificed to immediate gain. Capitalism is penny wise and pound foolish. If the State with its
broader interests and longer perspective had not stepped
in to restrain the avarice of industry and replace its kill-
ings, our country would now be stripped of fish and game.
Capitalism can cut down the timber which unaided nature
has grown through centuries, but it cannot afford the long
wait that is needed to grow new forests. It leaves the
exploited timber lands and turns elsewhere for new profits.
For any long-range care of nature capitalism is almost
useless. The Conservation Movement is a national confession that capitalism, in dealing with the natural resources of the country, is a national peril. In using up the
resources of nature faster than we can replace them, we
graft on our own children, for they will have to live in a
land of wasted forests, gutted mines, and dried water
courses. The avarice induced by our economic system sacrifices the future of the race to immediate enrichment.
From the point of view of a religious evolutionist that is
one of the greatest of all sins. God and nature are always
supremely intent on a better future. Now if capitalism
does this with the utilities of nature, what will it do with
her beauties ?

It is true that industry and commerce cater willingly to
the sense of beauty. Tirelessly they turn out new fabrics,
new patterns, new shades of color in glittering profusion.
But here again the fatal twist of Profit comes in. The
aim is not to sell a thing because it is beautiful, but to make
it beautiful because that will sell it. Show windows are
dressed to attract buyers; advertisements are brilliant to
attract buyers; buildings are radiant with incandescent
lights to attract buyers. This is beauty for profit, mere-
tricious beauty, the studied attractiveness of a painted
woman. There is a restless, self-assertive egotism in the
incandescent flashlights that points to self and yells for

cash. It lacks repose and moral quality. Much of the beauty created by commerce is full of lies, as adulterated as the food. It is made for mere appearance, and it has corrupted and vitiated the conscience of us all.

The relation of commerce to beauty comes home to us in the matter of woman's dress. Our women are the chief ministers of beauty in the life of most of us. They used to weave, dye, and make their own dress. Now industry makes it for them, and the industries that make and handle clothes far exceed in the value of their output those that make iron, steel, and machinery. The fact that the making of woman's dress is completely commercialized accounts for the fashions. They are not steps in the evolution of beauty, a permanent approximation toward some form of dress that will be comfortable, sanitary, and artistic like the robes of the Greeks. They are a succession of arbitrary changes devised by the commercial interests involved in order to keep women buying; for whenever fashion changes, there is brisk buying and fresh profits. If a female archangel should come down from heaven and reveal the eternally beautiful lines of dress to women, it would be to the interest of all the commercial concerns that cater to women to cry down that heavenly pattern after one season's run and obliterate the memory of it; for if that angelic style became permanent, what would become of trade?

Of course the changeableness of woman's dress is not wholly due to commercial stimulation. It is a manifestation of that feminine mutability which has ever been the delight and despair of men. A woman's dress is the resultant of two psychic attractions: the desire to be like other women, and the desire to be different from other women. That keeps dress on the move. But to many of the best women the merry-go-round of fashion is a nauseating vertigo. It plunges them in expense, labor, and worry, and when by taking thought they have worked out an adaptation of a given fashion to their peculiar slimness and height, another spasmodic contortion of fashion compels them to revise their canons of art and do it all over again. Some of the more serious Christian movements in history tried to break loose from the tyranny of fashion by adopting a type of dress that would be both simple and permanent, and an old-fashioned Quaker lady, a Catholic nun, and even a Salvation Army lass in her ugly bonnet are proof that simplicity sets off womanly sweetness and individuality wonderfully well. During the epidemic of big hats I noticed a nurse in hospital uniform coming into a room full of fashionable women, and she was by all odds the best-dressed woman there.

If left to their own taste, some women would prefer stability and some would enjoy change in their dress, but Business forces change on the former and stimulates the love of change in the latter, and for both creates a social driving force before which the individual woman is almost helpless. It hustles them into bizarre fashions because Business wants to turn over its capital and nothing sane happens to be in sight. For several years now our women have been wearing hats that were candle extinguishers of beauty and reduced thousands of charming heads to pitiable insignificance. When the wind blew, any grace of carriage became impossible. The women's clubs missed an opportunity in 1910. They ought to have organized great autos-da-fé all over the country to burn the big hats and to hang in effigy all those who compelled them to wear them. The world of men would have stood by to applaud, and it might have been the beginning of a great revival of morality and religion.

It is impossible to treat the matter of fashion without sarcasm, but truly it is no laughing matter. Women are the priestesses of beauty, and when their sense of beauty is seduced and distorted for years at a time, it is as bad as if the servants of the State yielded to corruption or ministers of the Gospel were willing to twist the straight word of God. Does it not concern the Kingdom of God on earth when an unregenerate economic system so invades our better life that good women wear immodest waists and indecent skirts, adapted to the professional needs of harlots, and trick out their heads with false and unclean things in order to look like the notorious mistress of a diseased French king?

There was once a little State which, for size and population, we could tuck away in our vast country and forget, but which has exerted a mightier influence in advancing the art and the intellect of humanity than our whole great nation has yet exerted or seems likely to exert. Athens in her palmy days used her wealth for the public good, building splendid temples and theaters, and giving her citizens leisure to enjoy the means of culture, and by this policy she created a community of productive intellects by whose side our professors and magazine writers are scrub growth. In our country we have followed the opposite policy. We have stripped the community and enriched individuals. We have handed over all the sources of wealth to private exploitation, and so our communities are poor, always on the edge of the debt limit and hardly able to keep clean. Few of our cities have any public collection of art. Few have any statuary to which the eye would care to turn often. Few have even fine public buildings.

Our age is an age of traffic. Our railway stations are in their nature great public buildings where men throng, and their size and vaulted interiors give scope for architectural treatment such as the builders of antiquity might have coveted. In the large cities of Germany the station buildings are imposing works of architecture, set in parked approaches. The cities turn their best face to the arriving

s

guest. Even cities of twenty thousand inhabitants have spacious stations with tiled subways to cross the tracks. On the other hand, in our American cities the streets about the station are usually the ugliest of all, a weedy back yard of commercialism and a congenial setting for the station building. The ordinary small station is a bald and dirty box. Of the larger cities on the great New York Central only New York and Albany as yet have ornamental buildings. At the great railway center of Buffalo the station is both plain and inadequate. The Union Station at Cleveland, the sixth city of the country, is dark, dirty, and nasty, and its passenger accommodations would be poor for a city of one tenth its size.[1] Why this difference? In Germany the railways belong to the various States of the German confederacy. They earn large incomes for the States, and the officials at their head are eager to show economy and a favorable balance. But their acquisitiveness is balanced by considerations of public welfare, and they coöperate with the governments of the cities in the interest of public beauty. Our railways are owned by private corporations and run for profit. They boast superior efficiency, but their efficiency, in so far as it is a fact, is the efficiency of capitalism, which is strong in anything that lowers cost and increases profit, and weak in anything that promotes the common good, but lowers dividends. Their strength is seen in the leveling of grades and other engineering feats, their weakness in their casualty lists and their disregard of beauty. In that respect our station buildings can fairly serve as demonstrations how public beauty fares when we surrender our public functions and our wealth to private and profit-making concerns, and let them erect our public buildings.

[1] A fine building is now under construction at Rochester, in which artistic idealism has found expression, and a new station has been planned for Cleveland. But why not long ago?

Some one ought to show the bearing of the doctrine of economic determinism on the history of art. The production of art is bound up with the general social system of production. The creation of an opera needs more than Mozart's head; it needs the Vienna opera house and all that pertains to it. The economic problem for the artist is how to get a living while he is producing his work, and then how to get it into permanent form and place it before the public. When wealth was in the hands of kings, nobles, and churchmen, artists were dependent on these patrons, and often had to prostitute their art in order to minister to the vanity of the powerful. A great hall in the Louvre is filled with eighteen huge paintings by the great Rubens, describing the courtship and marriage of Marie de' Medici and Henri IV of France in unappetizing detail and mythological embellishment. The whole series reeks with flattery and is a great painted lie. This was the task set by wealth in the hands of a prince to a great artist. Poor Rubens ! A penny for his thoughts ! The dethronement of feudalism and the rise of capitalism has shifted the wealth available for art into the hands of a new set of men, with greater intelligence and closer to realities, but with less artistic culture than the courts of many monarchs had acquired. So artists must paint the baggy faces of the Wertheimers and Laubentalers and their interesting wives, and choose subjects which such buyers are likely to select for their homes. This penalizes originality and democracy of conception. Artists are in the position of prophets who are in the pay of the rich. They must make their art say smooth things, and cannot be the bold interpreters of human life.

If artists have no access to the rich, they have to deal with middlemen, who take advantage of their poverty or bind them by contracts, so that poor artists in Europe are often sweated like Jewish tailors. With few exceptions the great modern French artists suffered for years or all their lives in misery. In the year when Millet was painting the Gleaners he was near to suicide. In 1859, the year in which he painted the Angelus, his wife was facing confinement and he had no wood in the dead of winter.[1] The only prosperous years he had, 1860–1863, he received $200 a month from a picture dealer, and was under contract in return to hand over everything he painted or drew. His Angelus was painted for an American, who was to pay $300 for it, but Millet had to sell it to another man for $200. The later high prices profited the dealers and not the artist. When artists are dead, there is an unearned increment in their pictures.

When rich men are the patrons of art, they usually place what they buy in their own homes where only a very limited public can enjoy it. This cuts the artist off from the spiritual touch with the common people, who might pay him the precious perquisite of admiration and love. Artists, like orators, are dependent on the answering vibrations of the common soul. Moreover, the working people with all their potential power of appreciation are cut out of the audience. They cannot afford to hear high-class music or plays, or to buy copyrighted books and pictures. Moving picture shows and canned music are their bill of fare. The intellectual élite of the working class are the most earnest of all hearers, but a large proportion of the workers lack the culture to appreciate art even if it is offered free. Like religion, art must be experienced in youth to be loved through life. In so far as our capitalistic system deprives the working class of the leisure and elasticity which would fit them for the higher pleasures, it deprives artists of their most stimulating audience.

The same causes destroy the soil in which creative artistic ability might flourish. In great art centers in the

[1] Romain Rolland, "Millet."

past handicraftsmen were able to graduate into art by easy stages. The modern factory worker would have to cross a chasm. The monotony of machine work gives no scope for the play of fancy or self-expression. The Lord knows what talent and genius dies stillborn in our factories. Capitalism is not happy with what is individual. It makes its profit in mass production; it revels in turning things out by the hundred thousand. It kills out the older craftsmanship, for instance in Japan. Artistic European workers who come to America feel that they are drowned in commercialism here.

So our economic system is not a sincere friend to beauty either in nature or art. If profit beckons, the beauties of nature are blotted out without remorse. If profit beckons, art is used, but only to be soiled somewhat. For the real development of beauty we need communities that have wealth of their own, a great public with leisure and culture enough to enjoy art, and a working class with leisure and vitality enough to develop the artistic talent in gifted individuals. Why have so many artists been revolutionists at heart?

CHAPTER IV

ONE of the glories of Christianity is the place it gives to love. It sums up all religious duty in love to God, and all ethical duty in love to man. It has set before humanity as the fullest revelation of God and the highest expression of manhood the life of Jesus Christ, whose name is a synonym of love. It has made love the dominant characteristic in the nature of God himself, and therewith has written love across the whole universe.

Love is the force that draws man and man together, the great social instinct of the race. It runs through all our relations and is the foundation of all our institutions. The friendship of classmates, the good will of chance-met strangers, the fellow-feeling of comrades in a cause, the sense of religious brotherhood, are merely different colors of the rainbow into which the white light of love is refracted. The social mission of Christianity is to make this natural instinct strong, durable, pure, holy, and victorious over all selfish and hateful passions. The spirit of Christ allies itself with all other social forces that make for love. It is at enmity with anything that checks love or propagates hate.

No other social organization is so distinctly the institution of love as the home. It is formed when a man and a woman love each other. In their case the natural friendship of two human beings is diversified by the play of sex difference and intensified by sexual love. If they have children, tremendous currents of love are added, running down to them and up from them. The loves of other members of the family, grandparents, brothers, sisters, relatives, converge and intersect in a home. Playmates, neighbors, guests, bring in their good will. As the knee joint of a man is a complicated system of ligatures, so a home is an interlocking system of loves. The more the economic activities have passed from the home to the shop, the more completely has the home become purely an institution of love.

Because the home is God's country, the valuation put on it by us all is exceedingly high. Most women feel that their life gets its full meaning and dignity only when they can have and make a home. Most men toil with little else in mind except to maintain their homes. From the point of view of society the home is an expensive institution. It would be possible to house us all in dormitories and feed us in institutions far more cheaply. To duplicate sitting rooms, dining rooms, and kitchens for every family is an economic waste unless higher interests justify it. Every separate house and cottage of the American type is an architectural and economic expression of the high valuation we put on the home as the institution of love and individuality. Christianity and the home have constituted an offensive and defensive alliance. Each has reënforced the other. Each is crippled when the other is hurt. Anything undermining the home is an invasion of God's country.

To-day the home is being hurt and crippled. Industrialism sweeps the workers together in tightly wedged masses in abnormally large cities. Private property in land turns over the unearned increase in land values to individuals and offers a bonus to anybody who will help to make land scarce for the users. Building materials have grown dear through the capitalistic exhaustion of the forests and through business combinations, and this registers itself in contracted homes.

The wages paid to industrial workers in many lines of employment will not support a home, not even a poor one. The average annual wage of industrial workers throughout the country is about $600, and 75 per cent of them earn less. The United States Commissioner of Labor, when investigating labor conditions after the strike at Lawrence, Mass., in 1912, found that 7275 of the 21,922 employees of the textile mills earned less than $7 even when working full time; 36 per cent of these were males.[1] The high price of the necessaries of life further cuts down the purchasing power of these wages. A couple with young children to support have to wade through the deep waters of poverty. Wife and children are forced to help in earning wages. But experience has shown that after this has become general in any industry, the temporary advantage of this sacrifice disappears again, and the whole family by incessant toil now earn no more than the father alone once earned.

Such an outlook deters many from marriage. The prudent go without children. When the wife is away at work, the home is bereft of the home maker and loses its meaning. Exhaustion and discouragement invite to drink and quarrelsomeness. The higher spiritual satisfactions of the home are washed away like the soil from a denuded mountain side.[2]

This poverty is not the sad necessity of a destitute nation, at least not in America. It is the direct result of an economic system in which property and power are in the hands of one class, and the other class is comparatively helpless. Wages are small in order that profits may be

[1] The report of the Bureau was made by resolution of the Senate, but proved to be so voluminous and thoroughgoing that the Senate ordered only enough copies to be printed to supply the Senate document room. Was this because it was voluminous or because it was thoroughgoing?

[2] I have stated some of these points more fully in "Christianity and the Social Crisis," Chapter V, especially pp. 271–279.

large. God's institution, the home, is being broken up to increase profit.

For an increasing portion of the wage-earning and salary-earning classes the home is becoming hard to attain at all. But when the shelter of the home is locked against men, they are exposed to all the storms of unsatisfied desire. In the home the primal sex passion is bound up with all that is noble, with loyalty, self-sacrifice, child life, common memories and hopes. Outside of the home it becomes predatory, marauding, piratical, a destroyer of existing homes instead of a builder of new homes. Unless we can give the people homes, they will have vice.

In three cities, Chicago, Minneapolis, and Kansas City, a thorough investigation of vice has been made of late, and in each the wretchedness uncovered has been appalling. One of the wisest of women, Jane Addams, has written an illuminating commentary on the facts in her book, "A New Conscience and an Ancient Evil." Every woman who looks forward to exercising the suffrage in coming years should read that book as a pledge to the Almighty that she proposes to take her citizenship seriously.

Miss Addams's book has a message of great hope, for she makes it clear that girls rarely prostitute themselves from any perverse and sinful preference for a life of vice. They are drawn into it by various influences in combination, which are all humanly comprehensible and natural, by instincts which we find in our own hearts and in our sisters and daughters, such as the love of ease, dress, and excitement. The white slave traffic has to maintain an international and expensive organization, play on the ignorance of foreigners and the womanly trustfulness of good girls, and finally use alcohol and physical force in order to recruit the women needed for the business. The girls are not crowding into vice; they have to be trapped and pushed in. If liquor did not paralyze their higher instincts and unleash the lower, most of the men too would turn in disgust from that beastly travesty of love.

There are many causes that are combining to multiply immorality: the ignorance of immigrants, the lack of restraint in city life, the volume of travel, erotic literature, and the lack of religious teaching in our schools. But the recent thorough investigations have driven home the fact that the most powerful creator of prostitution is our economic life. In nearly all sections of the industrial world the wages of women are too low to support them unaided. About 60 per cent of the women workers in the Eastern States get less than $325 a year; only 10 per cent get more than $500. Working under great strain, they are yet unable to make both ends meet or to eke out enough for some larger expense like a pair of shoes or a dress. Business is battering down their nervous capacity for moral resistance. "The increasing nervous energy to which industrial processes daily accommodate themselves, and the speeding up constantly required of the operators, may at any moment so register their results upon the nervous system of a factory girl as to overcome her powers of resistance. Many a working girl at the end of a day is so hysterical and overwrought that her mental balance is plainly disturbed. Hundreds of working girls go directly to bed as soon as they have eaten their suppers. They are too tired to go from home for recreation, too tired to read, and often too tired to sleep." [1] A girl in financial straits "does not go out deliberately to find illicit methods of earning money, she simply yields in a moment of utter weariness and discouragement to the temptations she has been able to withstand up to that moment. The long hours, the lack of comforts, the low pay, the absence of recreation, the sense of good times all about her which she

[1] Jane Addams, "A New Conscience and an Ancient Evil," pp. 72, 77.

cannot share, the conviction that she is rapidly losing health and charm rouse the molten forces within her. A swelling tide of self-pity suddenly storms the banks which have hitherto held her and finally overcomes her instincts for decency and righteousness, as well as the habits of clean living, established by generations of her forebears."

Our economic system is therefore a direct cause of prostitution by the fierceness with which it uses up human life to make profit. It also causes it by the atmosphere of idleness, ease, pleasure, and luxurious habits created in social life by those who live on unearned wealth. The women of the upper classes are an unconscious but very real source of temptation and enervation to the wage-earning girls who are thrown into contact with them. The force of temptation is greatest in those lines of employment where the two classes come into contact, for instance in the department stores and in office work; it is least in the factories where working girls have the stout morality and good sense of their own kind to hold them up. The most exposed situation of all is domestic service, where one or two working women live in social isolation and loneliness among people of a higher class.[1]

The men, too, find the way to hell paved by business. In former times it was militarism which gathered thousands of homeless men and established slimy pools of vice in which they could bathe. To-day similar masses of men are gathered in construction camps and wherever labor is shifting and poorly paid. What can we expect when low wages force men to live with a boarding-boss, sleeping in beds occupied by alternating shifts of men? Polygamy was maintained by the rich, who could afford to have many women; polyandry is maintained by the poor, where many men can afford to support only one woman. It has existed

---

[1] See the explanation of the peculiar temptations in domestic service by Miss Addams, pp. 167-178.

in poor communities, for instance among the mountaineers of Thibet; it has returned under other forms in the industrialism of the present day. Slavery was once the system by which the strong worked the weak, and polygamy was its sexual corollary; the female slave had to yield her womanhood as well as her labor force. Capitalism is the system by which the strong are to-day working the weak, and prostitution is its sexual corollary.

Sexual evils, such as adultery and seduction, will always exist in human society. Their frequency depends on the social control exerted by educated morality and religion. Prostitution differs from them by the money element. It is vice for gain. Some minimum of this, too, may be a permanent fact in society. Even in socialism a woman might prostitute herself to gain industrial advancement or political power for herself or for some one whom she loved. But mass prostitution, such as we know, is inseparable from poverty and from class differences. Socialism deserves our gratitude for insisting on this fact which the Church has failed to see or emphasize.

The economic influences, to which reference has been made, work indirectly and unintentionally toward the breakdown of the family and the multiplication of vice. The men and women who profit by our economic system would angrily and, in most cases, justly deny that they would knowingly take a dollar that had helped to push a girl into the life of a prostitute. On the other hand there are business interests that do it knowingly. The saloons that cater to women; the dance halls that encourage indecent dances and supply long intermissions for the consumption of liquor; pleasure resorts and excursion steamers; theaters, music halls, and moving-picture shows that use the ever ready attractiveness of sex interests, — are all smoothing the downward road — and they know it. The liquor trade is a big section of our economic apparatus, and it is inseparably bound up with sexual vice. Where recreation is supplied by commercial agencies and run for profit, they find it profitable to encourage the use of liquor and to play on the sex interest, because under these two influences money is spent most freely. That fundamental characteristic of the capitalistic system, the necessity of making profit, logically works out these results when capital is invested that way.

In recent years prostitution itself has become an organized business on a large scale, served by commissioned agents and using the modern means of communication. Just as capitalism generally has outgrown the little store and shop, so the white slave traffic is outgrowing the simple ways of the madame and developing systematic methods for getting and serving customers, and recruiting its service. It has to overcome many difficulties, pay taxes to the police and politicians, and keep the reformers from butting in, but the profits are enormous, and it overcomes the difficulties with that shrewdness and energy which Business always develops when big profit is in sight.

Prostitution destroys the health and degrades the personality of the victims. It is also the destroyer of the home as an institution. Every prostitute is the competitor of every wife. When prostitution is once set up and organized, it has to go out for trade like every other active business. From the house of prostitution secret lines of influence run into the respectable homes of the city. Incurable diseases contracted there leap over the chasm of social and moral separation, and blight the health and the affection of chaste and noble women. The memories and imaginations stocked by images of vice are a permanent suggestive force that undermines the single-minded loyalty of the home.

> "I've taken my fun where I've found it,
> An' now I must pay for my fun,

For the more you 'ave known o' the others
The less will you settle to one." [1]

Theories of free love get their active force through personal or social conditions. In all industrial cities are large bodies of men and women, many of them highly intelligent and thoughtful, who see no way of marrying without a drop in their standard of living which they do not care to risk. Business and modern ways of recreation throw the sexes together in a freedom formerly unknown. They feel all the old attraction of man and woman, but no hope of love under the old standards of morality. They are demanding to know what they are to do. Under such conditions the loose theories on sex relations, with which happily married people may toy in safety, spring into grim insistence. The wish will be father to the thought; desire will justify the intellect in breaking bounds. Socialist thought carries so large an ingredient of free-love theories because it is the product of these proletarian intellectuals. The ultimate blame for the theories rests with the conditions that secrete the theories as germ diseases secrete toxic forces in the blood.

If the home is the institution of love, and if love is of God, then the forces that cripple home life are an invasion of God's dominions. We have seen what a large direct and indirect influence our economic life has in breaking down the home and building up vice from the rotting remnants. If all the fallen girls of a city, including all those who lapse into evil occasionally and secretly, could be brought together and could formulate the causes of their sin and ruin intelligently, as God sees them, it would constitute an accusation against our unregenerate business life that would drive us frantic. If any one of us found an individual ruining his wife, his sister, his daughter, or his

---

[1] Kipling, " Barrack-room Ballads."

sweetheart, his moral indignation would probably grow so fierce that it would sweep all accustomed restraints away, and public sentiment would set the letter of the law aside to justify almost any violence he would commit in his anger. To any one who has learned to think socially, and to understand the collective forces of society which redeem or ruin their thousands, our economic system looms up like a great collective ravisher of our women, and what shall we do with him ?

CHAPTER V

Selfishness and the social spirit both belong to the make-up of human nature. Egoism is the original warp, and self-sacrificing devotion for others is the woof that is woven in if character develops well. Both are necessary and useful. They blend in different proportions according to maturity and elevation of character. Except in fine individuals or in special relations, as in the patriots and mothers of the race, the instinct of self-interest is stronger than that of devotion to the common interest, and if the two come in conflict, the common good suffers. Society always forms a self-protecting league to keep down the excessive selfishness of its members by various forms of condemnation, and to develop public devotion by education, patriotism, and religion. The ideal situation is created when self-interest and the common interest run in the same direction, and selfishness of its own will bends its stout shoulders to the yoke of public service. A community that does not solve the problem of yoking the able to the service of the common good finds its strongest sons its most insidious enemies.

The town, the city, the state, the nation are the most inclusive organizations for the common good, offering every citizen a thousand forms of protection and service. The problem for our selfishness then is, how to contribute as little in the way of taxes and service to the community, and how to get as many benefits from it as possible, — especially somewhat more than our neighbor is getting. If any man has never played at this game, he is a white raven. The "pull" is as old as history. Cain seems to have suspected Abel of working a pull on the Lord, and "influence" will last far into Kingdom Come. Every political community has the perpetual task of making its members toe the mark, just as every family has to work out a fair division of the chores on the one hand and the pudding on the other, and finds it an intricate business.

A community of equals, however, usually succeeds in protecting itself against the selfishness of its members and establishing a rough justice of paying and getting. The danger begins when any individual, or any organized group, becomes so strong that they can defy or paralyze the organization that serves the common good. For instance, under feudalism great vassals could become so powerful through the lands and privileges bestowed on them that they could defy the king's courts and the military powers of the Crown, and set up as a menacing State within the State. These feudal nobles were fundamentally great landowners, and their power corresponds to that wielded by the lords of industry in an industrial age. To take another instance, the Church is an organized group held together by the tremendous force of religion, and it, too, may become a dangerous power within the State, using political methods to extort special favors and concessions. Its power becomes intolerable when its spiritual cohesion is increased by large vested wealth and semipolitical power, as in the case of the Roman Catholic Church in the Middle Ages and the Mormon hierarchy to-day. The Mafia is a secret organization in Italy, which seems first to have grown up among disbanded mercenaries in Sicily. It has protected its members, levied tribute on others, punished its enemies, and paralyzed and defied the State. The East India Company and the Netherlands Company sent ambassadors and waged war like sovereign States, and hunted down interloping competitors like pirates. They

T

believed in the "closed shop." These are simply historical examples to show how individuals or social groups may set up special interests that antagonize the common good and threaten the very stability of the State as the organ of the common welfare.

Now, this is exactly the condition that is growing up among us under new forms. We have individuals in our country so rich and powerful that it is practically inconceivable that they should be brought to book and punished like ordinary citizens. In every community there is a group of propertied men who may not be organized, but who act in sympathy, and the community has to put forth tremendous efforts to enforce its will against their will, even for a short time. Our great corporations are States within the State; some of them employ more men and own more property than sovereign commonwealths; they enjoy semipublic powers in law, and in times of trouble build fortifications and assemble armed forces of their own. On many points the interest of these powerful groups is identical with the common good, and that is the saving element in the situation. But to some extent their interest is pitted against the common good. They need not only the ordinary protection of life and property which every citizen expects, but special legal privileges, protection against competitors, grants of mineral resources, franchises, and patent monopolies. They want these privileges as cheaply, securely, and permanently as possible. It is manifestly not for the common good to alienate coal lands permanently or give them away for a song. But that is what a corporation would like best. Its private interest runs one way, and the common good another. After they have obtained privileges men want freedom to exploit them with a minimum of State interference and restriction, and they now have their wealth and vested interests to back them in dealing with the officers of the community.

By granting away a multitude of public possessions and powers, we have armed the natural selfishness of the possessors with the means of blocking the common good. We have enlisted the interests of the ablest men in the community against its welfare. If a city built and owned a street railway, it would sell bonds at a moderate rate of interest. Every citizen would be directly interested in having efficient service, and in having politics clean in order that service might be efficient. Those who invested in the bonds would be interested in the financial stability of the city and its undertakings, but their bonds would earn no more, whether the railway charged a five-cent or a three-cent fare. On the other hand, when a corporation is given a franchise to use the streets for its business, it not only sells bonds with a fixed rate of interest, but also issues stock with a fluctuating rate of income. The dividends on the stock will be large if the company runs crowded cars, charges a five-cent fare and an extra for transfers, and works its employees twelve hours a day. On all these points the private interest of the stockholders runs against the common good, and as the stockholders are usually the wealthy and influential men, we have practically organized these able men into a force to hinder the welfare of the city. In order to protect its lucrative excesses from public interference the street railway must secure influence in local politics, and that again may paralyze the efficiency of the city government in every other direction.

The antagonism between private interest and public welfare is most glaring where private interest gets its profit out of social conditions which the moral sentiment of the community has outgrown and repudiated. The slave-holding oligarchy which ruled the South before the War numbered only about ten thousand men.[1] But to protect their private interest in an immoral source of profit, they

---

[1] References in Simons, " Social Forces in American History," Chapter XX.

forced an outgrown and inefficient form of labor on their communities, kept the poor whites in poverty, retarded the industrial development of the South by one generation or more, muzzled and perverted the social conscience of their people, and were willing permanently to disrupt the Union. The private interest that has invested its money in the wholesale and retail liquor business is seeking to fasten on an angry people a relic of moral barbarism which the awakened conscience and the scientific intellect of the world are combining to condemn. In such cases we can readily recognize the clash between private interest and the common good.

But there are other cases, more respectable and not so clear. For instance: the Tobacco Trust encouraging the cigarette evil; poisonous patent medicines and adulterated food breaking down the health of the people; yellow journalism pandering to the love of excitement and sex passion to increase sales; the Western Union hiring little boys to do its messenger work and sending them to saloons and houses of prostitution at night; respectable capital maintaining murderous tenements because they return 15 per cent to 25 per cent in rent. The gold-mining industries in and around Johannesburg in the Transvaal have concentrated a quarter of a million of kafirs in compounds, segregating them from their families because that is cheap. As a result of this unnatural condition the outrages on white women have put the whole community under terror and created a tension between the races which threatens massacres. By child labor the new industries of the present South are using up the manhood and womanhood on which the future South must build its greatness. High food prices are pressing on the health of every family that lives on its own work. The common good demands the elimination of the middlemen and their profits. But the middlemen do not want to be eliminated and block any public measure that will put the consumer in more direct touch with the producer, such as genuine public markets and the parcels post.   If a staple crop is short, public interest would demand that the supply be economized and distributed in such a way that prices will be kept as low as possible.   Private interest sees its opportunity in the public disaster, buys up the supply in advance, accentuates the shortage, and extorts extraordinary profits.   Public interest demands that a new invention be promptly added to the general equipment of civilization, and the inventor rewarded by a moderate royalty and by public praise.   Private interest has often taken advantage of the necessities of the inventor to buy him out for a trifle, and has then held up the progress of society during the life of the patent by monopoly prices.

Capital is cosmopolitan.   It does not follow the flag; it follows its one guiding star — Profit.   Individual business men may be keenly patriotic and loyal, but Capital collectively comes close to being "the Man without a Country." If higher returns are offered abroad, it will seek investment there with the dispassionate single-mindedness of water seeking its level.   American capital is now building up Chinese railways and industries, and so speeding the day when American industry will have to meet the full force of Chinese competition.   The American people have long taxed themselves in order to foster certain industries, and now these same industries, fed by tariff favors, are selling their goods more cheaply in Europe than in our own country.   Our nation has endowed the great railways with an empire of land five times the acreage of Ohio;[1] States and communities have given them millions in bonuses and bounties to aid railway construction.   As an expression of patriotic gratitude they have defrauded the people and corrupted the governments.   There is hardly a State that

[1] Railroads and other corporations have received from the Federal Government and from States 190,000,000 acres.   Homesteaders have been given only 115,000,000.   The Government has sold 180,000,000 acres.

has not been dominated by its great railway. The inflow of immigrants from the south and east of Europe was first set going by corporations that needed cheap and docile labor to keep down the wages and the spirit of the native American workingmen. Their coming has since been stimulated systematically by the great transportation interests that make their heaviest profits from the steerage passengers. These private interests have worked against the common good. They have burdened our cities with an undigested mass of alien people; they have lowered the standard of living for millions of native Americans; they have checked the propagation of the Teutonic stock; they have radically altered the racial future of our nation; and they have set a new destiny for our national religion. If in the next thirty years the Catholic population outnumbers the Protestant, and if the Church then applies Roman theories about Church and State to American life and politics, we shall owe that serious situation in part to the capitalistic interests that overcame the poverty and conservatism of the European peasantry and set this mass immigration moving.

A war is the occasion on which the maximum of self-sacrifice for the common good is demanded from the mass of individuals. The people have to bear heavy taxes, requisitions, and damage to their property. Countless families see their sons go to sickness or death for the protection of their country. In a popular war a passion of devotion seizes all. But when the men of the nation come out to fight, Capital goes into hiding. Securities fall in price. The nation has to pay a dollar to get a loan of ninety cents, eighty cents, seventy cents. The greater the need of money, the higher the price of it. Men are drafted; money is not, except in taxes. After the Civil War certain great capitalists took pride in the fact that they had bought government papers and staked their fortunes on the success of their country. They felt they had done something out of the ordinary. Yet, reckoned in terms of humanity, or judged by the eyes of him who praised the widow's mites, a money king losing half his millions and keeping the other half would not be in the same class with the plainest little woman who gave her boy, the fruit of her own body, the darling of her soul, and the hope of her old age.

High finance is often praised as a power making for the peace of nations. That is doubtless true. Money is timid and loves peace. A war hampers the free flow of business. But Capital is quite ready to push a nation to the verge of war if that serves its purposes. The big interests that build dreadnaughts and manufacture ammunition are a very powerful factor in keeping the nations armed to the teeth in times of peace. The capitalists who invest their money at high rates in the securities of shaky states like Turkey or some of the South American republics are always ready to use their country as a debt-collecting agency and to threaten the peace of the world. The activities of the Western nations in the far East all have as their objective the safety of investments and the extension of markets for the capitalist class. No war is fought without shouting the watchwords of the common good; but rarely, if ever, is any war fought in which private interests are not the real force demanding the war. On the other hand when commercial interests see no profit in a war, no moral or patriotic interest counts. It was Northern business that tried to suppress abolitionist agitation because sectional antagonism hurt trade. In 1812 New England merchants were opposed to our war with England for business reasons, and they did all they could to cripple our government, supplying food to the British ships, refusing to subscribe to the national loan, encouraging their militia to rebel, and advocating secession.[1]

[1] Babcock, " Rise of American Nationality," pp. 156–158.

Great numbers of capitalists laid the foundation for their fortunes in our Civil War. Army supplies opened up a tremendous market for uniforms and blankets, arms and ammunitions, and the unchanging character of these masses of goods gave the widest scope to the wholesale methods of capitalism. But Capital was not satisfied with legitimate profits. "So tremendous was the graft in connection with contracts for military supplies that most historians draw back in horror when they have lifted but a corner of the thick blanket of concealment that those who profited by the plunder have drawn over the mess. One Congressional committee, headed by Robert Dale Owen, son of Robert Owen, the Utopian Socialist, uncovered frauds of $17,000,000 in $50,000,000 worth of contracts."[1] One of the main objects of the Federal campaign was to prevent the exportation of cotton from the South in order to cripple Southern finances. From the point of view of the North, to assist in marketing cotton gave aid and comfort to the enemy and was treasonable. But when cotton was ten cents a pound in the South and fifty cents in the North, the profit was too great for patriotism. Northern merchants, in collusion with federal army officers, passed contraband cotton over the line, thereby prolonged the war, the outcome of which was inevitable, sacrificed the lives of additional men on both sides, and increased the debt resulting from the war. Private interest was against the common good.

The distorting influence exerted by private financial interests on American political life is so familiar that it scarcely needs discussion. It is fair to say that back of every chronic corruption has been some private interest that needed silence or favors. "As the smoke lifts we can mark just who are resisting law and corrupting government. In the cities the fight is chiefly with the vice caterers and the public-service corporations. The former want a 'wide-

[1] Simons, "Social Forces in American History," p. 280.

open' town.   The latter want unhampered enjoyment of
their monopoly power.   Battling along with these big
interests are bankers scheming for deposits of city funds,
rookery landlords in terror of the health-officer, business
men intent on grabbing an alley or a water-front, and con-
tractors eager to 'job' public works." [1]   When private
interests want something that is against public interest, they
are willing to pay for the favor.   After a time those in control get the appetite, and levy blackmail even on undertakings that serve the public in legitimate ways.   Corruption in politics is simply the application of commercial
methods and principles to the administration of government.   In business the middleman charges a commission
when he puts through a deal between two parties.   Why
should he not do so in politics?   In business a man who
controls a commodity will charge a monopoly price and
would be considered a fool if he did not.   A set of men controlling a legislature or a city administration have monopoly control of the machinery that turns out franchises or
contracts.   Why should they not charge a price to those
who want the goods?   It is proof of the regenerate condition of the State that what is legitimate in Business is a
crime in the State.

The most influential and permanent legislative body in
the nation, the United States Senate, was notoriously
under the control of the great Interests for years, and in
many respects they turned a body that is to serve the
common good into a force that betrayed it.   This is the
essence of treason.   The Senators were appointed by the
railroads and express companies, and they in turn nomi-
nated the federal judges and fixed in the courts, which are
now the most influential organization of government, a
number of men who are constitutionally predisposed to
side with the private interests against the common good.

[1] Professor E. A. Ross, "Sin and Society," p. 165.

The tenure of the judges is such that only the slow action of death or a revolution can change the bias thus set up for years to come. Even five years ago there was still general confidence that the courts had remained untouched by commercialism and faithful to the common good. That conviction is now slowly disintegrating as our political education is going on. The entire upheaval in the political alignment of 1912, the demand for direct primaries, for direct legislation, for the recall of judges, for the popular election of senators, are an expression of the profound and durable conviction of the nation, drawn from a fearfully costly process of education, that our whole political organization, as it stood ten years ago, had been turned into an instrument to victimize the people on behalf of private interests. Really, nothing more damning can be said than this tremendous verdict of a whole nation.

As business outgrows the automatic checks of competition the need for government inspection, investigation, interference, and control becomes constantly greater if the common good is not to be surrendered helplessly to monopoly extortion. Publicity and a clear recognition of the facts have become as essential to the body politic in its complex modern life as free and unobstructed action of the brain is to the physical body. But that is what the great private interests do not want. They invariably resist investigation and seek to paralyze all private and public agencies of scrutiny and publicity. "They are able to gag critics, hobble investigators, hood the press, and muzzle the law. Drunk with power, in office and club, in church and school, in legislature and court, they boldly make their stand, ruining the innocent, shredding the reputations of the righteous, destroying the careers and opportunities of their assailants, dragging down pastor and scholar, publicist and business man, from livelihood and influence, unhorsing alike faithful public servant, civic champion, and knight-errant of conscience, and all the while gathering into loathsome captivity the souls of multitudes of young men." [1]

We should expect that the persons in charge of an orphan asylum, a reformatory, or any charitable agency would turn their minds to the task of finding out what multiplies orphans, what demoralizes half-grown boys and girls, and what brings paupers and defectives into institutions faster than charity can put them on their feet.   Yet Mr. Edward T. Devine, editor of the *Survey*, in his presidential address before the National Conference of Charities and Corrections in 1906 said: "I have yet to find the report of an asylum or reformatory that deals intelligently and fearlessly with these questions."   He said that all forms of pauperism, degeneracy, and dependence require a conjunction between individual weakness and an overt temptation or unfavorable condition which would not exist if it were not to the advantage of some other party.   "The most profitable task of modern philanthropy is to find that other party and to deal by radical methods with him."   Yet philanthropy dares not undertake what is evidently its chief intellectual task. The horrible exploitation and robbery practiced by commercial concerns on helpless prisoners through connivance of the State is the one subject that cries for discussion wherever prisons are mentioned.   Yet the American Prison Association has apparently covered the subject of contract prison labor with decent silence, and it was only the persistence of one plucky woman, Miss Kate Barnard, State Commissioner of Charities in Oklahoma, that forced the convention in 1911 to give room for its discussion.   When she appealed to the religion and humanity of her hearers, she carried the audience by storm, and a strong committee was appointed to investigate the whole subject.[2]

---

[1] Professor E. A. Ross, "Sin and Society," p. 99.

[2] *Survey*, Nov. 4, 1911. Several magazines have published articles on prison labor in 1911 and 1912. See, for instance, the articles by Julian Leavitt, *American Magazine*, July, 1911, February, March, April, 1912.

If a man were caught in the house of an enemy, and he should perceive from indubitable symptoms that a subtle poison was being conveyed to him in his food, which was acting on his nerves in such a way that they no longer gave a clear and trustworthy report of what his eyes saw and his ears heard, but filled his mind with hallucinations, he would doubtless feel that his case was desperate, and that he must keep his brain in working order though he starved. The press performs for modern society the function of the nerves. It registers the facts, communicates them to the centers concerned, and spreads before the community the data on which public action must be based. If the press purposely states what is false, or colors and unbalances what is true, because it is controlled by some ulterior motive, then it breaks faith with the public and becomes a treacherous force to be watched. Hurry, carelessness, ignorance, and party passion we can allow for because they are human, but tampering with the public intelligence is a crime against the common good. But precisely this seems to be done, and very widely. As evidence of it we have the fact that the editorial page has almost lost its old-time power to lead the people, and we have repeatedly had the spectacle of all the papers in a city talking one way and their readers overwhelmingly voting the other way. Since the people have learned to distrust the editorials, the poison is administered by means of doctored news. The most important events, facts which tremendously concern a people that is fighting for its freedom and its property, are passed over with suspicious lightness of touch. Other articles opposing public ownership or direct legislation are so full of facts and so carefully written that we wonder what man in that newspaper office turned out such material, or whether perhaps it was furnished by the press bureau of some big Interest. The newspaper, like all the other higher organs of social life, has gradually come under the control of capitalistic organization and methods.   The days of the great editors who controlled their papers and made them serve their convictions, the days of Greeley, Dana, Halstead, Medill, are almost gone.   The journalist has become the hired man of a corporation.   A paper is owned and controlled by one or more capitalists, who are in the newspaper business for profit, directly and indirectly.   By their other investments, their business relations, and their social sympathies they are in touch with the interests of property, and if they were not, their advertisers would compel them to be.   Mr. William Marion Reedy, the brilliant editor of the St. Louis *Mirror*, speaking before his professional associates of the Missouri Press Association in 1908, drew a profoundly sad picture of the pseudoliberty of the press.   At the close he tried to cheer up by mentioning the agencies through which a path could still be kept open for free and honest thought. One was pamphlet literature, the other the comparatively free country newspapers.   The former would be a return to the one-horse methods of our fathers before the newspaper had been developed; the latter is an appeal to the rural and noncapitalistic portions of present-day society to come and save the rest of us.   This summary of Mr. Reedy's hopes is more eloquent of his despair than any of the black facts he recounted.   He warned the country editor who might attempt to speak freely, that "he will find that all the machinery for the making of public opinion is in the hands of people whose interest it is that public opinion shall in no way interfere with their graft.   He will find his every mail burdened with printed slips from various publicity bureaus, which he can use free, and in every case he will find that the purpose and purport of this slip matter is to bolster up some great private interest built upon public rights and property, or to discredit some man or movement proposing to put a check to the aggrandizement of such wealth by the restoration to the community of the rights which have been filched away from it through the connivance of corrupt representatives."[1]

Within an average lifetime we have watched the private interests grow as when boys roll a snowball on the ground in moist snow. They have amalgamated, combined, and come under centralized management with increasing swiftness and precision. In 1911 forty-nine railways with over four billions of capital stock were owned by 310,581 holders; sixty-seven industrial concerns with over three billions of stock were owned by 435,640 stockholders. But individuals often hold stock in a number of concerns. If all duplication of names was cut out, and all the little people were eliminated who hold a few shares as a nest egg, the ownership of this enormous wealth would probably simmer down to a hundred thousand persons. But the actual control of these seven billions is in the hands of far fewer still. It would be possible to assemble around one table a number of gentlemen who could control the bulk of the mobile wealth of a nation of ninety million souls. Mr. George M. Reynolds, of the Continental and Commercial Bank of Chicago, speaking to a family gathering of bankers in December, 1911, said: "I believe the money power now lies in the hands of a dozen men. I plead guilty to being one, in the last analysis, of these men."[2] A very few persons control the Clearing House Association and the Stock Exchange in New York. They can withdraw privileges from banks and corporations and put them out of business, withhold credit from new enterprises that would compete with their interests, create bull and bear markets, and if they should so determine, cause a national commercial crisis.[3] The safety

[1] Reedy, "The Myth of a Free Press." The address can be obtained from the *Mirror*, St. Louis, for five cents.

[2] Quoted in the autobiography of Senator La Follette, *American Magazine*, July, 1912. He says that the Proceedings in which this utterance was printed have since been suppressed.

[3] Many sober observers believe that the crisis of 1908 was purposely started by certain great financial interests.

and welfare of the nation is at their mercy and depends on their respect for the law and their concern for the public good. But great power inevitably weakens the force of moral restraint. Kings have always had a moral code of their own; the crimes of common people were the peccadilloes of princes. There is ample indication that our Lords of Capital are no longer on the ordinary plane of restraint, but, like Nietzsche's superman, have risen beyond the realm of Good and Evil. In the last panic, for instance, the banks refused to return money to those who had deposited it with them and created a new currency which had no more legal standing than any counterfeit, and no one was punished for it.

The tremendous power of the private interests has created a malaria of timidity in American life. When a great industrial plant has been established in a town for some years, the real estate values, the retail business, and the jobs of the workingmen are so dependent on its continuance, that if there is any threat of its removal, the whole community will kiss the feet of the corporation and promise to be good. The Illinois Steel Company for years made new land at South Chicago by dumping its slag in Lake Michigan, for which it had no legal sanction. Public Works Commissioner Joseph Medill Patterson, being a socialist, refused permission for further construction of that kind and brought suit to recover the land made. The citizens thought this obstacle was the cause for the erection of the great plant of the Company at Gary and two hundred of them went to the State capital at their own expense and lobbied for two weeks for a bill permitting the company to fill in the lake front at a nominal expense.[1] On Sept. 30, 1911, the great dam of the pulp mill at Austin, Pa., broke and a wave of death and destruction swept away the town. The dam had been cracked and unsafe, and the people knew it menaced their lives. The town authorities or any number

---

[1] John A. Fitch in the *Survey*, 1911, pp. 1146 and 1159.

of citizens could have sued for protection and the courts had power to order the dam strengthened or destroyed, but no such collective protest was made. Why not? " The answer is perhaps sadder than the little processions which tracked the wet ground about the morgue. It shows a predominantly American community so saturated with dependence upon an outside power from which it drew its livelihood that its very instinct for self-preservation was inhibited. Nor has it so far recovered itself, under the sting of the disaster, as to express an appreciable resentment toward those in whose power it was to do whatever might have been done to remove the danger. Two weeks after the catastrophe, not even a damage suit had been started." [1] The old American spirit of self-reliance that was bred on the Western frontier will weaken as the frontier disappears. The present insurgent movement in the West is the last chance to harness that splendid rebel force to the salvation of the nation. If that fails, we must look to the immigrant Jews and socialists to rescue the liberties of America for the native born.

To a Christian mind the ugliest fact is the vindictiveness with which the private interests fight righteousness. We can understand how honorable men have come to underpay their workers, employ child labor, demand rebates, and even bribe aldermen. But when the public conscience has awakened and seeks to end these collective wrongs, why do these men strike and hack at the hands that are trying to free them from a situation in which they are more or less forced to do questionable things? The real hindrance to every reform movement and philanthropic undertaking lies, not in the ignorance or viciousness of the people, but in the active and intelligent opposition of those who derive profit from wrong or inhumanity. Christian theology has been right in locating sin deeper than in ignorance. It

[1] Graham R. Taylor, " A Man-made Flood," in the *Survey*, Nov. 4, 1911.

is no slight task to wean a nation from the age-long customs of alcoholism, or to reconstruct a mass of unsanitary houses for the proper housing of the people. But if we merely had to save the present drunkards and teach the young to abstain from drink, and if we merely had to overcome the architectural and financial difficulties of the housing problem, we could shout for joy, for our salvation would be nigh. What makes these reforms hard is the malignant fighting force created by the profits of the liquor business and the rents of rotten tenements. The Pure Food Bill would have passed years before if the capital interested in adulteration had not fought action, and it would be administered more efficiently to-day if the same interests were not crippling its enforcement.

Wherever any reformer has shown persistent determination to loosen the clutch of privilege, he has been made to suffer for it. If he merely suppressed vice, he was endangered politically, though he might be supported by the high-class business community. But if he dealt courageously with the public service corporations, he found himself matched against a force with which few have wrestled successfully. Pingree in Michigan, Golden Rule Jones in Toledo, Henry George in New York, Tom L. Johnson in Cleveland, are through with their fight, and we can lay the civic crown on their graves. They fought for us. "There is not a man in the United States to-day who has tried honestly to do anything to change the fundamental conditions that make for poverty, disease, vice and crime in our cities, in our courts, and in our legislatures, who, at the very time in which his efforts seemed most likely to succeed, has not been suddenly turned upon and rent by the great newspaper publications."[1] And they were mere agents of larger interests. The labor movement has been one of the strongest and, on the whole, one of the most beneficent

[1] Reedy, "The Myth of a Free Press," p. 15.

U

reformatory influences in modern life.[1]   As for socialism, even its opponents are admitting that it has even now accomplished more to better the condition of the working class in Europe and to force the question of international peace on the military powers than any other influence. Yet both the labor movement and socialism have been bitterly opposed by the whole capitalistic world.

The self-interest of the individual is a necessary part of human nature and may be a beneficent force in human society.   It would be a calamity to rob this instinct of its incentives and its motive force.   We want free, strong, self-reliant men with elbow room for action.   But when a theory of so-called economic individualism has resulted in turning the property of a nation over to a limited group; in equipping them with rights and powers which only the community should wield; in pitting the self-interest of the most resourceful men against the public welfare; in giving them power to hold up the progress of humanity by extorting monopoly profits; in cowing public opinion, persecuting the truth tellers, and hog-tying the State, — then that theory has gone to seed and it is time to plow the ground for a new crop.   "It is a condition and not a theory that confronts us."   With unanimous moral judgment mankind has always loved and exalted those who sacrificed their self-interest to the common welfare, and despised those who sold out the common good for private profit.   The cross of Christ stands for the one principle of action; the bag of Judas stands for the other.   God's country begins where men love to serve their fellows.   The Devil's country begins where men eat men.   I submit the proposition that the overgrowth of private interests has institutionalized an unchristian principle, and that we must reverse the line of movement if we want to establish the law of Christ.

[1] See Ely, "Labor Movement in America"; Sumner and Adams, "Labor Problems"; Simons, "Social Forces in American History," Chapter XVII, on the early labor movement.

CHAPTER VI

THE TRAGEDY OF DIVES

A YOUNG settler and his wife are sitting at the door of their shack, looking off across the prairie where the heat lightning is playing around the horizon. It has been a long and grilling day, and they are too tired to talk. But they are content, for the crops promise fine, and inside the shack the baby is lying with its rosy limbs thrown out as if they were roots of a sturdy young pine gathering strength.

Under the same sky far to the eastward lies a hillside dotted with graves. The men that filled them were young, strong, and dearly loved, and they died untimely deaths, but all about them is their native land, undivided and under one flag. They ought not to have died, but they did not die altogether in vain.

Labor and death are our portion, but we can still sing our song at our work if only we know that we are spending ourselves freely for the folks we love and the cause we cherish, and that more abundant life will spring from the grain that falls in the furrow.

It is different when the sacrifices of our life are wrested from us without the free consent of our love. The working people are kept close to the line of bare necessities. The margin of ease and liberty, in which the finer joys can grow and blossom, is narrow and stony for many of them. What might make their life freer and richer goes to others. Some of their higher possibilities are stunted that the gifts of others may unfold the better. Perhaps such a sacrifice may be justified in the long range of evolution if it wins a permanent gain for the advancement of humanity. The upper classes are the beneficiaries of our unequal system of distribution. Are they at least really benefited? Are they developing that higher type of humanity which will at the last reorganize society, conquer want, and save the rest?

If we believed the teachings of Jesus, we could save ourselves the inquiry.[1] He said that riches have so fatal an attraction over the mind of man that his heart is sure to be bound up with his wealth. As a consequence the service of money and the service of God are mutually exclusive, and a man must make his choice.[2] A rich young man of fine character who longed for the true life was advised by him to dispose of his wealth in the most useful way and join the disciples on a footing of equality. When he could not wrench himself free, Jesus saw in this a confirmation of his belief that it is next to impossible for a rich man to enter the higher life.[3] He was deeply moved when Zacchæus, who had a Roman franchise to farm the taxes of a wealthy district, did cut loose and promised to make fourfold restoration of all his graft.[4] The only real picture of hell in the whole Bible was given us by Jesus to show the fate of a rich man who had apparently done nothing wrong except to eat and dress well, and let a poor man lie sick at his gate.[5]

The greatest and most searching moral teachers of humanity have agreed with Jesus in his moral diagnosis of the classes that live on unearned wealth. The demand for voluntary poverty which Tolstoy has repeated to our unbelieving age is simply the heroic corollary of the moral condemnation of unearned riches. The pathetic flight of the dying Russian was the last protest against the silken strands with which his home had still bound him to what

---

[1] See "Christianity and the Social Crisis," pp. 74–82.
[2] Matt. vi. 19–24.　　[3] Matt. xix. 16–24.　　[4] Luke xix. 1–10.
[5] Luke xvi. 19–31, to be taken in connection with xvi. 1–15.

his soul condemned. Wherever the modern novel brushes
romantic glamour away and reports the facts, it tells us
that the "best people" as a class are not good. Quite a
list of novels could be made up that deal with the very problem raised by Jesus: Can a rich man be saved? And the
general reply is: It can be done, but it takes an heroic cure
to do it. Howells bankrupts Silas Lapham; Mark Twain
turns a Prince into a Pauper; William Allen White breaks
the heart of a Certain Rich Man; and Rudyard Kipling,
that glorifier of the strong-armed class, rolls the son of a
railroad magnate from the deck of an Atlantic liner and
quarantines him on a Gloucester fishing smack among the
Captains Courageous in order to save his poor soul.

The man on the street nowadays is cynical enough about
the rich, but he would not stand for the radical teachings of
Saint Francis or Tolstoy. Nor has the Church ever backed
the judgments of her Master except with many qualifications. It sees too many genuine Christians among the
rich, — fine, lovable people, clean, sober, frugal, hard-
working, affectionate, kindly, spiritually-minded, abundant
in good works. How can it deny them salvation? Perhaps the Church has long meant something different by
salvation than Jesus did. The Church has meant getting
to heaven; Jesus meant living the right life with God and
man. He took the social view of salvation, and that explains his doubts about the fitness of the rich to enter the
Kingdom of God. Moreover, Jesus thought more scienti-
fically about moral questions than most of us. The common man looks at a given rich man and finds him a good
fellow. Jesus looked at the moral forces inherent in wealth
and inequality, at their assimilating power, and he feared
for the latter end when riches had done their work.

Many of the fine people whom we know among the rich
have come up out of poor and simple families, and their
habits of frugality and hard work are the endowment of

their youth, a foreign importation in the Land of Money, like the sturdy health of the peasant women that come to us from abroad. The old-fashioned Christian character of some wealthy saint is so attractive just because it contradicts its surroundings, like a simple, old ambrotype in a jeweled frame. The family, the Church, and the school with their regenerate influences create Christian characters, and wealth cannot disintegrate them in one generation. When such families educate their children and grandchildren in studied simplicity, and secure women of fine character to care for them and teach them, they are quarantining their loved ones with a very true instinct, and surrounding them with wholesome influences drawn from God's country. The question is whether their fight with the environment created by wealth will be permanently successful.

In old families of established wealth, also, we meet choice characters, simple-minded and democratic. Some of them have been saved by the new democratic or socialist spirit that has reached them, perhaps in diluted form, and has filled them with a saving indignation against themselves. Others are simply some of God's elect, some of the beautiful souls we find in slum and palace and cannot explain from their surroundings.

The rich are not all bad individually, and the poor are not all good. Ruskin sums up both with charming impartiality: "In a community regulated only by laws of supply and demand, and protected from open violence, the persons who become rich are, generally speaking, industrious, resolute, proud, covetous, prompt, methodical, sensible, unimaginative, insensitive, and ignorant. The persons who remain poor are the entirely foolish, the entirely wise, the idle, the reckless, the humble, the thoughtful, the dull, the imaginative, the sensitive, the well-informed, the improvident, the irregularly and impulsively wicked, the clumsy knave, the open thief, and the entirely merciful, just, and godly person."[1] The question is not so much whether some rich men are still good, as what their riches will ultimately do with their goodness. The monks had a proverb: "Godliness brings forth Wealth, but the daughter devours the mother."

Unearned wealth puts a man on the road to perdition by putting it in his power to quit work. He no longer has to work unless he wants to. He learns to take vacations often, at week ends, in midwinter to Florida, in summer to Europe, and the cables that anchor him to work are slipped as his wealth becomes ample and secure. There is a decreasing nexus between his income and his personal work. As long as his wealth is invested in one concern, he gets behind it and works hard. When he has many investments, bonds, mortgages, stock, his work comes to consist of "looking after his investments" and deciding where to place his accruing surplus. That is an important function, and if he does it poorly, he will have to go to work again. The decision of investors in the mass is also highly important for the course which industry takes. But it can hardly be called hard and productive labor. Now the community of true men is a community of labor, and when a man gets outside of the common work of mankind, he gets outside of the Kingdom of God. Except in sickness, childhood, age, and in spells of rest and play, it is ethically bad for any man to be idle. Every group instinctively feels so about its own members and resents the person who looks on while the rest work. The propertied classes have always felt the moral turpitude of idleness when they have seen it in the working class, and have even passed vagrancy laws by which an idle man on the road can be seized and put to work breaking stone, or making chairs for a corporation in prison. But within the social group to which the rich be-

[1] "Unto this Last," p. 106.

long this sound moral resentment against idleness does not apply. For a man who is rich, it is no disgrace to idle; and still less for a woman. We have double weights and measures for the rich and poor in ethics. But God's laws are not so easily set aside. "If any will not work, neither let him eat." Somehow, somewhere, and somewhen he will suffer for it if he turns his back on the great community of workers. If he will not work for God, the Devil will find something for his idle hands to do. And in any case he has shifted his work to others. If he were merely living on the hoarded results of his own work, he would eat up the hoard in the long run. He can make others work while he idles only because he owns what they need,—land, mines, machinery, something which God or humanity have made, but to which he holds title.

We shall be reminded that many men of very large wealth toil on till they drop in their harness. These are usually men of big brain power who learned to work when young, and feel the joy of existence best when they are putting forth their tremendous energies to make things move. They are playing the game of work, and they obey a true physical and moral instinct in going on as if they had no accumulated millions. They would probably work just as hard if they were harnessed to the public service and got five thousand a year with the perquisite of honor from the commonwealth, as they do now while they get millions and little honor. Their responsibility, however, is far greater when they are the autocratic owners of great railway systems and industries. Such a weight is more than any man should bear, and to see these great workers breaking down under the strain is one of the pathetic spectacles of our system. They are like the axis of a driving wheel that is getting fragile while the wheel grows in weight and speed. Even for their sake we need a decentralizing of responsibility through industrial democracy.

These strong men who obey the law of work are worthy of honor, but their position is illogical. Work is to meet want; they have no want; why should they work? Their sons, who have never had their hard training for work in youth and who may not have the big brain power of their fathers, will follow the logic of facts and lapse into semi-idleness. In so far as the fathers go on working, they are illogical, but highly moral; but in so far as they go on accumulating, they are illogical and immoral. The accumulation of wealth is justified if there is some sound human end in view, such as the education of a child. But when men make money merely to make some more money with it, the thing has become an obsession. Before the age of Capitalism Christian ethics condemned indefinite accumulation, and universal judgment still regards the miser as a moral abnormity, in whom the property instinct has escaped bounds just as the sex instinct is perverted in others. Capitalism has changed our ethics and made limitless accumulation decent. Formerly hoarding had its natural limits set by the bulk of coin; to-day millions can be stored in a bank vault in securities, and the physical limit to accumulation is gone. So a race of men has multiplied who are unlike the miser in being open-handed spenders, but like him in making it the end and aim of life to get money for its own sake. If there were only one such man in the country, we should study him with pity; because there are many, and these the most influential men, our moral instinct has been silenced and reversed. Our business system has perverted the natural instincts of the strong by denying them a nobler outlet. A strong man loves power; he feels the throb of living in exercising and gaining power. Our system of private ownership has disconnected the power of the strong from the service of the community and has concentrated it on the accumulation of private wealth. So their life runs out in tragedy whether they stop working or go on working, and the growth of the soul to its full stature is denied them.

The desire to serve our fellow-men and to feel that we are of use to mankind is ineradicable in human nature. Our economic system sets men to making profit for themselves only, but their social spirit gets a vent by giving away their profits again after they have made them. No matter if vanity and the love of power tinge their philanthropy, it is still an index of their higher nature. Even the love of a mother is alloyed with the pride she takes in the pretty frocks of her child. But the tragedy of their lives follows the rich in their giving. They find themselves surrounded by people who are anxious to become recipients, and who will use every art of persuasion for themselves or the organizations they represent. Unless careful investigation is applied, a large percentage of their gifts never accomplish their intention and only act as a reward to mendacity. "If they are wise, they delegate the task of dispensing their benefits to a brisk army of salaried officials, habitually underpaid, 'experts' in their several lines, who, according to temperament and function, develop in curious mixture the qualities of the saint and detective." [1] But by that intervention the human enjoyment of helping their fellow-men is sobered down for the rich givers. They also find that their contributions are apt to dry up the springs of benevolence in others. Why should the widow give her two mites to foreign missions if Dives stands ready to wipe out the deficit at the end of the year? Mr. J. D. Rockefeller's famous method of conditional gifts was developed as a wise way of preventing this danger. But the farther a man goes in the direction of charity, the more he realizes the dangers attending it. If he provides three-cent meals for the poor, they will accept still lower wages and cut under

[1] Professor Vida D. Scudder, "Socialism and Character," p. 210. This is a rare book, with a feminine wealth of insight and spiritual experience.

the self-supporting workers. If he feeds and clothes their children, he weakens parental responsibility. If he educates promising young men, he helps them to climb out of the ranks of manual workers and to leave the working class without intellectual leaders. If I had to examine a class of social workers as to their general intelligence, I should be willing to rest the whole examination on one question: "How would you give away a million dollars and inflict a minimum of damage in doing it?" The care, intelligence, and conservatism of those who make it a duty to give shows how the problem has pressed on them.

There is no sadder man than a disenchanted philanthropist. He has accumulated millions with the idea that some time he will do good with them, and then finds the good turning to harm. He rarely gets genuine gratitude. With an unerring instinct men reserve that for those who suffer for them. A gift out of unearned abundance has none of the blood of the cross on it. As the spirit of democracy spreads, men more and more resent the philanthropic attitude. So the rich man, if he is wise and has insight, will find himself baffled in his best impulses by the false situation in which he is placed. He has gathered millions in profit from the people, and cannot get them back to the people who need them. He has taken a little milk from thousands of small milk pails and filled a great tub; now he tries to pour it back into the small pails without slopping it on the ground, and finds it turning unclean and sour. It ought to have been left in the small pails in the first place.

Outsiders see still more elements of tragedy. As men and women grow rich, they get out of touch with the real needs of the poorer classes, and when they try to meet them, it is often like the Hallowe'en game in which two blindfolded persons try to feed each other molasses with a spoon. Older men think conditions are still as they were in their boyhood, and misjudge everything from that point of view.

The best thing millionaires could do would be to make the rise of further millionaires impossible, and it is too much to expect that of them.   In the whole realm of education the great givers are acting as a soft pedal on the piano.   There is probably not a teacher with a real message to our age who has not felt compelled by consideration for himself and his institution to soften and dull down the very things that most demand utterance.   The great givers have no intention of doing harm.   They want to help.   But the logic of a wrong relation works out that way.   That is the tragedy of Dives.

The immense power wielded by the rich is an intoxicant that few can withstand permanently.   Men defer to them, smooth their way for them, and make them the center of every occasion.   The morbid curiosity of the masses about their doings is unpleasant, but it is an expression of the sense of their importance.   They acquire the seigniorial habit of mind and expect all things, including the law, to make room for them.   The reckless driving of automobiles beyond the speed limit is one of the least dangerous expressions of that spirit.   Such an attitude of mind is inevitable under such conditions; nearly all of us would develop it; but it is a distortion of the moral sense, an hallucination of egotism.   Christianity gave a new valuation to the quality of humility in ethics.   Humility is the sense of dependence on others, the feeling that whatever we have has been received from God and our fellow-men, and that we find our true life only as serviceable members of the social organism. But wealth emancipates from that sense of dependence. Unless religion counteracts it, it displaces humility by pride. But therewith the rich become unavailable for social service, and a danger to the society that has equipped them with their wealth.

One of the simplest motives in acquiring wealth is the fact that wealth unlocks the house of pleasure.   Up to a certain point every increase in income really brings new and wholesome pleasures within reach. But there is a point of saturation in human nature as in physics. Our stomach has plain limits of size, and no skyscraper construction has yet been devised for it. After a man has eaten a thousand five-course dinners they give him little more enjoyment than country sausage and buckwheat cakes used to do, and after he has acquired a liver and a waddle, they give him less. After a week of hard work a social function gives a thrill. But when life is made up of social pleasures, they become a round of "social duties" and make us tired. To a school teacher a trip to Europe is the hope of years and a memory forever; to the leisure class it drops to the level of a sitz-bath or a shopping trip. The Lord has so balanced our nature that we get the best out of work and pleasure when we mix them like oxygen and nitrogen in the air. If a person tries to live on oxygen alone, he gets symptoms. Wealth tempts men and women to make a business of pleasure, and then nature makes a tragedy of them.

Men justly desire wealth because it will give them leisure to cultivate their intellectual life. To most paid workers, physical and mental, an increase of leisure and means would mean a richer blossoming of the intellect. Judging by their opportunities, we should expect from the wealthy class an enormous contribution of productive intellectual work. Actually there is very little. The feudal aristocracy contributed few great names to art, literature, and philosophy. Our own great money-getters have occasionally shown the possession of high literary ability, but business uses them up. Most of them read little, and their amusement has to be of the most frivolous sort. In their class the culture of the intellectual life is confessedly passing to the women. After a family has taken up its residence in the land of the lotus-eaters, the sting of necessity is gone. Let any productive intellectual worker ask himself how much work he would have turned out in his life if he had lived a life of leisure from the outset. Unearned wealth seems to have a benumbing influence on the intellect, something like adenoids. An operation sometimes works miracles in both cases. Men get out of touch with reality; they love antiquarian collections, romantic and antique art, and ritualistic religion. Dante makes Plutus the only one of the powers of the Inferno who cannot speak intelligently.

The motive which first sets men to accumulating wealth is the love of their families. They want to create happy homes, satisfy the desires of those whom they love, and secure them against poverty and misfortune. The tragedy is that in many respects wealth in the long run will ruin the descendants and destroy family happiness. Though the founder of a fortune may go on in a simple and hardworking life, his women and his children and their children are increasingly exposed to the temptations of idleness. Alcoholism always flourishes in idle society. Families whom the Church had saved from it have drifted back into it, and at their dinners waiters pour champagne for young girls without even asking whether they want it. But wherever alcohol is used in mixed society, the restraints of sex passion are weakened. Married women flirt and live for conquest. No healthy mind will call the "full dress" of society a modest dress. Sensational journalism has exaggerated their scandals, but there is no doubt that family life breaks down among the idle rich. Travel separates husband and wife and carries each into conditions of temptation. They do not share daily labor and the care of children as plain married people do. Even if romantic love cools, the ordinary man will feel reverence when he sees the mother of his children caring for them. But when a woman has no children and does no useful work for the home, what ground is left for reverence? So the family is poisoned by the wealth which was meant to feed it. The

young men and women are exposed to excessive temptations. Rich young men and poor young girls are a terrible
combination.

Wealth places men and women in moral danger because
it vastly increases the number of their inferiors and decreases the number of equals with whom they can associate.
Only our equals are in position to rebuff our conceit or
rudeness and thus make our manhood grow straight. The
white people of the South, as no others, know what lasting
scars it has left on their life that they have had a subject
race under them. Condescension to inferiors passes for
a virtue in the upper classes. Yet in the sight of Christianity and Democracy it is a pseudo-virtue. If any man
really desires the moral progress of the working class, he
ought to be glad of any increase in their self-confidence and
independence, for no virile character is possible without
a straight backbone. Yet arbitrary power has so demoralized the upper classes everywhere that even good rich men
regard a growing self-assertion of the working class as one
of the most dangerous results of the spread of democracy.
When the lower classes no longer cringe, the upper classes
are compelled to improve their own humanity, and that is
a painful necessity to us all.

Wealth confers leadership. It puts a man to the front,
gives him opportunity, throws him with able people, and
sets off his personality as a gilt frame sets off a picture.
The more wealth he commands, the more people are drawn
in the wake of his life. The plays that he and his kind like
are played, and the gallery must accept them or go without.
If Dives feasts, an army of people prepare his feast, and
their economic activities are decided for them, very often
not for their good. He is perpetually leading in a game
of "Follow the Leader," and when he jumps over a stump,
a trailing army of eager or weary people must do their best
to jump it after him. How great, then, is his opportunity

if he is also a man of intellectual ability and moral power, and determined to head toward righteousness and peace!

But, on the contrary, the fact seems to be that a man of great wealth has less chance of real leadership than a man of like caliber without it. If he goes into politics, he brings his party or his leader under suspicion, and his friends have to vouch for him that he is really not there for sinister motives.[1] If he goes in for religion, he is suspected of hypocrisy. The terrible fact is that large wealth neutralizes that love of the people without which all leadership is forced and short-lived. Marshal all the conspicuously wealthy men of our country in the last fifty years, and who of them was loved by great bodies of the people? Whose personality swayed men like that of Beecher or Phillips Brooks? Whose death brought a sense of personal loss like that of Longfellow or Mark Twain? Who now can hold a candle to Bryan or La Follette if personal loyalty and influence are in question? Washington was one of the wealthiest men in the colonies, but what won him the abiding love of a nation was not his wealth, but the fact that he shared in the sufferings of Valley Forge, and that he refused to fasten a permanent grip of power on the Republic. We prefer not to be told that he had a large financial stake in the success of the Revolution. His one rival for our patriotic devotion, Lincoln, was a plain country lawyer. Such wealth as a man can earn by evident ability and public service serves him well in gaining leadership, and nobody seems to grudge it. But no one has yet been able to persuade the common sense of the people that the great fortunes of capitalism are earned by useful ability. The people henceforth will believe it less and less. We recognize that the masterful men of wealth have done great things, but we see that they have mortgaged our children to their

[1] The campaign of 1912 staged several acts in the continuous performance of "The Tragedy of Dives."

children to pay for it, and we instinctively withhold our love. There are indeed a few rich men who have won the enthusiastic devotion of the people, men like Golden Rule Jones and Tom L. Johnson. But they won it by proclaiming their own wealth to be derived from injustice and by leading the people to an assault on the sources of it. Their civic religion began with an act of repentance and confession of sin, and that gave a solid foundation of sincerity to all they said and did.

The day comes for each of us when our work is done and we are gathered to our fathers, and a man's soul must be calloused indeed if he is indifferent to the verdict that his fellow-men will pass on him after he is gone. Our selfish lusts may be hot in us while they last, but when all is done, we want to be remembered in love for some good we have done, for some enduring help we have given to mankind. It might well break a man's heart to know that posterity will class him forever, not with the friends of Man who range about Jesus Christ as their leader, but with the oppressors and exploiters of the poor.

In so far as they have aided in the application of science to the production of wealth and in the perfecting of industrial organization, our captains of industry have had a great part in the permanent achievements of our age. The names of some of them, who have made epoch-making advances in the broader organization of industry, may be cited to students in centuries to come as marking the climax of capitalism and the unconscious transition to a new social order. But in so far as rich men have been mere accumulators of unearned wealth, they need expect no praise from the future. There is nothing in ethics, in politics, or in economics that makes the swollen fortunes of our day desirable or admirable. The indirect good done through them might have been accomplished in more direct ways. Their evil results will gather force far into the future. The

x

deadliness of sin is never sized up in one generation. Sin is always pregnant with Death, but it takes time to bring her terrible child to birth. From now on the great problem of statesmanship in the capitalistic nations will be how to stop the further accumulation of unearned wealth; how to dissipate the present great fortunes without causing a revolution; how to make way for human progress in spite of their obstructive influence; in short, how to undo what the profit makers have labored to do. Men hereafter will differ whether the great capitalists have done more good by their management or more harm by their accumulations. Before God they will have to answer for the fact that the main purpose of their industrial work was not social achievement, but private profit. As for their descendants, who become passive recipients of unearned incomes, they will probably pass into a merciful oblivion.

Since its advent, democracy has been busy revising the verdicts of political history. The first are becoming last, and the last first, as Christ foretold. Kings and generals are being transferred from the assets of humanity to the debit column. Patriots are coming out of prison and obloquy, and taking their place in the hall of fame. The more democracy becomes an instinctive part of our mental outfit, the less respect will merely selfish power get. Power will have to show moral qualities. The assizes of history will sit with Christ as the judge that charges the jury. The iniquities of their fathers are coming up to smite the living. During the debate on the Disestablishment of the Welsh Church in May, 1912, the Duke of Devonshire, in a political leaflet, charged the Liberal Party in England with "robbery of God." David Lloyd George, the Chancellor of the Exchequer, replied: "Doesn't he know that the very foundations of his fortune were laid deep in sacrilege and built on desecrated shrines and pillaged altars?" There were angry voices of protest, especially from Lord Hugh

Cecil. Mr. George replied: "These charges that we are robbing the Church ought not to be brought by those whose family tree is laden with the fruits of sacrilege at the Reformation. Their ancestors robbed the Catholic Church, the monasteries, the altars, the almshouses. They robbed the poor. They robbed the dead. Then when we try to recover some part of the pillaged property for the poor, their descendants accuse us of theft, — they whose hands are dripping with the fat of sacrifice." Lord Cecil denied that his family had profited by the robbery of church property, but historical proof was promptly furnished. This is the way in which democracy is sitting in judgment. "For the mills of God grind slowly, but they grind exceeding small." Within the last few years there has been an uncovering of secrets in our country, and some men fled into death because they could not bear the accusing eyes of their fellow-men. As the new industrial democracy gets control of the investigating power of government, and as it needs the information for dealing with the problem of unearned wealth, many facts will be brought to light that seem safe now. That will be part of the tragedy of Dives. When the British democracy was wrestling with the House of Lords in 1910, the Lords talked of calling on the people for vindication. Mr. G. K. Chesterton replied:[1] —

"Hamlets breaking, homesteads drifting, peasants tramping, towns erased;
Lo! my Lords, we gave you England, — and you gave us back a waste.
Yea, a desert, labeled 'England,' where you know (and well you know)
That the village Hampdens wither and the village idiots grow,
That the pride of grass grows mighty and the hope of man grows small.

[1] *London Daily News*, Jan. 15, 1910.

Will you call on croft and village? Let the rabbits hear your
    call.
Would you call upon the people? Would you waken these
    things then?
Call on God, whose name is pity; do not ask too much of men."

The great landowners of England have found it profitable
to diminish the number of people on the land; the great
owners of industry have increased their number in the cities,
but have made havoc of their quality.

The verdict of the future is even now confronting the
rich in their own children. The best of them are respond-
ing to the new spirit, and are suffering under the burden of
unearned wealth that has been laid upon them. They want
their human birthright of doing honest work for their
living, and of winning respect on their own merits. They
want to feel that they are giving more than they get in life,
and that they are not living on the sweat of others. They
are going into settlement work in order to have the sense
of their common humanity, and they feel that they redis-
cover their own lives when they can forget that they are
helplessly rich. Every father passionately desires the ap-
probation and reverence of his children. The spoiled
children of the rich will approve of their unearned income;
those in whom the religious spirit of their forefathers rises
in new form will condemn them. What kind of children
does Dives prefer?

In thus presenting the moral situation of the accumulators of unearned wealth, I have not been conscious of any
emotion of envy, class hatred, or personal grudge. I have
only good will and friendship for every rich man and woman
I have ever met. Some were among the finest characters
I have known, and if I should be informed on the day of
judgment that they all outrank me, it would only confirm
my secret suspicions. If my argument seems severe, I am
within my duties as a minister of Jesus Christ, pledged to

make men think as he thought and feel as he felt. This
chapter is simply a modern exposition of his saying on the
camel and the needle's eye. If the sermon is faulty and
one-sided, I have seen and heard others that were worse.
I appeal to the wise and Christian minds among the rich
to judge if their observations among their own class and the
history of their own spiritual temptations do not at many
points confirm what I have tried to set forth.

I have sought to show that my rich brothers are in a tragic
position. In a tragedy the leading character is placed in
a position where he struggles in vain with superior forces
that drag him down. It may be the battle of a strong and
guilty soul against the powers of the moral universe that
close in on him to visit retribution. It may be the conflict
of a righteous man with a seemingly blind and hostile
fate, or with the problem of obeying two incompatible
duties. I say in all soberness that every rich man is the
sad hero of a tragedy, and the more noble and wise and
righteous he is by nature, the more tragic is his fate.

The social order as it now is places its beneficiaries in a
position where they cannot escape wrong and unhappi-
ness. If they obey its laws, they enrich their own life, but
at the expense of others, and in the end their apparent advantage turns out to be their own curse. They escape
from the necessity of work, but in time idleness undoes
either them or their descendants. Their wealth seems to
promise large means of doing good, but they find their
philanthropy a heavy burden on themselves and a questionable blessing for others. Their money gives them
power, but that power is an intoxicant that undermines
their sense of human values. It piles up their pleasures,
but the more they surfeit, the less pleasure do they feel.
It offers them free scope for their intellectual life, but it
rusts the mainspring of their intellect. It holds out
happiness for their families, and does its best to ruin them.

It assures them of security, and makes them camp among enemies. It increases their sense of strength by surrounding them with inferiors, and thereby relaxes their virility. It forces leadership on them, and yet chills the love of the people which is the condition of all leadership. It seems to win all the powers of this world to their side, but it puts them on the wrong side in the final verdict of God, of humanity, and of their own souls. That is the tragedy of Dives.

At the beginning of this chapter we raised the question, if perchance the privations imposed on the working class by our economic system could be justified on the ground that the privileged classes are thereby helped to a higher footing which in the long run will enable them to help the weaker to rise to the same level. If our discussion has come anywhere near the truth, their unearned wealth unfits the rich to become saviors of anybody. It even robs them of their own salvation. They are themselves the victims of our social system. If they have suffered in the tragedy of their lives and have grown wise through it, let them save others from the same fate, and help to create a social order where the strong will get all they earn and no more; where the security of each will be guaranteed by the good will and help of all; and where honor and power are not gained by hoarding wealth but by giving life in the service of the common good. "You know that the ruling classes in a heathen social order lord it over the others, and their great men tyrannize the people. Not so is the rule of life among you. In your social order, whoever is ambitious for power let him be the helper of all, and whoever is ambitious for rank let him be the servant of society, just as the Son of Man did not come to get service but to render it, and to give his life as a payment to emancipate many." [1]

---

[1] Matt. xx. 25-28 in free rendering.

CHAPTER VII

LET us sum up the case of Christianity against Capitalism. We saw that the distinctive characteristic of the capitalistic system is that the industrial outfit of society is owned and controlled by a limited group, while the mass of the industrial workers is without ownership or power over the system within which they work. A small group of great wealth and power is set over against a large group of propertyless men. Given this line-up, the rest follows with the inevitableness of a process in physics or chemistry.[1]

Wherever the capitalist class remains in unorganized and small units, they will struggle for the prizes held out by modern industry. Capitalism in its youth threw off the restraints upon competition created by the older social order, and a fierce, free fight followed. Wherever the competitive principle is still in operation, it intensifies natural emulation by the size of the stakes it offers, enables the greedy and cunning to set the pace for the rest, makes men immoral by fear, and puts the selfish impulses in control. The charge of Christianity against competitive capitalism is that it is unfraternal, the opposite of coöperation and teamwork.[2]

Capitalism gives the owners and managers of industry autocratic power over the workers. The dangers always inherent in the leadership of the strong are intensified by the fact that in capitalistic industry this power is unrestrained by democratic checks and fortified by almost

[1] Part III, Chapter III, of this book.   [2] Part III, Chapter IV.

absolute ownership of the means of production and life. Consequently the master class in large domains of industry have exacted excessive toil, and have paid wages that were neither a just return for the work done nor sufficient to support life normally. The working class is everywhere in a state of unrest and embitterment. By great sacrifices it has tried to organize in order to strengthen its position against these odds, but the master class has hampered or suppressed the organizations of labor. This line-up of two antagonistic classes is the historical continuation of the same line-up which we see in chattel slavery and feudal serfdom. In recent years the development of corporations has added a new difficulty by depersonalizing the master. The whole situation contradicts the spirit of American institutions. It is the last intrenchment of the despotic principle. It tempts the class in power to be satisfied with a semimorality in their treatment of the working class. It is not Christian.[1]

The capitalist class serves society in the capacity of the middleman, and modern conditions make this function more important than ever before. But under the capitalistic organization this wholesome function is not under public control, and the relations created call out the selfish motives and leave the higher motives of human nature dormant. Under competition business readily drifts into the use of tricky methods, sells harmful or adulterated goods, and breaks down the moral self-restraint of the buyer. Under monopoly the middleman is able to practice extortion on the consumer. The kindly and friendly relations that abound in actual business life between the dealer and the consumer are due to the personal character of the parties and the ineradicable social nature of man, and are not created by the nature of business itself.[2]

In all the operations of capitalistic industry and commerce the aim that controls and directs is not the purpose

[1] Part III, Chapter V.   [2] Part III, Chapter VI.

to supply human needs, but to make a profit for those who direct industry. This in itself is an irrational and unchristian adjustment of the social order, for it sets money up as the prime aim, and human life as something secondary, or as a means to secure money. The supremacy of Profit in Capitalism stamps it as a mammonistic organization with which Christianity can never be content. "Profit" commonly contains considerable elements of just reward for able work; it may contain nothing but that; but where it is large and dissociated from hard work, it is traceable to some kind of monopoly privilege and power, — either the power to withhold part of the earnings of the workers by the control of the means of production, or the ability to throw part of the expenses of business on the community, or the power to overcharge the public. In so far as profit is derived from these sources, it is tribute collected by power from the helpless, a form of legalized graft, and a contradiction of Christian relations.[1]

Thus our capitalistic commerce and industry lies alongside of the home, the school, the Church, and the democratized State as an unregenerate part of the social order, not based on freedom, love, and mutual service, as they are, but on autocracy, antagonism of interests, and exploitation.[2] Such a verdict does not condemn the moral character of the men in business. On the contrary, it gives a remarkable value to every virtue they exhibit in business, for every act of honesty, justice, and kindness is a triumph over hostile conditions, a refusal of Christianity and humanity to be chilled by low temperature or scorched by the flame of high-pressure temptation. Our business life has been made endurable only by the high qualities of the men and women engaged in it. These personal qualities have been created by the home, the school, and

[1] Part III, Chapter VII.
[2] On the regenerate sections of the social order, see Part III, Chapter II.

the Church. The State has also made Business tolerable
by pulling a few of the teeth and shortening the tether of
greed. Thus moral forces generated outside of Capitalism
have invaded its domain and supplied the moral qualities
without which it would have collapsed. But capitalistic
business in turn is invading the regenerate portions of the
social order, paralyzing their activities, breaking down the
respect for the higher values, desecrating the holy, and invading God's country.[1]

Life is holy. Respect for life is Christian. Business,
setting Profit first, has recklessly used up the life of the
workers, and impaired the life of the consumers whenever
that increased profit. The life of great masses has been
kept low by poverty, haunted by fear, and deprived of the
joyous expression of life in play.[2]

Beauty is a manifestation of God. Capitalism is ruth-
less of the beauty of nature if its sacrifice increases profit.
When commerce appeals to the sense of beauty in its products, beauty is a device to make profit, and becomes mere-
tricious, untrue, and sometimes corrupts the sense of beauty.
Neither does the distribution of wealth under capitalism
offer the best incentives to artistic ability.[3]

Love is of God; the home is its sanctuary. Capitalism
is breaking down or crippling the home wherever it prevails, and poisoning society with the decaying fragments
of what was the spring house of life. The conditions
created by capitalism are the conditions in which prostitution is multiplying. Some sections of capitalistic
business are directly interested in vice and foster it. Because it is so immensely profitable the white slave traffic
would speedily become a great industry if the State did not
repress it; and where the State tries to grapple with it,
commercialized vice is corrupting the officers of the State.[4]

[1] Part IV, Chapter I.   [2] Part IV, Chapter II.   [3] Part IV, Chapter III.
[4] Part IV, Chapter IV.

Devotion to the common good is one of the holy and divine forces in human society. Capitalism teaches us to set private interest before the common good. It follows profit, and not patriotism and public spirit. If war is necessary to create or protect profit, it will involve nations in war, but it plays a selfish part amid the sacrifices imposed by war. It organizes many of the ablest men into powerful interests which are at some points antagonistic to the interest of the community. It has corrupted our legislatures, our executive officers, and our courts, tampered with the organs of public opinion and instruction, spread a spirit of timidity among the citizens, and vindictively opposed the men who stood for the common good against the private interests.[1]

When men of vigorous character and intellectual ability obey the laws of Capitalism, and strive for the prizes it holds out to them, they win power and great wealth, but they are placed in an essentially false relation to their fellow-men, the Christian virtues of their family stock are undermined, their natural powers of leadership are crippled, and the greater their success in amassing wealth under capitalistic methods, the greater is the tragedy of their lives from a Christian point of view.[2]

These are the points in the Christian indictment of Capitalism. All these are summed up in this single challenge, that Capitalism has generated a spirit of its own which is antagonistic to the spirit of Christianity; a spirit of hardness and cruelty that neutralizes the Christian spirit of love; a spirit that sets material goods above spiritual possessions. To set Things above Men is the really dangerous practical materialism. To set Mammon before God is the only idolatry against which Jesus warned us.

As Capitalism has spread over the industrial nations, a smoke bank of materialism has ascended from it and

[1] Part IV, Chapter V.   [2] Part IV, Chapter VI.

shut the blue dome of heaven from the sight of men. All the spiritual forces of society have felt themselves in the grip of a new, invisible adversary with whom they had to wrestle, and whose touch made their heart like lead.

The taste for pure literature, especially for poetry, has declined in the classes that once had it. A person who cultivates poetry as our fathers used to do must do it with a smile, or he will pass for a freak. In spite of the vast public created by the spread of education and reached by modern methods of publicity, the amount of enduring literature produced is slight. Authors who cannot produce what will make a commercial profit can get no hearing. Authors who do produce what is commercially profitable are overstimulated, rushed, and drained. Department store novels and Sunday editions are drowning the intellect of the people in a sea of slush. They furnish the sensations of thinking without its efforts. Cities that used to have several bookstores, with dealers who knew and loved books, can hardly support one store now, though they have doubled in population.

Our schools and colleges have felt the same subtle drag. In spite of the advance of educational equipment and method, very many educators agree that there has been an actual decline in the intellectual standards of the colleges and in the mental grip of the students. The business world sneers at anything in education that does not pan out immediate and material results. As its blaring band-wagon goes by the college walls, the students quiver to climb on board. They have lost interest in pure thought, which can never be converted into cash. The old love for the classics is gone, and the love of science for its own sake, which was to take its place, has failed to become general. The teaching profession, which is one of the chief supports and feeders of the spiritual life, has declined in relative standing and influence. To call an idea "academic" kicks it off the stage. A teacher has the choice between sharpening the claws of his students for the competitive struggle, or seeing their interest run away from his department. For several college generations there has been "an ebb of generous ideals and a mounting of precocious cynicism." "If such was the impression of triumphant lawlessness upon young men whose horizon had been widened by academic culture, what must it have been upon the multitudes of callow youth that from the schoolboy desk go ill furnished forth into active life?"[1]

The learned professions are still like islands amid the rising tide of capitalistic profit making, but as the yellow flood swirls about them and eats into their banks, the members of each profession watch it with sinking hearts, for "commercializing a profession" always means degrading it. Of the learned professions the Law is farthest gone. The most lucrative practice is the service of corporations, and they need the lawyer to protect their interests against the claims of the public. The learning, the moral independence, and the public standing of the profession have suffered as it has been commercialized. When a doctor urges an operation in order to get a commission from the surgeon who performs it, he adopts business methods, but if that is the spirit with which the healing profession will come to look at us as we lie helpless under their hands, we must betake ourselves to prayer. Every invasion of the nobler professions by the business point of view means a surrender of the human point of view, a relaxing of the sense of duty, and a willingness to betray the public — if it pays. When the news of the *Titanic*, for which half the world was waiting with tense faces, and for which thousands were gasping with breaking hearts, was held up by the wireless operator on the *Carpathia* because his superior officer advised him that he could get four figures

[1] Professor E. A. Ross, "Sin and Society," p. 153.

for his "story," the spirit of Capitalism invaded wireless telegraphy, which had hitherto stood in the public mind for a chivalrous agency of social help. The operator happened to have a monopoly of the goods that people wanted, and he had sole control of the line of communication. He used his chance for a business deal like every other monopolist. Why shouldn't he? After a short gasp of indignation, the world accepted the situation, and another light went out.

All the aggregative influences in modern life, which organize men in social groups and compel them to think and act together, are means of spreading the materialistic spirit that is secreted by business life. Even competition, which seems to disunite men, creates a spiritual solidarity among the competitors, so that if one of them sacrifices mercy for profit and underpays his employees, the others have to follow him. If one market man gives commissions to the cooks and servants, bribery becomes the law of that market. But in a large way the capitalist class has the leadership of the whole of society. We all have to follow the men who hold the purse, and these are the men trained by capitalistic business to follow profit first of all. Society has always accepted the morals and manners of the ruling class and standardized the rules of conduct on their pattern. The business class is to-day our ruling class, and their practical code of honor and morals in business is becoming the code of all.

So the materialistic spirit of Capitalism is pervading all our spiritual life and conforming our conscience to its standards. For great social classes this has meant a process of demoralization. Now, no man can bear the contempt of his own soul. When the drunkard feels his shame, he takes a drink in order to forget and feel like a fine fellow, and when a man has sold himself for money, he adopts a philosophy of life that justifies his conduct and gives him back his self-respect. This becomes infinitely easier when others are doing it with him. Then gray becomes the standard of whiteness, and sin becomes the moral law. So our social conditions create a social conscience to match them, and our social conscience evolves a philosophy of life to back it. There is a grim element of truth in the materialistic philosophy of history. If as religious men we fear materialism, let us beware of a social order which secretes materialistic ideas. When once the materialistic view of life has gained a hold on us all, there is no call of repentance to our souls and the way of regeneration is blocked. Dr. Jekyll remains Mr. Hyde. Pascal said truly, "More sinful than our acts are the thoughts by which we excuse them."

When literature, art, education, the learned professions, and all other organized expressions of the spiritual life are being blanketed by the materialistic spirit generated in our business world, how can religion and the Church escape?

The churches are the socialized expression of the religious life of men. They awaken the religious instinct in the young of the race, teach them spiritual conceptions of life, put them into historical continuity with the holy men of the past, hand down the socialized treasures of religion, the Bible, the prayers, the hymns of the Church, and give the people an opportunity to connect their religious impulses with the service of men. Presumably the religious instinct would live on even if the churches perished, but in many it would starve by neglect or relapse into barbaric forms if deprived of the social shelter given by the Church. But without some light of religion in our lives our spiritual nature would vegetate in an arctic night, and many of us would fall a prey to vice, discouragement, and moral apathy. Even those who do not believe in the reality of what the churches teach will acknowledge that religion has been the most potent form of idealism among the great masses of men throughout history.

The churches have to make their appeal to the spiritual nature of men, which is but slenderly developed even in the best of us, compared with the powerful instincts of hunger, sex, and pleasure. They are always like engines pulling a train on an upgrade, and they feel it if the brakes are set in addition. In every industrialized community the churches have had a hard time of it. They are weakest where Capitalism is strongest. If this does not suggest a causal connection, our mind is duller than it might be. Of course the decline of the churches is due to a combination of causes. They have lost force through their own faults, through traditionalism, narrow ecclesiastical interests, and opposition to science and democracy. But to a large extent they are victims of the same influences which have crippled all the other noble forms of social life. Instead of chastising the churches, those who believe in the spiritual values of life might inquire sympathetically why the strongest and most ancient institution devoted to higher ends languishes wherever industrialism grows. We are not so rich in fraternal and spiritual institutions that we can afford to laugh while any of them die.

In "Christianity and the Social Crisis"[1] I explained how the external interests of the churches are affected by the economic conditions about them. They are cramped for space by the rise of land values; straitened in their income by the poverty of the wage-earning classes; deprived of their volunteer workers by the exhausting toil of the week; endangered in the supply and spirit of their ministry; loaded down with the burden of caring for a mass of poverty; and compelled to work on human material that is morally debilitated. I have seen no contradiction of the line of thought presented there.

But beyond these external difficulties of the churches

[1] Chapter VI.

lies the spiritual antagonism between the genius of Christianity and the genius of capitalistic Business.

Religion declares the supreme value of life and personality, even the humblest; Business negatives that declaration of faith by setting up Profit as the supreme and engrossing object of thought and effort, and by sacrificing life to profit where necessary.

Christianity teaches the unity and solidarity of men; Capitalism reduces that teaching to a harmless expression of sentiment by splitting society into two antagonistic sections, unlike in their work, their income, their pleasures, and their point of view.

True Christianity wakens men to a sense of their worth, to love of freedom, and independence of action; Capitalism, based on the principle of autocracy, resents independence, suppresses the attempts of the working class to gain it, and deadens the awakening effect that goes out from Christianity.

The spirit of Christianity puts even men of unequal worth on a footing of equality by the knowledge of common sin and weakness, and by the faith in a common salvation; Capitalism creates an immense inequality between families, perpetuates it by property conditions, and makes it hard for high and low to have a realizing sense of the equality which their religion teaches.

Christianity puts the obligation of love on the holiest basis and exerts its efforts to create fraternal feeling among men, and to restore it where broken; Capitalism has created world-wide unrest, jealousy, resentment, and bitterness, which choke Christian love like weeds.

Jesus bids us strive first for the Reign of God and the justice of God, because on that spiritual basis all material wants too will be met; Capitalism urges us to strive first and last for our personal enrichment, and it formerly held out the hope that the selfishness of all would create the universal good.

Y

Christianity makes the love of money the root of all evil, and demands the exclusion of the covetous and extortioners from the Christian fellowship; Capitalism cultivates the love of money for its own sake and gives its largest wealth to those who use monopoly for extortion.

Thus two spirits are wrestling for the mastery in modern life, the spirit of Christ and the spirit of Mammon. Each imposes its own law and sets up its own God. If the one is Christian, the other is antichristian. Many of the early Christians saw in the grasping, crushing hardness of Roman rule a spiritual force that was set against the dominion of Christ and that found a religious expression in the cult of the genius of the Emperor. The conflict between that brutal force and the heavenly power of salvation was portrayed in the Revelation of John under the image of the Beast and the Lamb. If any one thinks that conflict is being duplicated in our own day, he is not far out of the way.

Whoever declares that the law of Christ is impracticable in actual life, and has to be superseded in business by the laws of Capitalism, to that extent dethrones Christ and enthrones Mammon. When we try to keep both enthroned at the same time in different sections of our life, we do what Christ says cannot be done, and accept a double life as the normal morality for our nation and for many individuals in it. Ruskin said: "I know no previous instance in history of a nation's establishing a systematic disobedience to the first principles of its professed religion." [1]

The most important advance in the knowledge of God that a modern man can make is to understand that the Father of Jesus Christ does not stand for the permanence of the capitalistic system.

The most searching intensification that a man can experience in his insight into sin and his consciousness of sin

[1] "Unto this Last," p. 88.

is to comprehend the sinfulness of our economic system and to realize his own responsibility for it.

The largest evangelistic and missionary task of the Church and of the individual Christian is to awaken the nation to a conviction of that sinfulness and to a desire for salvation from it.

The bravest act of faith and hope that a Christian can make is to believe and hope that such a salvation is possible and that the law of Jesus Christ will yet prevail in business.

The most comprehensive and intensive act of love in which we could share would be a collective action of the community to change the present organization of the economic life into a new order that would rest on the Christian principles of equal rights, democratic distribution of economic power, the supremacy of the common good, the law of mutual dependence and service, and the uninterrupted flow of good will throughout the human family.

PART V

THE DIRECTION OF PROGRESS

CHAPTER I

THE CHANNEL BUOYS

OUR argument has narrowed down, and we have arrived at the directly constructive part of our inquiry.

We have traced the social awakening of our nation and our churches, the rising tide of moral indignation against the needless sufferings of our fellows and against the inhumanities in which we are all involved, and the new sense of brotherhood that is drawing us all together. In these stirrings of the spiritual forces of our nation we recognized the voice of the living Christ, who is the soul of humanity, summoning us to complete the task of redemption.[1]

In this most modern task, which lies with a tremendous sense of destiny on the consciousness of all Christendom, we have back of us the original mission of Christianity, the purpose for which Jesus himself lived and died, the unquenchable hope which has always, at least in broken gleams, lived on in the hearts of Christian men, — the purpose and hope of founding on earth the Reign of God among men. Faith in the Kingdom of God commits us, not to an attitude of patient resignation, nor to a policy of tinkering and palliatives, but to a revolutionary mission, constructive in purpose but fearless in spirit, and lasting till organized wrong has ceased.[2]

[1] Part I of this book. [2] Part II of this book.

In the consciousness of this mission we then analyzed our present social order. We found that large portions of it have been so deeply affected by the spirit of Christianity that they have become fortifications of liberty and agencies to express good will toward all and to secure the common good. On the other hand, we found that the economic organization of society, while affected by Christian motives through personal channels, has not yet been christianized in its fundamental relations and methods, and that this is the cause of our misery and the source of the evil influences which are paralyzing and contaminating the regenerate parts of our social life.[1]

It remains now to inquire how a Christian economic order should be constituted, and by what methods our present order can be changed into one that will be Christian in its very constitution. "There is an order for human affairs which is the best. That order is necessarily not the one which now exists. If it were, why should we wish to change the present? But it is the order which ought to exist in order to produce the greatest possible welfare of mankind. God knows it and wills it. It is for man to discover and establish it." [2]

I can imagine the sad smile on the lips of the wise as they watch one more bark hoisting purple sails and laying its course for Utopia.

> "A thousand creeds and battle cries,
> A thousand warring social schemes,
> A thousand new moralities,
> And twenty thousand thousand dreams." [3]

Let them smile. I would rather meet God in a dream than not meet him at all. I would rather join in the Exodus and

[1] Parts III and IV of this book.
[2] The closing words of the great book, "De la propriété et de ses formes primitives," by the eminent Belgian economist Émile de Laveleye.
[3] Alfred Noyes.

lay my bones to bleach on the way to the Promised Land than to make bricks for Pharaoh forever, even if I could become an overseer over other slaves and get big spoonfuls from the garlicked fleshpots of Egypt. But I have no intention of furnishing blue prints of the castles we shall build in Utopia, or of predicting the course of human events. There is only one thing which I am prepared to assert with absolute confidence about coming events: that they will not happen in the way I expect them to happen. The forces working together in the mass of human life are so numerous, so intricate, so mysterious, that it baffles us to explain historical events after they are all over; and fore-telling them is slightly more difficult. But I do believe that it is not beyond the moral intelligence of man to get a fairly correct conception of the direction in which we ought to move, so that we may guide our practical decisions by our larger outlook.

We have a divine instinct for righteousness within us that acts as a guide. Like a compass needle, it is always quivering and shifting, always liable to deflections and aberrations that have led many a bold captain on the rocks. But it answers mysteriously to the cosmic will of God, and we disregard it at our peril. Many have been ruined by following its lead without scientific intelligence; but more by far have been beached on the mud flats by nailing a gilded stick to the bow and steering by that.

We also have the channel buoys to guide us which have been anchored by the historical experience of mankind. They too may be misleading, for the channel is always shifting, and the anchoring of the buoys has been badly done. History has always been written from the point of view of the dominant classes and edited to suit their needs. It has told all about kings and priests, and left the common people under the gravecloth of oblivion. It has erected monuments to the great destroyers of mankind, and stamped out the memory of the true leaders of the people whose wisdom might now offer us real guidance. Since the rise of democracy in the French Revolution the science of history has begun to speak a new language, and all the records are now being reread from new points of view. If that intellectual work were farther advanced, we could move with incomparably surer insight. History ought to serve us as the great experiment station of mankind, and even now we can get a clear verdict, for instance, on the question, if it is wise for a nation to have the bulk of its property owned by a small and irresponsible class.

For those of us who believe in Jesus Christ, there is still another sure means of guidance into the future. If the fundamental direction of his mind and his life was a revelation of the will of God for humanity, then he is to us a summons to go forward in the line marked out by him, and also a guarantee that we have the Almighty and his moral universe behind us as we move.

Whenever Jesus looked at any man singly, he saw and felt his divine worth; not on account of anything the man owned and knew, but on account of his humanity. The child, the cripple, the harlot, were to him something precious and holy, and he stood at bay over them when any one tried to trample on them in the name of property, respectability, or religion. He was always moving to break down the power of sin in the individual and of wrong in society, which corrupted or crushed this divine worth, and to furnish a faith, a spirit, a motive, and a human environment in which the life of man could unfold in freedom and strength.

Whenever Jesus looked at men collectively, he saw and felt their unity and brotherhood. To him sin consists in that which divides, in war and hate, in pride and lies, in injustice and greed. Salvation consists in drawing together in love, as children of one Father. If any member of the human family is weak or perishing, it concerns all. The solidarity of mankind was the great conviction underneath all his teachings.

These fundamental utterances of the mind of Christ are the supreme law of Christendom. Anything that contradicts them is anarchic. The chief business of Christian men to-day is to translate them into terms large enough to make them fully applicable to modern social life. Our economic organization will have to be transformed in these directions. It is unchristian as long as Men are made inferior to Things, and are drained and used up to make profit. It will be Christian when all industry is consciously organized to give to all the maximum opportunity of a strong and normal life. It is unchristian when it systematizes antagonism, inequality, tyranny, and exploitation. It will be Christian when it is organized to furnish the material foundation for love and solidarity by knitting men together through common aims and united work, by making their relations just and free, and by making the material welfare of each dependent on the efficiency, moral vigor, and good will of all.

In the following chapters I shall attempt to make the application of these fundamental demands of the Christian mind to the transformation of the economic organization of industrial society. In order to head off some of the misunderstandings into which men seem almost eager to slide in matters of this kind, I want to disavow formally any idea that we are to sit down and create a new set of social institutions out of our heads. Social institutions are the slow growth of centuries; they will not rise ready-made from the ground when we stamp our foot. Even religion is not powerful enough to make a break in the continuity of history. All that we can do is to take our social relations and institutions as we find them, and mold them whenever we find them at all plastic. In a previous chapter [1] I tried to show by what varied influences and how gradually the Family, the Church, the School, and the State have been christianized. I conceive. of the christianizing of Business as a similar process. Ethics and religion will exert their most valuable influence when they can get behind the great material forces which are constantly changing the social order, and coöperate with them. Our economic organization cannot be run into the repair shop to be made over. We should all be dead by the time it came out painted and varnished. Whatever happens, we want three meals a day, and our economic system must feed us. Any reorganizing process in the social order can only be like the minute cellular changes that transform a tadpole into a frog, or that heal over a wound in our own body.

When a novelist tells a tale that happened in our own world, our memory and imagination combine to supply the moving background for the story and the hum of life. On the other hand, in sketches of Utopia, like Bellamy's "Looking Backward," society seems thin, artificial, and monotonous, like a mechanical toy, and we get the impression that we are to trade off our own rich world for this papiermâché affair. I disavow any notion that all the world henceforth is to be made after one ready-made pattern and labeled "Christian." All the civilized nations for more than a century have been unanimously moving in the direction of democracy, but how much uniformity and monotony is there to-day in the political institutions of republican France and Switzerland, of New Zealand and Canada, of Oregon and Massachusetts? There is unity of movement, and yet endless diversity of life. The most monotonous thing in the modern world is the steam-roller progress of Capitalism, which creates the same conditions in Argentina, Bombay, and St. Petersburg. But even

[1] Part III, Chapter II.

Capitalism wears a different face in New York and Berlin. If, therefore, under some pentecostal inspiration all the world should begin to move toward the ideal of a Christian social order, every community would realize it in a different way. Nor would it be stationary anywhere. It would constantly have to meet new needs incident to growth, and would always be in danger of slipping back into new forms of tyranny and exploitation. Life will always be a strenuous and breathless game, playing tag among the teeth of Death. Yet we can move toward a Christian social order and get there.

Another lively misunderstanding will have to be scotched before we can proceed. The word "Christian" is so connected with the idea of self-sacrificing service that men get the impression that a Christian social order would have no room for the selfish interests. They justly conclude that such a contrivance would be too good to be good for anything. I hold with Edmund Burke that "the human system which is founded on the heroic virtues is doomed to failure and even corruption." I believe that there is incomparably more capacity for devotion to the common good in human nature than is now being brought out, and that a christianized social order would tap artesian wells of it. But unless the ideal social order can supply men with food, warmth, and comfort more efficiently than our present economic order, back we shall go to Capitalism. Christianity will have to validate its claims by productive efficiency. In his contest against the priests of Baal on Mount Carmel, Elijah proposed the test: "The God that answereth by fire, let him be God." Charles H. Spurgeon christianized the test: "The God that answereth by orphanages, let him be God." In our present conflict between God and Mammon we shall finally have to socialize it: "The God that answereth by low food prices, let him be God."

In the chapters that now follow I shall simply trace

those fundamental lines of social evolution along which society must move in order to leave inhumanity behind and to emerge in a social order that will recognize the worth of manhood and the solidarity of mankind. We really all know what these lines are, but a conscious formulation of them is mightily needed. The planlessness of our political and religious leaders is pitiable. Most of them have taken the advice of Jesus literally and are taking no thought for the morrow. Society would be drifting and yawing like a ship with a drunken crew, unless an invisible hand at the helm were steering us by means of our blind, primal impulses. In the prescientific age men lived in that fashion with Nature, taking her blessings and her blows as they came, and coöperating with her in a feeble and half-comprehending way. Science has given us directive powers, and we can now make Nature make us. As we are comprehending the great laws of social life, the time for large directive action is coming, and we shall make Society make its members. My appeal is to Christian men to use the prophetic foresight and moral determination which their Christian discipleship ought to give them in order to speed and direct this process. If any one thinks it cannot be done, let the unbeliever stand aside and give place to those who have faith. This thing is destiny. God wills it. What is morally necessary, must be possible. Else where is God ?

CHAPTER II

JUSTICE

THE simplest and most fundamental quality needed in the moral relations of men is justice. We can gauge the ethical importance of justice by the sense of outrage with which we instinctively react against injustice. If redress is denied us, we feel the foundations of the moral universe totter. Men have often gone to law and used up all their hard-earned property to satisfy their craving for justice, and if they thought it was permanently denied them, their whole nature has become hard and bitter. Until injustice between individuals is made right by restoration or forgiveness, fraternity between them is cleft, and only heroic love on the part of the wronged can bridge the gap. For a man who has overreached or wronged his neighbor, to offer him favors or charity is felt to add insult to injury. If he loves him, let him love him enough to be just to him.

So fundamental is justice between man and man. One of the prime requisites of a righteous social order, therefore, is to provide wise and prompt social tribunals to settle cases where private justice is in dispute. That the courts in our country have become slow, cumbersome, and inefficient, and that in some cases justice is defeated because the Law is tripped up by its own wool, is notorious and confessed. For a workingman suing against a corporation, dilatoriness in the courts is almost equivalent to a denial of justice. The moral injury which this condition inflicts by stunting the love of justice and by breaking down the confidence of the plain man in the righteousness of society,

is beyond calculation. The legal profession is formally
intrusted by society with the maintenance of justice.
Lawyers alone have the technical knowledge necessary to
remedy the existing evils. The fact that they have allowed
them to grow up, and that many of them are apparently
hardly aware that things might be bettered, lies as guilt
at the door of the entire great profession, just as any collapse in the work of the Church is brought home to ministers and priests.

As justice is the condition of good will between individuals, so it is the foundation of the social order. Any
deep-seated injustice throws the foundation walls out of
plumb. If one class is manifestly exploiting another,
there is no fraternity between them. Long-standing oppression has sometimes so dulled the manhood of a peasant class that they accepted injustice as part of the inevitable suffering of life, and received any act of justice from
the aristocracy with enthusiasm as a noble and generous
deed. Such patience is really the most pathetic symptom
of degradation. But the fact that the oppressing classes
have always vigilantly suppressed any social or religious
agitation that might waken the drugged sense of justice,
shows that such peace is always superficial. If any one can
read history without a sickening sense of the enormous
extent of injustice and oppression in all nations, he has a
mental make-up which I both envy and abhor. Practically all the internal upheavals recorded in history were
caused by the agonized attempts of inferior classes to resist or shake off the clutch of injustice. Nations die of
legalized injustice. It is more deadly even than sexual
vice or alcoholism.

When injustice becomes widespread and permanent,
it undoes the Christian character of the social order, because it makes human solidarity impossible between the
two classes concerned, and because it deprives both of them

of their full Christian manhood.   The class that profits
by injustice becomes parasitic.   All plant and animal life
shows that parasites may be brilliant in coloring, but they
are always defective in the essentials of life.   On the other
hand, the people of the exploited class are deprived of an
equal opportunity to develop their gifts.   Something of
the divine life in them is suppressed.

Revolutions furnish a curious proof of the extent to
which ability is suppressed under conditions of injustice.
A revolution is a time of lawlessness and of destruction of
life and property, which ought by rights to cripple a people
for many years.   But every successful revolution unhorses
privilege and flings open the door of opportunity to some
new class that has hitherto been shut out, and this has
sometimes set free such an opulence of intellectual ability
and moral power that all the damage and disorder of a
revolution were cheap.   The French Revolution loosed
an avalanche of ability and force over Europe.   The Puritan Revolution brought out the men of the Long Parliament, Eliot, Hampden, Pym, and Cromwell — the ablest
ruler England has ever had.   When Cromwell organized
the Ironsides, he disregarded the tradition which restricted
captaincies to men of noble birth, and that democratized
army made a new record in the history of fighting.   The
political ability of the plain people of England had been
shut out of the parliaments; in the Parliamentary Army
they found a social organization and a forum, and that army
launched schemes of political, social, and religious reforms
which England has been carrying into effect ever since.
The great migration of the Teutonic nations in the fourth
and fifth centuries was a terrible landslide of semibar-
barous people that buried civilization, overthrew the governments, and plundered the cities.   We should expect
only misery and destitution to follow such a first-class
disaster.   Yet the fact is that when the German Franks

conquered the Roman province of Gaul,[1] destitution diminished, the impoverished cities began to flourish, and the condition of the lower classes passed through an unparalleled improvement. The reason is that the destructive influence of the invasion was offset by an increase in justice. The Roman law had permitted the rich to monopolize the land and to enslave the working class. Gaul was full of huge estates with prison pens of slaves to work them. The Germans had a far milder form of servitude; they allowed the serf to live on his bit of land in return for a moderate rent and service. Their coming spread the slave population over the land and gave the poor man a chance, with the results aforesaid. How great, then, is the damage which injustice inflicts, if even a violent and destructive abolition of it can be a blessing?

Theoretically we have no special privilege in America. Our country was "dedicated to the proposition that all men are created free and equal." It is our boast that America spells opportunity. The belief in equal rights is so dear to us that when any special privilege is to be granted, it has to masquerade as an act for the public welfare. No party dared to support a high protective tariff on the plain ground that certain interests ought to be relieved from competition and enabled to make easier profits. But in reality our life is yeasty with special privilege. Whence have these huge fortunes grown in a single generation, if not from privilege? "By their fruits ye shall know them." Do we pick the pumpkins of millionaires from the grape vine of equality? In what do we differ from other countries when we foot up the result? Our aristocracy has no titles. But what's in a name? It is power that counts. Their wealth is not founded on solid square miles of agricultural land, like that of the nobility which grew up in an agricultural age. It is far-flung and

---

[1] The present France.

scattered, based on mines, railways, factories, building sites; but it involves rights to levy tribute which would have turned the Norman barons pale with envy.

Injustice is the obverse side of privilege. If one man has unearned wealth, others will have less than they have earned. It is a simple proposition in physics; money cannot be in two pockets at the same time. If any one wants to promote righteousness, let him put a stop to privilege; and if he wants to locate privilege, let him look for easy money. "In the sweat of thy brow shalt thou eat bread," is the law for all the sons of Adam. If a man does not eat his bread in the sweat of his brow, he is probably eating it in the sweat of other people's brows. If we see wealth bubbling up under a man's hands, broadening into a stream, and shooting up in a fountain, the community is justified in asking where it comes from. If he claims that he has a miraculous power to make money flow from the rocks, his claim deserves investigation, but meanwhile we ought to go on the assumption that he has tapped a public main, probably unknown to himself.

If any one wants to increase his social insight, it would pay him to study the historical processes by which special privilege has been built up. In olden times it was often by bold, rude seizure, as when some English lord fenced in the common land and called it his own, or when an Irish chieftain claimed as his personal property the lands of the clan to which he held title as the head of the commune We still have downright theft enough in our day, as the looting of the public lands in the West and the franchise grabs of our cities can testify. But usually the appropriation or increase of privilege is done by encroachments so quiet and automatic that even the beneficiaries are not aware that they are crowding any man from his property or tapping his earnings; they merely feel that things are coming their way and that they can afford to buy that limousine. And those who are suffering injustice are unable to discover how their labor is drained away; they merely know that after all their pumping the pail is only half full.

The fundamental step toward christianizing the social order, therefore, is the establishment of social justice by the abolition of unjust privilege. Logically this would be the first step; ethically it is the most important step; practically it is usually the last and hardest.

I have merely undertaken to point out the direction in which the christianizing process should move. It is not my business to locate and enumerate the forms of privilege in modern life. It would take a book. But lest any one should complain that I am leaving the matter up in the air, I will stake it down. The private ownership of land, of mineral treasures, of water power, etc., is just, only if the holder of such an exclusive privilege pays the full rental value for the opportunity granted to him by the community, which is, under God, the only real owner. If no adequate compensation is paid to the community, an injustice is committed, and this injustice grows as the population grows denser and the need for these natural opportunities grows greater. The private appropriation of the unearned increment of the land is the giant sequoia among the rich vegetation of injustice. The control of the means of traffic and intercourse also offers an opportunity for injustice in this age of traffic. Those who control them are exercising attributes of sovereignty, and if they use their power to levy tribute beyond a due reward for their services, they are unjust to those who have granted them their power. Those who control inventions and processes necessary to modern industry by means of patent rights are likewise in a position to levy tribute, and may take from society far more than a just return for the labor and service they contribute to the life of society. These are the three chief sources of monopoly profit to individuals, and of injustice

z

to the public: the private property in land which makes it possible to tax the propagation of life; the private control of the means of traffic which makes it possible to tax social intercourse; and the private monopoly of inventions which makes it possible to tax the progress of civilization. The first injustice can be eliminated by appropriating the unearned increment of the land through adequate taxation of land values; the second by the public ownership of the means of traffic, or — which is more difficult — by holding corporations down to a fair income; the third by rewarding inventors by public grants or a royalty system. In addition to these old and legalized forms of privilege, a modern form has grown up which gets its power from size and combination. Industrial corporations are able to fix prices for the public through the immensity of their resources; employers are able to fix the wages of workmen through the costliness of the productive plant and the impossibility of applying labor without machinery.

In one of the azure halls of heaven is the council chamber in which the Senate of the Immortals meets. Only the wisest of all ages have a seat there: Moses and Isaiah, Solon and Aristotle, King Arthur, Dante, and their spiritual peers. Equipped with the experience of their own nations, enriched by communion with men of all times, unbiased by selfish passions, uninfluenced by party interests, they sit to consider the course of human events.

To them entered one day that vivacious and versatile Personality who once came with the Sons of God and discussed the case of Job with Jehovah.[1] He had again come "from going to and fro in the earth, and from walking up and down in it," and he now reported that Columbus had just discovered America.

Immediately there rose before the prophetic minds of the great Immortals the sight of broadening streams of

---

[1] Job i.

human life pouring from the old world into the new, of communities colonizing the seaboard, pushing up the river valleys, clustering around the waterfalls, dotting the plains with homes, and building up commonwealths and nations. A great hope swept audibly through the Senate like the rushing of a mighty wind. In that new continent the best in humanity would find a free course; no inherited tyrannies seeking to perpetuate themselves, no embittering memories of bloody wars, no classes and castes cemented with injustice to baffle brotherhood and defy the liberty of States. Swiftly they began to plan a great Charter of Rights and Liberties that would forever bar out from the new land the forces which had ruined the older peoples.

Satan listened with an amiable smile. "Excuse me, gentlemen, but let us get down to common sense. We've got this all fixed. You forget that the people who occupy this country will need labor force. We'll let them use up the Indians, provided they can make 'em work. After that we'll tap the reserve force of Africa and put the black race at their service. You know that the venerable institution of slavery has been indispensable in the advancement of civilization. By restricting it to the colored races, we shall save the whites from the slight hardships which naturally accompany it." (The Senate moved uneasily.) "Then we've got to offer incentives to thrift and enterprise. We're going to introduce the system of private property in land which worked such remarkable results in the Roman Empire." (A shudder ran through the assembly.) "Those who first seize an opportunity can keep it and work it. That will promote industry and progress."

"But the land must not be sold in perpetuity," broke in the venerable figure of Moses. "Jehovah forbade it.[1] All must have a share in God's land. What shall they do who come after?"

[1] Leviticus xxv. 23–38,

"They'll have to make the best terms they can with the fellows on the inside. Every man for himself, and I'm always ready to take the hindmost, you know," and he winked at King Arthur, who gripped his staff with brawny fist, as if he would right willingly use it.

"As the population increases, it will be necessary for the sake of efficiency to consolidate the resources of the nation. The ablest men will come to hold all the important property rights and the lines of traffic. In four hundred years, say about 1892, they ought to have a pretty solid system. They can fix prices as they need them, and in that way they will have ample funds to finance the development of mankind and put society on a stable basis."

"Woe unto them that join house to house, that lay field to field," exclaimed Isaiah, lifting his hands. "What mean ye, that ye crush my people and grind the face of the poor?"

"This is death to the liberties of the people," cried Aristotle. "This is the very calamity from which every patriot of Greece sought to save his commonwealth. It was in vain. Greece became a desert." Solon covered his face.

They sat in silence, and darkness seemed to shroud the chamber. One of the attendant angels was reminded of the gloom that settled over heaven when word was brought of the fall of man. Even from the lips of Satan the smile vanished, and he passed out.

CHAPTER III

PERHAPS some reader, too sleepy or too sharp to understand my meaning, has gathered from the preceding chapters that I belittle the value of property and want everybody to live in a state of holy impecuniosity. On the contrary, I affirm that property is a means of grace and that none can experience a full salvation without it. When Jesus was charged with destroying the law and the prophets by his revolutionary teaching, he said, "I came not to destroy the Law, but to fulfill." In the same spirit I wish to vindicate the sacred right to property. A condition in which millions of people have no share at all in the productive capital of the nation, and hardly enough even of furniture, clothing, and food to cover their nakedness and nourish their bodies, debases humanity, undermines the republic, and desiccates religion. All the sweetest and holiest elements in life lean back on property for support. The dear memories that comfort us in loneliness and age cling about the pictures, the books, the trinkets that have come down the years with us and are now clothed in an aureole of love. The home has the respect of its inmates only if it contains some property that ministers to their comforts and pleasures. What ought to be the restful afternoon of life becomes a haunting specter if there is no property to support our failing strength. The philosopher Hegel was right: "Every man must have property." Schiller echoes it: —

"Etwas muss er sein eigen nennen,
Oder der Mensch wird morden und brennen."

Under the normal conditions of American life in the past, it was possible for the average man to support his family, raise his children, and still save something for a rainy day. Older men, who judge the present by their own past, feel that it must be so still and are inclined to regard a workingman as shiftless if he has no money in the bank. In fact, it is still so for great numbers, as our savings banks and insurance companies can testify. The brave, the wise, and the religious families succeed almost miraculously in educating their children and having a margin left on which to trust the Lord. But where Capitalism has broken down the defenses of the working class and forced the standard of income down to the line of bare support, it may be the part of larger wisdom for parents not to lay by money while they are raising children, but to use up their income to give the children the food and environment they need for their physical development. That is their best form of investment. But it submerges the parents in poverty during their vigorous years, and after their children are grown up, their own working force has declined, and their income is apt to become slender. If they do save, the accumulation of years is often swept away by a single illness or death in the family. I have often seen with what pitiful tenacity old people cling to the last $100 or $50 in their savings bank book because it may pay for their admission to a Home, or at least give them a decent burial. Before the pension system was introduced in England, a great proportion of frugal and hard-working people had to "go on the parish" in age.

But even if a workingman and his wife have $2000 in the bank and a home of their own, that does not equip them with property in the full sense of the word. It does increase their income, save them rent, and give them security, but it does not aid them in the act of production. The old-fashioned village mechanic could have taken the $2000,

equipped a shop of his own, and become his own boss. He
would have turned his little property into live capital and
if he was capable, could hoist his future higher with that
block and tackle. In the same way, the average farmer
has himself *plus* his farm, and the two make a strong combination. The modern industrial workman has only himself. The machinery with which he works is too expensive
for him to own. If he has property, it is divorced from his
work. It is not "capital." In point of fact, the industry
of our country is very largely financed by the savings of the
plain people. The banks and insurance companies collect
them, and thence they flow into the channels of business.
But therewith the money passes out of the control of the
owners. What a man deposits to-day may be used next
week to pay Pinkertons who will do things he abominates.
It may even help to buy a new machine in his own factory,
at which he will work, yet aside from the interest he gets
on the deposit, his money will not aid him in earning a livelihood.

This is an anomalous condition, and those who believe
in the sacredness of property would do well to consider it.
Modern industry has multiplied the amount produced by
the worker, but gives him little chance to save for age, and
next to no chance to use his savings as a leverage in production. The very bigness of modern industry defeats
him and reduces him to economic powerlessness.

My proposition is that the workingman needs property
more than ever, but that under modern conditions property
must take new forms. Under the simple conditions of
family production in the past, property took the form of a
small hoard belonging to one family jointly. Under the
complicated conditions of social production to-day, property
must consist in a share of and a right in a collective accumulation which belongs to a larger group jointly. I shall try to
explain my meaning by an example that comes home to all.

A French writer says: "To-day the child of a poor man falls to the ground naked, as if it were born in a savage state. It has no connections; it has no ancestry."[1] The spirit of that statement is fine, but the assertion runs far beyond the facts. Even the child of a poor man in a civilized community is a large property owner. He is part owner of a great network of streets, and when his baby carriage goes by, all concede his right of way and allow him to enjoy an amazing panorama of wonders in peace. There are great parks, with shade trees and lawns, with swings and see saws, with lakes and swans, and possibly with a zoo of monkeys and elephants, to which he has access — provided his folks can spare the time to take him there. In some cities skilled hands are working to eliminate microbes from his milk bottle. If he gets seriously sick, great institutions are open to receive him, — if they are not too full. When he begins to trudge about, the Kindergarten, once the privilege of the rich, teaches him games, songs, and stories. For years he has free use of a most expensive apparatus of schoolrooms and teachers. If he loses his way, an army of blue-coated giants hunt for him, wipe his nose, and take him home to his mother. If he has played with matches, another set of giants swarm up ladders and risk their lives to save him from his own naughtiness. And all this is not charity. It is his right. He is part owner of a great corporation. Its servants are his servants; its resources are his when he needs them. All this is property, and safer property than anything he will ever own. He may save ten years to buy a home of his own, and lose all his accumulation by mortgage foreclosure. But no one can foreclose on the property he holds in common with his fellow citizens. This property right is not the right of exclusive possession, but the right to use collective property whenever he has need of it.

[1] F. Huet, "Le règne social du christianisme."

When the child grows up, he will find that he has other property rights, which give him free access to public baths, libraries, lectures, and concerts. Public servants remove the ashes and garbage of his home without extra charge. If he is "down and out," the park bench will be his last resort for rest and reflection, and when he is old, he has a vested right to be supported at public expense in the poorhouse. This is not much compared with the similar rights of a citizen of Athens under Pericles, but it is better than nothing. Thus even now we all have rights in large collective properties, which supplement our exclusive and private possessions. This collective form of property admits of indefinite enlargement. It ought never to supersede the private form of property entirely, but it may well come to exceed it in value and importance.

This form of property is the truly modern form. A capitalist who holds stock in a railway, a gas company, and a factory cannot lay his hand on a single rail, pipe, or brick and say, "This is mine," as the farmer can say about his cow and his barn; in every case he is part owner of collective wealth, and this property right has a broader and securer basis than if he owned one fractional part completely. The system of insurance which has grown to such immense proportions in modern life is essentially a coöperative organization, with collective capital, which assures to every policyholder a contingent property right. If a man insures his house against fire, he has not bought tangible property, but he has bought a right. If he is never in a case to need assistance, he will never get a cent of returns for his insurance premiums; but in case of a fire his latent property right springs into active life and saves him from poverty. For the average man, which is the wiser way of providing for the contingency of disaster, to set aside a small hoard of his own to be used in case of fire or to hold an insurance policy and pay premiums on it?

Which would be the wiser way to provide for the contingency of protracted sickness or old age, to save several thousand dollars, or to earn the right to sick benefits and an old age pension ? The system of small family hoards went with the system of family production; the system of insurance and pension will have to be developed to go with the modern system of social production as its corollary.

Several European nations have struck out boldly in this direction in order to end the intolerable poverty of the working classes. Germany years ago began to develop a system of compulsory insurance against accident, sickness, and old age, and has recently expanded it further. Its administration has not been free from evil, but it has had a wonderful sanitary effect on the economic life of the working classes and on the industrial efficiency of the nation. Pauperism has disappeared from western Germany, and emigration to America has almost stopped. Under the leadership of Lloyd George, England has begun to move in the same direction. Her working people are hereafter to have support during sickness — and that includes maternity charges for women — and a pension of $1.25 a week in age. If now the liquor interests in Parliament and Church will allow the curse of drink in England to be abated, the human swamps of the nation will be drained in time.

Of course, if the working people are to have more property, the question is, who is to have less? The only way to answer that question is to cut into the unearned wealth of the privileged classes. In England the movement to abolish pauperism had as its counterpart the famous budget of Lloyd George which undertook to tax unearned incomes more heavily and for the first time to assess land values adequately. The impending increased taxation of the land has also inaugurated the breaking up of the great estates of England; many thousands of acres have already been sold to small owners. As sin breeds sin, so righteousness breeds righteousness.

Old age pensions and insurance against accident and sickness would give the kind of security which private investments have hitherto given, but it would not yet do for the modern workingman what the possession of a farm does for the farmer, and what the ownership of a shop used to do for the village mechanic. The industrial worker needs some property right in the industrial system in which he works. If he cannot be sole owner of a small shop, he must be part owner of a large shop. He must hold some fractional right like that of a shareholder in a joint-stock concern. Various lines of effort are converging on this end, voluntary coöperation, labor copartnership, profit sharing, etc. I am not discussing the methods here, but insisting that this is the direction in which the christianizing of the social order must move : the industrial worker must have property rights in industry.

The simplest and most effective form which such property right could take would be the right of a man to a job. When a child first enters school, friendly hands receive it, direct it to its place, set its tasks, hold it to work, train its faculties, and promote it when it deserves promotion. On the other hand, when the child leaves school and enters industry, there is no place ready for it, no socialized intelligence to direct it to a job, and none to estimate what its faculties are best fitted for. After some years of experimenting, some find the work they can love; some remain misfits. If a man has a good job, he has no security that he can hold it, even if he does good work. "The propertyless man is a dependent when work is plenty, and a vagabond when work is slack." [1] He needs a secure tenure of employment, to last as long as he is efficient and honest, so that he cannot be discharged arbitrarily; and he needs an organization of industry that will help him to a job.

[1] Professor John R. Commons, in "The Distribution of Wealth," pp. 79-85, has a brief but incisive discussion of the Right to Employment.

The right to employment is the next great human right that demands recognition in public opinion and law. If this seems incredible to any one, let him remember that the right to life and liberty, which seem to us self-evident and which the law protects with solemn sanctions, would have seemed equally preposterous in ancient times. A stranger could be killed at sight, and any unprotected man could be enslaved. The present social guarantee of the right of life and liberty to every individual has been the slow product of social and ethical evolution. The right to employment is now in the process of evolution. Unless that right is added to the others, the right to life and liberty remains a fragmentary right so far as the workingman is concerned. The business class have fought for and secured for themselves the "freedom of industry," which meant the right to have free access to nature and to produce wealth by manufacture and commerce. That right is valueless to the workingman under modern conditions; his form of the same right is the right to a job.

The moral instinct of the workingmen has long come to recognize this new right as among themselves. A man who does another out of his job arouses the same moral indignation among his fellows which a man who removes landmarks or shifts a line-fence would arouse among farmers. "Thou shalt not covet thy neighbor's house, nor his ox, nor his ass," was a demand for security of property and income under agricultural conditions. "Thou shalt not take thy neighbor's job," is the modern industrial equivalent for it. Employers, ministers, and other middle-class people have often misunderstood the ethical attitude of organized labor because they have failed to understand that the workingmen regard a job as a property right. Many actions for which we have most severely condemned them were warped efforts to establish a higher code of ethics under adverse conditions. The time is coming when this property right will have the sanction of law. While the landlords of England owned the law-making power in Parliament, they wrote their property convictions into the law. They believed, for instance, that the owner of the land owned the birds of the air and the fish of the streams; so they imprisoned and shot poachers for catching a rabbit or fish. As the working class wins political influence through the advance of democracy, they will certainly write their property convictions into the laws. Just as policemen, firemen, and other civil servants of the government have won security of tenure and can be discharged only for adequate cause, so the workingman must have security of tenure and a tribunal to which he can appeal if he is discharged arbitrarily. Public employment bureaus should put the best intelligence available at his command in finding a job, just as our consular service puts information at the command of business men seeking a market. Monopolistic business has inflicted harm on the working class in many ways; it should at least benefit them by making their employment steady by virtue of the superior stability and far-sighted management possible in noncompetitive business. If all other means fail him, the workingman should be able to fall back on the community itself for employment.

The right to employment would not only revolutionize the economic conditions of the industrial workers, but would dispel the curse of fear that is now on them, make the right to life and liberty effective, give them self-respect, and create a new attitude to their work. Wageworkers are often blamed for taking no interest in their work. When I consider how few motives they have for taking an interest in it, how little individuality they can put into it, and how little reward they have for doing it heartily, I rather wonder that almost every workingman still takes pride in his job. It is another proof of the ineradicable virtue in human nature. But if a man had a recognized status in his shop, a sense of belonging there, and a good expectation of remaining there, a new foundation would be laid for the morality of labor. Teachers and professional men, artists, writers, soldiers, and civil officers come to love their work for its own sake and to do their best work without reference to the material reward it may bring them. Why cannot the manual worker rise to the same moral dignity? He will when he becomes equally free. No slave of fear can be truly moral.

Every man should have property. Individual hoards are becoming an impossible and antiquated form of property to large classes. The workingman must be protected in sickness and age by the collective wealth of the community. He must have a recognized property right in the industrial organization. The minimum form of that right is the right to get employment and to stay in his job as long as he does honest and efficient work. How long it will take us to reach this condition I do not know. That we must move in this direction seems to me clear. A condition in which one fourth of the race holds all the opportunities of livelihood in its arbitrary control, and the other three fourths are without property, without access to the earth, and without an assured means of even working for a living, is neither American nor Christian. Property is a means of grace, and a good job is another.

In November, 1911, I received a declaration of principles from the American Liberty and Property Association, signed by a number of individuals and corporations for whom I have the highest respect. The Association opposes "paternalistic" legislation, i.e. government control and ownership. I was not able to approve the principles as they stood, but should like to reprint them here with some amendments. It may make the difference in point of view clear for all. My additions are given in italics: —

1. "As the proper function of government is to maintain equal liberty, we are opposed to all class legislation, whether directed against the rights of individuals, or of corporations," *or of the community.*

2. "Every man has a right to labor at whatever useful occupation he chooses, and is entitled to all that he earns by proper mental or physical exertion," *and no more.*

3. "It is not the duty of the Government to save men from the results of their own improvidence, or to make them virtuous by law," *but to protect them from injury and impoverishment by those who are stronger.*

4. "Our system of taxation should not discourage the accumulation of capital by taxing the results of superior ability, industry or thrift," *and still less by taxing the results of inferior ability, industry, or thrift more heavily.*

With these additions I should find myself in closer agreement with these four propositions and should regard them as more adapted to our real dangers. The fifth I should have to alter more radically. It reads: —

5. "The best results to the community are attained under such open competition and personal liberty as does not interfere with the equal liberty of others."

I would suggest as a substitute: The best results to the community are attained by combining the highest degree of personal liberty with the most effective coöperation of all.

CHAPTER IV

WHEN Jesus, at the beginning of his public career, came to the synagogue of his home city of Nazareth, they handed him the roll of the prophet Isaiah, and he singled out these words to read : —

"The spirit of the Lord Jehovah is upon me,
    Because Jehovah hath anointed me to proclaim glad tidings
        to the poor;
    He hath sent me to bind up the broken-hearted,
    To proclaim liberty to the captives
    And the bursting of the prison to them that are bound;
    To proclaim the year of Jehovah's favor,
    And the day of vengeance of our God." [1]

When these words were first written, they had promised an exiled nation freedom and restoration of its national life. Jesus declared that he found the purpose of his own mission in fulfilling this prophecy, and thereby he adopted it as the pronunciamento and platform of Christianity. The words reverberate with freedom, and wherever the Gospel has retained even a breath of the spirit of Jesus in it, it has been a force making for freedom. If its official exponents have ever turned it into a chain of the mind, may God forgive them.

Christianity necessarily must be on the side of freedom if it is to fulfill its twofold purpose of creating strong and saved characters, and of establishing a redeemed and frater-

[1] Isaiah lxi and Luke iv.

nal social life, for neither of the two is possible without freedom.

Freedom is the life breath of a christianized personality. A servile class or nation lacks virility. Slaves and flunkies cringe, lie, and steal. Oppressed peoples resort to conspiracies and assassinations. Free people organize. The general judgment of past ages that woman was a clog to the higher aspirations of able men was really true in large part. As long as women were a subject class, they had the vices of a subject class. Men kept them ignorant and oppressed, and then were cursed by pulling with unequal yokemates. Freedom is to character what fresh air is to the blood. This is the truth in Nietzsche's contempt for the morals of servility.

Freedom is also the condition of a christianized social order. Men can have no fraternal relations until they face one another with a sense of freedom and of equal humanity. Despotism is always haunted by dread, and fear is not a symptom of the prevalence of fraternity. In tracing the moral evolution of the Family, the School, the Church, and the State,[1] we saw that every social organization is on the road to redemption when it finds the path of freedom.

We are told that democracy has proved a failure. It has in so far as it was crippled and incomplete. Political democracy without economic democracy is an uncashed promissory note, a pot without the roast, a form without substance. But in so far as democracy has become effective, it has quickened everything it has touched. The criminal law, for instance, has lost its bloody vindictiveness since the advent of democracy; men are now living who will see our penal institutions agencies of human redemption and restoration. Democracy has even quickened the moral conscience of the upper classes. The most awful poverty has always existed before the eyes of the rich, yet they

---

[1] Part III, Chapter II, of this book.

2 A

failed to see it till the lower classes became articulate through democracy. Is the cure of such blindness not a moral achievement?

Some forms of evil merely seem to multiply in a democracy because they get publicity there. Things that remain discreetly hidden in a despotism are dragged into the open by the impertinent curiosity of the plebs. What an aristocracy calls hereditary rights, a democracy calls scandalous graft. When Roman patricians or French seigneurs unloosed the anger of the common man, they could retire within the haughty class consciousness of a solid social group as into a bomb-proof shelter. In a democracy the extortionate rich must trust mainly to the thickness of their private skins.

Rightly considered, even the sins of democracy have some background of honor. Three of our presidents have been assassinated within fifty years. Few despotisms have such a record. But let the czars and sultans mingle with their people as our presidents do, and who will carry their insurance risks? A former czar is said to have asked the king of Prussia to lend him a Prussian officer to massage his imperial back, for he had no servant whom he could trust.

Other things being equal, a free State is always stronger, for it commands the devotion of the people. The boasted military efficiency of a despotism goes bankrupt when the trained armies are used up; a republic can stamp the ground and new armies will rise from the dust, as the history of Switzerland, Holland, the first French Republic, and the Boers testify. Switzerland has a citizen militia practicing marksmanship constantly with guns furnished by the government. Russia would not dare to arm and train its people; neither would Germany and Austria.

If the faults of our American democracy depress the mind of any one, let him consider this problem. When our Constitution was adopted, the suffrage was so restricted that only about 120,000 inhabitants out of 3,000,000 had a vote.[1] During the colonial period a very large percentage of the immigrants arrived in a state of unfreedom; not only the black people imported from Africa and the Antilles, and the subjugated Indians, but about half of the white immigrants.[2] Some were criminals sent by England; many thousands were children and young people kidnapped for the colonial trade; most of them were persons who had bought their passage by selling themselves for a term of years as "indentured servants"; all these were sold at the wharf when a vessel arrived or hawked about the villages in chains. Given such beginnings, what would be the social condition of our country to-day if democracy had not meanwhile established manhood suffrage and prohibited slavery and peonage? Is democracy, then, a failure?

Whatever theorists may say, the verdict of the people is all one way. No nation wants less freedom than it has. The people always seek to remedy the faults of democracy by still more democracy. For five hundred years democracy has widened its concentric circles. The Renaissance of the fifteenth century began the democratizing of Education and the Intellect. The Reformation of the sixteenth century began the democratizing of the Church (which has taken more than three hundred years). The Revolution of the eighteenth century began the democratizing of the State and the political order. The Industrial Revolution of the nineteenth century began the democratizing of property. For let us not forget that Capitalism in its youth raised the battle cry of freedom. It was a revolutionary force bursting the rusty chains of feudal privilege and bringing property down where plain merit and ability could own it. It is true, the blessings of freedom and property were mainly confined to the merchants and manufacturers, and

[1] Simons, "Social Forces in American History," p. 97.
[2] Commons, "Races and Immigrants in America," pp. 34-36.

when Capitalism now raises its old watchwords of liberty, it is usually to defeat some movement for real liberty. The democratizing of property was only begun by Capitalism. A new form of aristocracy has been built up. To-day we have neither free competition for business men, nor free contracts for workingmen, nor free markets for the consumers. Capitalism set out as the opponent of privilege and the champion of freedom; it has ended by being the defender of privilege and the intrenchment of autocracy.[1] The democratizing of property and industry must be resumed under new leadership.

The ideal of Capitalism — in so far as it has a moral ideal and is not frankly mammonistic — is the wise and benevolent employer, who can manage the affairs of the workingmen better than they can do it themselves, and whose plans for their welfare will be rewarded by their respect and gratitude. A great deal of good will, earnest thought, and faithful effort have gone into the realization of this ideal, and not without permanent results. The danger which dogs it is that it leaves the working class in a dependent attitude and fails to call out the qualities of independence and initiative. It is the ideal of paternalism, and it is very funny to hear men who put their trust in it cry down labor legislation and public ownership as "paternalistic." In point of fact, the benevolent-employer theory is as utopian as any scheme of socialism in its infancy. The weight of experience is against it. Only scattered individuals have had enough moral vigor to act on it. In the long run it is easier to educate the workers to govern themselves than to educate a set of superior persons to do the governing for them. Moreover, it is more lasting. The benevolent employer dies or sells out, and therewith the constitutional guarantees of his happy employees are swept

[1] Part III, Chapter V, of this book. The present chapter presupposes the former.

away. In politics the drift is away from one-man power; in industry we shall have to move the same way.

The alternative for an aristocracy of superior persons is the democracy of labor. John Stuart Mill formulated the ideal of industrial democracy finely: "The form of association which, if mankind continue to improve, must be expected in the end to predominate, is not that which can exist between a capitalist as chief, and workpeople without a voice in the management, but the association of the laborers themselves on terms of equality, collectively owning the capital with which they carry on their operations, and working under managers elected and removable by themselves." [1]

Two great movements are pushing toward the realization of this idea. The more radical of the two is Socialism. It stands in the midst of capitalistic society like a genuine republican party in a monarchical State, and seeks to lead the working class from "the kingdom of compulsion into the republic of freedom." The more conservative movement ·for industrial democracy is Trades-unionism. Just as a liberal party in a strong monarchy leaves the dynasty and its fundamental rights untouched, but demands parliamentary representation and the right to vote on the budget, so Trades-unionism recognizes the rights of the owner and employer under the present social order, but seeks constitutional guarantees and a Bill of Rights for the working class.

In the long view of history I think there is not a shadow of doubt that the powerful employers and associations of employers that have set themselves rigidly against both of these movements toward industrial democracy, have chosen the wrong side. They have aligned themselves with all the absolutist kings who resented the demand for a parliament or a douma as an interference with God-given rights, and yielded to compulsion as slowly and ungraciously

[1] Mill, "Principles of Political Economy," Vol. II, p. 357. 1868.

as they could. The determination of great corporations to allow no labor organization to lift its head in their works is a present-day echo of the famous challenge of Louis XIV, "L'État, c'est moi !" These employers speak of their "private business" and resent the interference of outsiders in it; they use illustrations and maxims that might have been proper when a master mechanic employed three journeymen in his own home. Yet they command an industrial army of thousands; the bread and life of great industrial towns is dependent on their decisions; personal touch with their men is practically impossible. How can they call that a "private" business? In all respects except legal property rights it is a public affair and the concern of all society. When one corporation combines the ownership of coal mines with the ownership of the railway that carries the coal, the business world protests against such a combination of powers as dangerous. But some corporations have twisted all the strands of a workingman's life into one rope in far different fashion. They have fixed his wages and given him no voice about them; they have provided the conditions under which he must work; they have housed him in drab-colored shanties in a fenced village in which the company owns every foot of the soil as landlord, even the roads; they have compelled him to run an account at the "pluck" store of the company and to accept their prices and measures. If then the man proved troublesome, they can twitch the man's living, his home, his friendships, his whole existence from under him as the sheriff springs the death trap of a condemned man. Yet even such employers think there is no call for labor organizations. The belief in hell has waned at a time when we need it badly. Some think we shall be born again on this earth under conditions such as we have deserved. It would certainly be a righteous judgment of God if he placed us amid the conditions we have created and allowed us to test in our own body the after effects of our life. How would a man feel if he knew that the little daughter that died in his arms twelve years ago was born as the child of one of his mill hands and is spinning his cotton at this moment?

If industrial democracy is coming, the workingmen as a class must be trained for the responsibility which the future will put upon them. In their own organizations and under their own leaders they must learn by practice that fairness and self-restraint without which democracy cannot work. If the labor organizations are suppressed and stunted, and if their energy is consumed in fighting their enemies instead of educating their members, the transition to the coöperative commonwealth will find them untrained, factious, and without tried leaders. Then we shall reap the results of the policy of suppression.

The errors of the Unions, their excesses, and their brutalities have been spread out for all to see. Their opponents and the newspapers have not allowed us to underestimate the number of dynamite outrages. But after the worst is said — they have never inflicted as much wrong as they have suffered. They have never been as rotten as the political parties we have supported and cheered. Social workers and upper-class people who come into inside contact with the organizations of labor usually gain a deep respect for their moral soundness. As individuals the workingmen have all the faults of raw human nature, but their organizations act on higher and more humane principles than the corresponding organizations of the commercial class.[1]

It is not enough to give the organizations of the workingmen legal toleration. The Law must facilitate and regulate the organization of the industrial workers. They must have legal recognition and honorable rights and duties as

[1] See Part V, Chapter VII, of this book.

important groups within the social body. Subject always to the supreme interests of the whole community, every trade must have jurisdiction over the qualifications of its members; the workingmen must have the right to bargain collectively with their employers; and jointly with the latter they must constitute tribunals of conciliation and arbitration. If any group can organize coöperative production and dispense with an employer entirely, it is to the interest of the commonwealth that they shall have all facilities to try the experiment.

Some men see behind the slightest recognition of organized labor the specter of a "labor trust," combining all the labor of a given industry and charging extortionate prices for their work. It is true that a legalized trade organization may become a nest of privilege, but at present that danger seems remote. Capitalistic monopolies unite the corporate powers bestowed by law with the rights secured by private property, and the real grip of their extortionate power lies in the latter. A monopoly of labor would at least not own the earth in addition, and any revolution which our children may have to start against the extortionate labor prices of the coal miners would be far more hopeful and easy than our revolution against the extortionate coal prices of the mining corporations.

The transition to industrial democracy will put every employer to a moral test, perhaps the severest of all. Is he willing to relinquish autocratic power and trust increasingly to superior moral and intellectual efficiency for the leadership he claims? If he heartily consents to that, he proves that he is an American indeed, and that Christianity is more than a fine emotion to him. Even if he is willing, he will encounter misunderstandings, suspicions, unreasoning waves of emotion, and malicious demagogism among those whom he is trying to meet halfway. If so, he will suffer vicariously for the sins of other employers, of foreign nations,

and of past generations. This stunted life and these instinctive antagonisms are the results of generations of wrong,
and it will take time to outgrow them. On the other hand,
if he has sober expectations, he may find himself rewarded
beyond all his hopes by the good will of his workmates.
And whether he fares well or ill, the old despotic relation is
played out. It is becoming intolerable to both sides. The
finer spirits among the employing class are ready for a new
deal. If they have to choose between the present industrial
war and the possible troubles of industrial democracy, the
latter may be a real relief.

Economic democracy means more than the right of the
organized workers to control their own industry. It means
also the control of the people over their own livelihood.
It means the right and power to straighten out the line of
communication that runs from the farm to the kitchen and
the elimination of the middleman's profits that make food
prices dear. It means the power to cut all monopoly prices
out of business and to base prices solely on service rendered.
Democracy means the absence of class rule; monopoly
contains the essence of class rule. The power to charge a
monopoly price shows that part of the taxing power of the
government has gone astray into private hands, and that
a privileged class is exercising the attributes of sovereignty
over the rest. Therefore every lessening of monopoly
profit is a step toward economic democracy. When we
limit the price charged by common carriers so that they
earn only a reasonable return on the capital actually invested; when we prohibit capitalization that has no actual
investment behind it; when public ownership converts the
lucrative stock of a corporation into the modest bonds of a
city or state, we are moving away from economic aristocracy
and modern feudalism.

Every genuine advance in economic democracy in history
has involved a fight for political democracy. The larger

economic and political movements are invariably two sides
of the same thing.   The possessing classes are also the governing classes.   They have to control the government and
make the laws in order to exercise their economic privileges
in safety.   Consequently if the people want to stop exploitation, they must get control of government.   When the
English democracy tried to tax unearned wealth for social
purposes, a political crisis promptly arose.   The Lords
tried to block the Commons and had to be curbed.   In our
country the effort to curb the arrogant power of the monopolies and lessen their unearned profits has resulted in a political conflict all along the line.   The smoke of masked batteries has risen from every political hilltop, showing how
completely the enemy had occupied every strategical position.
The movements for direct primaries, for commission government, for direct legislation, for the recall, and for the direct
election of senators are the political counterpart of the
struggle for economic democracy and emancipation.   The
political confusion and bitterness of the presidential campaign of 1912 get their significance and dignity only from
the economic issues involved and the immense social forces
struggling for the mastery of the country.   The genuine
leaders of these movements are not fighting for names and
forms, but for realities, for our homes, our children, and our
manhood.

In their struggle with economic aristocracy the people
are handicapped by their inveterate morality.   The great
Interests have had no mercy on the public; they have
crippled the public good for private profit, resisted public
control, hired the best lawyers to thwart the law, and tampered with the poorly paid servants of the people.   On the
other hand the people are more than fair.   They fall in
with the point of view that when graft has been enjoyed
securely for some time it becomes a vested right.   They are
merciful toward those who have accommodated themselves

to unearned wealth. A mature democracy, such as the Swiss, the English, and our own, is usually highly conservative. Democracy constantly balances conflicting interests, and so becomes a college of compromise. But when public opinion is convinced, it moves with the finality of a landslide. Democracies seem vacillating, but they stay put when they move.

Democracy has become a spiritual hope and a religious force. It stands for the sanitation of our moral relations, and for the development of the human soul in freedom and self-control. In some future social order democracy may possibly stand for the right to be unequal. In our present social order it necessarily stands for more equality between man and man.

Men are unequal in their capacities, and always will be, and this inherent inequality of talent will inevitably be registered in some inequality of possessions. But beneath the superficial inequalities of intellect lies the fundamental endowment of human personality, and in that we are all equal. Wherever we get close enough to our fellows to realize their humanity, we feel an imponderable spiritual reality compared with which all wealth-getting gifts are trivial. Our children may differ widely in physical perfection and intellectual ability, but the strong child and the crippled child are alike life of our life, and the same mysterious human soul gazes at us out of their inscrutable baby eyes. Outsiders may rate the gifts of a husband and his wife very unequally, but the gifted partner often knows that all his cleverness is like autumn leaves and that in human worth his quiet mate outranks him. In the family it is love which acts as the revealer of this profound human dignity and equality. In society at large the Christian religion has been incomparably the strongest force in asserting the essential equality of all souls before God.

Democracy aids in christianizing the social order by

giving political and economic expression to this fundamental Christian conviction of the worth of man.   We do not want absolute equality; we do want approximate equality.   We can at least refrain from perpetuating and increasing the handicap of the feebler by such enormous inequalities of property as we now have.   To assert that they really correspond to the actual differences in intellectual ability is idle talk, and it becomes more absurd with every year as we see the great fortunes grow.   They are an institutionalized denial of the fundamental truths of our religion, and Democracy is the archangel whom God has sent to set his blazing foot on these icebergs of human pride and melt them down.

Men say that equality would hold ability down under a dead weight of mediocrity.   If ability can be held down it is not very able.   If the time ever comes when the strong are oppressed, I shall gladly join a crusade for their emancipation.   Meantime I judge with the old German composer Zeller: "A genius can do anything.   A genius will shampoo a pig and curl its bristles."   Disciplined intellect will ask no odds except of the Almighty.

CHAPTER V

SUPPOSE, now, that we had such a social order as we have been praying for in the preceding chapters, — an order in which justice and economic democracy prevailed, in which all unearned incomes were stopped, in which men had the right to a living as they now have the right to life, and in which the chances of prosperity and distinction were open to all on fairly equal terms. How, then, would these free and equal men act together in their economic relations? Should they compete? Should they coöperate? Should the bulk of productive work be done by small economic units in open competition, diversified, perhaps, by the public management of some great natural monopolies? Or would the christianizing of the social order call for the creation of a great coöperative system of production, diversified by small and scattered sections of private and competitive effort?

The former was the ideal taught by the old political economy, and has been the inspiration of many of the finest upper-class champions of democracy and human rights. It takes its most militant and influential form to-day in the philosophy of the Single Tax, and we could ill spare the brave spirit and indoctrinating power of that movement from our public life.[1] But it seems to me to exhaust its great moral force in the opposition against unjust privilege, and to lack constructive faith. In the noble

---

[1] The movement is represented by the *Public*, of Chicago, one of the ablest weeklies in the country, a stanch friend of all real democracy.

motto of the French Revolution, "Liberty, Equality, Fraternity," the first two terms are mainly negative; the chief positive value is contained in the third. Economic individualism is strong in its emphasis on liberty and equality, but weak in the economic basis it offers for fraternity. Is fair and open competition really the last and best word of the social hope? Are we to live like the little lobsters in the tank of a government hatchery, each wolfing for itself, and preying on its neighbor when the food supply runs low?

In the first century of our era a new social organization spread through the Roman Empire. It had a force of cohesion so strong that it bound men of all races and social classes into fraternity, resisted the crushing pressure of the Roman despotism, and survived all the shocks and changes of European society for nineteen hundred years. One of the earliest leaders of this remarkable organization formulated its social philosophy from the biology of the human organism. The ideal society, he said, has an unlimited diversity of organs and functions, but a fundamental unity of life, motive, and purpose; it is perfect in the measure in which every member has the support and protection of the whole body, and in turn serves the whole in its due place.[1] Paul's philosophy of the Christian Church is the highest possible philosophy of human society. The ideal society is an organism, and the christianizing of the social order must work toward an harmonious coöperation of all individuals for common social ends.

Fraternity needs an economic basis if it is to be made a vigorous and substantial part of social life. In turn fraternity alone offers a spiritual faith strong enough to inspire the mass movements necessary to overthrow inherited privilege. Individualism has pounded the protective tariff for generations and not yet rooted up its worst

[1] 1 Corinthians xii.

evils. The ideal of coöperative fraternity has found its most coherent and dogmatic form in socialism, and socialism has an incomparably stronger moral appeal with the masses than economic individualism ever had. In his Autobiography [1] John Stuart Mill has sketched the gradual maturing of his social hopes, and the course traversed by that bold, clear mind has since been followed by social thought at large. At first he looked only for some slight mitigation of the inequalities of property by the abolition of primogeniture and entails in England, by the education of the working classes, and the voluntary restraint of propagation. In time he passed from mere democracy to socialism: "We were now much less democratic than I had been, because as long as education continues to be so wretchedly imperfect, we dreaded the ignorance and especially the selfishness and brutality of the mass; but our ideal of ultimate improvement went far beyond Democracy, and would class us decidedly under the general designation of Socialists. . . . The social problem of the future we considered to be, how to unite the greatest individual liberty of action with a common ownership in the raw material of the globe, and an equal participation of all in the benefits of combined labor. Between communism and all its chances, and the present state of society with all its sufferings and injustices, all the difficulties, small or great, of communism would be but as dust in the balance."

If the christianizing of the social order involves ultimately the evolution of a coöperative economic organization as wide as society, we confront the largest constructive moral task ever undertaken. It is hard enough to get four or five men to work together without serious friction. To induce a hundred or a thousand to coöperate without tyrannous coercion is a work of strategy and art. Humanity took centuries to consolidate the patriarchal family,

[1] pp. 230–234.

the village commune, or the modern State. A coöperative commonwealth would join in associated work millions of people of low intelligence and education, but of strong passions and egotisms, who will have to render honest and faithful service in the main, and subordinate their passions to a higher reason and the common good, if the coöperative system is not to break down and relapse into some form of despotism. If any one thinks such an organization can be evolved by the mere propaganda of an economic doctrine or the creation of a strong party, let him take a contract to build a suspension bridge with a clothesline. But if any one thinks it is beyond the possibilities of human nature, let him rub his eyes and look around him.

The evolutionary process by which a great coöperative system will eventually be built up is now going on all about us. Intellectual persuasion and moral conviction are invaluable factors in the process, but they would never by themselves overcome the resistance of selfishness and conservatism. In this business the rude hand of economic necessity is fortunately on the side of the moral ideal, shoving and jamming and hauling the obstinate factors around into their places. The very hugeness of the modern machine, both steel and human, demands teamwork, the orderly interlocking of more and more, and bigger and bigger units of productive force. The story of modern industry is the story of the aggregation of labor and the coöperation of intellect. The first half century of capitalism per-fected the business firm; the second half century wrought out the corporation. The corporation marks a long stride toward social coöperation. The time was when the best observers held that the corporation could never develop enough initiative and devotion to business to compete with the swift powers of decision and the keen personal interest of the single owner or the business firm. Yet the corporation is steadily superseding the old-fashioned private busi-

ness in all the large and distinctively modern forms of
undertaking. The private firm was evolved from household
production and was based on personal efficiency and family
coherence. The corporation is the product of modern
traffic. It is a higher stage in the education of society in
the difficult art of coöperation, combining vastly more
units of labor and capital. The claim that human nature
could not furnish the moral qualities necessary to make
the corporation work has been disproved by the course of
events. Have we now reached the limits of the coöperative capacities in human nature, or is the corporation the
stepping-stone to something larger still?

Whenever any one holds up the hope of a coöperative
commonwealth, the question is almost invariably raised:
"Where will you get the kind of men to make such a social
order work?" The question involuntarily betrays the
consciousness that the present order is not producing a
sufficient stock of conscience and public devotion to equip
any social order resting on a really ethical basis. Capitalism has overdeveloped the selfish instincts in us all and left
the capacity of devotion to larger ends shrunken and atrophied. But a little observation of actual life will show us
that it is not dead. Whenever an individual enters a social
group that calls for free obedience and devotion, there is
some response of his moral nature. When a selfish man
marries, he begins to labor with all his might to support
the family group and even to protect them against want
after he is dead. When a self-willed and obstinate little
child from a lonely home enters the kindergarten, it soon
submits to the higher will and the orderly collective life of
the schoolroom. When a half-grown boy enters a shop, it
may be no ideal place for him, but it is an organized community of labor, and it assimilates him and helps to make a man
of him. The love with which men freely work for their
church, their lodge, their union, their philanthropic society,

2 B

their party, their city, their country, demonstrates what enduring loyalties a true social organism can evoke in its members. Make a man a trustee of an institution, let him serve it for years, and it becomes part of his life. He prays for it, plans for it, and endows it when he dies; yet it never did anything for him except to give him an honorable chance to serve his fellow-men. Would that same man be too selfish to serve the coöperative commonwealth with devotion? In our present economic order the accumulation of private property has been the only means of securing personal safety and advancement. Year in and year out men have to plan and labor intensely for their own business profit. Is it any wonder that the roots of their minds are coiled inside of that flowerpot? Compel them to think for the common good, connect their personal welfare and wealth with the prosperity and opulence of the community, spur them with the fear of public shame or the hope of public distinction, and see what heroic exertions they will put forth in the service of the commonwealth!

There is a great stirring of public spirit in all kinds of organizations, chambers of commerce, trades-unions, women's clubs, churches, publicity associations; they all want to serve humanity, but there is no harness available in which to hitch them. If the pent-up moral willingness of our nation could be set free to move toward organized fraternity, the forward rush would probably astonish us by its swiftness. We are forcibly held back from larger coöperative undertakings by the unsocial perversity inherent in Capitalism. In many of our cities the people are morally and intellectually ready now to undertake the coöperative management of their gas and electricity and street railways by means of municipal ownership, but the capitalistic group wants the profits and uses all its powers to frustrate and discourage public ownership. If the nation could vote by referendum on the government ownership of telegraphs and telephones, the people would probably seize the chance to widen the scope of their coöperative efforts, but the profit-makers refuse to let them. The flower of the working class is bending all its efforts to stop the suicidal system of pitting every workingman against his fellows and to substitute the principle of solidarity for that of anarchy. But Capitalism opposes their efforts for coöperation because the organization of labor would impair the profits of capital. Capital itself is anxious to unite still further, for the large coöperative organization of capital is manifestly sensible and profitable. But the public has found out by terrible experience what the enormous powers of association signify when they are wielded by an irresponsible financial aristocracy for purposes of extortion, and the public is afraid. The nemesis of its greed has come on Capitalism. The moral forces of the community are lined up to prevent Business from moving toward larger coöperation. The guerrilla warfare of petty competition has come to look like a paradise of peace to the suffering public. The Government, as the guardian of public interests, is forced into the attitude of an obstructionist of social progress. Our public life has become a huge tragi-comedy in which we are all trying not to do what we all know we shall have to do anyway. This is the enchanted maze into which the wily Devil of Profit has conjured us, and here we go milling around in sweaty stupidity.

CHAPTER VI

AN unchristian economic order tempts men and debases character, sets individuals and classes into unfraternal antagonism to one another, and institutionalizes widespread disloyalty to the common good. A Christian economic order would aid in training sound and strong individuals by its assimilating influence, would place men in righteous relations to one another and to the commonwealth, and so promote the Christian purpose of giving all a chance to live a saved life.

In the foregoing chapters we have inquired in what direction our economic life must move in order to approximate a Christian condition.

A Christian order must be just. Unjust privilege and unearned incomes debase the upper classes by parasitism, deprive the lower classes of their opportunity to develop their God-given life, and make genuine fraternity impossible between the classes.

A Christian economic order must offer to all members of the community the blessed influence of property rights. If modern industrial conditions no longer permit the workers a chance to own their productive plant and to accumulate enough for security, property must take the new form of a share in social wealth which will guarantee security in sickness and age and give a man an assured position in the workshop of the nation.

Our economic order must work away from one-man power toward the democratizing of industry. It must take the taxing powers of monopoly from an irresponsible aristocracy and put the people in full control of their own livelihood. It must do away with the present unethical inequalities of wealth and approximate a human equality.

A Christian economic order must organize all workers in systematic and friendly coöperation, and so create the material basis for Christian fraternity.

These fundamental demands of the Christian spirit are all simple and almost axiomatic, but they cut deep and are revolutionary enough to prove that they are really the laws of the Kingdom of God on earth.

Every forecast of the future lies under the suspicion of being the iridescent dream of a single mind, interesting perhaps, but without authority for the rest of us. The "practical man" sets all things new aside and rests contentedly on the things to which he is accustomed and which he supposes to be universal and eternal. We could make out an excellent case to prove to the social conservative that polygamy, slavery, alcoholism, and monarchical government have the almost universal consent of mankind through all the ages, and of the larger part of humanity to-day, so that we ought to view with seasoned suspicion any revolutionist who tells us that we ought to keep sober, have one wife, run a republic, and refrain from buying and selling women and babies.

Yet the practical man is right at bottom. What is wholly new is not likely to be true. The common sense of mankind ought to have weight with us. We all feel surer of our convictions when we find them held by great numbers and running far back into the past. The Catholic Church bases its claim to authority on that feeling. It claims to teach that doctrine which has always and everywhere and by all been held as the substance of the Christian faith, and by that traditional wisdom to brush aside the novel inventions of heresy. Only we must be very sure that we are really listening to the voice of God in history, and not to the unanimous consent of human sinfulness. Majorities do not necessarily stand for truth and justice. They stand for the customs and convictions of the past. They embody the solid experience and common sense of millions, but also their stolid prejudices and superstitions. The higher moral purposes which are now stirring unborn beneath the heart of mankind, and maturing toward that day of birth which God alone knows, are not registered in majorities. God's pioneers are always few. To trace the movements of God in history, we must not look to the broad bulk of mankind, but to the forward movements of the choicest members and segments of the race in whom the spirit of God got a lodgment and worked his will. They, and not the Sanhedrin and the crowd before the palace of Pilate, constitute the true Church of Jesus Christ, whose consent should have weight with us.

The ablest, purest, bravest, and most Christlike men have always headed in substantially the same direction. The noblest and most fraternal social groups have always reached out for the same essentials of a righteous social life. The richness and fullness with which such men were able to unfold the faith that was in them depended on their personal gifts and on the favor of circumstances. The form in which such social groups cast their social life depended on their historic environment. Usually they emphasized some special form of righteousness because that was the protest against some special form of iniquity which oppressed them. But wherever God got a foothold among men, we find an irrepressible drift in the same direction, an effort always renewed and reawakened in spite of defeat, always seeking to realize a just, free, and fraternal community life. This I hold to be a true consent of the saints of God, that faith of the Kingdom of God which has always and everywhere and by all true souls been held in spite of suffering and death, the *quod semper, quod ubique, quod ab omnibus* of the Church Catholic. The blood of the martyrs surely attests it. If to-day we find the faith of these elect groups becoming the clear faith of millions; if the hand of prince and priest is no longer able to stifle it; if the pace of freedom is quickening, and increasing freedom is used to achieve increasing justice, — we may well feel that the great day of Jehovah is near for which our fathers waited and strove.

Wherever historical investigation has uncovered the early history of our Aryan race, we see communities of free men in organized fraternity of life. These forefathers of ours met in assembly to govern themselves, choosing their leaders freely as needed. The land, which was then the one great instrument of production, was owned in common, and citizenship involved not only the right to vote, but the right to share in the common property. The combination of community property with private property was the characteristic feature of their economic organization. The forest with its wood and game, and the water with its fish, were common wealth which could be used by all according to regulations made by all. Every family owned its cattle, but it was pastured by the village herdsmen on the common pasture land. The plowland was divided in severalty to the families, but still owned by the community and redivided when changes in the population demanded it. A building site in the village was assigned to every family, and all helped a young couple erect their home, just as our farming communities still give their friendly help at a barn raising. New ground was often cleared in common. The larger buildings of the community and all extensive enterprises were undertaken in common. Approximate equality of possession was maintained and the aggressive acquisitiveness of individuals was kept in check as a menace to the freedom and property of all. All the concrete institutions of society were based on the sense of solidarity and trained men to fraternity. Outsiders were under no protection of law, but for those inside it was "all for each and each for all." Within the community every man had security for life, every woman protection of her honor. Before the courts of the nation the community answered for its members and bore their fines.

Thus the essentials of a righteous social life, justice, property, democracy, equality, coöperation, were embodied in the rude and simple conditions of these communities. Here the social supremacy of the Aryan race manifested itself and got its evolutionary start. Here the traditions of democracy and justice were dyed into the fiber of our breed so that they outlasted ages of despotism and reasserted themselves whenever the grip of tyranny slackened.

In time these simple fraternal democracies were everywhere weakened or disrupted by the inroads of the strong. Perhaps it had to be so. Chiefs intrusted with temporary authority by the community held fast their power and made it hereditary. The stronger members of the community took more than their share of the common land and its advantages, and claimed its permanent use. When kings rose in war, they stretched their powers in peace and gave away the property rights of the people to their underlings. The Church was given a share of the common lands and then amassed more. The old customary law, in which the rights and freedoms of the community were laid down, was twisted or set aside by the powerful men who made the new laws. At last the Roman law, with the deadly exaggeration of private property rights and lordly power which it brought down from the imperial despotism, legalized injustice and swept away the remnants of popular rights. So primitive democracy was slowly broken down and monarchical and aristocratic power was built up. The law of fraternity expressed in land communism was supplanted by the law of force and covetousness. The rich and poor moved apart. Primitive democracy and fraternity had been based on blood kinship and neighborhood feeling. It broke down as the community outgrew those moral ties.

But not everywhere alike. Some nations and some communities retained far larger elements of their early democracy and communism than others. Where the law of private covetousness had free swing, the common people were impoverished and lost their virility. Wherever a community succeeded in combining popular liberty with common property rights and capacity for united action, the intellectual ability and moral integrity of the breed was preserved and further trained. Thus the republics of Greece and Rome developed their famous life because they fought off the oppressors longer than others. The history of the Greek republics is a history of the struggle of democracy with the encroachments of the strong, and the question at issue always was the use of the common lands and the fraternal property rights of the people. The great names of Hellas and Rome, Solon, Lycurgus, Manlius, and the Gracchi, were the men who led in the struggles to limit the amount of land to be owned by individuals, to restore the use of the common lands to the people, and to save their nation from an utter denial of the principle of human fraternity. If we could translate the struggles of their agricultural age into the modern industrial equivalents, we should find that they were fighting against trusts, franchise grabbers, labor crushers, and party bosses just as we are.

It is wonderful with what tenacity the institutions of fraternal democracy maintained their life. For instance, the common meals that were customary at Sparta, Athens, Rome, and many cities were remnants of an early communistic organization and nuclei of happiness and fraternity. The village communities, the town guilds, the city republics, the religious fraternities of the Middle Ages, were continuations under changed forms of older communistic democracies. The finer breeds of vegetable and animal life are one of the most precious acquisitions of civilization. They can be transmitted and perfected easily, but who could reinvent the Northern Spy or the Jersey breed if it perished, or reorganize the vocal chords of the nightingale or mocking bird? So the higher strains of social organization are rarely invented; they are transmitted. Those communities in which the essentials of fraternal democracy were rescued from the inroads of tyranny, furnished other communities, often in distant continents and ages, with the model and inspiration of democracy. Our American democracy was no new invention; English and Dutch liberties merely grew to bolder size on the new soil. The influence exerted by the republican traditions of Greece and Rome on the intellectual classes has been beyond computation. The Swiss communities, which by the favor of their mountains have always preserved large fragments of their primitive community life, such as the town meeting and common forests and pasture rights, for centuries held up before northern Europe the models of democracy. When the Reformation took root on Swiss soil, it there developed a type of church organization that proved one of the most powerful allies of democracy and education. The initiative and referendum, the last-forged weapons in the hand of our own insurgent democracy, were forged in the smithy of Swiss self-government. What would humanity be by this time if the free institutions of the Aryan village community had everywhere been preserved and developed in unbroken historical continuity as they have been in Switzerland?

Christianity itself is such a strain of higher social life derived from one of the breeding grounds of righteousness. Israel was one of the unsubdued communities in which the love of freedom and justice was kept alive through all disaster. The sacred writings of the nation carried the burning words of its religious revolutionists down the centuries. The social passion for fraternity was enormously intensified through the influence of Jesus himself. With that social impetus derived from the prophets and from Jesus Christianity entered the Roman world like a young mountain torrent. For three centuries it was as much in opposition to the existing society as socialism is now. If any one wants to understand the spirit with which some Christians regarded the Empire, let him read the seventeenth and eighteenth chapters of the Revelation of John and imagine that he were reading about the impending destruction of London or New York. Even after Constantine accepted the Church as his ally, the Christian spirit was still in protest against the social order. The Church Fathers were practically unanimous in holding that the State and private property had come into the world through the Fall; in other words, the despotic State, as they knew it, with its coercion and cruelty, and the system of exploiting wealth, were not a wise institution of God, but a product of human sin, and would disappear if the power of sin was broken.

When the Church gained its wonderful ascendency over the social life of the Teutonic nations, it set itself against those economic tendencies which have since resulted in capitalism. It prohibited the breeding of money from money by interest. It discountenanced the unlimited accumulation of wealth. It condemned monopoly profit and taught the doctrine of the "fair price" as a just reward for labor cost. To take advantage of a man's necessity to raise the price was regarded as extortion. The Jews, who were not under the law of the Church, were free to practice the principles of capitalism centuries before its time. That made them rich; it also made them hated and despised. In the long run the Church was not able to hold back the commercial hunger for profit and has modified its teaching to suit the code of business, but it deserves more credit than it has ever received for the stand it made against exploitation.

The medieval monasteries were the pure cultures of the social bacillus of Christianity. Here the Christian spirit went out of the world to fashion a little world of its own. The asceticism of the monasteries was one thing; their social organization was another. Every monastery was essentially a communistic republic. Whoever entered an order left all distinctions of rank and wealth behind; they were blotted out in the uniform garb, the name of "Brother," and the simple life common to all. In most monasteries the governing power was vested in the brethren. The abbot or prior might exercise stern powers of command, but it was understood to be for the common good, like the discipline of a teacher or parent. The property of the order was owned in common and usually worked in common. The vow of poverty meant the abjuring of private property. The monastic orders were always falling away from their social ideals because they were always invaded by the life of the world about them, just as the nobler social organizations and professions to-day are invaded by capitalism. Secular society was full of idle and lascivious men, living on rent and the labor of others. Is it strange that cliques of monks developed in the monasteries who domineered over the poor lay brethren and left the manual toil to them? Or that entire monasteries became parasitic groups living on the surrounding secular community by means of rents? Whenever a monastery or convent grew rich by gifts, the nobility quartered their landless younger sons or unmarried daughters in it, and so wrested it from its purpose. But the pride and exploitation that were a matter of course in secular life were at least felt to be a shame and degradation in monastic life, and the Christian spirit was incessantly striving to rescue its own peculiar community life. In spite of all corruptions, these fraternal democracies were the haven of all idealistic spirits and the fountainheads of all nobler spiritual and social impulses for centuries. The Roman Catholic Church still points to these communistic settlements as the finest flower of its spiritual life. To-day socialism is seeking to establish on a world-wide scale some of the essential principles of the monastic societies, the abolition of rank, the duty of work, the combination of manual and spiritual labor, and fraternal property rights. The Catholic Church feels compelled to oppose socialism. Is it then in some other form putting its sentence of condemnation on existing society with the same clear severity as in the medieval monastic communities?

Radical Protestants may not be moved by arguments drawn from Roman Catholic monasticism, but what will they do with the fact that the evangelical sects of the Middle Ages, in whom they are accustomed to see the remnants of the true Church, had practically the same social ideals? They too demanded simplicity and voluntary poverty, fraternal love, and sharing with the needy. Therewith they repudiated as unchristian the class pride, the ostentatious luxury, the commercial covetousness, and the enthronement of money which Christians who take their ethics from capitalism can stomach without qualms. Existing society seemed to some of these old evangelical bodies so sinful that they would not allow their members to get mixed up in its iniquities by holding public office. They were too bitterly persecuted to have a full opportunity for organizing their social life according to their own convictions, but when they did have a chance, they tried to create little coöperative commonwealths. Our own country has given the spiritual descendants of some of these bodies the freedom of action which Europe denied them, and they have dotted America with coöperative colonies. These communistic colonies are profoundly pathetic. Whether a colony succeeds or fails financially, its members are withdrawn from the rich life of human society and condemned to isolation and narrowness. But considered as protests against the cruelty, covetousness, and unbrotherliness of our civilization, they are deserving of far more attention than they receive. To lift a body of people out of the old grooves of life, to make them give up their private property and risk their lives on a great venture in fraternity requires a tremendous moral force. Yet for every hundred Christians who have actually joined a coöperative colony, there have probably been ten thousand who have wished that they might.

Our college and university communities offer their contribution to an inductive study of fraternal community life. Why do we all look back to our college days with such strange attachment? It is not merely the glamour of youth that lights those sunlit spaces of our memory, for we were young before college and after it. It is not necessarily the ease and comfort we enjoyed; some of us worked hard and have never again been so pinched by poverty as when we earned our education. Why, then, do the college days seem set apart from the rest? Is it not because we were members of a fraternal community life? A college is essentially a democracy. There is authority; work is exacted; but the authority of the faculty is leadership for the common good, and the work does not use men up, but builds them up. The individual is impelled by great collective loyalties to do his best. He is made free of the campus, the library, and a large endowment of collective property rights. Worth and manhood count; if wealth and social rank also count, the college is ashamed of it. The faculty and president receive honor, often extravagant honor, but they are not in a social class apart. The youngest freshman can sit at prexy's table and court the dean's daughter. The faculty differ in salary and standing, but the extremes are rarely farther apart than $1000 and $10,000, and the career is open from bottom to top. For such financial rewards many of the ablest intellects of the world have always gladly given the best that was in them.

The traditions of university life have been slowly built up by generations of intellectual and more or less idealistic men, and may therefore count as a prophecy of the social life toward which the best in humanity is feeling its way. They also connect historically with the communistic community ideals which we have just sketched. The medieval student bodies were molded on the model of the monastic communities. The stately colleges of Oxford and Cambridge have grown up around the common kitchen quite as much as around the lecture room. Without its democratic and communistic elements every college would be stripped of its glow of affection. If our economic life could be organized at all on the same basis, it would prolong the spirit of youth for us all, and initiate the working class into the delight of teamwork, collective enthusiasm, and the combination of work and play.

Thus the fundamental demands of a Christian economic order which we have laid down, justice, collective property rights, democracy, approximate equality, and coöperation, are nothing new-fangled. They are the basis on which all men of noble mind have sought to build the social organizations in which they were interested, and all communities that have made distinguished and permanent contributions to the social traditions of mankind have preserved and developed these essential elements of social righteousness in some combination. The tyranny and covetousness of the strong have in the past held down or broken down the free development of fraternal democracy, so that only broken gleams of the Reign of God flash down to us from history. The question is if now at last the spiritual forces of humanity have gained enough conscious purpose and continuity of action to overcome the destructive forces of sin and found a fraternal commonwealth on the laws of God and Christ.

CHAPTER VII

"THE POWERS OF THE COMING AGE"

WE have seen that the social intuitions of the Christian spirit are confirmed and verified by history. Our fathers moved in the same direction as we.

Our ethical foresight is also verified by the young life of our own times. The new economic order is even now growing up and maturing among us, and we can begin to discern its fundamental bent.

Our age is like a family circle in which three generations are grouped around the same fireplace: the grandparents who ruled the past, the parents who are carrying the burdens of the present, and the children who are growing up to take their place. None of the three generations realizes how swiftly they are moving across the stage of life. So three economic orders are combining to make up the total of modern life: the precapitalistic which is passing away, the capitalistic which is in the flush of its strength, and the collectivistic which is still immature. Most farmers, some mechanics, and many small business men are still to some extent living according to the methods and the spirit of the age before capitalism. Capitalism, both in its competitive and its monopolistic form, is dominating our business, our legislation, our institutions, and our thought, and thinks it always has been and always will be. But on all hands a new order is growing up, young, vigorous, and clamorous, eager to inherit the house and run it in its own way.

Each of these three stages of social evolution is affected by the other two. None is able to express its peculiar spirit

and genius in logical severity and simplicity. But there
is a deep difference discernible, not only between their
economic methods, but between their ethical spirit and their
philosophy of life, and those social movements and organizations which most distinctly belong to the future, most
clearly embody the characteristics of the Christian economic
order. This is another corroboration of our faith. I have
no space for an extended study of the embryonic social
organizations of the future order, but shall present a few
evidences to back my claim.

Few people in America, unless they have given special
attention to the matter, as yet have any idea of the scope
and importance of the modern coöperative associations.
In Europe they have developed by thousands, especially
since 1870.[1] The network of these associations has become
an economic and social fact of first-class importance, and
in some countries, such as Belgium, Denmark, and Ireland,
they have begun to change the economic and·social character
of the nation.   There are coöperative retail stores, associated in large wholesale associations which manufacture
for their own market; building and loan associations to
furnish cheap credit; purchasing associations to buy raw
material for mechanics, or seeds, fertilizers, and agricultural
implements for farmers; societies to sell handicraft products or market-garden truck and farm products; coöperative mills, bakeries, slaughterhouses, creameries, cheese
factories, and grain elevators.

Their immediate aim is to save the middleman's profit
for their members, to insure them clean and unadulterated
goods and honest weights and measures, to save them from
the parasitic trickery of the petty middleman and the usury

[1] Germany in 1908 had 24,652 coöperative societies with 3,658,437 members. Denmark with a population of only 2,500,000 had about 1200 retail
stores, with 200,000 members, and has developed productive coöperation as
no other country has. Basle with 125,000 inhabitants had 28,000 coöperative buyers. Since 1908 the figures have grown very much.

2 C

of the money shark who exploit the poor, to train their people to frugality by cash payments and small savings, and to secure for the working class and the lower middle class some share in social wealth and profit. Every cooperative association encounters the same initial difficulties as any other business concern. They have to meet the most efficient survivors of capitalistic competition. They usually start with little capital and less experience, a double lack that would almost certainly be fatal to an ordinary business undertaking. There have been many failures, especially at first before the conditions for success had been worked out by experience. In some fields of enterprise they have not succeeded. But taking them in the large, they have demonstrated their economic fitness just as convincingly as the corporation. Yet they rest on a different moral basis.

The corporation is a product of the business class and takes its psychological coloring from that class. The cooperative is an organization of the earning classes, the industrial workers, the small farmers, and the lower business class, and it draws its strength from their peculiar moral qualities. The corporation is an association of capital; money counts in it; the members vote by the number of shares they hold; the small stockholder is practically a cipher in the management. The coöperative is an association of men; one man has one vote, regardless of the number of shares held. They have learned to appreciate the technical efficiency of salaried officers, but their directors give unpaid service for love of the cause, and the general business meeting of the members is the real power, at least in the smaller associations. "The number of bankruptcies and defalcations by directorates and officials is infinitely smaller in the world of the coöperative associations than in the corporations and big private business concerns."[1]

[1] Schmoller, "Volkswirtschaftslehre," I, 447.

The capitalistic corporation is after profits; its stockholders have no use for the goods they help to produce except as they earn profit; it accepts the brute struggle for existence as the law of business. The coöperative has a far stronger sense of humanity; it thrives best where the sense of solidarity is stoutest; its abler members seek to lift the weaker with them as they rise to economic prosperity. They do try to save money; they do not try to exploit men to make money. They refrain from taking business away from the ordinary dealer by cutting the market prices, though they might, in many cases, drive them out of business. They distribute the benefits to those who have made actual use of the coöperative plant, and according to the amount of use they have made of it.

Thus the coöperative associations represent a new principle in economic life, clearly of higher ethical quality than the principle dominant in capitalism. They combine a wholesomely selfish desire to get ahead with genuine fraternal sympathy and solidarity, and the combination works and holds its own against the most efficient business concerns in those fields where the coöperatives have learned to master the situation. They have appropriated the business system and calculating keenness of capitalism, but they draw the lower classes whom capitalism has almost deprived of initiative into the management, and train them to industrial and moral efficiency. Their methods have been adapted from the joint stock company, but their spirit is drawn from the older communal organizations, from the new socialist hatred for exploiting methods, and from the depths of uncontaminated human nature. There is no prospect that the coöperative associations will displace capitalism, but they have a great future and no limit can be set to their possibilities. They have proved what a fund of good sense and ability lies unused in the lower classes. They have demonstrated the economic efficiency of fraternal coöperation. They are creating everywhere trained groups, capable of assuming larger responsibilities when the time comes, and a new spirit that can afford to look down on the exploiting spirit of capitalism. Thus the achievements of these humble coöperators are the beginnings of a higher business morality. They are part of the newly forming tissue of a Christian social order and are one of "the powers of the coming age." [1]

The organizations of labor are also part of that new economic order which is growing up in the midst of capitalism.

From some points of view the unions are just as brutally commercial in their tactics as any capitalistic corporation. They sell labor wholesale as others sell goods, and they seize every advantage of the market as shrewdly and ruthlessly as any trust. But there are human and ethical values in trades-unionism which put them on a different footing, and explain the wonderful hold which the unions have on the loyalty of the élite of the working class.

Wherever their influence reaches among the workers, they substitute the principle of solidarity for that of competitive selfishness. They train their members to stand together loyally and to sacrifice their private and immediate advantage for some larger benefit to be won for all. It is true, they seek the advantage only of their own group, and not directly of all society. But what class does? Few loyalties have been world wide. Even patriotism is a limited devotion, bounded by the nation. Christian love itself checks its pace when it crosses the threshold of its own particular Church. Why should we demand of one of the lowest classes, fighting on the borderland of poverty, an unselfish devotion to all society which the upper classes

[1] See Holyoke, "History of Coöperation in England "; Beatrice Potter (Mrs. Sidney Webb), "The Coöperative Movement in Great Britain "; Acland and Jones, "Workingmen Coöperators "; Henry D. Lloyd, "Labor Copartnership."

have never shown? The group selfishness of the unions is at least a larger and nobler selfishness than that of the strike breaker whom the public sentiment of capitalism praises and rewards. The capitalistic class finds it hard to understand the ethical value of the solidarity exhibited by organized labor, because commercial practices have fatally disintegrated its own capacity to stand together for similar sacrifices.

When the unions demand a fixed minimum wage, a maximum working day, and certain reasonable conditions of labor as a security for health, safety, and continued efficiency, they are standing for human life against profits. With capitalism the dollar is the unit of all calculations; with unionism it is life. With capitalism the main purpose of industry is to make as large a profit as possible, and it makes the margin of life narrow in order to make the margin of profit wide. With unionism the purpose of industry is to support as large a number of workingmen's families in comfort as possible. Capitalism and unionism fail to understand each other because they revolve around a different axis.

We have seen that the perversities of our economic order force the business men into false positions. The workingmen are put in the wrong in the same way. Their noblest impulses often lead to actions that shock the moral judgment of outsiders. For instance, the sympathetic strike is condemned by law, by public opinion, and by the cautious prudence of the leaders of labor, yet the labor organizations are often quivering on the verge of it. And as a demonstration of altruism and solidarity it is sublime. Like the charge of the six hundred at Balaklava, it is not war, but it is magnificent. Thousands of men and women giving up their job, their slender hold on subsistence, imperiling the bread and butter of their families for the sake of men in another trade with whom they have only a distant economic connection, simply to help their fellows in a fight which they feel to be their own, — where in the transactions of the business class, and where in church life do we find such heroic self-sacrifice of great bodies of men and women for a common cause?

Organized labor is blamed for limiting the pace of work in a shop and restraining the capable workers from doing their best. It surely seems dishonest for a workman not to give his employer the best work that is in him, and it levels the standard of work down below the maximum of efficiency. In a coöperative democracy of labor such a condition would indeed be against the common good and ethically intolerable, but as long as the workers are on the defensive against a superior force that seeks to get the maximum of labor from them for the minimum of reward, this unnatural condition may actually be moral. The men know by bitter experience that in some shops the pace set by the young and able is soon demanded of all and made compulsory by speeding up the machinery or cutting the price of piecework. The few may gain if the capable do their best, but the mass would lose. The older and slower workmen could not keep up at all; the strength of the others would be drained. Under such conditions the workers are in a moral dilemma, cornered between two wrongs or two duties. When they limit the pace of the capable, they enforce the law of solidarity: "Bear ye one another's burdens, and so fulfill the law of Christ." But with what right can the capitalist class blame them, which everywhere seeks to limit the output in order to maintain its monopoly prices? The Steel Trust fixing prices for all steel manufacturers by a gentleman's agreement, and a shop of workmen enforcing the "ca' canny" policy on all the men, are both doing the same thing. The Steel Trust does it to keep up its enormous profits. The workingmen do it to preserve their health against premature exhaustion, and in order to help the older men to hold their job. If there must be limitation of output, who has the better cause?

Labor unions are fighting organizations, and fighting always abridges personal liberty and stiffens the demand for obedience and subordination. In the long fight of labor the odds are nearly always against it, sometimes enormously so. The employers have the tremendous backing of property rights and the long wind given by large resources. The Law, which ought theoretically to be impartial, has always been made by the powerful classes. It used to treat the organization of workingmen as conspiracy, and still takes a grudging attitude toward demands which are clearly just. The battle of labor is fought by a few for all. Only a minority of the industrial workers is sufficiently strong economically, and sufficiently developed morally, to bear the strain of organized effort. Unorganized labor reaps the advantages of the sacrifices made by the unions, yet often thwarts their efforts and defeats the common cause. Bitterness, roughness, and violence are inevitable in such a conflict. The danger of tyranny is real enough. But underneath the grime of battle is the gleam of a higher purpose and law which these men are seeking to obey and to bring to victory. They are standing for the growth of democracy, for earned against unearned income, for the protection of human weakness against the pressure of profit, for the right of recreation, education, and love, and for the solidarity of the workers. They doubtless sin, but even the errors of labor are lovable compared with the errors of capitalism. The seed of a new social order is in them. They too belong to "the powers of the coming age."

The coöperative associations and the organizations of labor are practical efforts to secure immediate benefits for the persons who unite in these movements. Two other great movements, the Single Tax and Socialism, offer no direct advantage to their supporters. Each is a missionary movement and bears a gospel of social salvation to our capitalistic age. I point to them here as proof that the moral and spiritual convictions on which a new social order will have to be based are gaining force and are even now preparing that new order.

"All the evils under which civilized people suffer can be traced back to private property in land as their cause." [1] All tyranny and exploitation is based on the control of the natural resources of the earth. Whoever owns the earth can exploit the people who live on it. In our industrial era the increase and concentration of population have enormously increased land values and enabled the owners of the land to levy a tribute on the working population beyond compute.

Wherever the demand for justice has become intelligent and thorough, it has included a demand for the restoration of the land to the people in some form. But a continuous, world-wide agitation, based on a scientific theory, and offering a simple and practicable reform, has begun only with the man Henry George and his book, "Progress and Poverty." Editorial wiseacres still keep on informing us that the Henry George movement failed. God grant all good men such failure! It failed in its first attempt to carry politics by storm, but it betook itself to the education of the public mind. Henceforth it distrusted party organization and put its faith in intellectual conviction. Its teachings dropped into the minds of the young and grew up with them. Now that the men who were young twenty-five years ago have come to maturity and influence, the teachings of Henry George are everywhere entering practical politics, though supported by the slenderest sort of organization. The budget of Lloyd George in 1910, which precipitated the constitutional revolution in England, was only the beginning of a movement to socialize the income from

---

[1] Zachariæ, "Bücher vom Staat."

the land, and it is well understood that radical land taxation will be the next great step in the social revolution going on in Great Britain. Since 1900 a number of cities in Germany have been taxing the unearned increment whenever land is sold, and the tax proved so simple, painless, and profitable that the Imperial Government has begun to draw on the same source for its revenues. New Zealand has a local option law in taxation under which nearly a hundred municipalities derive their local expenses from land values exclusively. The young cities of the Canadian Northwest are doing the same. In several of our older States movements are on foot to deal with the housing question by gradually shifting taxation from improvements to land values, thus forcing idle land into use and encouraging building. The whole procedure and administration of taxation has been deeply affected by the spread of Single Tax convictions.

But this movement is not simply the propagation of a new tax device, but the proclamation of a new social order. It is the uncovering of the most fundamental form of unearned wealth, and a democratic protest against the economic aristocracy built up on the unearned increment. Scratch a single-taxer and you find a genuine democrat who can be depended on to oppose all other forms of unjust privilege. Tom L. Johnson, who was won from the aimless acquisition of riches to the service of the people by the gospel of Henry George, applied the insight gained from the Single Tax doctrine to the knotty relations between the American municipalities and the public service corporations. He was only a conspicuous example of a new generation of public men whose souls and intellects have been saved from the vice of unearned money by that doctrine, and who are now occupied with the practical problems of political and economic democracy. The Single Tax movement has not appealed to the working class as powerfully as Socialism, but it is a system of thought exactly adapted to middle-class intellectuals and to religious individualists. I owe my own first awakening to the world of social problems to the agitation of Henry George in 1886, and wish here to record my lifelong debt to this single-minded apostle of a great truth.

Socialism, on the other hand, has laid hold of the industrial working class with the grip of destiny. It promises these propertyless men that they shall once more own the tools of their work, share in the profit of their toil, take part in the management of their shop, and so escape from their insecurity and dependence. It holds out the hope that in the socialist commonwealth they shall plant the vineyard and eat of the fruit thereof; they shall be full heirs of the science and art and education which they now labor to maintain, but into which, like Moses when he saw the Promised Land afar, they cannot enter.

Socialism always makes headway slowly at first. It requires hard thought. A man has to view all things from a new angle and revise all his maxims and value judgments. The leaders of the working class in any nation need a generation to assimilate it, and after that they have the task of popularizing it for the masses. But it never goes backward, and no industrial nation can escape its influence. It trusts more to intellectual conviction and less to emotion than any great movement of our day. Socialists appeal to the theoretical and historical intellect with almost wearisome exclusiveness. In Milwaukee nine tenths of the party funds used to go for literature. The socialists are to-day the only preachers who love doctrinal preaching. Not since the days when Calvinism was convincing the intellect of northern Europe has any system of thought been expounded with such evangelistic zeal.

The fact is that Socialism is the necessary spiritual product of Capitalism. It has been formulated by that class which has borne the sins of Capitalism in its own body and knows them by heart. It stands for the holy determination of that wronged and embittered class to eliminate those sins forever from the social life of mankind. Thus Socialism is the historical Nemesis of Capitalism and follows it like its shadow. The only influence that can long seal the minds of the industrial working class against the doctrines of Socialism is the power of religion in the hands of a strong Church. That influence has created solid organizations of nonsocialist workers in Europe. But socialism seeps in, even there. If those Catholic federations of workingmen which resist Socialism in Germany were transferred bodily to America, their presence would be felt as a tremendous reënforcement of the socialist drift in our trades-unionism. There is no way of taking the wind out of the sails of the socialist ship except to sail alongside of it and in the same direction. As a clever Irishman in Wisconsin puts it, "The only way to beat the socialists is to beat them to it." But when the enemies of a cause are compelled to aid it in order to oppose it, the stars in their courses are fighting against Sisera. The opponents of the Progressive Party in 1912 called its platform socialism; Mr. Roosevelt called it a corrective of socialism; the *Boston Common* called it "an adaptation of the more imminent teachings of socialism for middle-class neophytes," and added, "Out from among the lowly and despised once more has come a message of guidance for humanity."

For the present argument the important fact is not the growing political power of the socialists, but the moral power of their cause. The Russian despotism also exerts vast political power, but that is in defiance of the conscience of mankind. Socialism appeals not only to the working class, but to the idealistic intellectuals. A great number of artists and literary men are socialists at large. Many of the magazine writers and political leaders to whom we owe much of the present awakening are near-socialists. The same thing is true of the teaching profession and of social workers. An eminent banker, a former Secretary of the Treasury, said in an address to college alumni as early as 1909: —

"I am alarmed at the trend toward socialism in this country to-day. If there is any power in this country to stem it, it ought to be the trained minds of college men. Four out of five commencement-day orations are purely socialistic. I have met many of the teachers of sociology in our schools and universities. With few exceptions these teachers are socialists, though they hesitate to admit it and most of them will deny it. Unconsciously there is a great deal of socialism being taught in these days from the pulpit. The Chautauqua is also full of it. I do not recall a Chautauqua popular speaker who is not talking and teaching socialist doctrines. The trend of the newspapers is towards socialism, and, I repeat, the trend is dangerous to this country."

Such a statement is correct only if we accept our definition of socialism from the timidity of a banker. But it is interesting to see this man call on the college men to come to the rescue, and yet confess that the college men have gone over to the enemy. But if in any great historic movement the men of property are on one side and the young and idealistic intellects are on the other, on which side is God?

The religious idealists constitute a special variety of the intellectual class. In their case, the power of religion is added as a potent ingredient to their higher life. No one can deny that the ethical life of our religious leaders is deeply tinged with a diluted socialism. Wherever a man has the prophetic cast of thought, the broader moral outlook, and the tongue of fire, we can discover clear affinity for socialist ideas. Those men who have kept their mental balance against the dogmatism of the cruder type of socialism, who have guarded the purity of their life against the

looseness of modern morals, who have cherished the devout-
ness of intimate religion in the drought of skepticism, but
who have also absorbed the socialist analysis of our collective sins and the socialist hope of a fraternal democracy,
stand as a class marked by God as his own. The best of
them belong to "that small transfigured band whom the
world cannot tame."

Religious men are forced into a tragic dilemma when they
face organized Socialism. On the one hand they realize
in its ideas the most thorough and consistent economic
elaboration of the Christian social ideal. It is far and
away the most powerful force for justice, democracy, and
organized fraternity in the modern world. On the other
hand, these moral elements are fused with an alloy that is
repellent to their Christian instincts.

There are religious people who are not Christians. Their
sympathies are not with the common people, but with the
parasitic classes. They do not trust in freedom, but want
a strong Church to lay down the law to the common man.
If Jesus appeared in modern dress among such people,
they would not know what to do with him. To such persons, of course, Socialism is horrid. I am not concerned
for them. I speak for men who have drawn their economic
insight from Socialism, and their democracy and moral
ardor from Jesus himself, and who yet find it hard to co-
operate whole-heartedly with party socialism as they
actually find it.

When they attend socialist meetings, they encounter a
rougher, directer, more dogmatic, more acrimonious tone
of discussion than they are used to in gatherings of the
educated classes. Also an entire absence of respect for
many of their conventional objects of respect. But if
they have the right stuff in them, they will get used to it
and even come to like it as a proof of unvarnished sincerity
and profound interest in the subject. But they will also

find an almost universal attitude of suspicion and dislike against the Church, which often rises to downright hate and bitterness, and expands to general antagonism against religion itself. The materialistic philosophy of history as the average socialist expounds it, emphasizes the economic and material factors of life so exclusively that the spiritual elements of humanity seem as unimportant as the coloring of a flower or the bloom on the grape. In large parts of the party literature the social and economic teachings of Socialism are woven through a web of materialistic philosophy, which is part of "scientific Socialism." The party platform declares religion to be a private affair, but that declaration of neutrality does not exclude persistent attacks on religion by official exponents of the party. The practical deductions drawn from materialistic philosophy and from historical conceptions of the family, have combined with modern impatience of moral restraints to create in some of the intellectuals of the party loose views of sex life against which all the instincts of Christian training warn as poisonous.

If a Christian man sees the good in Socialism and identifies himself with the organized movement, he is suspected of atheism, free love, and red-handed violence, and he cannot repudiate that charge against his party friends as mere slander. A man of mature religious convictions may discriminate between the economic doctrines of Socialism, which are its essential, and the philosophical teachings, which are an adventitious historical taint of it. But others, who may be drawn into the party through his influence, may not be able to keep the two things apart.

Socialist leaders in America have committed an enormous tactical mistake in allowing Socialism to be put in antagonism to Christianity. Why should they permit some of their agitators to go out of their way to belie the neutrality promised by the party platform? Why should they erect a barb-wire fence between the field of Socialism and Christianity which makes it hard to pass from one to the other? Organized Christianity represents the largest fund of sobriety, moral health, good will, moral aspiration, teaching ability, and capacity to sacrifice for higher ends, which can be found in America. If Socialists will count up the writers, lecturers, and organizers who acquired their power of agitation and moral appeal through the training they got in church life, they will realize what an equipment for propaganda lies stored in the Christian churches. As soon as the Socialist party came to the point of being able to elect mayors and city officials, it found that Christian ministers somehow made up a large percentage of the men elected, which seems to argue that they have capacities that are not wholly contemptible. Many Socialist leaders misread the situation in America because they are obsessed by theories developed in Europe on the basis of the bad experience which Democracy has had with the Roman Catholic Church and with the Protestant State Churches. They know too little of religious history to be aware that religion is a very different thing in England and America where it has been loved and sustained for centuries by the free sacrifices of the plain people in their own little religious democracies. The autocratic Churches of Europe have long done their best to suppress any spontaneous religious movements of the common man, and have succeeded very well in making personal religious experience almost unknown in large sections of the population. In England and America millions of the people have experienced the power of religion in their own lives, and when Socialism undertakes to pull up Christianity, it will find it rooted deeper than in Europe. Surely Socialism has its job cut out for it in overthrowing Capitalism. Why should it force into the hostile camp the multitude of Christian men who are so close to it in their moral point of view? In England the best leaders of the Labor Party are Christian men and active church workers. The leaders of German Socialism are at a loss to understand a situation where Christian men can be also avowed Socialists. But that proves that the continental leaders are unfit to guide the policies of American Socialism. If Socialist philosophy does not reckon with the actual facts of social life, it is not "scientific," but a stock of imported misinformation.

As long as Socialism was an intense insistence on a few fundamental doctrines, and was upheld by a small body of minds bent on driving these doctrines home, it is comprehensible that the religious desires and emotions of the human soul were slighted or forgotten. But the more Socialism aspires to become a rounded expression of all sound and wholesome human life, and the more it embodies the great masses of humanity, the more sectarian and narrow-minded will the traditional contempt for religion become. Jaurès, the brilliant French Socialist leader, heralds a broader view: "I believe it would be wearisome and even fatal to stifle the aspirations of the human conscience. I do not believe at all that the material and social life suffice for man. We want him to be able to rise to a religious conception of life by means of science, reason, and freedom. The hour has come for democracy no longer to mock or outrage the ancient faiths, but to seek whatever they contain that is living and true and can abide in an emancipated and broadened human conscience." [1]

[1] Paul Sabatier, in his "L'Orientation Religieuse de la France Actuelle" (p. 38), tells an interesting anecdote. At a great church festival in Lyon, at which all the bishops of southeastern France were present, the bishop who had preached the sermon was receiving the compliments of ladies and priests at a dinner. He told them he had just read one of the most beautiful sermons he had ever read in his life, and begged permission to read them extracts. When he finished, all demanded the name of the preacher. He asked them to guess. They ran through the list of the celebrated preachers of France, but in vain. At last he announced that it was an address by — Jaurès.

The Socialists are not nearly as unbelieving as some of them try to make us believe. Their theories may make everything turn on "economic class interests"; they may scoff at moral ideals, and insist that it is all a "stomach question"; but they appeal to men to act contrary to their economic interests on behalf of humanity, and they themselves labor with a moral enthusiasm and a power of self-sacrifice which look most suspiciously like religion. "Nothing in the present day is so likely to awaken the conscience of the ordinary man or woman, or to increase the sense of individual responsibility, as a thorough course in socialism. The study of socialism has proved the turning-point in thousands of lives, and converted self-seeking men and women into self-sacrificing toilers for the masses. The impartial observer can scarcely claim that the Bible produces so marked an effect upon the daily, habitual life of the average man and woman who profess to guide their conduct by it, as socialism does upon its adherents. The strength of socialism in this respect is more like that of early Christianity as described in the New Testament." [1] Jesus surprised the religious people of his day by telling them that the publicans and harlots had more religion than they. Between a church member who lifts no hand against commercial inhumanity because it would "hurt business," and an atheist who endangers his position and consumes his energies in fighting it, we might be in doubt who of the two really believes in God.

Time and experience will balance the philosophy of Socialism. No great mass movement in history was ever free from one-sidedness and error. When Christianity was pervading the pagan world of Rome, it feared and repudiated art, because art had grown up in the service of paganism and seemed inseparable from it. But in time the Church became the great patron of art. In the Reforma-

[1] Professor R. T. Ely, "Socialism and Social Reform," p. 145.

2 D

tion the Protestant minority was wrought to such a fighting pitch that it hated the entire Catholic Church as anti-christian and devilish, and the Puritans cleared their churches of music and art because Catholicism had stamped them with its spirit. That dogmatic intolerance of a young movement fighting against the overwhelming pressure of an older social force is duplicated in Socialism to-day. Religion bears the stamp of the older epoch in which it was developed, and Socialism treats the Church as the Church treated pagan art and philosophy, and fears its gifts as Protestantism fears Catholicism. This seems intolerable, but it is human. While a movement is fluid and plastic, it takes the impress of its first environment and casts its doctrines and institutions in that mold. Jewish apocalypticism, Persian demonology, and Greek philosophy saturated early Christian thought and seemed part of the essence of Christianity to the early Church Fathers. Calvinism was molded by the stern, keen mind of John Calvin and by the civic institutions of Switzerland and proclaimed these equipments as part of the eternal gospel. Compared with the tenacity with which religion clings to its early prejudices or superstitions, Socialism has shown a very sweet reasonableness in the speed with which it has left some things behind.

To me the greatest danger seems to lie in the loss of that teachableness. When I try to look at Socialism as coming centuries may look back at it, I fear the solidity of the Socialist parties and the intensity of their party spirit. An organization created for fighting purposes does not melt away when the fighting is done, but its maintenance becomes an end in itself and therewith the organization becomes a drag on social progress. The history of the Republican Party and the useless perpetuation of many of our religious sects prove that. Pure love of the truth and independent thought do not flourish in the midst of party spirit. The internal history of Socialism shows how quickly a narrow and jealous orthodoxy springs up within the party and forbids the prompt assimilation of larger knowledge. Important sections of the party fear "the intellectuals," just as religious sects have feared their educated men. I realize that Socialism needs a steel edge to cut through the obstacles that confront it, and only party loyalty, party dogmatism, and even party hatred can temper that edge, but I wish the coming generations could be spared what we are preparing for them. Whoever solidifies the opposition to Socialism, inevitably solidifies Socialist party spirit, and when it is a Church that does it, it solidifies Socialist irreligion. The Roman Catholic Church laments and despises the sectarian divisions of Protestantism, but it is itself chiefly responsible for them. Its arrogance, its egotism, its refusal to be reformed by anything except the sledge-hammer blows of the Almighty's chastisement, necessitated the agonies that bled Christendom white and consolidated the reforming elements into fighting bodies which still perpetuate the dead issues of that fight after four centuries. Socialism inevitably involves a menace. It is our business to make its menace small and its blessing great.

Aside from the dangers involved in party orthodoxy we may safely trust that Socialism will slough off its objectionable elements as it matures. Those qualities against which the spirit of genuine Christianity justly protests are not of the essence of Socialism. The loose views of marriage in some individuals are largely a bacterial contagion contracted from the outside.[1] The materialism of the Socialist philosophy of history is the result of throwing a great truth out of balance; Christian doctrine, too, has often been one-sided by overemphasis of some truth. Atheism is in no way essential to Socialist thought. Socialists have no monopoly of it. It was the popular philosophy

---

[1] See Part IV, Chapter IV, of this book.

of continental liberalism in the '50's and '60's, and the leaders of the working class absorbed it as true "science." Christianity was the religion of the possessing classes and was used as a spiritual force to hold down Socialism; consequently revolutionary thought seized the philosophy that seemed most effectively to maul Christianity.[1] The Socialists found the Church against them, and thought God was against them too. They have had to do God's work without the sense of God's presence to hearten them. When a great moral movement has been infected with dogmatic unbelief, partly through the sin of the European churches, shall we back away from it in fear, or have we confidence enough in our own religion to take part in it? Can we prove in our own personality that the highest type of Socialism is that which combines the economic intelligence and political force of Socialism with the character and faith created by religion?

Whatever the sins of individual Socialists, and whatever the shortcomings of Socialist organizations, they are tools

[1] Professor Werner Sombart, "Sozialismus und soziale Bewegung," p. 91, thinks the hostility of the proletarian movement against religion has a theoretical and a practical cause. The theoretical cause is that Socialism in its youth absorbed the bald atheism which was the philosophy of the semi-educated classes in the middle of the nineteenth century. This dogmatic atheism is now definitely outgrown by science. "No serious representative of science will to-day dare to assert that science demands atheism or excludes religion." Therefore the proletariat would now be free to come out of the atheistic dogmatism into which it backed up. But practical causes still keep it there. The enthusiasm for unbelief was caused by the feeling that the philosophy of materialism was a mighty revolutionary explosive, fit to break the hold of the existing authorities. It opposed the Christian philosophy of the ruling classes. "For no one ought to be in doubt that in the great majority of cases official Christianity was utilized by the ruling classes against the proletarian movement for greater liberty. The fate inflicted on dissenting Christians is the best proof for that. As long as monarchy and capitalism are defended as divine institutions, every social movement of our day had to turn against the church and against religion." He adds that these causes will disappear as soon as Christianity takes a neutral position, or becomes friendly to Socialism.

in the hands of the Almighty. They must serve him whether they will or not. "He maketh the wrath of man to praise him, and the remainder of wrath he turneth aside." Whatever tares grow in the field of Socialism the field was plowed and sown by the Lord, and he will reap it. Socialism is one of the chief powers of the coming age. Its fundamental aims are righteous, not because they are socialistic, but because they are human. They were part of the mission of Christianity before the name of Socialism had been spoken. God had to raise up Socialism because the organized Church was too blind, or too slow, to realize God's ends. The Socialist parties, their technical terms, and their fighting dogmas will pass away into ancient history when their work is done. The only thing that will last and the only thing that matters is the Reign of God in humanity, and the Reign of God is vaster and higher than Socialism. The great danger is that our eyes will be blinded by ecclesiastical prejudices so that we do not know God when he comes close to us. The Jewish Church had the sacred book and the heritage of the prophets. Yet when He came who fulfilled the law and the prophets, they turned against him. He was identified with publicans and sinners, and he seemed to overthrow morality and religion.

PART VI

THE METHODS OF ADVANCE

CHAPTER I

THE PACE OF ADVANCE

IN Part V of this book we have tried to chart the course
for our effort by laying down the main lines of direction,
drawing our wisdom as best we could from the teachings of
Jesus Christ, from the general convictions of the Christian
conscience, from the common consent of the best social
groups of the past, and from the bent of the most prophetic
movements of the present.

I should be glad to stop here and leave the practical
application of these Christian principles to every man's
conscience. A man who has his eye on God and his hand
on his job ought to know better than any one else how he
can make room for more righteousness in and around the
place where he stands. But I know by experience how men
love definiteness. There is at present more honest will to
"do something" than clear understanding of what is to
be done. So I shall try to explain in these closing chapters
what practical methods seem to me indispensable in bringing about the fundamental regeneration of our social order.
The reader must remember that it is not my business here
to enumerate all the constructive philanthropies which
help individuals and social classes,[1] but to state the prac-

[1] The regular weekly reading of the *Survey* ($2 a year) will give an
education to any man or woman who wants to follow with sympathetic

tical steps by which the social order itself can be put on a
more Christian basis.

But first a word about the pace of advance. The pace
has been slow enough to sicken faith; so slow that some
have doubted if there is any real advance at all, or if mankind is trapped like a squirrel in a cage, treading the wheel
of vain endeavor. Inevitably movements arise again and
again which try to hasten the pace of the governing classes
by putting the fear of death on them or to block the machinery of society by destructive action. If we belonged
to the class that suffers, we might do the same. If we saw
our wives compelled to leave the home and toil in the shop
and our children slipping down into vicious temptations
amid tenement-house life; if we felt our strength prema-
turely drained and our years slipping away without ever
bringing us the full taste of life; if we realized that our
loved ones were in want only to give additional luxuries
to some who already surfeit; and if all this came home to
us with the intimacy of persistent torture, — we too might
try whether the hiss of fear would not bring to reason those
who refuse to listen to the calm voice of justice or pity.

Recent events have already thrown the shadow of
social terrorism across the future of our country. It is
certain to come, for America itself breeds it. All classes
of society in our country are swift to take justice into their
own hands and to invoke the awful arbitrament of Death.
The prevalence of brutal lynching; the slugging and dyna-
miting of labor struggles; the "strong arm" methods and
"third degree" of the police; the prompt cry of corporations for Pinkertons, constabulary, militia, and regulars,
— it is all the same spirit of raw and untamed life. When
that same American spirit meets us in some revolutionary

intelligence what is actually being done for the protection and salvation of
the weak. If a man reads the Bible and the *Survey*, he ought to find salvation.

organization of the working class, standing at bay, may we remember that we are all jointly responsible for it and find some wiser answer to violence than violence.

I do not hold that the use of force against oppression can always be condemned as wrong. Americans are estopped from denying the right of revolution, for our nation was founded by revolutionary methods, employed too by a minority of the population for class purposes. The test of brute strength is the *ultima ratio* when all higher arguments have proved vain. The great Roman historian expressed the general conviction of nations: "War is just for those for whom it is necessary, and arms are holy for those to whom no hope is left except in arms." [1]   Quivering fear has sometimes sobered mortals drunk with power and self-will, and restored their lost sense of humanity. But the sight of blood is quite as apt to rob men of their reason as to bring them to reason. The ruling classes in the past have never been more murderously cruel than when they were panic-stricken. The game of organized violence is the game they can play best. The Socialists in Germany are careful to abstain from any show of violence, for the government knows all their leaders, and on the first pretext of public safety would close the dragnet, stand them up against a wall, and so scoop the brain out of the Socialist movement. The old days of hand-to-hand fighting are gone, and no streets were ever less adapted for barricades than American streets.

Moreover, if a sudden rising did put a revolutionary movement in control, the real difficulties would still be ahead of the leaders. They must make the revolution succeed in a week, or it will be thrown back for years. When every household was an independent economic enterprise, stocked with supplies in barn, cellar, and attic,

---

[1] Livy: "Justum bellum, quibus necessarium, et pia arma, quibus nulla nisi in armis relinquitur spes."

a nation could bear political disturbance for months.   Our
cities live from hand to mouth.   Any break in the complex
machinery that feeds them would plunge New York or
Chicago into a famine, and that would be fatal to any party
that caused it.

Force always seems a short cut to the promised land.
In reality it may be the longest way of all.   Whoever
figures out the time-table of progress must count in the
long reactions that follow force.   The idea that violence
can suddenly establish righteousness is just as utopian as
the idea that moral suasion can suddenly establish it.
Wherever workingmen have had a chance to gain experience by the practical handling of power, they have ceased
putting their hope in force and have settled down to a
slow climb.   Socialist thought represents the widest and
most continuous body of revolutionary thinking, and its
development has been steadily away from faith in suddenness.   As compared with the utopian socialism that preceded it, Marxian socialism is a great philosophy of patience,
and in so far as scientific socialist thought of late has moved
beyond Marx, it has further abandoned the expectation
of a breakdown of society and accepted a program of
evolutionary tactics.   The great body of the Socialist
Party has no desire for a force revolution.   The revolutions
of kings against the people far outnumber in history the
revolutions of the people against the kings.   The danger
of a force movement with us will come when the great
interests feel that their control of the political and military
power is slipping away from them.   Then they will use a
coup d'état to snatch the rightful control from the popular
movement and thus will force the people to fight.   As soon
as the Republican Party elected Lincoln, the slave oligarchy forced secession.

But this call to patience is not for those who are at ease,
especially not for those who are in any sense the benefi-

ciaries of our wrongs. Let us "go slow," but let us hurry
up about it. The capacity of the nation to throw off injustice and go through a social transformation is lessening
in many ways. Wherever the physical and moral stamina
of any portion of our people is breaking down, the active
forces of health are weakened and new toxic forces are
generated in our national organism. When all the intellectual professions have taken the bit into their mouth as
tamely as the lawyers have done, who will lead us? The
relative decline of church life means a lessening of the fear
of God and of all religious motives throughout our people.
Our nation is losing its youthful elasticity and crossing the
dead line of middle age. Young communities always have
an immense advantage in social progress. To-day the
banner of economic and political freedom is fluttering most
bravely in New Zealand, Oregon, Vancouver, and Arizona.
Some of the progressive qualities of American life in the
past were due to the rawness of our continent and the youth
of our social organization quite as much as to any spiritual
convictions about freedom and justice. But now the
Western frontier and its glorious race of rebels is disap-
pearing forever. The present insurgent movement in the
Western States may be the last great rising of the old American spirit. If that fails, we must look to the new Americans
who are coming to us with the social rebellion of the old
world in their hearts. So this is no time to put on the
brakes, but to stoke the fires.

The doctrine of gradualness may be overworked. It is
true enough that the capacity of the social organism to
adapt itself to change has been very limited in past periods,
but it has grown immensely within the last four centuries
and again in the last four decades. Society in the past
would not move because those in power did not want it to
move, and the people had so little chance to think and act
together that their forward push was spasmodic and in-

effective. To-day the area of popular intelligence has widened; the means of common action have improved; progress has become fairly continuous. Religious dogmatism and superstition, which used to lubricate the axis of progress with rubber cement, has lost some of its strength. Political power is still in the hands of selfish interests, but democracy has put the levers where the people can reach them whenever they need them badly. Reformers are at least no longer hurled down the Tarpeian Rock or burned by the Inquisition. Every position captured by the people is a point of vantage for the next move.

This is not an affair of legislators and public men alone. When the social body has to rebuild its diseased tissue, every cell must do its part, and every leucocyte should keep its eyes open to arrest and swallow alien microbes. Every honest man and woman and every wholesome social group is needed. For instance, public school-teachers have no business to use their position for partisan agitation; yet nothing would so aid the christianizing of the social order as to have all teachers enlightened with a mature understanding of the essentials of social righteousness. No matter how just a social change may be, the social class affected by it will resist it. The reluctant class must be shouldered along the ways of wisdom by the other classes whose selfishness may be equally great, but is not called into activity by this particular issue. Business is the unsaved part of the social order. It is reluctant to be saved, yet salvation would be a blessing to it. The saved portions of the social order must stand together in the consciousness of moral and religious superiority and go after the lost Brother.

CHAPTER II

WE charged our industrial system with mammonism. Industry ought to exist for the support of life; actually it exists to make money, and it is in constant danger of sacrificing the life of the many to the profits of the few.[1] All the powers of Christianity should react against this irrational and immoral perversion of the great organization of society. The conservation of life is the first duty of every Christian factor of the social order. But the most insidious enemy against which life at present needs protection is the insatiability of industry.

In every attempt to build firmer shelter for the weak against industrial exploitation we encounter the legal and economic doctrine of "freedom of contract." No State in this country, for instance, has yet been allowed by the courts to establish a legal minimum wage in private employments, however sweated they may be, because that would violate the right to "freedom of contract." That doctrine was introduced into law by Capitalism and is one of its chief legal supports. Imagine a man who has been out of work for six weeks. His baby is sick, his credit at the grocery exhausted. He has stood in line with fifty other men, and his heart is in his throat when the foreman passes him in. He may not know that eleven hours are a day's work in this shop, and that skilled hands rarely make more than $9.20 a week. He would take the job on almost any terms; he has to. But the law calls this procedure

[1] Part IV, Chapter II, of this book.

412

a contract, and it protects the man's "liberty" to take as low a wage as he wants. Between equals and in theory this may be equity; in practice it is iniquity.

We have broken with a good many orthodoxies; we shall have to break with this legal orthodoxy of Capitalism. We do not allow the workman the freedom to commit sudden suicide; why should we allow him to commit slow suicide? We do not allow another man to maim him with a club, even in a free fight; why should we allow a corporation to drain him with overwork, even in a free contract? The police powers of the State ought to be enough to cover the case as soon as we have judges who know as much on the bench as the man on the street. The self-interest of the community also demands interference. The diseases of the workingman, his immoralities, the children he breeds in his fatigue, and the poverty of his premature age are thrown on the community. Above all, the Christian doctrine of the brotherhood of man and of the value of life make this legal fiction of free contract an intolerable fraud.

Our first concern is for the weak. "Women and children first!" This law of the sea is the law of Christianity and of evolution, for women and children stand for the future of the race. We cannot afford to have bright-eyed children transformed into lean, sallow, tired, hopeless, stupid, and vicious young people, simply to enable some group of stockholders to earn 10 per cent. The absolute prohibition of factory labor for children under fourteen; the limitation of labor to eight hours for children under eighteen; the exclusion of the young from night labor and from hazardous and poisonous employments, — are the minimum which the industry of the richest country in the world, amid the technical efficiency of the twentieth century, ought to be able to afford.[1]

[1] In this chapter I accept the "Social Standards for Industry" formulated by the Committee on Standards of Living and Labor of the National Con-

Women, too, demand special protection because life springs from their bodies. They alone can exercise the sacred function of maternity, which is higher than the production of goods. Their capacity to bear and rear sound children is the most important physical asset of the race. Pregnant women should not be allowed to toil under the incessant strain of shopwork. Nursing the child with her own milk is part of a mother's duty to God, who made her breast the only fountain of pure and fit food for the babe. To take the sucking child from its mother's breast and harness her to a machine seems an indecency. For all women the hours of steady labor must be limited; night work and hazardous employment must be eliminated; and we must see that these measures designed for their protection do not push the women of the poor farther into starvation.

What the hours of labor in the coöperative commonwealth may come to be, we do not know. For the present an eight-hour day and a rest of forty consecutive hours at the week-end are the ideal of organized labor. The maximum working-day and the living wage together mean the chance to live. The living wage will vary as to dollars and cents, but it must be enough not only for a lonely man in a boarding house, but for the father of an average family, who keeps his family in a sanitary home, provides nourishing food, sends his children to school till they are sixteen, and saves or insures himself against sickness and old age. The wage scales of employers should be on file for public purposes like the statistics of public health. Minimum wage boards should be established in every state to determine the standard that can be sanctioned as a minimum.[1]

ference of Charities and Corrections, of which I had the honor to be a member. The literature on the questions which I touch here is too immense to quote. Those who have no time for thorough study will find the digest of information in the report of that Committee (1912, 48 pp.) full of valuable material.

[1] Such boards are in operation in the Australian States; England established them in 1910; Germany has provided for them; other countries are

Where wages are paid according to weight or tally of work, the workers and the public through their representatives should have the right to inspect the instruments and methods of accounting, just as the customer and the public have a right to inspect the weights and measures in a store.

Modern machine work both multiplies the dangers of accident and lessens the ability of the individual to protect himself adequately. Its dangers are social; it demands social protection. The community must act for its members. It must prevent unnecessary crippling and occupational diseases by standardized regulations imposed on all employers by law and enforced by competent inspectors, whose character, intelligence, and social sympathies must be satisfactory to the working class on whose behalf they act. To keep a scientific record of the injuries and diseases incident to labor should be one of the prime intellectual functions of the organized community, and a high percentage of human wastage should bring any employer or trade under public scrutiny and reprimand, just as unusual breakage and wastage of goods would cause the dismissal of an employee. A high rate of accidents raises the presumption of technical inefficiency and moral callousness.

When accident and occupational disease do occur, it is unfair and inhuman to throw the financial loss on the suffering family, or to put the burden of legal proof on them, and to waste a large part of the damages they may secure on lawyer's fees and court expenses. Either the industry employing the man, or the whole community, should support the man during his disability or compensate his family in case of death, so that they will not be sucked into the quicksands of pauperism by their disaster. Since Germany has begun to protect her working people against the ravages of absolute poverty in such times of distress,

preparing to do so. Practically all continental countries have industrial courts to which aggrieved workmen can appeal.

her industrial life has been built on solid foundations. Childbirth is the professional period of danger for housewives, and if their family resources are not sufficient to secure them rest and care, the community has enough at stake in their welfare to arrange for their care in maternity hospitals, and if necessary to provide by some form of insurance or pension for the extra expenses of the lying-in period.

The care of the aged, where they are not sheltered by the family institution, is one of the unsolved problems of our national life. Our communities have handed over their resources to individuals for exploitation, and our privately owned industries do almost nothing for their workers when they have passed their prime. They should be saved from the stagnation of idling in a poorhouse. As long as they have some capacity for work and any desire for work, they ought to have that sense of worth which goes with productive work, and should earn some part of their support without the drive and strain of wage labor. To organize the industry of the handicapped by furnishing them material for light labor in their homes, or by locating them in rural colonies and putting them in touch with the soil, is one of the tasks that awaits Christian social initiative in most of our communities.

The proper housing of the people is essential to the conservation of their life. The campaign against tuberculosis has taught us that it is possible to kill people with a tenement as neatly as with a stiletto. Lack of air and sunshine bleach the blood and darken life. An investigation in Berlin some years ago showed that the death rate for families occupying one room was 163.5 per thousand, for families occupying two rooms 22.5, three rooms 7.5, and four rooms or more 5.4 per thousand.[1] The poor pay a larger proportion of their income for rent than others and get more death for it.

[1] Jacob A. Riis, "Charities and the Commons," Vol. XVIII, p. 77.

The most simple and immediate remedy for a shortage of homes is to tax land and untax houses. Our tax on houses has checked their production; a higher tax on vacant lots would stimulate building. A vacant lot should be taxed as high as any other lot of equal site value. It represents an opportunity granted by the community to the owner; if he cannot make use of it, let him sell it to one who can. To keep land vacant for speculation in a crowded city is a form of immorality about which we must develop a conscience. "Any one who speculates in real estate ought not to enjoy the general respect of his fellow-men." [1]

The housing problem is a big thing that can be handled economically only in a large way. Capitalism is manifestly failing to provide the kind of houses that are most needed. The situation calls for community action. Moreover landlordism is one of the most active forms of exploitation. If tenants increase their thrift or cities beautify the neighborhood, the landlord increases his rent. On the other hand, he will make no improvement in the quality of workingmen's homes until it is forced on him by law. If municipal governments considered the landed interests less and the poorer class of tenants more, the barometer of Christianity would rise.

The conservation of physical life and health is only the basis for the conservation of the real thing, — the personality and manhood of men. Our so-called individualism blunts the individuality of millions by the monotony of machine labor, and the docile regimentation of the workers. The more specialized and monotonous labor is, the more do the workers need leisure, recreation, and educational and artistic stimulus to balance it. The more modern industry calls for the subordination of all to a single will, the more

---

[1] A remark made at the fourteenth annual session of the Evangelisch-Soziale Kongress in Germany by Professor Wagner, one of the most eminent economists of Germany.

2 E

does it need the self-respect of democracy to keep the soul of men erect within them. In the Sermon on the Mount, Jesus revised and expanded the moral standards of his nation. The current law forbade murder and made killing justiciable in the common court. Jesus pushed up the whole schedule of crimes, and made it an offense justiciable in the High Court even to call your brother a worthless fool.[1] To break down a man's sense of his own worth murders his power of aspiration. It chokes the god in him just as surely as faith in his higher possibilities awakens the soul in a lost man to a new birth. The conservation of life demands the emancipation of the soul.

[1] Matt. v. 21–22.

CHAPTER III

In the preceding chapter we have called for compensation in case of disablement or death through industrial accident or occupational disease, for pensions in old age, and for the care of working women during the period of maternity. But where is the money to come from for all these new expenditures? Will not taxes become excessive and discourage thrift? Manifestly we cannot increase the public expenditures without increasing the public income. Our American communities are all poor, all in debt, and many are perpetually near the debt limit. They usually have plenty of wealthy people among their citizens, but as communities they have often been threadbare, out at the elbows, and apparently without soap to clean up. There is plenty of property, but it is not available for social purposes. If we want to conserve life, we shall have to resocialize property.

What do we mean by socializing property? If a farmer who has a spring on his land near the road should set up a trough on the road and allow the public the use of the water, he would socialize the spring and be a public benefactor. If a man closed up a vacant lot and refused the boys permission to play ball on it, he would desocialize it. If a Scotch laird forced crofters from the land and converted it into a game preserve, he would desocialize it. When the London County Council opened the many small parks to the public, to which hitherto only a few adjoining property owners had had access, it socialized their use. When the

robber barons along the Rhine levied tribute on the merchants teaming along the road, they partly desocialized
the great trade route of the river valley. When the
burghers of the commercial towns bought them off for
a lump sum, they partly resocialized the public highway,
and when they finally razed the barons' castles as nests of
social vermin, they socialized the road more fully. When
the Interstate Commerce Commission in 1912 compelled
the Express Companies to improve their antiquated service and to lower their extortionate charges, it partly socialized a great branch of transportation, and when Congress
at last established the parcels post, it socialized the same
branch more fully.

By "socializing property" we mean, then, that it is made
to serve the public good, either by the service its uses render
to the public welfare, or by the income it brings to the
public treasury. In point of fact, however, no important
form of property can be entirely withdrawn from public
service; human life is too social in its nature to allow it.
If a rich man builds a ten-foot wall around his estate and
admits nobody, the birds will still nest and sing there to
the poorest passer-by, and his trees will produce oxygen
that is wafted to the slum. Socializing property will mean,
therefore, that instead of serving the welfare of a small
group directly, and the public welfare only indirectly, it will
be made more directly available for the service of all.

The socializing of property at times becomes of life and
death importance to society when the slow accumulation
of great social changes has turned old rights into present
wrongs. That is the present situation in our country.
When our great territory was being settled men took possession of the land, hunted and fished, cut down the forest,
and encroached on no right of society in doing so. In
fact, they were effectively socializing the land by using
it as their private property. If they were enterprising

enough to use water power for a dam and mill also, or opened a mine, they were serving the common good. But as the country fills up and its resources are needed for the use of thousands, the old rights change. Cutting or burning the forest becomes a menace to far-off farming tracts which are deprived of their rainfall and to cities in the valleys which are threatened by flood. Defiling the watershed from which cities draw their water may become more deadly than murder. The modern wholesale methods of utilizing the natural resources make inroads on the common wealth of the nation of a wholly different character from formerly. Fishing with a rod or hand-net is one thing; scooping the whitefish out of the great lakes by steam power is a very different thing. No one feared the settler with his axe; a lumber company slashing square miles of timber and replanting none may be a public menace.

Thus the mere expansion of society has caused a shifting of right and wrong in all property questions. Our moral and legal theories about the rights of the individual in using the resources of nature and in operating his tools to get wealth, are based on the assumption of a sparse population and of simple methods of production which we have largely outgrown. What was once legitimate and useful is now becoming a dangerous encroachment on the rights of society. Property rights will have to be resocialized to bring them into accordance with our actual moral relations. If all memory of past property rights were miraculously blotted from our minds overnight, no sane man would think of allotting property as it is now allotted. All would realize that the great necessities of society, our coal and iron mines, our forests, our watersheds and harbor fronts must be owned by society and operated for the common good. But the plain path of justice and good sense is blocked by the property rights brought down from a different past. We can blame no one for holding and defending what he has bought or inherited. But what is society to do? The same question confronted the world when it was emerging from the feudal into the industrial age at the end of the eighteenth century. The rising business class found the world divided up between the Church, the feudal nobles, and the city guilds. It cleared the deck to suit its needs by abrogating old property rights wholesale. Whenever it suited its needs, Capitalism has been the great expropriator *par excellence*. May it not be done by as it did, for it rode into power roughshod, reckless of the suffering it inflicted.

One universal problem of civilization is how to resocialize the land on which our cities stand. Public health and public wealth alike demand its social ownership. The time was when the land on which lower New York now stands was worth a trifle. If it had then been acquired by the community and leased to the citizens at moderate rentals, increasing as the value of the land increased, New York would always have had ample funds for all public needs without raising a dollar of taxes, and it would be incomparably the richest and most sumptuous city in the world. All the graft inevitably fastening on such wealth could not, in the nature of things, have made away with quite so much public property as the private appropriation of the unearned increment has actually sequestered. That the city lands would have been built up under a system of leaseholds is proved by the fact that the lands of the Astors, the Goelets, the Rhinelanders, and of Snug Harbor are well built up. If the land could be Astorized, why could it not have been socialized? England has been owned by a few people; the people had to pay the State taxes and the landlords rent; yet the English nation has grown rich. Would it not have grown richer if the nation had owned the land, and the people had paid their rent to the State and no taxes to anybody?

The question is how to socialize the land now that the enormous social values are in private hands, and to wrong nobody in the doing of it. There would be no wrong if the community decided by law to take any unearned increase of value accruing after a given date; that would leave all past values intact for the present owners. There would be a minimum of suffering if the taxation of land values were gradually increased through a term of ten or twenty years until it came near absorbing the whole annual rental value. If buildings were simultaneously relieved of taxation, the earnings of private thrift would go into private hands, and the results of social growth would go to society. The man that can get no wisdom from the Singletaxers has padlocked his intellect.

The Single Tax would leave the title to the land with the present owners and merely socialize the unearned rental values. But it would be highly desirable for every community to own outright far more land than our communities now own, as a basis for a larger and finer community life, for more spacious public buildings, and for the housing of the poorer classes. Some English cities have bought up their slum districts, torn down the old tenements, and laid out new and splendid streets, at great profit to the public treasury and great detriment to the death rate. When New York laid out Central Park, it seemed like riotous finance, but the park has long ago paid for itself by the increase of taxable values around it. When city planning is going on, why should not the cities themselves get the increased values they create by buying land affected and leasing it under restrictions as to architectural excellence? German cities buy large suburban tracts, lay them out in lots of assorted sizes, fence them, and rent them out as gardens to people who enjoy spending their evenings and Sundays in open-air life, raising flowers and vegetables. As the city grows, the entire tract is laid out for building lots in accordance with plans made long ahead. In several countries taxpayers are allowed to fix their own assessments, but the community has the right to buy the property at the figure they name. There is material for a delicious comedy in the agonies of a clever taxpayer who tries to beat the devil around the stump under these conditions.

The time is coming now when large capital will invest in agricultural lands. Would it be for the public good for a corporation to own a half or a quarter of a State and control the tenant farmers on it? All history answers that any approximation to such a condition would be a peril. If so, this is the time to make it impossible. New Zealand levies a progressive tax on large holdings. Our States and the federal government should keep all the land they still have and henceforth lease it instead of selling. And if the conditions of any land grants have not been fulfilled, they should be revoked. The Conservation Movement has come too late for the good of our nation, but we still have a remnant of our heritage to hold for our children.

Mines, oil wells, and natural gas wells are specialized forms of land, of the highest importance to an industrialized nation. While mines were small and operated competitively, private ownership was the best way to socialize their products. Now that mines are great social undertakings, and their products are sold at monopoly prices, has private ownership any basis in reason or ethics? The idea that there can be any absolute ownership in a mine, as in a coat, is preposterous. Did the Almighty stock the rocks of Pennsylvania with anthracite for the benefit of a few thousand stockholders, or did he provide for the use of a great nation? God made the coal; the mining companies made the holes in the coal; they have a right to what they made. Mining rights are essentially like franchises; the obligation to render public service is an expressed or implied condition of the grant and the sole moral basis of it. If a corporation uses the gift of the people to charge the same people extortionate prices for the necessaries of life, the action is morally base and forfeits most of the claim to consideration that property owners otherwise have.

Water power, too, a joint product of the sun and the strata of the rocks, is a social possession and should never be alienated outright by the community. The laws governing riparian rights need overhauling.[1] The absurd legal assumption that the beds of rivers, and even lakes, is owned by the abutting property owners, was imported from England, a land of tiny rivers and huge landlords with law-making powers. My city of Rochester is cut in two by the Genesee, a river of dangerous floods, with three great falls and a deep gorge within the city limits. The city bears the expense of costly bridges and liability for damages by flood, but it gets no compensating income from the river. The water rights were alienated long ago, and are now mostly held by a single corporation. Even under private ownership the river has helped to make Rochester. If all its possibilities were socialized, the city would become splendid.

The problem of socializing property becomes most acute wherever private ownership has established a virtual monopoly and charges monopoly prices. In that case private ownership has become positively unsocial. "The very purpose of monopoly is to secure unearned income," [2] and how can such a purpose be either social or moral? The problem with which our nation is now wrestling is how to resocialize monopolistic corporations that refuse to bow

[1] The Hon. Geo. P. Decker of Rochester, N.Y., who had to give special attention to the matter as counsel for the State of New York, has discussed "Riparian Right and Power Conservation in New York" in a valuable pamphlet, 1912.

[2] Professor R. T. Ely, "Socialism and Social Reform," p. 272. His whole treatment of the socialization of monopolies, pp. 253–300, is very sane and thorough.

their mighty necks under the yoke of public service. We are proceeding at present under the assumption that government inspection and control, publicity and the pressure of public opinion, can socialize them. But can it? Is not the form of their organization too exclusive, and the purpose of their profit-making too unsocial, ever to make them more than forced servants of the common good?

Private property is an indispensable basis of civilization and morality. The per capita amount of it ought not to lessen; it ought to increase. But for the present the great ethical need is to reëmphasize and reclaim social property rights which are forgotten or denied. Society has rights even in the most purely private property. Neither religion, nor ethics, nor law recognizes such a thing as an absolute private property right. Religion teaches that all property is a trust and the owner but a steward. Ethics makes the moral title to property depend on the service the owner renders by means of it. The law can dispossess me under the right of eminent domain if the community needs my property. In war the State can commandeer anything I have, even my body. Private property is historically an offshoot of communal property and exists by concession and sufferance. The whole institution of private property exists because it is for the public good that it shall exist. If in any particular it becomes dangerous to the public welfare, it must cease. *Salus reipublicæ summa lex.* Religious teaching can do much to make the partnership of the community in private property a conscious force in public thought. The doctrine of stewardship must be backed by knowledge of law and history, and become more than an amiable generality.

The right of a man to his home, his clothing, and any simple savings of his labor is not practically questioned by anybody. The social use of that can easily be controlled by law. It is different with great fortunes. Even if their accumulation is just, their perpetuation is dangerous. The community may allow the man who has collected a great fortune its undisturbed possession during his lifetime, but the moral claim to it weakens when he tries to govern it by his will after he is dead and gone. The right to make a will and to have the community enforce it is historically a recent right, and all governments limit it. A man cannot do what he will with his own; in America he cannot completely disinherit his wife, and in Germany his child. The law recognizes the right of the State to take a share, and a large share, of an estate at death. A progressive inheritance tax is one of the most approved ways of resocializing large fortunes, and it should be applied far more thoroughly than hitherto, not only to add to the public income, but to protect the social order.

Every successful effort to better the pay in depressed industries, to shorten the hours, to increase the comforts and safety of the workers, to provide for them in case of disablement, and to put a larger proportion of the profits of business at the service of the working class is a partial socialization of business. The social dividend, which arises through the coöperation of all social factors in production, is to-day appropriated by limited private groups, and divided among them according to their ability to seize it. The people have lost control of it. How far society will go in coming days in resuming control, no one can now foretell. But it is plain that it must get a far different grip on the social property and social rights involved in so-called private business. A private business that employs thousands of people, uses the natural resources of the nation, enjoys exemptions and privileges at law, and is essential to the welfare of great communities is not a private business. It is public, and the sooner we abandon the fiction that it is private, the better for our good sense.

Finally I want to mention, what logically ought to go first,

— the socialization of public money.   Taxes are a beneficent
social institution; they buy more for us than any other
money we spend.   But they have been put to very unsocial
uses.   Conquerors and despots have taxed nations, not in
order to have funds for public improvements, but to carry
off the swag and consume it in riotous living, which they
called regal magnificence.   We still have duodecimo kinglets, who use some of our taxes for giving themselves or their
courtiers easy jobs or junketing trips.   They desocialize
the public income.   The best way to put a stop to them is
to socialize the machinery of government still further by
direct nominations, direct legislation, and the recall.

The method of collecting taxes has also been made to
accomplish side purposes profitable to private interests.
Rome used to farm out the taxes of provinces as we farm out
street railway franchises, and the Roman business men who
bought the right to collect the taxes used them to collect a
great deal more for themselves besides.   These were the
"publicans" whose underlings appear in the New Testament as persons so detested that it took the religious insight
of Jesus to discover any good in them.   We have similarly
tried to make our system for collecting taxes on imports
serve the additional purpose of exempting our business men
from the stress of foreign competition, in the hope that they
would, of their own free will, socialize the benefits of their
"protection" for their workingmen and the public.   We are
not at present enthusiastic about the results of our generosity, and find it urgently necessary to resocialize our revenue
system.   The surest way to make our taxation serve public
uses only is to collect direct taxes only.   Indirect taxes are
supposed to be easy to collect because the people do not
feel them.   In other words, they are a device to hoodwink
the people.   They are, in fact, an invention of unsocial
governments, of an age when Government and the People
were not identical, but hostile interests.   Indirect taxes

are a cover for all kinds of deceptions, and in the end the most costly of all taxes.

The resocializing of property is an essential part of the christianizing of the social order. If we can give back to the community which creates them the unearned ingredients in rent and profit, we shall make commerce and industry honest, and at the same time increase the public wealth available for the protection of life, for the education of the young, and for the enrichment of culture and civilization. If we can resocialize the public property which is now in private possession, we shall democratize industry, secure far greater attention to the problems of public welfare, and win more genuine respect for what is truly private property.

The problem is how to accomplish these very righteous ends without inflicting too much incidental suffering. Some suffering there is bound to be. It is humanly impossible to straighten a crippled limb without pain. We shall have to set over against the possible cost of suffering inflicted by a Christian reorganization of property the far greater suffering that is now inflicted every day and hour by the continuance of ancient wrongs, and the still vaster suffering that will grow out of our sins if we fail now to right them. For "the wages of sin is death," and humanity is so closely bound together that the innocent must weep and die for the sins the dead have done. In his second inaugural Abraham Lincoln said : —

"Fondly do we hope, devoutly do we pray, that this mighty scourge of war may pass away. Yet if it is God's will that it continue until the wealth piled by bondsmen by two hundred and fifty years of unrequited toil shall be sunk, and until every drop of blood drawn with the lash shall be paid with another drawn with the sword, as was said three thousand years ago, so it must still be said, that 'the judgments of the Lord are true and righteous altogether.'"

CHAPTER IV

COMMUNITY LIFE AND PUBLIC SPIRIT

An increase in socialized property and an increase in public functions go hand in hand. They are obverse sides of the same thing. Every function of the community is based on public property.

For generations we have been taught to regard every increase of public property and public functions with a sort of instinctive dread. The doctrine that the best State governs least has been drilled into us as civic orthodoxy. In fact, it is a dangerous heresy.

As in most heresies, there is a modicum of truth in it. As long as the State was run for the benefit of a class of aristocratic idlers, who regarded the wealth of the industrious classes chiefly as an object of extortionate taxation and interference, the people might well pray for an indolent government that would let them alone. A bad man is most amiable when he is asleep. On the other hand, the more democracy makes the State and the People to be identical in extent and interest, the less reason is there to fear state activity. Under true democracy state action comes to mean action of the People for their own common good, and why should we fear that?

As the State becomes democratic, the old situation is reversed. The people now desire an extension of state functions and the aristocratic class fear it. They do not want the community to interfere with the profits of child labor and adulteration. They do not want public ownership to cut under the unearned income of their monopolies.

They want to be let alone. Let Government swing the policeman's club to protect Business, and let Business do the rest.

Against the doctrine that the best State governs least, I set the assertion that the finest public life will exist in a community which has learned to combine its citizens in the largest number of coöperative functions for the common good.

We often wonder why, with such vigorous moral feeling, we have so little public spirit. How can we have it? Would we breed a strong family spirit if we had no family furniture except a garbage barrel and confined the parents to the function of spanking the children when they were naughty? Public spirit grows up around public property. Go over the list of your city property, and you will find that the classes of property there enumerated, the schools, parks, playgrounds, markets, baths, libraries, and hospitals, are the feeders of the public spirit in your community. What difference would it have made to the resonance of public spirit in Boston, for instance, if Boston Common had been sold a century ago and built up with private business blocks? Public spirit grows by common action. Some people feel that war is actually desirable as a kind of regeneration of patriotism. The reason is that war is a tremendous common action that generates collective consciousness. It is not the killing, but the solidarity that has thrown a halo of glory even about the brutality of war. Those cities which have made most progress in recent years in expanding their communal activities and in reasserting the rights of the people over their public service corporations have shown an increase in public spirit and civic mind that has braced all other cities. The long lethargy of China has largely been due to the fact that outside of the powerful bonds of the family and clan, there has been no public activity, no communal property, and consequently no social mind.[1]

[1] Professor E. A. Ross, "The Changing Chinese."

The whole capitalistic business world by its instinctive predisposition is in a silent league against public ownership. A corporation president who comes out for an extension of public functions is quoted with wonder as a sort of freak of openmindedness. All academic political economy used to preach the doctrine of *laissez faire*. The press, too, obeys the influences of wealth that control it. A bureau organized for that purpose has long supplied it with tainted news crying down public ownership.

But in spite of these persuasive influences the whole civilized world is calmly gravitating toward ever greater community functions. The social achievements created by civilization before the present age of inventions have all been taken out of private hands. Toll roads and toll bridges owned by individuals or corporations are becoming extinct. In a list of municipal property I failed to find any mention of the streets at all; they are so much public property that we hardly know it. The organization for fighting fire used to be run by corporations for profits; the excited owner enjoyed "freedom of contract" to make terms with them while his house was burning down. Courts and prisons used to be owned and operated by the feudal nobles as valuable adjuncts to their methods of getting money. War used to be the private privilege of gentlemen; the two buttons on the back of our frock coats still remind us of the sword belt our fathers wore. The schools have been socialized almost completely. Would any one care to revert from these community functions?

The new outfit of civilization created since the invention of steam and electric machinery will have to go the same way. Most communities have developed some economic functions, and after the first difficulties have been overcome, there is never any desire to go back to private ownership. Our postal service certainly has some moss-grown spots, but a referendum to hand it over to the express companies would probably not get a record majority. Some cities could be persuaded to get along without their traction companies; none wants to get rid of the municipal water system. Public ownership of gas and railways seems to us next door to socialism and heathenism. In England, where some cities have long enjoyed municipal gas for fifty or sixty cents, and in Germany, where state railways are a source of common comfort and profit, they think these things are just common sense. Every community wants at least those public functions which it now has, and usually more. Every public officer who takes his duties seriously and enthusiastically wants to increase public functions and property at some point. Every reformer is charged with socialism, because no constructive reform is possible without taking a leaf from the book of socialism. The tendency toward community action at present is like a ratchet wheel; it moves only one way. This sort of historical verdict outweighs all academic theories and all reports of investigating commissions. Back of the present demand for home rule for cities, commission government, the referendum and recall, is the desire for more public ownership. We have not dared to expand the activities of our cities because our politics were dishonest. Therefore we are getting a firmer grip on the men who are to manage our public property in the future so that they will find honesty the best policy.

When Capitalism was superseding the antiquated handicraft system at the end of the eighteenth century, it developed the doctrine of *laissez faire*. Its attractive element was that it stood for the free and natural play of economic forces, while state activity stood for artificial interference. To-day Capitalism is becoming antiquated, and if economic forces were allowed free play, they would run swiftly toward community ownership in some large sections of economic activity. *Laissez faire* to-day means public ownership.

2F

But economic forces are not allowed free play; the Interests block the way; they are now the power of artificial interference. One postmaster-general after the other has advocated government ownership of the telegraph system. Ours is the only great nation that has left the telegraph in private hands, and for years we have had the worst service in the world. But the Western Union has barricaded the path of common sense. Our post office has cheapened its letter rates again and again; its parcel rates it could not cheapen because the express companies stood in the way. The banks long blocked the postal savings bank experiment which had proved its usefulness in other countries. When public sentiment forced it through, the banking influence turned the new postal savings banks into feeders and collecting agencies of the banks. They can receive only small amounts, can offer only 2 per cent interest, and must redeposit 95 per cent of their deposits in the private banks at $2\frac{1}{2}$ per cent, leaving the more profitable end of the deal to the banks. Philadelphia years ago had a fair municipal gas system. But private interests held up appropriations for improvements until it ran down and was sold back to them. The socialists at Milwaukee have had similar experience of active interference with community activity. Every community may well say to the Interests now, "*Laissez faire, laissez aller!* Let us alone. Let things follow their natural course."

As an illustration of a judicious form of coöperative action on a large scale I should like to refer to the Public Trustee Act which went into effect in England in 1908. Some of us know to our cost that the duties of an executor or trustee of an estate are troublesome and arduous. Private persons rarely have the necessary information; they may die; they may prove dishonest. This Act created a Public Trustee "who will never die, never leave the country, and never become incapacitated, and whose responsibility is guaranteed by the Consolidated Funds of the United Kingdom." The Act was opposed, of course; it was predicted that the work would be expensive, tangled in red tape, done without consideration of human interests, and there would be little call for it. Instead of that the business increased swiftly; the staff by 1912 had grown to 208 persons, housed in 53 rooms; 2993 cases had been accepted, administering property worth $120,000,000; 2200 intending testators had applied for the services of the Public Trustee and the total value of business negotiated had mounted to $340,000,000. The Trustee may decline to accept a case, but not because the property involved is small; the purpose is that the specialized skill and experience of the office shall be at the command of the common man and woman. A trust company has the experience, but it exists to make a profit for its stockholders even when it is investing funds; the Public Trustee, if he is honest at all, has no such dual allegiance. There is no profit to be earned for any one. The fees are simply to cover the expenses of the staff and office and insure the public funds against loss. They were fixed as low as any in the world, yet a slight surplus has been earned. There was certainly danger that an impersonal public office could not develop the necessary human interest to receive the most intimate secrets of people and to care for orphans and queer old ladies, but under the leadership of Mr. Charles J. Stewart the staff has apparently entered with genuine public spirit into its varied obligations, even providing Christmas and wedding presents.[1]

The natural monopolies, — railways, surface lines, elevated roads, subways, water ways, telegraph and telephone systems, gas and electric light and power systems, — these are the irreducible minimum which must come under public ownership. They are all monopolies in their very nature. Competition in their case is economic nonsense. But if

[1] For information address "The Public Trustee, London, England."

we must have monopoly, then a monopoly over which the people have clear jurisdiction and which will turn its monopoly income into the public treasury, is by far the best kind of monopoly. Any loss through graft tapping the public income will never be as great as the loss of the entire profit through private ownership; any undue influence of the public employees will never be as corrupting as the influence of the public service corporations has been in every city and State of our Union. Professor Franklin H. Giddings, one of the most eminent economists of our country, says: "If I may venture an opinion as to the most important question in political economy before the American people, it is this: Shall the chief and controlling means of production in the United States, including mineral and forest resources, water power sites, railroads and means of communication, patent rights, and the enormous funds of loanable capital be owned by a billionaire Four Hundred, who, in virtue of such ownership, will be able for all practical purposes to own a hundred or more millions of us ordinary human beings; or shall we ordinary human beings, in our collective capacity, own the means of production ourselves and proceed to work out the reality of a democratic republic?"

The natural monopolies must become public property not only for the sake of efficient and coherent management, but for the sake of civic morality and public spirit. The corporations managing them for us have been the most unsocial influence in our public life, and even if they managed their business well, we cannot, in the interest of the higher community life, afford them any longer. When we have left them uncontrolled, they have devoured us. When we have tried to control them, they have escaped control by corrupting our legislatures, our executive officers, and our judges. Able men who might have been powerful servants of the common good have been hired by the great salaries and fees drawn from unearned monopoly profit, and have used their wits to circumvent the agents of the people. The points where the corporations have touched politics have been the points of decay. They have turned in the large campaign contributions that have invited to corrupt practices. The financial means with which the party boss has done his work on us have come from their need of franchise extensions and public favors. The whole class of investors, the most influential class in our cities, has, through the public service corporations, been made a party at interest in opposing many measures of public utility. The treatment of the public by these monopolies has been so surly and oppressive that when the people did get a powerful champion to protect them, as in the case of the Public Service Commission in New York, it was felt to be an immense relief from tyranny. They fill the calendars of our courts with the most intricate and tedious cases, and the whole procedure of our courts would be relieved if these monopolies were public property. They exist to make money, and are not even efficient at that. Before the railways were compelled to submit to government regulation, an eminent authority said: "Management of the public finances so corrupt as that which has characterized the private railways of the United States would have produced a revolution long ago."[1] Many a time when their nerves were shattered by financial debauches, the government appointed a receiver, and this public officer had to nurse them back to health.

We fritter away precious time by dallying at the halfway house of mere public supervision and control. The outside interference of government officers will prove inefficient, meddlesome, and irritating. We must come to public ownership some time, and any one whose thinking parts are in order ought to see it by this time. When an

[1] R. T. Ely, "Socialism and Social Reform," p. 270.

industry arrives at the stage where prices are uniform and fixed, where genuine competition has ceased, and where the size of net income indicates unearned profits, the clock has struck. Henceforth it should be only a question of ways and means. Not that we should plunge into public ownership at any cost. We have long been too slow; we may become too swift and repent at leisure when we find a great bonded debt saddled on a municipal industry against which the best management can make no headway for a generation. The people are always infinitely more fair and generous to the corporations than the corporations are to the people, but there is no ethical obligation on us to buy them out at their own inflated capitalization. Why should we buy back at a fancy price the very franchise we have given as a gift or for a song, and which they may have corrupted our government to obtain? Let us first have enforced publicity about their actual conditions and methods, and adequate taxation of their landed wealth, their franchises, and their mineral holdings. After that, their capitalization will be nearer the truth. Why should we pay for a lie?

Success in public management is nothing automatic. Our communities will have to work out success by experience, and at present our nation is more backward in that important form of social knowledge than others. Some cities and States may find their public service unenterprising and inefficient. But has corporation service never been so? The question is in which case the public has the prompter and more effective remedy. In his admirable arguments against socialism Professor Ely lays stress on the danger of "a concentration of public dissatisfaction." [1] He concedes that the service is far better under public ownership, but the people grow impatient over every slight delinquency in the public service, whereas they submit to

[1] pp. 199–204.

the miseries of corporation service with the patience of helplessness, and an accumulation of such dissatisfaction might overthrow a socialist government. Let us agree to that possibility; but which kind of service meanwhile is more likely to be kept in a condition of efficiency? Where public ownership has long been in practice, as in the Australian commonwealths, it has proved very enterprising. It constantly invites to larger service. The rural delivery service has tugged at the leash and demanded the parcels post. Where trolleys and railways are owned by the public, they can carry the people to homes in the suburbs by giving free transportation to school children and cheap transportation to the working people at the hours when they travel. City planning is almost impossible without extensive public ownership. A monopoly has no incentive to extend its service when the point of maximum profit is reached. It has to be pried loose to make it go farther.

The problem of creating a body of willing and hard-working employees for an expanding network of community service is a real problem, but a splendid and hopeful one. Our civil service was poor in the past because it was outside of the spirit of democracy. The spoils system which controlled it was essentially a recrudescence of feudal despotism. Your party boss was a miniature imitation of a feudal king, distributing office and largess to his courtiers, demanding the same unthinking loyalty, and viewing the public as an unusually large oyster. These kinglets are to-day fighting the invasion of the new democratic measures with the same moral indignation and immoral craft with which the European dynasties fought the inroads of democracy when it first began, and for the same reason. If direct nominations, home rule for cities, uniform accounting, commission government, direct legislation, and the recall succeed in really democratizing our political business, we shall soon see the rise of a new type of public officers who will be leaders

of the coming social order.   There are plenty of forerunners
of that type now at work.   These men will then have to
put their own spirit into their subordinates and that requires high talents for education and organization.   Indeed,
the efficient management of the public service will call out
human qualities of a higher order than capitalistic business.
They will find themselves compelled to summon the public
spirit to their aid at every turn, and to intensify and educate it, while the managers of corporations are quite willing
to let the public spirit drowse on with the sleeping dogs
whom none cares to stir.

We have dwelt so long on the socializing of the great
public utilities because these are the backbone of community life, and all higher efforts are hampered as long as
these are run for profit only.   But the enrichment of community life is needed in other directions and can be begun
on a smaller scale.

Our American life as a whole is in great need of wholesome social pleasures.   Pleasure resorts run for profit are
always edging along toward the forbidden.   Men spend
most freely when under liquor or sex excitement; therefore the pleasure resorts supply them with both.   Where
profit is eliminated, the quieter and higher pleasures get
their chance.   The institutions of pleasure maintained by
the people for their own use, such as parks, playgrounds,
museums, libraries, concerts, theaters, dance halls, are
always cleaner than the corresponding ventures of Capitalism, provided some rational supervision is maintained.   I
spent an evening in a small Missouri town, waiting for a
train.   The streets were in possession of an amusement
company and lined with tents and booths.   The company
evidently tried not to offend the public sense of decency
and to supply a "moral show."   The saloons were doing a
rushing business, but the crowds flowing along the side-
walks were composed of clean American farmers with their

wives and children or their sweethearts, trying to have a good time with the facilities offered. But those facilities were so meager and so monotonous! You could pay a nickel for pop corn and soft drinks; or pay a quarter to see the clowns and the girls in brilliant tights perform in a variety show; or pay a quarter to throw balls, or toss rings, or shoot a rifle to win a prize. That was all; pay, pay, pay, and nothing but a gambling thrill or satisfied curiosity to show for it. This is what Capitalism can do for our people in catering to their desire for recreation. Can the people do no better for themselves?

Under competent leadership almost any neighborhood can organize a real festival with home talent, and develop a knack and a reputation along special lines. Such a festival may become a great moral asset of the community. A certain suburban ward some years ago had a simple. Fourth of July celebration with a procession, a speech and song, races for the children, and fireworks from a hilltop. In the course of a few years it had become a feature of the day for the whole city and was imitated by other wards. The City Club of Rochester gives an annual banquet to the citizens naturalized during the year. Why should not these citizens, together with the young men and women who have attained their majority during the year, march in procession to the town hall and take a pledge of allegiance to the common good, like the young Athenians? The fine sports of swimming, boating, skating, kiteflying, and choral dancing get a still keener tang of pleasure and interest when they are made social by games and competitions, and become the center of attraction at a public festival. Such civic undertakings are a wholesome outlet for vital energies that easily turn to vice; they educate to chastity and beauty; and they breed public spirit.

The time will come when every village and every city ward will have a noble social center, a building that will offer space for great meetings and little meetings, for the sparkling play of children and the electric play of young people, a gymnastic arena and a swimming pool, and when the so-called pleasures of the saloon and sex hell will be relegated to the place from which they ascended. Meanwhile the awakening community spirit of our nation is looking around and taking stock of its possessions, and it finds — the schoolhouse and the Church. For generations the churches and the homes have been the only resorts for untainted social recreation in countless communities, and it is simply a question of social intelligence for those in control of church buildings to make them once more the centers of a wider community life. The appropriation of the schoolhouse for more varied purposes is a master stroke of the new democracy. The social center idea is opposed by amusement caterers, who want people to come to them and spend money; by the old-line politicians, who shiver when the people begin to think for themselves on political questions; and by some priests of the Roman Catholic Church, who set their Church above all public interests and hope to quarantine their people against the public school and the common spirit of the nation.

Nothing is foreign to community action which concerns the common welfare. Our forefathers had sense enough to hunt and fish together when united action promised more food than solitary effort. We too shall have to develop coöperative action if we want clean and plentiful food and drink. We have learned to do that about our water supply. Our municipal reservoirs and conduits are simply the village pump raised to the fourth power. Individualistic pumps would kill us under city conditions.

If our city sells us liquid water, why should it not sell us frozen water? Ice is a necessity under modern conditions, yet we all buy it at artificial prices. If ice is dear in summer, babies die. It is not appetizing to inquire where the ice was cut that tinkles in our glass. Most of the ice used in New York City is cut on the Hudson River after Albany, Troy, and other industrial towns have discharged their sewage into it. Our health officers protect the purity of our water. If the city supplied our ice, would we not have better assurance than at present that our frozen water would be clean? And would the price of ice be as high as now? Uncle Sam has installed ice machines in nearly all the great department buildings at Washington. When the Post-office Department first installed its own plant in 1909, private dealers were charging $7.65 a ton; the Department now calculates the cost at $2.25.

In summer we want much ice and little coal; in winter we want little ice and much coal. If our cities dealt in both necessities, they could balance the two. The employees and teams that carry ice in summer could carry coal in winter. In regard to both staples the ordinary family has no guarantee that they are getting the weight they pay for. The retail price of coal is absolutely fixed by the coal trust; the local dealers have become mere distributing agents. What moral obligation has a community to leave its members at the mercy of a monopoly? The whole question of coal prices would get a new ventilation if great cities entered the market as wholesale dealers in coal.

Milk is the one hold on life for the little children. This most vulnerable part of our population, the most decent and respectable citizens we have, are dependent on the cleanliness and purity of the milk supply for their health and their life. We know that our health officers have to keep up an incessant fight against dirty and tuberculous milk, and that their efforts are never really successful or their successes permanent. The milk business is too vital a part of human life to be left to those who have no interest in it except their profit. Every city should run at least a small dairy that would supply the nursing babies with clean milk. That would save many a little life ɑear to the mother that bore it, and would popularize new standards of cleanliness. Here is a means for the enfranchised women to prove that they are able to teach men some new arts in municipal housekeeping.[1]

The trade in drugs should be taken over by the community as part of the care of public health. That drugs at present are very commonly adulterated is a notorious fact. Adulteration is easy, for who can test their genuineness? Most drug stores show by their very appearance that medical science has been crowded into one corner, and that commercialism runs the establishment. Every advance in rational living and in true medical science lessens the amount of drugs used. The drug stores cannot live on their legitimate business, and are gradually forced in the direction of debased trade. Some become purveyors to all kinds of vices and have helped to fasten the various drug habits on our people which are secretly undermining the health and character of uncounted individuals. They are dragging the doctors down with them into commercialism. We must either standardize the drug stores or municipalize them. In Germany they are licensed; their number is limited; and they are restricted to the compounding of prescriptions. This eliminates the temptation to price-cutting and adulteration to a large extent. But why should not the Board of Health, under the advice of the organized medical profession, supply drugs at cost? Our cities now supply vaccine and antitoxin. All the real drugs needed by a large city could be stored and compounded in a single laboratory of moderate size. Then we could hope to deal with the drug habits.

The community alone can save us from the scandal of

[1] Dr. G. W. Goler, the health officer of Rochester, N.Y., has done very successful work in this direction which has attracted attention throughout the country. He will doubtless be glad to furnish information.

our burial customs. All the appurtenances of death are sold at monopoly prices. When men and women come to bury their beloved dead, they are in no condition to be on the watch against avarice, and they have a right to the fraternal protection of all their fellows. Instead of that all the professional interests connected with burials have pushed one another into the custom of extortionate charges; undertakers, cemetery associations, liverymen, and even priests stand in together. It is stated that undertakers charge five and even ten times as much for coffins as they pay for them; yet the casket manufacturers charge trust prices and are said to make enormous dividends. Family pride and the holiest affections are played on to draw the poor into tawdry display and ruinous expenses which cap the misfortune of the illness that preceded death and the destitution that may follow it. This is a case for community action. The community prohibits the individual from burying his dead privately; then it is under obligations to furnish him the proper facilities for burial and to protect him against overcharge. Cemeteries and crematories should be public property; if religious or charitable organizations desire sections of the cemetery set apart for their use, that ought not to be difficult. The work now performed by undertakers should either, as in most countries of Europe, be done by licensed associations whose price schedules are prescribed by the city, or, as in Switzerland, be treated as a public service to be supplied to all citizens alike and at public cost. The Jews had hired mourners; Jesus turned in anger from their commercialized grief. What ought the Christian Church to do when it is compelled constantly to coöperate with the exploitation of the sacred grief of the poor and the paganizing of the solemn majesty of death? [1]

[1] See articles by Graham Taylor in the *Survey*, Sept. 2, 1911, and by Quincy L. Dowd, in the *Independent*, June 13, 1912.

A noble community life is a great aid to every family that has fine aspirations. When the community life is vicious, it is hard to keep the serpents out of our homes. The community has the power of praise and blame; our social appetite craves the good opinion of our fellow-men; if their good opinion is obtained by folly, then for folly we shall spend our substance. Innumerable hard-working parents are straining to overdress their children because other people are overdressing theirs. Any one who has ever had to go to school in patched pants or a made-over dress to sit on the seat with the scornful, knows what children suffer, and most parents will give up almost anything to save their children from heartache. So we dress them up; not because their beautiful bodies need it, but because we must keep the pace set by others who may be just as much driven as we are. Why should not a community adopt a simple school uniform for all? Such a custom, without compulsion, exists in Germany; also in some Catholic parochial schools. It actually improves the looks of the children. If desired, each school can have some special color device to distinguish its pupils and so create school spirit. Every mother can see how this would simplify the clothing problems, save time and nerves, and save money. The school clothes, like army uniforms, would be produced in great quantities and ought therefore to be produced cheaply.

The public spirit of our nation is mewing its wings like an eagle and trying its strength at new tasks. If we deny a community the right to undertake larger public functions, we cripple the public spirit and deny it the right to growth. If we forbid a community to increase its public property, we deny the public spirit its necessary tools and the ground to stand on. In the palmy days of Greece and Rome the rule prevailed that private life should be simple and public life ample and rich. The glorious remnants of the literary and artistic life that developed under that rule still justify its wisdom. We have reversed that principle, making private men rich and our cities poor, private houses sumptuous and our public buildings mean. If the unearned rent of the land flowed into our public treasury, and if our public utilities were a source of public income and a means of public service, private citizens might not have such fortunes to waste on the housing of their poor mortality, but our cities would rise clean, symmetrical, and splendid, planned by the genius and adorned by the love of their sons and daughters.

> "O beautiful for patriot's dream
> That sees beyond the years
> Thine alabaster cities gleam
> Undimmed by human tears.
> America ! America !
> God shed his grace on thee,
> And crown thy good with brotherhood
> From sea to shining sea !" [1]

[1] From the hymn, "O beautiful for spacious skies," by Katharine Lee Bates, — the most beautiful patriotic hymn we have.

CHAPTER V

THE condition of the working class has been considered from various angles in the course of our argument, but this final summary of the practical steps that would lead to a Christian social order would be a maimed and futile thing if the rise of the industrial working class were omitted from it. Modern humanity can never be saved until the working class is saved. The absolute mass and the relative weight of this class are steadily increasing in all nations. Other social classes are being ground up and their fragments increase the bulk of the industrial working class. How can society as a whole have peace and health if this great segment of society is left without property and security, and if large parts of it are demoralized and submerged? In fact, our whole national life lacks health and peace because it is constantly wrenched and shaken by the struggles of this class to escape economic and moral drowning.

Moreover, the importance of this class for the moral future of humanity reaches far beyond its own membership. It is the most modern of all classes, the product of to-day, the creator of to-morrow, the banner bearer of destiny. Its rise to-day parallels the historic rise of the business class from the feudal social order. The feudal barons despised the merchant class. To levy tribute on the traders by highway robbery was considered a far more honorable occupation than to make or sell cloth. Yet the future belonged to the men of the ell and bale, and history was digging the grave in which the gallant barons were to rest from their peculiar labors.   So the working class is making its way through contempt and opposition, but its rise is the salient fact of present history, and if the banner of the Kingdom of God is to enter through the gates of the future, it will have to be carried by the tramping hosts of labor.

We have discussed the conservation of life.[1]   The industrial wage earners have the same right to life and health as all others, but to them vitality and vigor are doubly essential because the working force of their body and mind is their whole asset and capital.   If the working class is to rise, its physical fitness must be protected.   The farmer can hardly escape fresh air at his work; the factory and mine worker can rarely get it.   Hand labor set its own pace and the automatic safeguards of the body protected it against exhaustion; in machine labor the pace is set for the workman by fellow-workers with muscles of steel that never tire.   Therefore the industrial worker needs added protection against exhausted air and poisonous gases, and against a pace of work that drains and poisons the body with an accumulation of its own waste products.[2] The man who works alone in his own home or shop can make his own conditions of labor; the man who works in another man's factory can control the conditions only through joint action with his fellows or through community action. Therefore the industrial worker needs more social protection than other classes.   A maximum working day and a legal minimum of safety and comfort in the conditions of shop and mine labor are a concern of civilization and a step to a Christian social order.

It would aid the rise of the working class if the sufferings of labor could be appreciated as vicarious sufferings, just

[1] Part VI, Chapter II, of this book.
[2] Josephine Goldmark, "Fatigue and Efficiency."

2 G

as we appreciate the sufferings of soldiers who have bled for their country. Our industrial communities as yet have no adequate sense of their joint responsibility for the needless accidents of industry. The Church ought to be the organized social conscience; has it done its part to convict us of our guilt? A medieval pope is said to have put himself under church discipline because a man had starved in his city of Rome. Would it not be a fit function for the Church to summon the people once a year to an act of common mourning for those who died while doing the dangerous work for all, and to an act of common contrition in so far as their death was preventable and needless? At Gloucester, in Massachusetts, when the fishing fleet is home for the season, the town unites in a service, calling the roll of those who lost their lives at sea and thereby taking on the common heart the grief of those who are bereaved, and then the children cast flowers on the outgoing tide to be carried out to sea where the dead are buried. Why should not the churches of an industrial community unite with its labor organizations to find a fitting religious expression for what we ought to feel when men die at their posts where they labored for all, and when strong bodies are crushed that might be enjoying the light of life but for our neglect?

Since the wage earner sells, not goods, but life, the community is even more concerned in the fairness of his bargains than in other commercial transactions. As weights and measures are inspected to protect buyers, and as railway freight rates are reviewed and fixed to protect shippers, so the wages paid to workers and the methods by which they are paid should be scrutinized by the community through duly authorized wage boards to protect the individual workers against misuse of their ignorance or helplessness.

The rise of the working class involves an increase in their share of the profits of business. Modern business is a social process, and the community is a partner in every phase of it; most of all where public rights and resources are needed to carry on the business, as in the public utilities and in mining. Capital should have its fair return, but after that is paid, the other factors of industry should get their share of the social dividend by increased wages and lower prices. Social peace and a Christian social order will never come without a juster distribution of the joint profits of industry.

As consumers the industrial wage earners are concerned with all others in getting honest goods at prices that contain no monopoly charges and no unnecessary middlemen's profits. Their rise as a class would be greatly aided by coöperative organizations.[1] The housing problem is peculiarly pressing for this class because they are massed in industrial centers. Communities that solve the problem of local transportation and of land taxation will thereby solve in large part the housing problem.[2] Because workingmen live close together and under uniform conditions their housing invites community action on a large scale. Their homes are in a peculiar danger of invasion by tenement-house manufacturing, which harnesses women and children and the home itself to industrial production and uses them up to save the employer part of his expenses. It should be prohibited entirely.

Nothing so holds down the rise of the working class as the dragging fringe of unemployed workers. Its chronic existence charges our whole social system with incompetence and anarchy. Our political parties have dodged that vital question, lavishing their enthusiasm on issues that seem paltry by the side of this. If, as is alleged, some employers purposely maintain a body of unemployed workmen in order to keep a thorn bit in the mouth of Labor, I have no words to characterize so inhuman a policy. The best work

[1] Part V, Chapter VII, of this book.   [2] Part VI, Chapter II.

on this baffling problem has been done by the labor unions, and this alone would justify their existence. We need a connected system of employment bureaus, such as the longer experience of older countries has worked out. But it must be controlled by the class it is to serve and not by any interest hostile to it.

The wage earners are now a propertyless class; if they are to rise to even worth with the other social classes, they must have the security and moral stimulus of property rights. Public opinion and the law must come to recognize the property right of a worker in the business to which he contributes his energies. This right can best be recognized by giving him, like the civil servants of the government, a claim on his job unless dismissed for cause.[1] Social insurance against industrial accident, occupational disease, and old age would act as a property right, and would save workingmen from dropping into the bottomless pit of poverty and from the constant fear of it.

The rise of Labor and the spread of education are inseparable. All except the higher machine labor dulls the intellect by its monotony and demands extra educational stimulus to offset it. Every workingman should have enough technical education to understand the productive process of which he is part; such comprehension would support him in the dullness of his own labor. As industry becomes socialized, it can be put into coöperative relation to the higher schools, so that industrial and educational work, each fertilizing the other, can go on side by side after adolescence. If the problem of unemployment were solved, the working people would not have to be as suspicious as they now are of vocational schools and industrial training. The intellectual earnestness with which assemblies of workingmen handle their problems, the absence among them of the dilettant tone with its unreality, and the tire-

[1] Part V, Chapter III, of this book.

lessness with which they listen to anything that seems to them to concern real life, impress every one who deals with them and guarantee their intellectual future. To feed their intellectual hunger is one of the simplest services which men and women of the professional classes can render them. But the eight-hour day and a workless Sunday would be the surest aids to their intellectual development.

As humanity is constituted, the rise of the working class can be neither easy nor painless. Its desires conflict with the interests of the most powerful classes, and its progress can come only through class struggle. The Christian forces of society must not block that struggle, but ease and speed it, so that a minimum of class hatred will cloud it, and a maximum of class valor will be generated. For the advancement of this class the organizations of labor are indispensable. If outsiders have been doubtful about that, the instinct of the working class has never wavered. Even if the progress of the working class were likely to be achieved for it by outside influences, it is not morally desirable that it should be. They must win their own prizes and qualify for them by effort. We are told that trades-unionism is an affair of a minority of the wage earners and not a movement of the whole class. Every upward movement of humanity is carried upward by a minority; except at the highest emotional moments the mass is sluggish. "The many are called, but few are the elect." The fewer they are, the more worthy of honor and aid.

Public opinion and the law must uphold the working class in their demand for collective bargaining. No other form of bargaining puts the two parties to this contract on a level so that the bargain is free from coercion. In the long run collective bargaining will prove to the advantage of the capitalist class, too. The wage contracts between capital and labor to-day involve issues so large that they are not private affairs. The community has a stake in them and should be represented by wage boards and boards of conciliation and arbitration to protect the public interest and to add the impartial fairness of outside public opinion in case of disputes.

The rise of the working class in the last century would have been impossible without the political rights of free speech, free assembly, free organization, and free press. Every advance in genuine political democracy is a further gain to the working class, and unless the working class ultimately attains economic democracy, political democracy will come to be a hollow and dishonest form.[1]   In the future too the struggle of the working class will have to be fought out in part on the political field.   The business class is now in control of our political machinery and is using it with tremendous effectiveness.   The working class can secure equal justice only by a readjustment of political power. On the economic field the number of the workers is their weakness, for they bid against each other; at the ballot box their number is their strength.   The old parties have neglected or fooled their working class constituency in the past, and any alliance hereafter between an organized working-class group and the management of the old parties would certainly lead to scandals and betrayals.   The Socialist Party represents the point of view and the interests of the working class just as accurately as the old parties have represented Capitalism.   Even if a man dissents from the philosophy of Socialism and is dubious about its ultimate aims, he cannot help recognizing that in Europe this minority party has done more to force the working-class problems to the front and to secure labor measures from the upper classes than any other influence in politics.

A man who has his eye on history would be rash indeed if he denied that the rise of the working class involved serious risks for the rest of society.   No class that pushed its

[1] Part III, Chapter V, of this book.

way up has ever held the balance of justice even; the business class certainly did not; yet it would have been far worse for society if it had been left with the feudal aristocracy and clergy in control. If the working class secures the legal right to organization, employment, insurance, and pensions, it may create privileged groups that will keep others out and down in order to make these privileges worth more. In the village communes and in the guild system an aristocracy of Labor grew up that took to special privilege just as kindly as any other form of aristocracy. We must trust to the modern spirit of democracy and the political grip of our grandchildren to deal with the centipede of Labor as we now have to deal with the octopus of Capital. Our present duty seems clear, and that is all we can ask. If men had always waited till no possibility of evil had lurked in their ventures, neither the American Revolution, nor the Protestant Reformation, nor the discovery of America, nor the founding of the Christian Church, nor the creation of Adam would ever have happened. To strike for what is plainly good and right, and to risk the rest, is faith.

At any rate, the working class embodies an immense fund of moral energy which we need to equip the Christian social order. The members of good trades-unions feel that their influence is a great moral force. That influence is much more searching and forcible because exerted by their own fellows than if it were professionalized or exerted by a higher class. The support and comfort given by the unions to their members in time of trouble is also ethically higher than the charity of an upper class would be; it is coöperative and thereby cleansed of degrading elements.

The working class lays the stress on the human virtues differently than the middle class and the churches, and this makes it hard for each of the two sections to appreciate the qualities of the other. The churches have laid chief stress on the conquest of animal passions; the working class appreciates social solidarity above all things. The churches will exclude a man who drinks, and tolerate a man who over-reaches in trade; the working class will tolerate a man who drinks, and loathe a man who takes another man's job away from him. Each side would be the better if it adopted the virtues loved by the other in addition to its own. The churches are tainted with the money morality of Capitalism; the trades-unions have not emerged from the barbarity of alcoholism. Probably no one thing would do so much to increase the fighting capacity of the working class and to win the moral confidence of that great body of virtue which is organized in the churches, as for the labor unions to follow the almost unanimous verdict of science and the call of their best leaders and to break with alcoholism. The individual physical impairment after drink, which continues for several days, becomes a social peril amid machine and gang labor. The impairment of self-restraint and good judgment by even a slight dose of alcohol endangers the cause of labor in times of trouble when everything depends on the judgment of the leaders and the crowd. During the last fifteen years there has been a long advance in sobriety in the trades-unions. It would be a great step in the rise of Labor if the unions refused to meet in any hall connected with a saloon or to pay their rent in the form of drinks. The churches could render no better service to Labor and to temperance than to assist the unions in securing a labor temple in every city, or else the right to meet in the schoolhouses. If only the churches had the affection of the trades-unions, there would be still an easier way; the churches have the buildings which the unions need; their lecture rooms, let at a small rental, would solve the problem in many cases. At any rate, let us cheer organized Labor when it encourages its members to come out for abstinence, and when it recognizes that it has no part nor lot with that most voracious form of Capitalism, the Liquor Business.

I know of one large city where nothing but lemonade is served at the annual ball of the Barkeepers Union, and a number of the members of that union are total abstainers.

But temperance is not the only virtue. No union is built up and maintained without financial expense and self-denial, without foresight and sagacity, without fortitude and suffering. They gather their members from all nationalities, parties, and religions, and by the warmth of a new fraternity melt down the old anti-fraternal immoralities inherited from other social relations. They teach their men to stand together in mutual defense against wrong and indignities, and though they may prove overloyal to the unworthy at times, surely the doctrine that "the injury of one is the concern of all" is higher than that individualistic doctrine, "Every man for himself," which was first formulated in the question of Cain, "Am I my brother's keeper?"

The men who are now organizing the working class are the same brand of men who organized our continent as pioneers. The heroisms and privations going on, out of sight of most of us, would be fit material for artists and poets, and may yet be their finest theme. A man who has no sympathetic comprehension of the rise of the working class may be very clever and widely informed, but he has no vital grasp either of the present or of the future; he is not really a modern man; nor is he a friend of men. The members of the working class individually are probably no better than those of other classes; they may even average worse; but collectively their class stands for a higher morality than Business. It is one of the powers of the coming age.[1] Its rise is one of the agencies essential to the christianizing of the social order. The pillar of cloud and fire which once moved before a nation when it broke from the servitude of Egypt and marched to the promised land of freedom and plenty, is now moving before the industrial working class.

[1] Part V, Chapter VII, of this book.

CHAPTER VI

IN looking back over the field traversed in this book, it may seem to some as if our argument had fallen away from the high religious ground taken at the outset and had sagged down to the level of mere economic discussion. That impression would be superficial. This is a religious book from beginning to end. Its sole concern is for the Kingdom of God and the salvation of men. But the Kingdom of God includes the economic life; for it means the progressive transformation of all human affairs by the thought and spirit of Christ. And a full salvation also includes the economic life; for it involves the opportunity for every man to realize the full humanity which God has put into him as a promise and a call; it means a clean, rich, just, and brotherly life between him and his fellows; it means a chance to be single-hearted, and not to be coerced into a double life. I believe with the great historian Von Ranke that "the only real progress of mankind is contained in Christianity;" but that is true only when Christianity is allowed to become "the internal, organizing force of society."[1] We have scouted around our economic system, mined under it, and aëroplaned over it, because this is the fortress in which the predatory and unbrotherly spirit still lies intrenched with flags flying. It is the strategical key to the spiritual conquest of the modern world.

But, on the other hand, no outward economic readjust-

[1] Fichte.

ments will answer our needs. It is not this thing or that thing our nation needs, but a new mind and heart, a new conception of the way we all ought to live together, a new conviction about the worth of a human life and the use God wants us to make of our own lives. We want a revolution both inside and outside. We want a moral renovation of public opinion and a revival of religion. Laws and constitutions are mighty and searching, but while the clumsy hand of the law fumbles at the gate below, the human soul sits in its turret amid its cruel plunder and chuckles. A righteous public opinion may bring the proudest sinner low. But the most pervasive scrutiny, a control which follows our actions to their fountain-head where the desires and motives of the soul are born, is exerted only by personal religion.

But here again we are compelled to turn to our economic life. What if the public opinion on which we rely is tainted and purposely poisoned? What if our religion is drugged and sick? The mammonism generated by our economic life is debilitating our religion so that its hand lies nerveless on our conscience. Jesus told us it would be so. He put the dilemma flatly before us: "Ye cannot serve God and Mammon. If ye love the one, ye will hate the other." Every proof that we love Mammon with all our heart and all our soul raises the presumption that we have lost the love of God and are merely going through the motions when we worship him. We can measure the general apostasy by noting the wonder and love that follow every man who has even in some slight degree really turned his back on money. Men crowd around him like exiles around a man who brings them news from home.

So we must begin at both ends simultaneously. We must change our economic system in order to preserve our conscience and our religious faith; we must renew and strengthen our religion in order to be able to change our economic system. This is a two-handed job; a one-handed man will bungle it. I have discussed the economic system in many chapters. In this closing chapter I shall talk about revolutionary religion and the need of converted men for the christianizing of the social order.

When Archimedes discovered the laws of leverage, he cried Δὸς ποῦ στῶ. He thought he could hoist the bulk of the earth from its grooves if only he had a standing place and a fulcrum for his lever. God wants to turn humanity right side up, but he needs a fulcrum. Every saved soul is a fixed point on which God can rest his lever. A divine world is ever pressing into this imperfect and sinful world, demanding admission and realization for its higher principles, and every inspired man is a channel through which the spirit of God can enter humanity. Every higher era must be built on a higher moral law and a purer experience of religion. Therefore the most immediate and constant need in christianizing the social order is for more religious individuals.

I believe in the miraculous power of the human personality. A mind set free by God and energized by a great purpose is an incomputable force. Lord Shaftesbury was naturally a man of rather narrow type and without brilliant gifts, but he gave himself with religious devotion to the cause of the oppressed classes, and so became one of the prime forces that swung England out of its carnival of capitalistic inhumanity.[1] If we in the West have been correctly informed, the emancipation of China from the Manchu oligarchy has been chiefly due to the personal teaching and persuasion of one man, Sun Yat Sen, and the band of devoted men whom he raised up. One of

[1] The Duke of Argyll in 1885 said: "My Lords, the social reforms of the last century have not been mainly due to the Liberal Party. They have been due mainly to the influence, character, and perseverance of one man, Lord Shaftesbury." "That," said Lord Salisbury, "is, I believe, a very true representation of the facts."

the most fruitful intellectual movements in Germany [1] owes its beginning to one man, Professor Albert Eichhorn. His health has been so frail that he has published nothing but a sixteen-page pamphlet, but by personal conversations he inspired a number of able young minds, setting them new problems and fertilizing their thinking by his unselfish co-operation. The Democratic Convention of Baltimore in 1912 will stand out in our memory chiefly for the dramatic power of a single personality, strong in his sincerity and the trust of his countrymen, to wrest the control of his party at least for a time from evil hands. The history of the new democracy in recent years is the history of small groups of men of conviction and courage who stood together for the new democratic measures. Often without official standing or financial backing they have shattered political redoubts that seemed impregnable. The Inquisition of the Middle Ages and the Siberian exile system alike testify to the fact that the powers of tyranny are afraid of single-handed faith.

This power of the individual rests on the social cohesion of mankind. Because we are bound together in unity of life, the good or the evil in one man's soul affects the rest. The presence of one heart that loves humanity shames the selfish spirit in others and warms the germs of civic devotion in the chilly soil, so that they grow and bear seed in turn. One brave soul rallies the timid and shakes the self-confidence of the prosperous. One far-seeing man can wake the torpid imagination of a community so that men see civic centers where they saw only real estate deals before. Hopes and convictions that were dim and vague become concrete, beautiful, and compelling when they take shape in a life that lives them out. No torch is kindled of itself, but when one man has lighted his at the altar fire of God, hundreds will take their light from him. So the faith

[1] The so-called *religionsgeschichtliche Schule.*

of the pioneers becomes socialized.   The belief of the few in
time becomes a dogma which does not have to be proved
over and over, but is a spiritual fund owned in common by a
great social group.   We need new dogmas that will raise
the old to a new level and give them wider scope.   "You
have heard that it was said of old time — But I say unto
you." [1]   Such a lifting of moral conviction comes through
those who can speak with authority because they speak
for God.

Create a ganglion chain of redeemed personalities in a
commonwealth, and all things become possible.   "What
the soul is in the body, that are Christians in the world." [2]
The political events of 1912 have furnished fresh proof that
after individuals have preached their faith long enough, the
common mind reaches the point of saturation, and moral
conviction begins to be precipitated in solid layers.   At such
times even poor Judas thinks he would like to join the
Messianic movement and be an apostle, and the rotten
nobility of France follow the peasant girl : —

"The White Maid, and the white horse, and the flapping banner
    of God ;
Black hearts riding for money ; red hearts riding for fame ;
The Maid who rides for France, and the king who rides for
    shame ;
Gentlemen, fools, and a saint riding in Christ's high name." [3]

"Force and Right rule the world ; Force till Right is
ready." [4]   The more individuals we have who love the
Right for its own sake and move toward it of their own will,
the less force and compulsion do we need.   Here is one
of the permanent functions of the Christian Church.   It
must enlist the will and the love of men and women for
God, mark them with the cross of Christ, and send them out

[1] Matt. v.
[2] The Epistle to Diognetus, Chapter VI.   Probably of the 2d century.
[3] Theodore Roberts, "The Maid."   [4] Rochefoucauld.

to finish up the work which Christ began. Is the Church supplying society with the necessary equipment of such personalities? Let us grant that it can never reach all; but is it making Christian revolutionists of those whom it does teach and control? Jesus feared the proselyting efforts of the Jewish Church, because it made men worse than they were before.[1] Some people to-day who carry the stamp of ecclesiastical religion most legibly are the most hopeless cases so far as social spirit and effort are concerned. The spiritual efficiency of the Church is therefore one of the most serious practical questions for the christianizing of the social order. We have shown[2] that the American churches have been to a large extent christianized in their fundamental organization, and every step in their redemption has facilitated social progress and increased the forces available for righteousness. But the process of christianizing the Church is not yet complete.

To become fully Christian the churches must turn their back on dead issues and face their present tasks. There is probably not a single denomination which is not thrusting on its people questions for which no man would care and of which only antiquarians would know if the churches did not keep these questions alive. Our children sometimes pull the clothes of their grandparents out of old chests in the attic and masquerade in long-tailed coats and crinolines. We religious folks who air the issues of the sixteenth century go through the same mummery in solemn earnest, while the enemy is at the gate.

To become fully Christian and to do their duty by society the churches must get together. The disunion of the Church wastes the funds intrusted to it, wastes the abilities of its servants, and wastes the power of religious enthusiasm or turns it into antisocial directions. Civil war is always bad; it is worst when a nation is threatened by outside

[1] Matt. xxiii. 15.   [2] Part III, Chapter II.

enemies and the very existence of the fatherland is in danger. Some churches are so far apart on essential matters that union is hopeless for the present. But the great body of Protestant Christians in America is simply perpetuating trivial dissensions in which scarcely any present-day religious values are at stake.

To become fully Christian the Church must come out of its spiritual isolation. In theory and practice the Church has long constituted a world by itself. It has been governed by ecclesiastical motives and interests which are often remote from the real interests of humanity, and has almost uniformly set church questions ahead of social questions. It has often built a sound-proof habitation in which people could live for years without becoming definitely conscious of the existence of prostitution, child labor, or tenement crowding. It has offered peace and spiritual tranquillity to men and women who needed thunderclaps and lightnings. Like all the rest of us, the Church will get salvation by finding the purpose of its existence outside of itself, in the Kingdom of God, the perfect life of the race.

To become fully Christian the Church must still further emancipate itself from the dominating forces of the present era. In an age of political despotism our fathers cut the Church loose from state control and state support, and therewith released the moral forces of progress. In an age of financial autocracy we must be far more watchful than we have been lest we bargain away the spiritual freedom of the Church for opulent support.

We do not want to substitute social activities for religion. If the Church comes to lean on social preachings and doings as a crutch because its religion has become paralytic, may the Lord have mercy on us all! We do not want less religion; we want more; but it must be a religion that gets its orientation from the Kingdom of God. To concentrate our efforts on personal salvation, as orthodoxy has done, or on soul culture, as liberalism has done, comes close to refined selfishness. All of us who have been trained in egotistic religion need a conversion to Christian Christianity, even if we are bishops or theological professors. Seek ye first the Kingdom of God and God's righteousness, and the salvation of your souls will be added to you. Our personality is of divine and eternal value, but we see it aright only when we see it as part of mankind. Our religious individuality must get its interpretation from the supreme fact of social solidarity. "What hast thou that thou hast not received?" Then what hast thou that thou dost not owe? Prayer ought to be a keen realization of our fellows, and not a forgetfulness of the world. A religion which realizes in God the bond that binds all men together can create the men who will knit the social order together as an organized brotherhood.

This, then, is one of the most practical means for the christianizing of the social order, to multiply the number of minds who have turned in conscious repentance from the old maxims, the old admirations, and the old desires, and have accepted for good and all the Christian law with all that it implies for modern conditions. When we have a sufficient body of such, the old order will collapse like the walls of Jericho when the people "shouted with a great shout" and "every man went straight before him" at the wall. No wrong can stand very long after the people have lost their reverence for it and begin to say "Booh" to it.

Mending the social order is not like repairing a clock in which one or two parts are broken. It is rather like restoring diseased or wasted tissues, and when that has to be done, every organ and cell of the body is heavily taxed. During the reconstructive process every one of us must be an especially good cell in whatever organ of the social body we happen to be located. The tissues of society which it will be hardest to replace by sound growth are represented

2 H

by the class of the poor and the class of the rich.   Both are
the product of ages of social disease.   Christianizing the
social order involves a sanitation of the defective and de-
linquent classes, and of the classes living on unearned incomes.   All these need religious salvation.

Suppose that we had successfully democratized our government, made our laws just, and socialized our industries.
We should still have with us a great body of people who have
been crippled by war or industry, exhausted by child labor,
drained of vitality in their mothers' wombs, unbalanced
by alcoholism, or made neurotic by drug habits and sexual
excesses.   These would be the legacy bequeathed by the old
order to the new, and surviving it for at least fifty years;
perhaps a hundred and fifty years.   To-day we have that
same body of defective people, constantly replenished and
increasing in proportion to the population, hanging as a
dead weight on society and on the working class especially.
Whatever decreases that weight will give us elbow room for
constructive work.   The men and women who are helping
to organize the defective members of the community so that
they will get the maximum enjoyment out of their life and
will present the minimum of hindrance to the present social
transition, are not mere ministers of mercy, but constructive agents in the christianizing of the social order.   If
the selfish political henchmen who have run our public
institutions can be replaced by regenerate intellects, our
institutions of mercy will come out of their conspiracy of
silence with the workers of cruelty, and we shall begin to
find out who and what is throwing all this burden on the
community.

The problem of healing the social tissues is even more
difficult in the case of those who break the laws.   The old
vindictive method of punishment has manifestly been in-
effective.   It is also unchristian; for nothing is Christian
that is not impelled by love and the desire to redeem.   It

becomes increasingly intolerable as our clearer psychological knowledge reminds us that we all in youth had the same wayward and brutal instincts, and that the majority of youthful criminals are just such immature human beings as our own children. We are realizing that the social disorder which we ourselves have helped to create is responsible for a large part of our lawlessness. "Society stands in the docket with every criminal who is there."[1] We need redeemed minds to deal with the delinquents of society. The men and women who deal with offenders should be the wisest and most Christ-like persons in the community. To save the young and wayward from losing their honor and to fan the dying fire of manhood in older criminals, is a great ministry of Christ, and Christian men ought to enter the police force with the sense of enlisting for God and their country. Within this generation our prisons should become redemptive institutions. But the consciousness of doing productive and honorable work is an essential condition of true salvation. Our penal institutions must become coöperative industrial establishments, where offenders can still support their families, lay by for the day when they will be thrown on their own resources, and, if possible, make restitution to those whom they have harmed. Our prisons must cease to be slave pens where the State lends its physical compulsion to some predatory industrial concern that wants to make big profits by underselling outside labor, grafting on the State, and draining the prisoners. The participation of our States in contract prison labor is an indefensible business that ought to rob us of our sleep.

The sanitation of the wealthy classes is another problem; there we deal, not with the misery and waywardness of the poor, but with excessive material power. Some think it is idle to appeal to the rich to change their own lives; it

[1] Victor Hugo.

will have to be changed for them. I do not believe it.
As a class they will doubtless go their way, eating and
drinking, marrying and giving in marriage till the flood
comes. But individuals will respond; more of them, I believe, than in any similar situation in history before. Large
groups of them have of late traveled miles in the direction
of the fraternal life.

Even if there are only a few, their coming counts. Something happens when Moses leaves the palace of Pharaoh
and joins the fortunes of his people. At a directors' meeting a single steady voice lifted for humanity and 6 per cent
and against inhumanity and 8 per cent, cannot be disregarded forever, and that voice may mean health and
decency for hundreds. Socialists justly say that there is
no instance in history where one of the possessing classes
has voluntarily given up its privileges. But is there any
case where a poor and oppressed class has made a permanent and successful advance toward emancipation without
help from individuals of the higher classes?

The desire for social esteem is one of the strongest and
most subtle forces in social life. The individual always
toils for whatever his class regards as the game. He will
collect scalps for his belt, Philistine foreskins for a bridal
gift to his beloved, silver cups or wreaths of wild olive as
athletic trophies, funny titles, shady millions, — it's all the
same thing. Now, a few self-confident men can create a
new basis of esteem in their class and therewith change the
direction of effort. If a few redeemed minds in a given business community begin to yawn at the stale game of piling
up and juggling money, and plunge into the more fascinat-
ing game of re-making a city, others will follow them.
They cannot help it. God and the instinct of imitation
will make them.

Social institutions can be hit hardest by men who have
grown up inside of them and know their weak spots. Phari-

saism was hit by the Pharisee Paul; monasticism by the monk Luther; the aristocracy of France by Count Mirabeau; alcoholism by John B. Gough; militarism by the ex-officer Tolstoy; frenzied finance by Lawson; the traction system by the traction magnate Tom L. Johnson. Even a few renegades from the rich are invaluable. It takes a sharp blow from the outside to crack an eggshell; the soft bill of a chick can break it from within.

Every rich man who has taken the Christian doctrine of stewardship seriously has thereby expropriated himself after a fashion and become manager where he used to be owner. If a man in addition realizes that some part of his fortune consists of unearned money, accumulated by one of the forms of injustice which have been legalized by our social order, it becomes his business as a Christian and a gentleman to make restitution in some way. There is no sincere repentance without restitution and confession of wrong. If I discovered that I or my grandfather had, knowingly or unknowingly, by some manipulation or error of the survey, added to my farm a ten-acre strip which belonged to my neighbor, could I go on harvesting the crops on it and say nothing? It is true that restitution of wealth absorbed from great communities through many years is a complicated matter, and that the giving away of large sums is dangerous business which may do as much harm as good. Yet some way must be found. Since the rich have gained their wealth by appropriating public functions and by using the taxing powers which ought to belong to the community alone, the fittest way of restitution is to undertake public service for which the State in its present impoverished condition has no means, such as the erection and running of public baths, playgrounds, and civic centers. But the moral value of such gifts would be almost incalculably increased if some acknowledgment were made that these funds were drawn from the people and belonged to them. Every time any rich man has indicated that he felt troubled in mind about his right to his wealth, the public heart has warmed toward him with a sense of forgiveness. If some eminent man should have the grace and wisdom to make a confession of wrong on behalf of his whole class, it would have a profound influence on public morality and social peace.

If a rich man has a really redeemed conscience and intellect, the best way to give away his unearned wealth would be to keep it and use it as a tool to make the recurrence of such fortunes as his own forever impossible. The Salvation Army sets a saved girl to save other girls, and that is the best way to keep her saved. By the same token a man whose forefathers made their money in breweries or distilleries ought to use it to fight alcoholism; a man who made his by land speculation should help to solve the housing question or finance the single-tax movement; a man who has charged monopoly prices for the necessaries of life should teach the people to organize coöperative societies; and so forth.

Men and women of the wealthy class who have been converted to the people as well as to God can perform a service of the highest value by weakening the resistance which their classes will inevitably offer to the equalization of property. That resistance has been by far the most important cause why humanity has been so backward in its social and moral development. The resistance of the upper classes has again and again blocked and frustrated hopeful upward movements, kept useful classes of the people in poverty and degradation, and punished the lovers of humanity with martyrdom of body or soul. The cross of Christ stands for the permanent historical fact that the men who have embodied the saving power of God have always been ill treated by those who profited by sin. Reference has been made to the work of Lord Shaftesbury.[1] In Lanca-

[1] Hodder, "The Life and Work of the Seventh Earl of Shaftesbury," 3 vols., 1886.

shire alone he found 35,000 children under thirteen years of age, many of them only five or six years old, working fourteen and fifteen hours a day. It took Shaftesbury and his friends fourteen years of agitation to get a ten-hour bill passed, and even then it was so impeded by legal difficulties that successive Acts, chiefly instigated by him, were required to give it effect, and the ten-hour standard was not fully secured till 1874. He and his friends were loaded with denunciation and insult for years. Few clergymen stood by him; they were indifferent, or cowed by the cotton lords. Men whose names are revered because they led the fight of the capitalistic class against landed wealth, Cobden, Bright, and Gladstone, were at that time the malignant opponents of the protection of the working class. Machiavelli said that men will forgive the murder of their parents more easily than the spoliation of their property.

Of course the road is smoother since democracy has leveled it. In 1567 under the Duke of Alba a man was condemned to death for the treasonable assertion that "we must obey God rather than man." It would probably be safe to say that now, especially if chapter and verse were quoted. But the opposition of the powerful classes against every movement that seriously threatens their privileges is one of the most formidable facts with which we have to reckon. All the dynasties of Europe combined against the first French Republic. All capitalistic governments would combine to trip and cripple the first Socialist Republic. If our Interests found their control of government really in danger, it would be comparatively easy to embroil our nation in war; that is always the last trick of a tottering dynasty. Therewith the President would be vested with almost dictatorial powers; martial law could be proclaimed wherever needed; State rights could be overridden; and the popular movement could be forcibly suppressed as treasonable.

A minority of wealthy men and women, who stand for the democratic American ideals and sincerely believe in the necessity and justice of the impending social changes, would do a great deal to avert the heading up of that spirit of anarchy among the rich and to prevent such a *coup d'état*, which would be the beginning of the end for our nation.

I estimate that about two thirds of my readers have read the foregoing pages about the conversion of the rich with a smiling sense of unreality, as the amiable dreams of a "good man." The late Duke of Cambridge had a way of talking aloud to himself, even in church. One Sunday the lesson about Zacchæus was being read, who gave away half of his goods to the poor. "Gad," said the Duke, "I don't mind subscribing, but half is too much." The rich young ruler was asked to give the whole and went away sorrowful. He wanted the goods, but the price staggered him. He missed his chance by not being game. He stood shivering on the shore and feared the plunge from which he would have come up in a tingle of life. He might have traveled day by day in the company of Jesus, with the Master's words in his memory, his eye on him, his friendship coaxing every good thing in the man's heart up and out. He might have become an apostle, one of the guiding spirits of the young Church, handling growing responsibilities, seeing the world, facing kings and mobs, tasting the fullness of life. His name might to-day be a household word wherever the Gospels are read, and millions of boys might be named after him as after John and James. Instead of that he probably lived and died as the richest man of his little Galilean town, carrying in a frozen heart the dead seed of a great life, unless, indeed, some Roman official squeezed him dry or the Jewish War did for him by force what he would not do freely.

So far from being dreams these suggestions are hard sense. If I were rich myself, I could state them far more strongly. The call to place unearned wealth at the service of the people's cause is to-day the daring short cut to great experiences, to the love and confidence of all good men, and almost the only way to fame open to most rich men. It is the "open but unfrequented path to immortality." [1] It is also the path to peace of heart and the joy of life. The sacrifices demanded by a religious conversion always seem sore and insuperable, but every religious man will agree that after the great surrender is made, there is a radiant joy that marks a great culmination of life. All the remaining years are ennobled. God is the great joy. Whenever we have touched the hem of his garment by some righteous action, we get so much satisfaction that we can be well content even if we get no further reward or recognition, or even if we suffer hurt and persecution for it. Not the memory of power wielded, not even the memory of love, is so sweet as the consciousness that we once suffered for a great cause. When Thomas Jefferson gave directions about his epitaph, he made no reference to having been Governor, Secretary of State, Vice President, and President of the United States. He did boast of having been the father of the University of Virginia, the author of the Declaration of Independence, and of the Virginia statute guaranteeing religious liberty.

"Now I saw in my dream, that the highway up which Christian was to go was fenced on either side with a wall, and that wall is called Salvation. Up this way therefore did burdened Christian run, but not without great difficulty, because of the load on his back. He ran thus till he came at a place somewhat ascending; and upon that place stood a Cross . . . . So I saw in my dream that just as Christian came up with the cross, his burden loosed from off his

[1] John Howard died in Russian Tartary, trying to find the cause for the plague and a remedy for it. On his grave in St. Paul's Cathedral are the words: "He took an open but unfrequented path to immortality."

shoulders and fell from off his back. . . . Then was Christian glad and lightsome and spoke with a merry heart." It is a sober fact that for many a Christian the load that burdens his soul is unearned money. If he returned it in some wise and redemptive way to the people from whom it came, he would once more own his soul, be a friend of all men, and a happy child of God. It is truly at the Cross alone that freedom of the soul is won.

I call on the old to make a great act of expiation and love before they go hence. Why will they descend to join

"the melancholy souls of those
Who lived withouten infamy or praise.
Commingled are they with the caitiff choir
Of Angels, who have not rebellious been
Nor faithful were to God, but were for self." [1]

In 1909 Chauchard, the proprietor of the Magazins du Louvre, one of the great department stores of Paris, died, leaving behind a fortune of $20,000,000, a colossal fortune for French conditions. His 8000 employees, who had helped him make this money, had been given to understand that he would leave them at least five millions. Instead, he left them $600,000, the amount of their annual tip. To the poor he left $40,000. His casket of precious wood and bronze, made under his care, cost $100,000; his shroud was cloth of gold; the pearl buttons on his waistcoat were valued at $100,000; opera singers performed at the burial service; the Grand Cross of the Legion of Honor was borne on a cushion before the hearse. Paris turned out to give him the honor that he seemed to have deserved. Grand stands had been built; hundreds of thousands lined the roads to the Père la Chaise to see what they called the Chauchard Carnival, a carnival of contempt and mockery. With blasts from motor horns, whistles,

---

[1] Dante, "Inferno," III, 34.

hisses, shouts, and catcalls, the plumed hearse swept along. The efforts of the police to check the roar of execration was in vain. This dramatic burst of emotion, with its mingling of selfish anger and righteous moral indignation, is prophetic of the judgment that democracy will pass on selfish wealth and display in coming days when it becomes more class conscious.

Set over against that the verdict on a Roman patriot: "In the following year died Publius Valerius, by common consent the foremost man in the arts of war and peace. His fame was immense; his private property was so scanty that there was not enough to pay the expense of his funeral. He was buried at public cost. The matrons mourned him as they mourned Brutus." [1]

When a few princes and cities in 1530 avowed their faith in the principles of the Reformation by presenting the Augsburg Confession, Prince Wolfgang von Anhalt was warned not to sign because it would bring down on him the anger of the Emperor Charles V. The old man replied: "Many a time have I ridden to war to help my friends; so now for once I'll take horse for my Lord Christ."

But the call is not to the old alone. It is to all. "The Kingdom of God is at hand. Therefore repent and believe in the Gospel." I wish the Student Volunteers could add another pledge by which those who do not go to the foreign field would bind themselves to give some term of their youth at least to social work in the trenches. If necessary, young men and women should be willing to secure their freedom for poorly paid work by postponing marriage. Childless men and women are under a special law to make good to the race what they are not putting into the bearing and rearing of children. Those whose love has suffered a great loss should fill the gap with a wider love, and do for humanity what their loved one would have been worth

[1] Livy, II, 16.

to his fellow-men if he had lived. Those who have suffered
through some social sin can give a meaning and value to
their suffering by making it serve the redemption of the
race from that sin. For instance, if a man has borne the
curse of alcohol or drug poison in himself or in the degradation of a friend, he is under holy bonds to warn others and
stamp out that evil; if a woman has felt sex sin cutting
into her heart or her body, she has a special call from God
to save humanity from that silent ravager, and if she is
deaf to the call, her suffering, in place of being part of God's
salvation, becomes a mere waste and loss. On the ancient
minster at Basle are two sculptured groups: St. Martin
cutting his cloak in two with his sword to clothe a beggar,
and St. George spurring his horse against the dragon that
devastated the country. Every Christian man should
embody both kinds of sainthood in one life.

> "Trumpeter, sound for the splendor of God!
> Sound the music whose name is law,
> Whose service is perfect freedom still,
> The order august that rules the stars!
> Bid the anarchs of night withdraw.
> Too long the destroyers have worked their will.
> Sound for the last, the last of the wars!
> Sound for the heights that our fathers trod,
> When truth was truth and love was love,
> With a hell beneath, but a heaven above.
> Trumpeter, rally us, rally us, rally us,
>   On to the City of God."

INDEX

A

Ability, suppression of, under unjust conditions, 333–335.

Accidents, industrial, the community's support of expenses of, 228; figures of, 242–243; increase of, with spread of power machinery, 245; need of scientific record of, 415; compensation in case of, 415.

Accounting, uniform, 3.

Accumulation of wealth, extent of justification for, 297.

Addams, Jane, quoted, 249, 266–267; "A New Conscience and an Ancient Evil," by, 265.

Adulteration, of goods, 206–210; of food, lowers physical efficiency of working people, 246; of food, an illustration of the clashing of private interest with public welfare, 276; avoidance of, in case of drugs, by public ownership, 444.

Advertisements, disfiguring, 253.

Advertising, effects of, on character, 210–212.

Æsthetic life, treatment of, by industry and commerce, 252 ff.

Age, increase in conservatism with increasing, 32; saving for, 342, 343.

Aged, care of the, an unsolved national problem, 416; an act of expiation and love asked of, before death, 474–475.

Agricultural land, proposed socialization of, 424.

Alcoholism, in idle society, 302; complete break needed between working class and, 456. *See* Liquor trade.

America, difference in attitude of socialism toward religion in Europe and in, 108–109, 398–400; debt of education in, to Christianity, 146–147; inequality and privilege in, 335–336.

American Federation of Catholic Societies, anti-socialist propaganda of, 27.

American Liberty and Property Association, declaration of principles of, 350–351.

Amusement and social pleasure, public provision for, 440–442.

Anabaptists, the, 83.

Andover House, 20 n.

Andover Seminary, pioneer in study of social problems at theological seminaries, 20 n.

Anglo-Saxon communities, blending of religion and freedom in, 154.

Anhalt, Prince Wolfgang von, story of, 475.

Anthracite coal monopoly, 229, 424.

Anticlericalism in continental socialism, 109–110.

Apocalypticism, development and significance of, among the Hebrews, 54–55; still a living force, as shown by the Book of Daniel and the Apocalypse of John, 55; how it came to dominate the Christian view of future history, 55–56; necessity of the idea of the Kingdom of God to get rid of, to meet demands of the modern social world, 56; pre-Christian utopian form of the Kingdom-of-God hope held by, 65; revival of, and new meaning, in twelfth century, 83–84.

Arbitration, boards of, 454.

Argyll, Duke of, quoted, 460 n.

Aristocracy, building up of a capitalistic, 356; the democracy of labor *vs.*, 357.

Arnold of Brescia, 85.

Art, commercialism a smothering atmosphere for, 257 ff.; close relation of, to the general social system of production, 259; the hand of the middleman in, 259–260.

Aryan village communities, 375–376; survivals of, in ancient Greece and Rome and modern Switzerland, 377, 378.

millionaires' fortunes springing from, 230–232; danger in subtlety of this form of spoliation, 232–233; the essence of class rule in, contrasted with the absence of class rule in democracy, 361; problem of resocializing monopolistic corporations, 425–426; natural monopolies, 435–437.

Moral efficiency, dependence of, on religious faith, 41.

Morality, evil effects of profit-making business on standards of, 212–213.

Mormon Church, a dangerous power within the State, 273.

Mortality rate of tenement dwellers, 416.

Mother, meaning accompanying word, 128.

Municipal ownership, 370–371.

N

National Progressive Party, socialism and the, 395.

Natural monopolies, 435–437.

Natural resources, abuse of, by capitalism, 254, 421.

Nearing, "Wages in the United States," cited, 248.

Newspapers, capitalistic control of, 284–286, 289.

New York City land, 422.

New York Sun, list of rich men published in, 231 n.

New York Tribune, cited on sources of millionaires' fortunes, 230.

New Zealand, influence of the Single Tax doctrine in, 393.

Niagara Falls, onslaught of commercialism on, 253.

Noël, Conrad, cited, 70 n.

Noyes, Alfred, quoted, 325.

O

Old-age pensions, 346, 347, 416.

Open shop, autocratic aspect of employers' insistence on the, 357–358.

Other-worldliness, effect of, in eclipsing the social ideal of Christianity, 73–76; value of this type of religion, 75–76; not the atmosphere in which Jesus lived, 76; conclusion to be drawn from, as to force of the Christian religion, 76;

reduction of abnormal, by the Protestant Reformation, 86–87; religion of the faith of the Kingdom of God contrasted with, 96–97, 98; neglect by, of effect of sins on society, 100.

Owen, Robert Dale, 280.

P

Pace-making, 390, 449.

Palisades, commercialism and the, 253.

Papacy, loss of temporal power of, 140.

Parcels post, the express monopoly and the, 219, 420, 439.

Parks, public, 440.

Patent medicines, 209, 246; an illustration of the antagonism between private interest and public welfare, 276.

Paternalism, analogy between benevolent-employer theory and, 356.

Patriarchal family, the, 129–130.

Patterson, Joseph Medill, 287.

Peabody, Francis G., 20 n.

Personality, power of the human, 460–462.

Personal religion, moral force exerted by, 103; question of effect of social Christianity on, 103 ff.; anxiety about, due to lack of faith in, 105; causes of collapse of, in certain cases, 106; rediscovery of the value of, by enthusiasts who have turned away from, 107; dangers to, from the influence of the social interest are temporary, 111; tinge of self-seeking in some types of, 111–112.

Personal work, loss of interest in, from interest in social work, 113–114.

Pfotenhauer, F., quoted, 24–25.

Philanthropists, burdens of, 298–299, 309.

Philippines, the school and the commercial corporation in the, 146.

Phillips, Wendell, 8.

Philosophy of Calvin and of socialism, 110.

Phosphorus poisoning in match industry, 247.

"Pilgrim's Progress," the religion of other-worldliness illustrated by, 75; quoted, 473–474.

Playgrounds, public, 440.

Pleasure, limitations to, 300–301.

Pullman Company, an example of business under monopoly conditions, 217.
Pure Food and Drug Act, 209, 213, 289.

Q

Quakers, the, 75; superiority of, to the tyranny of fashion, 256.

R

Ragaz, Leonhard, 117 n.
Railways, selfishness of private interest illustrated by, 277–278; concentration of control of, 286; public ownership of, 433.
Railway stations and railways, lack of art in, 257–258.
Real estate, speculation in, 417; resocialization of, 422–425.
Recall, the, 3, 181, 282, 362, 428.
Reedy, W. M., on the "Myth of a Free Press," 285–286, 289.
Referendum, the, 3; Swiss origin of, 378.
Reformation, characteristics of radical movements that preceded the, 83–85; theology of, not concerned with social teachings, 85–86; profound changes inaugurated by, and their bearing on modern science, democracy, and social renovation, 86–87; part enacted by, in the christianizing of the Church, 140–141.
Reformatory institutions, traces of selfish private interests in, 283.
Reformers, obstacles placed in paths of, 288–290.
Religion, power of, beneficent and otherwise, 34; moral force exerted by personal, 103; question of effect of social Christianity on, 103 ff.; alienation of working classes from, in Europe, 108; hostility of continental socialism to, 108–110; practical test of, to which social Christianity measures up, of creating a larger life and the power of growth, 113; is not dying, but changing to meet the needs of the time, 120–121; escape of, from materialistic sway of capitalism, 319 ff.; necessary steps toward the revival of, 458 ff. See also Personal religion.
Religious Education Association, 17.

Religious men and the question of socialism, 396–400.
Revenue system, resocialization of our, 428.
Revival of religion, 458 ff.
Revolution, rejection of, by Jesus, 58–59; smallness of risk of, from socialism, 408–409.
Revolutions, suppression of ability under conditions of injustice proved by, 334–335.
Reynolds, George M., on concentration of control of money power, 286.
Rich, tragic position of the, 291–310; problem of the conversion of the, 467–475.
Right to employment, the, 347–351.
Riis, Jacob, cited, 416.
Riparian rights, need of changing laws governing, 425.
Ritschl, Albrecht, quoted, 70 n.
Roberts, Theodore, quoted, 462.
Rochefoucauld, quoted, 462.
Rochester, N. Y., lack of art in railway station at, 258 n.; illustration in, of need of socializing water rights, 425; banquet to newly naturalized citizens in, 441.
Rockefeller, J. D., 298.
Rolland, Romain, cited on Millet, 260.
Roman Catholic Church, attitude of, to the social movements, 25–27; illustrations of conservatism of, 34–35; part taken by, in American Revolution and in Latin American revolutions, 37–38; question of consistency in opposing socialism, 381; opposition of, to social center idea, 442.
Rome, relations of private and public life in ancient, 446–447.
Roosevelt, Theodore, on the Progressive Party as a corrective of socialism, 395.
Ross, E. A., works by, cited and quoted, 185, 280–281, 282–283, 317, 431.
Rubens, enforced lowering of genius of, 259.
Ruskin, on the "economic man," 185; on the five great intellectual professions, 221; on art and the moral life, 252; summing-up of the rich and the poor by, 294–295; quoted, 322.
Ryan, John A., program of reform of, 27.

S

Sabatier, Paul, "Life of St. Francis" of, 84 n.; anecdote of Jaurès by, 400 n.

Salvation, attainment of, always a social process, 114–115; is a social force and is exerted by groups charged with divine will and love, 116–117.

Sangnier, Marc, 35 n.

Savings of the average American family, 342.

Schaff, Philip, "Creeds of Christendom" by, cited, 21.

Schiller, on the possession of property, 341.

Schmoller, quoted, 386.

School uniforms for children, 446.

Schools, the christianizing process shown by, 142–147.

Science, conflicts between religion and, ended by social Christianity, 118; triumphs of our era due to, rather than to capitalism, 236–237.

Scudder, Vida D., quoted, 298.

Self-restraint, the want of, due to profit-making business, 211.

Senate, United States, corruption of, 2–3, 281–282.

Senators, direct election of, 362.

Service, glorification of mutual, by the religion of the Kingdom of God, 98–100.

Shaftesbury, Lord, work of, for the oppressed classes, 460, 470–471.

Sheldon, Charles M., influence of books of, 46.

Shoe-making, industrial revolution illustrated by, 160–161.

Sickness, insurance of working classes against, 346, 415.

Sillon, the, in France, 35 n.

Simons, "Social Forces in American History," cited, 275, 280, 290, 355.

Sin, viewed as a social force, 116.

Single Tax philosophy, individualism of the, 365; discussion of, as a creed of social salvation, 391–394; method recommended by, of socializing land, 423.

Skepticism of socialists, 110.

Slavery, inefficiency and dearness of labor under, 195–196.

Social centers for communities, 441–442.

Social Christianity, effect of, on personal religion, 103 ff.; is a distinct type of personal religion, 104; dangers from, are of a temporary character, 111–113; larger life and power of growth created by, 113; wherein an improvement on the evangelism of the individualistic gospel, 114; is especially adapted to win and inspire modern men, 117 ff.; ends the conflicts between religion and science, 118; removes the obstacle that religion is "against the people," 118–119; fusing of, with old religious faith, 122; examples of working of, in the family, the Church, the educational system, and the state, 123–155; is not, then, an untried or unsuccessful venture, 155; urgent need of application of, to business, 199–201.

Social conservatism. See Conservatism, social.

"Social Creed of the Churches, The," 15 n.

Social efficiency of early Christian churches, 77–78.

Social Ethics, chairs of, at theological seminaries, 21.

Social ideal of early Christianity, reasons for long eclipse of, 69 ff.; in the emancipation of Christianity from its early Jewish environment and its transition to the Greek environment, 70–71; in the change of the form in which the social hope was presented, 71–73; in the ascendency of the other-worldly hope, 73–76; in the ascendency of the organized institutionalized life of Christianity, — the Church, 76–81; emergence from eclipse dating from dawn of modern democracy, 83.

Socialism, fight of Roman Catholic Church against, 27; position of, toward the Kingdom-of-God ideal, 91; hostility of continental, to religion, 108–110; ingredient of anticlericalism in, 109–110; modern science and skepticism in, 110; mercifulness of criticism by, 200; use that science may be put to under a régime of, 236–237; free-love theories found in, 270, 403; a beneficent influence, but opposed by the capitalistic world, 290; view of, as a great movement for the democracy